...ARE IN FRANCE

For any company or individual deciding to live or work in France, it is important that they understand the workings of the French National Health System.

Health care and health facilities in France are excellent, probably. Amongst the best in the world. France spends a greater proportion of her GNP on health than on defence or education. Standards are high, the public and private systems operate alongside one another and the quality of treatment offered by each one is virtually the same. It should be noted also, that there is no lack of capacity. You will not have to wait for treatment or a bed and unless you are hospitalised in an emergency, you can go into a clinic or general hospital of your choice. It is worth comment that a ward in a French hospital generally consists of no more than four beds and usually only two in the more modern establishments. Private rooms are readily available.

It is worthy of note that establishments and practitioners in France are comprehensively classified by the state. the two principal classifications are Conventionée and Non-conventionée.

Conventionée means that the doctor, consultant, hospital or clinic etc. has agreed to observe the price levels negotiated by their associations or in the case of hospitals by themselves with reference to their annual budgets. The price level is known as the Tariff de Convention and on it the whole system of charging and reimbursement is based. Both the state service and the French insurance companies use percentages of the Tariff de Convention to define the payments they will make.

Anyone working in France or those from other European states who have reached normal retirement age join the French system, but those who have retired prior to the normal retirement age are not entitled to state cover.

The French National Health Service (C.P.A.M.) is not a complete reimbursement system and each person may have to contribute towards all treatments. Certain operations are covered 100% but on average visits to doctors are only covered for 70%, Pharmacy costs 65%, specialists fees 50%, dental fees 70% and other operations 70%. This could mean that even a person who believed they were fully covered by the C.P.A.M. could face a bill of thousands of pounds.

All persons moving to France should, therefore, consider carefully the benefits of private insurance, whether or not they are covered by the state system. Most French nationals purchase a top-up (or complementaire) policy to supplement the C.P.A.M., offered by a number of French companies. There is now, however a top-up policy offered to expatriates by a British company - Columbus Insurance. This covers the full difference between the payments made by the C.P.A.M. and the total bill and all claims are settled quickly through an associate French office. For those not entitled to join the French system full private medical insurance is a necessity and many international companies like Columbus, offer suitable products for France.

Good advise is essential for all people planning to live or work in France and Columbus offer an expert, impartial service to all expatriates. Please see so... ...ent for details.

Doing
Business
With
France

Doing Business with France

Consultant Editor
Roderick Millar

Foreword by
Jean-Daniel Tordjman

Published in association with
 Chambre de Commerce Française
de Grande-Bretagne

With support from

PRICEWATERHOUSECOOPERS

KOGAN PAGE

First published in 1998

Kogan Page Limited
120 Pentonville Road
London N1 9JN

© Kogan Page and contributors, 1998

British Library Cataloguing in Publication Data
ISBN 0 7494 2564 4

Typeset by Saxon Graphics Ltd, Derby
Printed in Great Britain by Bell & Bain Ltd, Glasgow

PRICEWATERHOUSE COOPERS

The biggest name in professional services is now, well, the biggest name in professionnel services

www.pwcglobal.com

Contents

PART ONE: BACKGROUND INFORMATION

PART TWO: INVESTMENT ISSUES

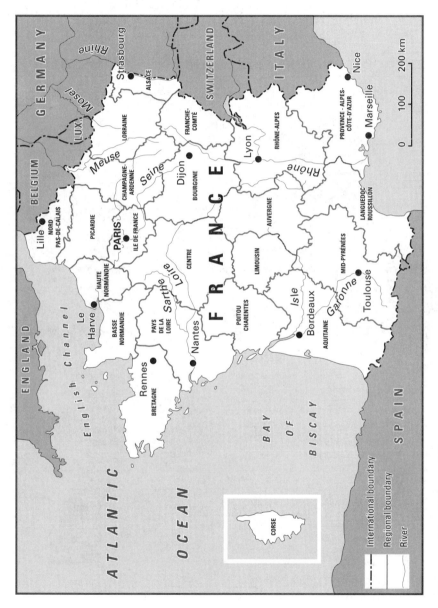

Geographical Map of France

France :
A competitive base for the European market

TOYOTA, Japan's largest manufacturing company, has selected France as the site for its second European automobile plant.

The decision follows similar moves by DAIMLER-BENZ, FEDERAL EXPRESS, IBM, MOTOROLA, PHILIPS, GENERAL ELECTRIC and GENERAL MOTORS, all motivated by the features that have made France the world's third host country for direct inward investment.

France is an affluent market, with sound economic fundamentals: low inflation, attractive interest rates, a stable currency and overall competitiveness reflected in healthy trade surpluses.

At the heart of Europe, it offers a variety of sites backed by excellent transport infrastructure, leading-edge scientific and technical expertise, a productive workforce, competitive telecommunications and power supply, and the

resources of a vast array of sub-contractors.

France is a country of the future, with a strong industry and open to international business.

Jean-Daniel TORDJMAN
Ambassador at large
Special Representative
for International
Investment

MINISTÈRE DE L'ÉCONOMIE
DES FINANCES ET DE L'INDUSTRIE

139 rue de Bercy - Teledoc 334 - 75572 Paris Cedex 12 France
Tel. : (33) 1 44 87 70 21 - Fax. : (33) 1 44 87 70 26

Foreword

Toyota, Japan's largest manufacturing company, has selected France as the site for its second European automobile plant. The decision follows similar moves by Daimler-Benz, Federal Express, IBM, Motorola, Phillips, General Electric and General Motors, all drawn by features that have made France the world's third host country for direct inward investment.

France is the world's fourth largest economy, Europe's second largest market, the second largest exporter of agrifood products and third largest exporter of services. It is the only country with direct links to Europe's six largest markets: Germany, the UK, Italy, the Benelux, Switzerland and Spain.

At the heart of Europe, it offers exceptional sites backed by outstanding transport infrastructure, leading-edge scientific and technical expertise, a productive workforce, competitive telecommunications and power supply, and the resources of a vast array of subcontractors.

Performances reflect a range of strengths that have attracted 8,000 international businesses, as well as the commitment of government and regional authorities to improving conditions for investors. Significant advances have been made recently in the sphere of taxation with the implementation of a competitive system for company headquarters, logistics and distribution centres. The accumulated total of direct investment stocks in France rose from $23 billion in 1980 to $184 billion in 1997.

With a combined GDP of $8 trillion, the European Union is the world's largest market. And the move to its new single currency, the euro, in which France and Germany have played a central role, will transform Europe profoundly in a very short time. The new currency will lead to greater integration, transparency, competition and efficiency. The euro will spur cross-border investments, mergers and acquisitions, generating numerous new opportunities for trade and investment. As the euro zone's leading host country for foreign direct investment, France provides an excellent base for supplying Europe's markets of the 21st century.

I strongly recommend *Doing Business with France*, a comprehensive guide for both newcomers and companies already present on the French market, covering the different aspects of investment, finance and business culture.

Jean-Daniel Tordjman

Ambassador at large, Special representative of France for international investment

The Contributors

Contact details for all contributors are listed in Appendix B.

Association Française des Banques (AFB)

The AFB (French Association of Banks) is the professional association and trade union for French banks. Any credit institution which is, legally speaking, a bank has automatic membership, regardless of whether activities are general or specialised, of whether the bank has regional, national or international status, is French-owned or not. There are 405 full members of the AFB with some affiliated members among other credit organisations and investment enterprises. Building Societies, specialised financial institutions and cooperatively or mutually run banks are not eligible.

The AFB's role is to defend its members' interests and to represent them before public and elected authorities, economic and social institutions, professional associations, consumer groups, the media and also the EU and other international bodies. To these ends, the AFB carries out studies and prepares statements on issues which concern the banking profession; informs its members of any major legislative, administrative and judicial decisions which might affect their activities; has a policy of information and communication which aims to further public understanding of the banking profession and to explain its role in the economy; and represents the profession in the dialogue with business and in negotiations with union bodies.

Association Française des Investisseurs en Capital (AFIC)

AFIC, the French Venture Capital Association, is an independent professional association of French equity capital investment companies.

The key business activity of AFIC member companies is to take equity positions in unlisted companies and, by working with their management, generate profits through capital gains upon sale of the investment.

AFIC now has 168 company members, 131 of which are full members, ie equity investors in unlisted companies, while 37 are associate members whose professional activity is closely related to equity capital investment activity (law firms, accountants, consultants, etc). All members, including their personnel, are bound in writing to respect the Association's professional code of ethics.

AFIC membership accounts for 90 per cent of all French venture capital's investors, represents more than 7 billion fr invested per year, and has thus become the profession's representative body.

Chambre de Commerce Française de Grande-Bretagne

The mission of the Chambre de Commerce Française de Grande-Bretagne is to develop and promote trade and investments between France and Britain and to provide both business communities with specialised services and a forum to future its members' interests.

The Chambre de Commerce Française was established in London in 1883 as a private organisation dedicated to the improvement of trading relations between Great Britain and France. The membership is represented by senior business executives from over 600 companies.

Jean-Marie Bergman has been Managing Director of the Chambre de Commerce Française de Grande-Bretagne since 1995. He was born in Paris in 1943. He attended the Paris Institut d'Etudes Politiques and the University of Puget Sound (USA). He then moved to Canada where he taught political science until 1975. His previous positions are: Senior Policy Adviser to the President of the Canadian Development Agency, Director General of the Champlain Regional College (Quebec), President of Basic Manpower Training International (Calgary) and Director of the Centre Parisien de Technologie Export, part of the Paris Chamber of Commerce.

Florent Belleteste is Regional Co-ordinator at the Chambre de Commerce Française de Grande-Bretagne. He is in charge of relations with French local authorities and the development of the chamber's network of branches all over the UK. He is a graduate in Economics and Politics and holds a research diploma in European Studies entitled 'Local Government Responses to Europe in Britain and France'.

Coopers & Lybrand CLC Juridique et Fiscal

Coopers & Lybrand CLC Juridique et Fiscal is one of the largest French law firms, with 280 lawyers and with offices in Paris, Lyon, Marseille, Strasbourg, Lille, Bordeaux, Sophia Antipolis, Rennes, Grenoble and Annecy.

Coopers & Lybrand CLC Juridique et Fiscal offers its clients a full range of services, particularly in business and tax law, both in France and at international levels.

Conseil National du Patronat Français (CNPF)

CNPF is the French Employers' and Businesses' Organisation, representing over 1.5 million companies.

Department of Management Studies, Paris Panthéon Sorbonne University

Professeur Jean-Francois Amadieu is Professor of Management Studies at the Sorbonne University in Paris, and is on the board of the Human Resources Management Association of France (AGRH). His publications include *Le Management des Salaires* ('Salary Management'), 1995, and *Gestion des Relations Sociales* ('Social Relationship Management'), to appear in 1998, both published by Editions Economica. His many articles and reports include commissions for the French Minister of Employment and the EU as well as for business corporations. He also acts as a business consultant, specialising in the fields of social relationship dynamics and human resource management.

Department of Trade and Industry (DTI)

The Department of Trade and Industry provides help to British companies seeking to establish new markets for themselves overseas.

E.M.LYON

E.M.LYON is a leading European business school in France with a specific focus on international management education and research. It offers a range of postgraduate management programmes, as well as high-level tailor-made executive programmes. Over the past 14 years, it has developed overwhelming expertise in the field of entrepreneurship.

Ian Tovey studied Modern Languages at Oxford and Business Administration in Lyon. Since 1984, he has taught Comparative Business Studies and International Management at E.M.LYON. He was also Assistant Dean for International Relations at the school from 1989 to 1996.

Freight Europe (UK)

Freight Europe UK Ltd is a subsidiary of French Railways. It was created in 1996 to promote business within the continent. As a UK-based freight operator (situated in London near Waterloo station), Freight Europe specialises in all transport logistics to and from continental Europe via the Channel Tunnel, using conventional wagons.

Particularly experienced in meeting the transport needs of companies operating in the steel, chemicals, consumer goods and wood/paper sectors, Freight Europe focuses principally on providing UK manufacturers and distributors with a freight service that is reliable, efficient, flexible and competitive.

Its efficiency has been distinguished by the Institute of Transport Management which has selected Freight Europe UK Ltd to receive an Award of Excellence for 1998.

Healey & Baker

Healey & Baker is an international partnership, established in 1820, providing real estate consultancy and agency advice. It specialises in all types of commercial property and acts for a range of prominent clients across the corporate, public and private sectors. The firm's global network covers 132 offices in more than 40 countries.

Huglo, Lepage & Associés Conseil

Huglo, Lepage & Associés is a Paris-based law firm specialising in environmental and administrative law. With fifteen Attorneys at Law holding at least postgraduate qualifications relating to environmental protection, administrative management and international relations (including Community Law), Huglo, Lepage & Associés is able to tackle diverse legal issues through its specialised departments.

Established at the end of the 1960s by Christian Huglo and Corinne Lepage (both Doctors of Law), Huglo, Lepage & Associés was one of the first legal firms in France to use the law to serve the interests of the environment, at a time when environmental regulations had not yet been imposed. It has won recognition in many international pollution cases, including 'Amoco Cadiz', 'North Holland Rhine Pollution' and 'Red Sludges of Montedison'.

The founder members have been active in the development of French Environmental Law, through judicial proceedings but also with many legal publications, written collaboratively and separately.

Corinne Lepage was appointed French Minister of the Environment in May 1995. She held the post until June 1997.

INSEAD

Founded less than 40 years ago in 1959, INSEAD is today widely recognised as one of the most influential business schools in the world. The school has 101 permanent faculties and 45 visiting professors from over 20 countries. Each year INSEAD teaches over 500 postgraduates representing about 200 nationalities in the MBA programme and provides management development for 4,500 executives from all over the world. There are now more than 18,000 INSEAD alumni.

INSEAD has corporate partnerships with many of the leading firms in Europe, the US and Asia. Extensive research assures the relevance of the teaching in today's highly competitive and constantly changing business environment.

Olivier Cadot is Associate Professor of Economics at INSEAD and has also taught at UCLA, NYU, and McGill University, among others. He worked at the OECD and the IMF, and has done research on international trade and industrial policy issues for the French government, the European Commission and the World Trade Organisation. Professor Cadot is also a frequent contributor to executive programmes on international issues.

Invest in France Agency

The Invest in France Network is an association founded in 1992 at the initiative of DATAR, the body charged with economic development and regional planning in France. Members include regional development organisations, public utilities and financial institutions, as well as consulting and engineering firms. Together with DATAR and with the assistance of Invest in France Agencies around the world, it encourages industries and services from abroad to set up in France.

Invest in France agencies are located at the eighteen DATAR offices around the word: eight in Europe, four in North America and six in Asia. Agencies offer potential investors services which include: information concerning sites suited to business goals and requirements; assistance in defining projects and related options; organisation of visits to suitable sites and premises; assistance in contacts with authorities and businesses; establishing contacts with local partners. All these services are strictly confidential.

Joint Venture Research Centre, Ecole Européenne des Affaires de Paris (EAP)

The Joint Venture Research Group is dedicated to the study of all forms of cross-border collaborative structures (joint venture, strategic alliances, cross-border partnerships). The research group disseminates results of systematic and multi-disciplinary research on the setting up, the management and the evolution of inter-company cooperation. It assists firms in their international development.

The EAP, European School of Management, is a French graduate business school operating on four European campuses: Paris, Oxford, Madrid and Berlin. It delivers a 3-year 3 country European Masters in Management programme, has several MBA programmes and an International Executive Centre.

Jackie Vasseur is Associate Professor of Strategic Management at EAP and at the Sorbonne (Université Paris IV). She is a specialist in Alliance and Cooperation mainly with SME; she also created the Joint Research Venture in Paris.

Jane Kassis is Associate Professor of English for International Business at EAP. She specialises in intercultural communication in the context of management.

PricewaterhouseCoopers

PricewaterhouseCoopers, the world's largest professional services organisation, helps its clients build value, manage risk and improve their performance.

Drawing on the talents of more than 140,000 people in 152 countries, PricewaterhouseCoopers provides a full range of business advisory services to leading global, national and local companies and to public institutions. These services include audit, accounting and tax advice; management, information technology and human resource consulting; financial advisory services including mergers & acquisitions, business recovery, project finance and litigation support; business process outsourcing services; and legal services through a global network of affiliated law firms.

In France, PricewaterhouseCoopers currently employs 3,900 people. In addition to offices in Paris, it operates through more than forty regional offices, the main locations being Bordeaux, Cognac, Dijon, Grenoble, Lille, Limoges, Lyon, Marseille, Metz, Montpellier, Nantes, Nice, Pau, Quimper, Rennes, Rouen, St Quentin, Sophia Antipolis, Strasbourg and Toulouse.

Roderick Millar

Roderick is an experienced financial editor and writer specialising in foreign trade, development economics and business start-ups.

Union Nationale des Entreprises de Travail Temporaire (UNETT)

On 1 June 1998 the UNETT (National Union for Temporary Employment Agencies) merged with Promatt (Syndicat des Professionels du Travail Temporaire – Union for Professionals in Temporary Employment) to become the SETT (Syndicat des Entreprises de Travail Temporaire – Union of Temporary Employment Agencies), an employers' association whose aim is to defend the interests of temporary employment agencies. With its 400 business members the SETT brings together 85 per cent of the temporary employment market's volume of business activity and represents a turnover of at least 70 billion fr.

The SETT is a member of the CNPF, the CGPME (Confédération Générale des Petites et Moyennes Entreprises – General Confederation of Small and Medium-sized Businesses) and the CIFTT (Confédération Internationale des Entreprises de Travail Temporaire – International Confederation of Temporary Employment Agencies).

Christiane Pacotte is a legal expert at the SETT, having originally worked for the UNETT since 1995.

HAMMOND SUDDARDS
SOLICITORS

BUSINESS LAWYERS
A NATIONAL BASE. AN INTERNATIONAL NETWORK

ADDRESS:	7 Devonshire Square, Cutlers Gardens London EC2M 4YH
TELEPHONE: FAX:	0171 655 1000 0171 655 1001
ACTIVITY:	Solicitors. Contentious and non contentious
CONTACTS:	John Heller, Chris Jones, Peter Simpson, Christopher Haan, Corinne Bouffandeau (French Clientele)
DEPARTMENTS:	Corporate; Banking and Financial Services; Commercial Litigation; Derivatives; MBO; Tax; Aviation; Property; Construction; Insolvency; Employment; Advertising; Entertainment and Media; Environment; Information Technology; Intellectual Property; Insurance; Pensions; EC Law (Brussels office).
ADDITIONAL INFORMATION:	The firm has a team of bilingual English and French qualified Lawyers with dedicated expertise in both legal systems thereby minimising the culture and language gap.
	With its national base and its international network (correspondent firms in Europe - including Eastern Europe - and in Asia Pacific) HS is well equipped to meet the needs of its clients wherever their location.
	With a staff of over 1,000 including 72 Partners, the firm has enjoyed swift expansion and internationalisation. It has doubled its fee earning capacity in five years and is now among the top UK business law firms.
OTHER OFFICES:	*Overseas:* Brussels: Avenue Louise 250, 1050 Brussels, Belgium Tel: (32) 26 27 76 76 Fax: (32) 26 27 76 86 NB: The list of our correspondents in Europe and Asia Pacific is available at the London Office.
	UK: Leeds, Manchester, Bradford

Part One

Background Information

1

Recent Political Past and Policy Stance

Jean-Marie Bergman, Chambre de Commerce Française de Grande-Bretagne

POLITICAL PARTIES AND THE 1997 ELECTION

On 3 June 1997, Lionel Jospin, the leader of the Parti Socialiste, became the most important person in French politics, his Left coalition having won 319 seats to the Right's 258 in the 577-member National Assembly. This was a resounding victory for the Left, because in the previous Assembly they had had 114 members only compared to the Right's 463. This sea change was largely unexpected and commentators are still divided as to why the President (Jacques Chirac) called an election more than one year ahead of schedule. A re-elected *député* on the Right, is quoted as saying: 'Chirac found himself in a dark apartment with a smell of gas, so he lit a match to see better.'

As a result, the French Right has many bitter ex-members of the National Assembly and is plagued by internal conflicts which are reflected in the seemingly genuine differences of opinion Right party leaders have about what the Right stands for in France.

There is a minority on the Right who consider themselves to be 'liberal' but are considered by a majority of the population to be 'ultra-liberal'. This small faction, sometimes called a sect by its opponents, received 2 per cent of the popular vote, and is currently led by Alain Madelin who served briefly as Minister of Finance in 1995. In France to be 'ultra-liberal' means that you trust market forces and fundamentally believe that the state should not be involved in business. In this respect, they would dispose as soon as possible of the many state enterprises still run by the government.

Most other French conservative leaders are more or less interventionists. Half of them belong to the Rassemblement Pour la République (ie are Gaullists), which received 23 per cent of the popular vote, and believe that France is by definition a great power and that therefore the state has a duty to insure that there are 'national champions' in as many economic sectors as possible. The cost of such grandeur is never a serious obstacle, as de Gaulle illustrated when he said 'L'intendance suivra' ('I don't care about the costs, just do it!'). This quiet disregard for economic reality is a popular stance, it reassures the electorate that France is still a great, independent power, not governed by the 'invisible (Anglo-Saxon) hand'.

The other half, more market-oriented, identify with the Union pour la Démocratie Française, which received 21 per cent of the popular vote, and are followers of Giscard d'Estaing. The party is in fact an unstable coalition as no leader has really emerged to define a programme and a strategy.

Finally, on the extreme Right is Jean-Marie Le Pen, who runs a populist xenophobic campaign with some success in the south-east of the country and generally where there exist some relatively large visible minorities. In fact, much of the debate on the Right revolves around the issue of how to convince the 5.64 per cent of the electorate who voted for Le Pen's Front National to rejoin the 'respectable Right'.

The French Left is also divided. The Parti Socialiste is the Left's largest party, with 38 per cent of the popular vote). The party of Jacques Delors, his daughter Martine Aubry, François Mitterand, Michel Rocard and Lionel Jospin, it is trying to be realistic and become a modern social democratic party on the Scandinavian model. It is generally in favour of greater European integration, and is very concerned with educational issues as its strongest support has always been from the academic establishment. The party is slowly coming to terms with the necessary structural reforms of the French economy, including privatisation of more and more state enterprises, but has to remember that many of its electoral support comes precisely from the employees of these state concerns.

The Communist Party, led by Robert Hue, is the second largest party of the Left with 37 seats and 3.84 per cent of the popular vote.

The Greens polled less than 2 per cent and other parties of the Left a further 4 per cent.

The French electoral system with its run-off procedure does not generally give rise to large majorities because the forming of electoral alliances is always possible between the first and second round ballots. Nevertheless, the percentages above represent a realistic picture of French political opinion in 1997.

THE BIG ISSUE: UNEMPLOYMENT

French unemployment at 12 per cent is perceived by and large as a consequence of globalisation. Unemployment in France is well compensated by an insurance scheme. The greatest problem is that young people who are not insured because they have never paid the insurance premiums, have no income and very little prospect of finding full-time private sector jobs if they are not well qualified. The parties on the extreme Right and extreme Left are convinced that a more protectionist European Union would avoid this calamity. The mainstream parties usually disagree mildly and hope that a strong and growing European Union will make the problem to go away. The employers' federation typically argues that they cannot hire staff because the market is not there and that French labour is globally too expensive. The unions reply that French labour productivity in the private sector is the highest in the world (which is probably true) and that wages are too low, thus demand is depressed and hence unemployment grows.

Words such as 'liberal' and 'flexibility' are anathema to the French mind as far as labour market operations are concerned. The thought that the very protective labour laws are themselves the main cause of precarious employment is not easily conveyed to anyone in France except employers.

THE EURO

Since the referendum on the Maastricht treaty was ratified by a small majority, the debate in France has almost entirely been concerned with the mechanics of meeting the famous criteria. There has been a general consensus that it ought to be done for political as well as economic reasons. Politically the Euro is sold in France as the only way to insure that interest rates will be set on a Europe-wide basis rather than simply by the Bundesbank (BUBA). In other words, France is buying a right to influence the value of the Euro by accepting the German economic model, the famous social market economy.

It is a matter of historical record that many of the principles of the continental welfare state were defined by Bismark around 1870. As a consequence of the Franco-Prussian war, Alsace and Lorraine were annexed by Germany and therefore enjoyed the same level of social protection as all other residents of the Reich. In 1918, when these eastern provinces returned to French jurisdiction, they kept their welfare system. The rest of France adopted similar laws, especially around 1936 during the Popular Front government. It is therefore not very surprising that these two systems are somewhat similar and that creating a common currency appears to be a fairly natural progression, even if last-minute horse-trading may give the impression of conflicts.

THE STATE

'L'État c'est moi', 'Le Roi gouverne par lui-même'. These maxims of autocratic government which are proudly displayed in Versailles are still very much part of the French collective psyche. Of course there have been several revolutions (1789–92, 1830, 1848) which eliminated the monarchy but led to Napoleon. From Napoleon to de Gaulle, the autocratic benevolent leader is one of the popular models of French governance. Indeed, between such periods, the democratic system of checks and balances is so efficient that change appears to be blocked. The inability of France to move forward in a quiet way remains one of its structural characteristics. 'Plus ça change plus c'est la même chose' are both reassuring to the conservative and infuriating to the reformer. Yet the solution to this dialectic appears to pile reforming institutions on top of old ones which survive indefinitely. This is one of the reasons why 25 per cent of the workforce is employed by public bodies compared to 16–20 per cent in other European countries.

In many ways the very size of the state is the big French issue. Since Colbert, in the 17th century, France has always relied on the state to define economic goals. While some of the most brilliant liberal economists have been French – J B Say for example is as seminal as Adam Smith – the general consensus has been a reluctance to trust the market. It has been easy to justify big, heroic, costly, technically exciting projects to the French people, for instance small French investors funded the Suez and Panama canals, Eurotunnel etc, and the French taxpayer has been only too pleased to fund Concorde, TGV, Ariane Rafale and Minitel ventures. The technostructure has usually been able to capture the imagination of the politicians for such uneconomic adventures. In some sense French R&D has remained very strong thanks to these projects which of course have led to considerable spin-offs and very profitable ventures among the private contractors who effectively produced the plane parts, Minitel terminals etc. It is much easier for any French government to sell a bank than an electronics producer. Financial institutions are considered as far less important than prestigious industrial concerns.

It is therefore probable that new spectacular initiatives of a technical nature will continue to be popular with the French electorate and that they will naturally expect the European Union to share in funding this techno enthusiasm.

DEATH AND TAXES

France has the highest level of overall taxation after the Scandinavian countries. The bulk of tax revenue is indirect, VAT, fuel, etc. 80 per cent of income tax is paid by 10 per cent of taxpayers. Social security taxes collect more revenue than income tax, which remains much lower for most people than in the rest of the European Union.

Recent developments include a deliberate effort to shift social security funding from payroll taxes to income from all sources. This is closer to the German model and should alleviate some of the crippling labour costs which make it difficult to justify employing low-skill labour in France. French people are by and large very supportive of their health-care facilities, and not very receptive to cost-cutting in that field. Life expectancy is comparable to all the other European countries even if it costs 1–2 per cent more of GNP to achieve. The system is, however, much more user-friendly than the British scheme. Waiting lists are very rare and the problem seems often to be oversupply rather than shortage of resources.

THE ENVIRONMENT

The arrival of a Green Minister of the Environment, Dominique Voynet, is having an extraordinary effect. As was mentioned above certain projects have been cancelled but more importantly the tech-nostructure is being questioned about its strategic choices. Should France continue to encourage the use of diesel cars, should nuclear generation be the only significant source of electricity? To have such questions asked at that level is extraordinary in a country where the press is traditionally fairly deferential to the government on such issues.

She is also basking in the glory of having imposed the first ever reduc-tion of automobile traffic during a pollution peak in September 1997. The French press was absolutely astounded to report that 95 per cent of the people had complied gladly with the ban on even numbered licence plates for that day. Civic duty was accepted for a Green cause, and the other politicians were taking great care not to disparage the minister whom they more or less openly dismissed a few days earlier. On that day many ministers drove to work in electric Peugeots and Renaults which find more and more plug-ins to recharge their batteries in progressive French cities such as Paris, La Rochelle or Montpellier. Again an example of substituting national atomic energy for imported oil, which France finds a natural way of doing even if it costs more in the short term.

CONCLUSION

The political sphere in France is an ever-present subject of conversation and a low-level cause of anxiety because of its considerable call on resources. At the same time genuinely erratic or arbitrary decisions are very rare. The modern infrastructure could not have been built without a considerable degree of political consensus. France and Britain are very experienced nation-states. In many ways they have defined the main political and constitutional options which are available to rich countries.

2

The System of National Government

Roderick Millar, Consultant Editor

BACKGROUND AND HISTORY

The current system of government might be described in commercial terminology as the product of a series of aggressive restructurings. Since 1958 France has operated under the Fifth Republic when General de Gaulle returned to power following the collapse of the Fourth Republic after a period which began with military defeat in IndoChina (1954) and culminated when insurrection in Algeria led to the threat of civil war in France. The French system of government obviously has roots that run much deeper than the last 50 years and while the current government structure may appear more modern than that of the United Kingdom, say, the forces that have shaped it go back over 1,000 years.

The endeavours of Charlemagne and the Capetian monarchs that followed began to unify the country around the turn of the first millennium, but it was not until the end of the One Hundred Years war against England in the late 15th century that the monarchy finally gained the upper hand over the feudal nobility and a solid system of centralised authority began to take shape. The 16th century saw France caught up in the Wars of Religion, where the Catholic majority defended itself against the Protestant-Huguenot forces, to allow centralised government to develop significantly. The absolute power of the monarchy was considerably strengthened in the 17th century, where Louis XIII and Louis XIV ruled over an increasingly centralised France managed by powerful ministers, Richelieu, Mazarin and Colbert. France's borders were secured and commerce as a national activity was encouraged.

At this time the overarching power of 'prime ministers' caused the traditional aristocracy to feel excluded. So too did the *parlements*, unelected bodies which acted as high courts and administrative and tax-collecting councils on a local level and tried, ineffectively, to challenge some of the centralised powers. The relationship between the *parlements*, particularly the one in Paris, and the king's ministers became increasingly strained as they tried to overrule and outwit each other, until finally, government business and its wish to raise taxes to cover its debts was in such disarray and the executive's actions so peremptory that the system of government collapsed and the Revolution ensued in 1789. The Revolution while a pivotal event in fact did little to establish an effective governmental system out of the chaos it had created.

The rise of Napoleon Bonaparte from 1799, however, saw him instigate a series of institutions that can be taken as the basis of modern French government, if not democracy. He redesigned the tax system, created the Bank of France, instituted a corps of *prefets* answerable to himself, made judges part of the state system and most enduringly founded the Civil Code legal system. Napoleon was replaced by a more liberal monarchy but it slid back into its old ways and in 1848 the Citizen King, Louis-Phillipe, Duc d'Orleans fled to England and France ceased to be a kingdom as the provisional government ushered in the Second Republic.

The Second Republic was radically liberal. It enacted universal male suffrage, the first time this had happened anywhere, and it tried to alleviate unemployment through a system of national workshops. Again new taxes designed to offset the country's financial burdens brought the government down and in 1852 Napoleon's nephew was elected to office on a liberal ticket. That quickly changed, however; once in power, he proclaimed himself Emperor. Despite the expansion of trade and industry, introduction of trade unions, extension of public education and the granting of a liberal opposition the regime fell against the rising forces of Germany's Bismarck. The Third Republic was created in 1870 with the election of a national assembly. This was peculiarly monarchist and failed to represent the aspirations of the working classes. After World War I the French Left failed to unite effectively and split into a pro-Leninist Communist Party and the Socialist Party, a division that endures today. After the Second World War the country would only accept General de Gaulle as interim president; it was believed that only he was capable of uniting the diverse factions in the country at that time. The Fourth Republic was created and elections, for the first time with female suffrage, brought in a left-wing government; however, Marshall Plan reparation restrictions ensured that the administration was commerce based. De Gaulle returned as prime minister and then president in 1958 and rewrote the constitution giving the president vastly greater powers and so creating the current Fifth Republic.

GOVERNMENT STRUCTURE

The structure of the French government has been shaped by these events and experiences and it is useful to bear them in mind when trying to understand why and how the processes of government operate. The role of the executive has always been pivotal in the French system and its alienation from the people too often the cause of riot and revolution. The Fifth Republic endeavours to check this power by dividing duties and powers between the President of the Republic and Parliament. De Gaulle insisted that the president should be capable of maintaining the due process of government should Parliament dissemble and prevaricate in such a way that would lead to administrative chaos, which had been the cause of much French distress through the years.

The Constitution

The constitution of the Fifth Republic was established on 4 October 1958. The second article of the constitution states:

> The language of the Republic shall be French. The national emblem shall be the blue, white and red tricolour flag. The national anthem shall be La Marseillaise. The motto of the Republic shall be 'Liberty, Equality, Fraternity'. Its principle shall be: government of the people, by the people and for the people.

The President of the Republic

It goes on to outline the structure and responsibilities of the government. The government is headed by the President of the Republic who is elected by absolute majority (in two rounds if necessary, the second round contested between the two leading contenders from the first election) every seven years.

The president nominates a prime minister who suggests a council of ministers that the president appoints. The prime minister will tend to be from the leading party in the National Assembly. The president presides over the council of ministers. All Acts of Parliament need to be signed by the president before they become law. One of the president's most effective powers is his right to ask Parliament to reconsider an Act if he disapproves of it. Parliament does not have the right to refuse to reconsider. Clearly the use of this power has political implications. A president is unlikely to use it too often but his threat to use it is often sufficient to persuade Parliament to legislate in a way that the president will find acceptable. Under certain conditions the president can refer Acts to a referendum by the people, the result of which is binding.

The president's other major power, unique amongst leading democratic nations, is his right to dissolve the National Assembly and force a general election. The reasons for so doing can be either purely political opportunism, such as in 1997 by President Chirac, or to establish the will of the people on issues that are being inconclusively effected by Parliament.

Further to these two statutory powers the president can enact emergency powers (after consultation with the prime minister and presidents of the assemblies), however, these powers are temporary and subject to later ratification. The president also appoints ambassadors, senior civil and military posts, he is Commander-in-Chief of the armed forces and he negotiates and ratifies international treaties.

The Prime Minister and Government

The government is headed by the prime minister and 'determines and conducts the policy of the Nation'. It is responsible to Parliament, not the president. The prime minister directs the operations of government and ensures the implementation of legislation and can deputise for the President of the Republic in certain circumstances. The government is responsible for the defence of the nation.

Members of government may not be simultaneously members of either assembly or hold a national occupational representation or other public employment. Frequently senior government members are also mayors of a local authority.

Members of government may address either assembly whenever they so request and in return Parliament may question members of government on relevant issues.

Parliament

The French Parliament consists of two assemblies, the National Assembly and the Senate. The National Assembly is elected by direct suffrage for a maximum term of five years, with each of France's *departements* returning a number of deputies depending on their relative populations, the smallest returning 2 deputies, the largest 24. Similar to the presidential elections the deputies must be elected by absolute majority through the two-round process. All members of the assembly have parliamentary immunity from prosecution during their terms of office. This immunity can only be retracted by the Assembly Bureau, a 22-member committee that is presided over by the President of the Assembly and is elected each session, and runs the Assembly's administrative programme.

The National Assembly sits from October through to June each year, although special extra sittings can be arranged in exceptional circumstances. The members are grouped into different political groupings (see Box 2.1), each group consisting of a minimum of 20 members (*apparentes*). These groupings put forward members for different positions within the Assembly's structure, such as the six functional commissions and the parliamentary delegations. Those members who do not join a political grouping (*non-inscrits*) sit as independents.

The Senate is the second of the two assemblies. Unlike the National Assembly the Senate is never dissolved; this is part of the checks and balancing system to counterweight the President's authority. The Senate instead has one-third of its 321 seats elected every three years for a nine-year term. The elections to the Senate are conducted by indirect suffrage, through an electoral college predominantly constituted of local councillors along with deputies and regional councillors.

Political Parties and Groupings in the National Assembly   Box 2.1

Parti Socialist (PS) – the main left-wing party of President Mitterrand, that ran the country from 1981 to 1995.

Parti Communist Français (PCF) – not as Stalinist as it sounds, this party holds the furthest left ground of the mainstream parties, with close links to the trade unions and local government.

Radical, Citoyen et Vert (RCV) – a grouping of smaller parties including the environmentalist Green Party.

Union pour la Démocratie Française (UDF) – the breakaway wing of the right, set up by Valerie Giscard D'Estaing

Rassemblement pour la République (RPR) – Gaullist right-wing party led by Jacques Chirac.

Also Front National (FN) – the racist right-wing party led by the charismatic and enduringly colourful Jean-Marie Le Pen. Hold no seats in the National Assembly following the abolition of proportional representation in 1988. They are still a force in local politics and have 11 European Parliament seats.

This manifests itself with a large number of local councillors being elected as Senators. The President of the Assembly is elected every three years with each new Senatorial intake. He is also the deputy-president of the Republic and would temporarily carry out the president's duties in the event of a vacancy. In strict protocol terms he ranks after the president of the Republic and the prime minister. The Senate, in similar fashion to the National Assembly, has a Bureau of 22 members who administrate its functioning and business and is presided over by the president of the Senate.

The Senate's role is primarily as legislator, though being less directly sensitive to political trends the house presents a more stable, long-term perspective. The Senate considers legislation proposed by the government, the National Assembly and their own private members bills. The Senate is able to examine all legislation before the National Assembly, except finance matters which must go through the National Assembly first.

The process of legislation is similar in both houses. The proposed legislative text is sent to the house's standing committees, a *rapporteur* is appointed who will explain any modifications made to the house, the committee will accept written reports and amendments modifying the bill and then gives advice on amendments submitted by non-committee member Senators (or deputies). The bill then goes to public session, where the minister in charge presents the bill, the *rapporteur* presents the amendments. Senators who have registered to debate can then give their points of view and ask questions of the government. The bill then goes to the amending process where votes are taken on the various sections of the bill. Finally, a vote on the whole bill is taken either by a show of hands (if this is inconclusive, by a standing vote where Senators are counted) or failing this by a balloted 'recorded vote'. The bill will then proceed to the other house, or if it has already been there to the President of the Republic.

Where Senate amendments are not accepted by the National Assembly they are arbitrated by a joint committee of Senators and deputies, and failing a harmonious outcome there, the bill with or without Senate amendments is presented to the National Assembly for a final binding vote.

Other Institutions

There are three other important governmental institutions: the Constitutional Council, the High Council of the Judiciary, and the High Court of Justice. The Constitutional Council is composed of nine members serving nine-year terms, again one-third elected every three years. The President of the Republic, the Senate and the National Assembly nominate a representative (from outside the parliamentary world) for each election. All former Presidents of the Republic are also ex officio members of the council. The Constitutional Council can declare Acts 'unconstitutional' and their decision is final with no appeal.

The High Council of the Judiciary is presided over by the President of the Republic and the Minister for Justice is ex officio vice-president of the council. The council sits in two sections, one which oversees the judges, made up of the president, the minister, five judges and a public prosecutor plus a representative from the Consel d'Etat and three prominent citizens. The other section oversees the public prosecutors and has the same make up except that it has five public prosecutors and one judge on its body.

The final institution is the High Court of Justice which is made up of an equal number of National Assembly deputies and Senators, and is the highest court in France.

CURRENT POLITICAL SCENE

President Jacques Chirac was elected President of the Republic on 7 May 1995 and appointed Alain Juppé as his prime minister. This was the first time since the early years of François Mitterrand's presidency that the president and the prime minister were from the same party, and was possible only because Chirac's RPR held the majority in a coalition with the UDF in the National Assembly.

In the summer of 1997, with the National Assembly still having some two years of its term left to run, President Chirac felt that the time was ripe to reaffirm and consolidate the RPR's position as the majority party within the National Assembly and give M. Juppé a better mandate for government. This was considered a surprising and risky move as the Juppé administration was not popular at the time and had been experiencing difficulties in reforming the employment and welfare legislation. Chirac's risk did not pay off and he was left with the embarrassing situation of his prime minister being defeated by the socialist candidate Lionel Jospin, previously considered to be something of a political lightweight in relation to Juppé.

In the National Assembly following the 1997 general election the socialists had 250 seats to the UDF/RPR's 253. But the balance was swayed by a socialist coalition with the 34 Communist Party seats and the 33 RCV seats. There are also 5 independents in the National Assembly. The President of the National Assembly is Laurent Fabius, a previous prime minister under President Mitterrand back in 1984.

The Senate last held elections in October 1995. The RPR have the most seats with 30 per cent of the house. There are five other political groupings and eight independent Senators. The President of the Senate, M. René Monory, is a member of the Groupe de L'Union Centriste, and was elected in 1995.

CURRENT POLITICAL ISSUES

M. Jospin was returned as prime minister on a classic left-wing ticket to increase social benefits and support and help the unemployed. The economy in the early months of 1998 is going his way with manufacturing output up by 3.3 per cent, low interest rates, inflation at just over 1 per cent, a foreign trade surplus of over $30 billion, GDP growth at 3 per cent, unemployment edging down and crucially (to meet the single European currency entrance criteria) government debt at 3 per cent. However, the government is fighting the temptation to distribute the recovery's dividends 'before we know it is durable' as Jospin announced on introducing some modest social benefit increases in February 1998.

This tight control on spending is causing tension within the left-wing alliance and Jospin's personal rating is beginning to slip. Meanwhile the RPR/UDF right-wing alliance is regrouping under the leadership of Philippe Seguin, who is forsaking his *dirigiste* credentials and putting together a set of policies marked by their free-market and welfare reform policies.

With the National Assembly still having four years left of its term, unless President Chirac braves a further dissolution, the right-wing have plenty of time to fine-tune their policies. There is a possibility that they may unify completely if they can manage to bury the leaders' personal ambitions. However, free-market reforms have a history of being encouraged in concept but thwarted in practice in France. The moves to privatise Air France under Prime Minister Balladur in the early 1990s almost brought the country to a standstill. More recently, roads and ports have been blockaded by lorry drivers protesting against employment law reforms that would be considered mild in many western economies. Thus M. Jospin's cautious progress in reforming the economy is to be expected while the out-of-power right-wing can make grand plans for more extreme policies.

The French have a deep-seated belief in the role of the state to manage the economy in a more interventionist manner than is accepted in other capitalist countries. Their principle of 'government of the people, by the people and for the people' is heavily ingrained and the relinquishing of government control of state-owned companies to private interests is frequently viewed as a loss of control for the employees and citizens rather than a positive competitive move.

This belief in the grandeur of national government is clearly seen in French foreign policy where wielding influence greater than its economic weight is a paramount concern. A strong hand in a strong Europe to counterbalance American 'hyper-power' is also a central tenet of French government policy regardless of party politics.

France maintains its position as a world leader through the use of sophisticated and often courageous foreign policies, often hoeing its own row and standing aloof from the crowd. Its insistence on maintaining an interventionist economy is similarly idiosyncratic yet appears to continue to confound the free-marketeers.

3

The System of Regional and Local Government

Florent Belleteste, Chambre de Commerce Française de Grande-Bretagne

Is France today what it used to be? I mean the archetype of a centralised state or the country with more local authorities than anywhere else in Europe following the path of decentralisation?

We will see first that the current situation stems from the past and the ideas advocated by two opposing factions, the 'Jacobins' and the 'Girondins'. Then, we will tackle the influence of the radical programme of decentralisation implemented in the 1980s. Finally, we will concentrate on the organisational structure which will probably remain the same for the foreseeable future.

'JACOBIN' STATE VERSUS 'GIRONDIN' TENDENCIES

Since the *ancien régime*, two different ideas of how power should be organised in a unitary state have been in conflict: should it be centralised or decentralised? Until the early 1980s the centralists had won the argument.

The Jacobins, like the monarchs of the *ancient régime*, imposed centralisation as their means of strengthening the regime against internal opponents and external enemies. Napoleon perfected it and future regimes consolidated the centralising work of the Jacobins. During the

20th century centralisation tendencies have been further accentuated by Jacobins such as General de Gaulle and Michel Debré, first Prime Minister of the Fifth Republic.

Why then did centralisation seem to take such a hold on the national psyche?

One explanation is that France has to be understood as a country of great geographical and cultural diversity and was created by bringing together people as distinct as Basques and Bretons, Béarnais and Burgundians, Alsations and Auvergnats, Normans and Provençals.

Also, parts of France such as Nice and Savoy are recent acquisitions only (they were annexed in 1860), and Alsace has twice this century (1918 and 1945) been taken back from the Germans.

Centralisation was the inevitable result of the need to impose minimum standards in areas such as education, housing and health. It was always felt by French politicians that centralisation was the only means of holding together a people so prone to social, political and religious strife.

It was a response to the egalitarian aspirations of the French.

As the result of historical, cultural, social and economic pressures, decision-making became increasingly concentrated in Paris, traditionally depicted as the centre of revolution which, in 1789, 1814–15, 1830, 1848 and 1871, disturbed the peace-loving province. Also, as Vincent Wright outlines in *The Government and Politics and France*, although Ile-de-France region, of which Paris is the regional capital, covers only 2 per cent of the national territory, it dominates the country's political life. Thus strong, unified and centralised authority became the basis of 'the one and indivisible republic'.

A 'RADICAL PROGRAMME' OF DECENTRALISATION

The framework of relations between national and local government, before 1982, was routinely centralised, thanks to a pyramid-shaped structure, from state to *commune* (parish), going through intermediate levels such as the *région* and the *département*.

Elected in 1981 the socialists embarked upon a decentralisation process in order to generate new life into French regions. Gaston Defferre, Mayor of Marseilles, was appointed Minister of the Interior and Decentralisation and his proposals were among the first acts of the new government.

The reforms of the 1980s were an attempt to clarify the situation, directly opposed to the logic of the central Jacobin state, laying the emphasis on daily democracy with new possibilities for freedom and responsibility. Juridically, the institutional principles are all visible in the the law enacted 2 March 1982: *Rights and liberties for the communes, départements and régions.* The emphasis is placed on both rights and freedoms.

The first major step in the process, the March 1982 Act, affected all levels of local government. Between 1982 and 1986, 48 laws were passed, 269 decrees adopted, and numerous circulars distributed in the push to implement the decentralisation programme. The following are some of the measures undertaken:

- The government increased the political power of locally elected officials by transferring executive responsibility to them in the *régions* and the *départements*. New powers were granted to the local authorities: the *communes* received increased powers in urban planning; the powers of the *départements* were enhanced in areas such as health, social welfare, education, road maintenance and school bus transport, the *régions* were given new powers in planning, land-use planning, economic intervention and professional training.
- Not only was the power of elected officials increased, but the regional councils were to be elected by the people.
- Local finance was somewhat rationalised. Some specific grants were transformed into block grants, and new financial resources were made available to local governments.
- Certain tasks previously carried out in Paris were transferred to local state services through the prefects.

It will be several years before the final shape of centre–local relations is discernible, and it is therefore premature to draw up a balance sheet of the socialist reforms.

THE ORGANISATIONAL STRUCTURE

Despite the decentralising measures of the 1960s, 1970s, and above all the 1980s, the position of the centre remains powerful.

Three main sources of central power can be underlined:

- the statutory weakness of local authorities and the obsessive control exercised by Paris and its provincial agents, the prefects and the technical services, even if the power of the latter has always been exaggerated and its nature misunderstood;
- the archaic nature of present structures which renders local government sometimes ineffective and vulnerable to central pressure, even if the state depends on the localities in certain respects and state officials are often sensitive to local requirements;
- the financial dependence of local authorities on Paris even if local government has its own taxes.

No one disputes that France is a unitary state, where most major decisions are taken in Paris. However, it is important to know not only where decisions are taken but from where they emanate and where they are shaped. In this respect, relations between the centre and the periphery are more subtle and complex than one can imagine. There is frequently a great measure of agreement between them, a mutual system of interdependence and self-interest exists.

Another key theme is the Europeanisation of French politics during the 1980s. Most politicians and ordinary citizens now acknowledge what de Gaulle vehemently denied for so long: that France is an integral part of a supranational European Union. Its economy is interdependent with those of other members, its monetary policy is tied and its economic policies in most areas are now made jointly through the European mechanisms based in Brussels. Europeanisation also means that domestic politics are increasingly normal, in that they resemble those of France's similar-sized European neighbours, like Britain.

The permanent presence of Europe in the French political arena is today an important and fundamental theme. This is reflected in the relentless struggle being fought between the three different levels of government in that they all fully appreciate the consequences of Europe becoming an important instrument of power.

Major problems were and are still not tackled. No attempt was made to rule the respective powers of the various local authorities in any over-

Table 3.1 Number of *communes* in France according to size

Number of inhabitants	Number of *communes*	Population
0–699	25,792	6,984,603
700–1,999	6,621	7,584,091
2,000–4,999	2,402	7,308,516
5,000–9,999	817	5,588,695
10,000–19,999	412	5,693,608
20,000–49,999	285	8,702,912
50,000–99,999	68	4,503,062
100,000–299,999	31	4,752,294
300,000 and more	5	4,178,858
Total	**36,433**	**55,296,639**

Source: 'Les cahiers Français', *La documentation Française* 239

Table 3.2 The 22 régions of France

Régions	Superficie (km^2)	Population 1986 (000s)
Alsace	8,280	1,599.6
Aquitaine	41,308	2,718.2
Auvergne	26,013	1,334.3
Bourgogne	31,582	1,606.9
Bretagne	27,209	2,763.8
Centre	39,151	2,324.4
Champagne-Ardenne	25,606	1,352.2
Corse	8,680	248.7
Franche-Comté	16,202	1,085.9
Ile-de-France	12,012	10,249.7
Languedoc-Rousillon	27,376	2,011.9
Limousin	16,942	735.8
Lorraine	23,547	2,312.7
Midi-Pyrénées	45,348	2,355.1
Nord-Pas-De-Calais	12,414	3,927.2
Basse-Normandie	17,589	1,372.9
Haute-Normandie	12,317	1,692.8
Pays-de-la-Loire	32,082	3,017.7
Picardie	19,399	1,773.5
Poitou-Charentes	25,810	1,583.6
Provence-Alpes-Côte d'Azur	31,400	4,058.8
Rhônes-Alpes	43,698	5,153.6
Total	**543,965**	**55,279.3**

Source: 'Les cahiers Français', *La documentation Française* 239

all or rational way: the existing powers of each were left intact and new ones were simply added.

Nor was there any restructuring of local government boundaries. France will continue to live with its 36,000 *communes* (see Table 3.1), 96 *départements* and 22 *régions* (see Table 3.2) – the most fragmented system of local government in western Europe (see Table 3.3) and probably the world. Centralising pressures are poised to remain.

The fact that all the different levels of administration are listed without distinction means that they work along the same lines and have an identical goal. Each has its own specific issues to deal with, issues being allocated to the level considered most suitable to cope with the citizen's needs. That is to say, roughly, the *régions* manage the Lycées, professional training and direct economic aid for firms, while the *départements* look after the *collèges*, school transport, social assistance and indirect aid for businesses. Finally, the *communes* deal with primary schools and urban issues. Thus we can speak, as the French do, about the three 'Ps': *'Proximité'* for the *commune, 'Péréquation'* (adjustment) for the *département* and 'Promotion' for the *région*.

Table 3.3 Number of local authorities in Europe

Country	Local government levels
Germany	8,839
Austria	2,309
Belgium	608
Denmark	289
Spain	8,077
France	**36,564**
Greece	6,073
Ireland	115
Italy	8,188
Luxembourg	126
Netherlands	726
Switzerland	3,023
United Kingdom	954
Portugal	277

Source: 'Les cahiers Français', *La documentation Française* 239

4

Comparison with Main Trading Partners

Olivier Cadot, INSEAD

France's somewhat lukewarm support for the Uruguay round of multi-lateral trade liberalisation and its recent drive to reinforce the EU's already awesome antidumping arsenal, together with the uneven penetration of French products on markets outside Europe, project the image of a country feeling threatened by globalisation. At the same time, France justifiably boasts of being the world's fourth largest exporter and has been recording rising trade-balance surpluses for five years in a row. Can these conflicting images be somehow reconciled through a candid assessment of France's economic health?*

---

* I will deliberately avoid using the term 'competitiveness'. Whereas corporations in the same line of business compete with one another, the best ones becoming the most profitable (something that can be readily verified at the bottom of their balance sheet), nations trade more than they compete with each other and have no clear-cut bottom line, so that analogies between corporations and nations are in this regard at best approximations. Only one line of argument may suggest that there is some degree of competition between nations as far as industrial policy is concerned – namely, that because some industries are characterised by technological spillovers and barriers to entry (eg civil aeronautics or semiconductors), governments may actively compete to attract or nurture them. The limit to this line of reasoning is that industrial policies are unlikely to succeed in the absence of local inputs that are key to their success, such as infrastructure, skills, R&D capabilities, and so forth. Looking at national market shares in those industries is then a round about way of inferring the quality of those inputs (or the effectiveness of industrial policies, when applicable) without introducing the dubious notion of 'national competitiveness'.

FRANCE'S FOREIGN TRADE IN PERSPECTIVE

Figure 4.1 shows France's 'import-coverage ratio' (ICR, computed as total exports to the world divided by total imports from the world) over the 30-year period 1967–97. It suggests two observations. First, the short-term volatility of France's ICR has been reduced significantly over time. In France's case, the ICR's volatility in the first half of the sample was mainly attributable to imports, which have traditionally included a substantial proportion of oil and raw materials whose world prices fluctuate. As the share of intra-European trade (mostly made of manufactured products) rose in France's overall trade, this source of volatility gradually lost weight. Secondly, and perhaps more import-antly, the mid-1970s marked the beginning of a severe deterioration in France's external position, from which the country recovered only 15 years later. Was the 1973 oil shock the only problem? Whereas the perception during those years was that the source of France's difficulties was primarily external, additional internal factors, whose effects have lingered on until now, were also at play. First, as rising oil and raw-material costs reduced

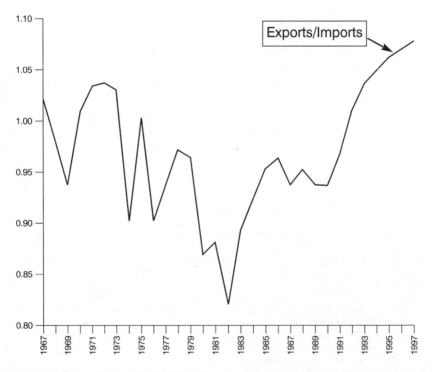

Source: Chelem 1996, *OECD Main Economic Indicators*, February 1998

Figure 4.1 France's import-coverage ratio, 1967–96

the share of sales revenue that could be used to remunerate labour and capital, governments were faced with a dilemma: should they attempt to preserve the purchasing power of wage-earners through rising minimum wages and negotiated collective agreements, albeit at the expense of the return on capital, or should they attempt to maintain corporate profitability? It turns out that successive French governments, be they of the Right or the Left, all chose the former option; in doing so, they bought social peace but at the price of a severe loss of competitiveness. Secondly, an inflationary environment traditionally accommodated by a weak currency turned suddenly – as in the rest of the OECD – into a deflationary one, characterised by very high real interest rates and a strong currency. Thus, during the 20-year period extending roughly between 1974 and 1994, French corporations found themselves squeezed on multiple counts: high material costs, high labour costs, high interest rates, and a depressed domestic demand. In response to this hostile environment, they spent much of the 1980s restructuring, reducing their indebtedness, and cleaning up their balance sheets; they were, as a result, hardly in a position to seek market-share gains. By the early to mid-1990s, the restructuring was over: the share of profits in value added was back to 32 per cent (from a low of 26 per cent in 1980) and the ratio of debt service to gross operating surplus was down to 20 per cent (from 35 per cent in 1980); with the return of profitability, French firms could regain some of the lost market share, and the trade balance improved rapidly, as Figure 4.1 shows.

Beyond the temporary macroeconomic difficulties just described, the country's foreign environment has undergone three major changes in the last 40 years: first, the erosion of dominant positions in ex-colonial markets where sales were comparatively easy; secondly, the elimination of trade barriers within Europe and the emergence of a fiercely competitive single market; thirdly, the end of the franc's repeated devaluations, which, in the 1960s and 1970s, allowed the country to accommodate rising labour costs and buy social peace. In fact, not only did the franc stop its regular slide downward: it started appreciating alongside the Deutschemark, to which it has been virtually pegged since 1987. Thus, the franc's 'effective exchange rate' (a weighted average of its rates against the currencies of France's major trading partners) appreciated by more than 10 per cent over the period 1990–96. The return of a strong export performance under such radically altered conditions sanctions equally fundamental changes in management, technology and labour relations. French products have made tremendous progress in terms of manufacturing quality, and their brand image in Europe has improved markedly in this regard. Labour relations have improved, not just because unions are weaker than they used to be (an average of 8 days per year per thousand inhabitants have been lost to strikes over 1993–95, against 44 in Italy, 19 in the USA, 7 in the UK, and 4 in Germany; in 1996, only 444,000 days in total were lost to strikes, against 1.3 million in the UK) but also because empowerment and participative management styles are – albeit slowly – gaining ground. Finally, continuous innovation and a drive to export are now spreading to small and medium-sized companies which used to rely entirely on the domestic market.

If this optimistic analysis is true, one may wonder why the French are so worried about globalisation. As a matter of fact, in spite of the vigorous restructuring of the last two decades, two dark spots stubbornly persist. First, France suffers from a syndrome that is, unfortunately, common to most of Europe – namely, an apparent inability to make strong headway in high-tech industries. Figure 4.2 shows the export market shares of France, Germany, the UK, Japan and the USA, for an aggregate of high-tech products. It is readily apparent that France's export market share in high-tech products has never reached 10 per cent and shows no sign of improvement – although an optimist would remark that it shows no sign of decline either, unlike that of Germany

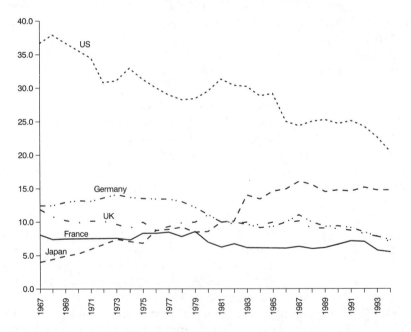

* Pharmaceutical products, aeronautics, electronic components, computer products, telecom equipment and precision instruments. Consumer electronics are excluded

Source: Chelem 1996

Figure 4.2 Export market shares in high-tech products*, 1967–94

or the United States. Be that as it may, France undoubtedly suffers from a competitiveness gap in high-tech industries. Such a gap is a paradox: like the rest of Europe, France has a highly educated labour force and world-class research capabilities – although the UK performs better by a Nobel-prize count and Germany by a patent count. Given France's capabilities, the theory of comparative advantage predicts that it should export skill- and R&D-intensive products, whereas the trade data show just the opposite; moreover, of all OECD countries only Japan, a relative newcomer in global R&D, is making headway in those industries. Why this is so is a puzzle, and only piecemeal explanations have been offered so far. One of the most convincing – at least for France – has to do, paradoxically, with governments that were too well-wishing. Starting with General de Gaulle's *Plan Calcul*, governments have for years laboured to establish national champions in the electronics and computer industries through engineered mergers, state ownership, subsidies and a forceful use of procurement. But all these policies backfired. Forcing a relatively efficient firm to merge with or acquire less efficient ones, for instance, inevitably clouded the former's balance sheet, diverting scarce managerial talent and producing a hardly manageable commercial entity with few internal synergies, no corporate culture and little drive for internal growth. Forced mergers would typically be followed by waves of downsizing, renewed subsidisation and further rounds of mergers. The result, it is now recognised, was an unmitigated disaster. If France did retain in Bull a national champion in the computer industry and in Thomson one in consumer electronics, the costs of doing so for the taxpayer were staggering, and by all accounts out of proportion with the benefits – especially given that the majority of the jobs were anyway lost to relocation in southeast Asia. The deep political embarrassment that followed the aborted sell-off of Thomson to Daewoo in 1996 illustrated vividly the contradictions and dead ends of industrial policy *à la française*; in fact – although it may still be early for such a claim – this unfortunate incident provoked an unprecedented domestic debate about the usefulness of *dirigisme* and is likely to prove a watershed in official doctrines about industrial policy.

If France could not nurture a local IBM – General de Gaulle's dream – it did not produce a local Microsoft either. Long-standing mistrust between academia and business, an extremely risk-averse banking system, disproportionate penalties for bankruptcy and the absence of a well-developed venture capital market or, until recently, of an equivalent of America's NASDAQ, have all contributed to stifle incentives for start-up creation, especially in high-tech industries. Indeed, part of the justification for governmental drives to 'pick winners' among existing large firms was the absence of a fabric of small firms capable of emerging on global markets through internal growth. But until recently, few in official circles would recognise that the absence of such a fabric was itself the consequence of a hostile business environment largely attributable to a multiplicity of bureaucratic hurdles. Is this changing? Although any serious change is hardly noticeable so far, some signs are encouraging. In spite of strong union opposition, the left-wing government elected in 1997 views the development of pension funds favourably; such a development, together with the recent creation of Europe's EASDAQ, would have key implications for the access of start-ups to capital markets. Similarly, the current government is considering regulatory reforms designed to improve the incentives for scientists in academia to start their own businesses. While such reforms are only piecemeal and would in any case take time to become effective, it is fair to say that the climate is changing, both in Parisian officialdom and at the grass-roots level. In the long run, there is no reason why France – like the rest of Europe – could not leverage its extraordinary wealth of human capital into successful entrepreneurship. The success of Ariane, Airbus, or the TGV demonstrates that France can excel in large-scale projects combining infrastructure and technology development. Independent entrepreneurs have found it more difficult to blossom in their homeland, and French talent can be found, in increasing numbers, in California or the United Kingdom. But this willingness to venture abroad should itself be taken as a good sign, for if an increasingly open and dynamic Europe (together with nostalgic memories of sweet France) ultimately lures some of them back, they will bring with them a broader experience, more openness and a familiarity with global markets that are still too rare among French entrepreneurs.

The second weakness of France's industry is the combination of a heavy focus on European markets and of a weak penetration of high-growth markets – although the definition of a 'high-growth market' is bound to be affected by the 1997 Asian crisis. Table 4.1 shows where French exports went in 1996, in comparison with German exports. Contrary to a common perception, the geographical spread of exports, and in particular the importance of extra-European exports in the total, do not differ dramatically between France and Germany: whereas the share of intra-European exports in total exports is 70 per cent for Germany, it is only marginally higher (72 per cent) for France. What is slightly different, however, is where those extra-European exports go: including Japan, the once-booming Asia–Pacific region accounts for 11.5 per cent of Germany's exports, against only 9.5 per cent for France's; similarly, the NAFTA region (made up of the United States, Canada and Mexico) accounts for 9 per cent of Germany's exports, against 7 per cent of France's; by contrast, Africa and the

Table 4.1 Destination of French and German exports, 1996

Destination	France	Germany
Europe (EU 15 + non-EU)	71.63%	70.14%
Eastern Europe & CIS	1.72%	3.73%
NAFTA	7.14%	8.72%
Latin America	1.84%	1.96%
Africa & Middle East	8.14%	3.99%
Japan	1.91%	2.71%
Other Asia & Pacific	7.62%	8.75%

Source: OECD, *Monthly Statistics of Foreign Trade,* February 1998

Middle East, two regions having experienced slow growth over the entire postwar period (except for the Middle East's oil boom) still account for as much in France's exports as in Germany's.

By and large, these differences are minor, and one can say that the structure of France's foreign trade is fairly similar to that of Germany. However, from a corporate perspective, this similarity can hide significant differences. The automobile sector is a case in point. Over the last decade, capacity growth in Europe has been outpacing demand by a wide margin. As ever more excess capacity is added to an already glutted market, the stage is set for a bloodbath reminiscent of the one that took place in the steel industry in the 1970s – except that, given new budget constraints, the automobile sector is unlikely to benefit from a rescue package on the scale of the steel industry's *Plan Davignon*. Whereas car-makers with a more global reach, like Germany's Volkswagen, can use rear bases to withstand a price war in Europe, French producers, with their exclusive European focus, lack this capability. The key difference here is not so much one of *exports*, but of *investments*, as for example Volkswagen has non-European subsidiaries that can contribute to the group's overall profitability should the European unit run into trouble. Renault is undoubtedly forcing the pace of its globalisation, but time is running out; as for Peugeot, precious time and resources wasted in failed Chinese and Indian ventures will be difficult to make up. In this regard, the automobile sector is quite representative of the problems faced by French industry, although it paints a picture that is probably darker than the overall one: first, the oil shock revealed a host of structural problems, including deficient processes and quality management, a weak financial structure, and adversarial labour relations. Then, within 15 years – under the threat of trade liberalisation – the sector reduced its indebtedness, shook itself up and improved its performance in all respects, an effort showing up in a rate of productivity growth that jumped from 3 per cent to 5 per cent annually after 1980. But while the industry was getting its act together, the world was not sitting idle; and by the time Peugeot and Renault were finally in shape, it was very late. Problems such as these are hidden in Table 4.1, because they have to do with direct investments and relocation decisions, which are not recorded by trade data (Volkswagen cars made in Brazil are counted by the OECD as Brazilian products); but they are no less real.

On the other hand, emerging markets – be they Asian or Latin American – have not reserved only good surprises in the past. European markets are growing slowly, but they are, by and large, stable and predictable; penetrating riskier markets demands not only a global vision, but also financial muscle which, for reasons explained earlier, corporate France has been lacking until recently.

In sum, France's export performance, particularly in the last decade, suggests underlying changes in management, labour relations and the climate of public policy. These microeconomic changes, whose analysis is beyond the scope of this chapter, are deep-rooted and, to a large extent, irreversible; they provide ground for further growth and modernisation, and it is fair to say that the country should welcome rather than loath the intensification of world trade. In this regard, the country's performance is ahead of its spirits. However, new challenges (see below) lie ahead; moreover, the favourable diagnosis that, we have argued, is suggested by trade figures needs to be further substantiated by a look at productivity data, to which we now turn.

PRODUCTIVITY

As in the rest of the OECD, the growth of labour productivity has been steadily slowing down in France over the last three decades. However, the French productivity slowdown has lagged behind that of its main trading partners, so that French rates of productivity growth have been, in comparison, relatively high. Table 4.2 shows the growth of two productivity measures: labour productivity, ie output divided by the labour force, and total factor productivity (output divided by a weighted average of the labour force and the capital stock). Whereas the first measure can record either increased efficiency or substitution of capital for labour, the second records only increases in productive efficiency due to technological progress, improved production processes, or the accumulation of human capital.

The fact that France was, over the three sub-periods covered by Table 4.2, among the sample's two or three best performers in terms of total

Table 4.2 Productivity growth in the business sector (annual averages)

Labour productivity	1960–73	1973–79	1979–96
France	5.3	2.9	2.2
Germany	4.5	3.1	1.1
United Kingdom	4.1	1.6	1.8
Italy	6.4	2.8	2.1
United States	2.6	0.3	0.8
Japan	8.4	2.8	2.2
Total factor productivity	**1960–73**	**1973–79**	**1979–96**
France	3.7	1.6	1.3
Germany	2.8	1.6	0.8
United Kingdom	2.7	0.7	1.5
Italy	4.4	2.0	1.2
United States	1.9	0.1	0.6
Japan	5.7	1.1	1.1

Source: OECD *Economic Outlook* **62**, December 1997, Table A58

factor productivity growth tends to confirm our earlier interpretation of the trade data: namely, that France has been witnessing improved managerial performance, technological upgrading, and enhanced worker education on a scale significant enough to be recorded by aggregate statistical data.

As for *labour* productivity, because of the rapid growth recorded in Table 4.2, current levels are very high in France. GDP per employee-hour, for instance, was in 1996 $40.4, against $39.4 in Germany and Japan, $33.2 in Italy, $31.6 in the US, and $22.6 in the UK. In industry, French productivity ($64,000 of annual value added per worker) is second only to Japan ($84,000). But this rapid growth can be interpreted in two ways. On the one hand, it is consistent with the previous interpretation – namely, increased process efficiency. On the other hand, it is necessarily related to one of France's most daunting problems: the failure of growth to create new jobs in sufficient numbers to reduce unemployment. It is precisely because output growth – itself relatively slow: over the last five years, it averaged 1.1 per cent per year, against 2.6 per cent in Germany, 0.8 per cent in the UK, 1 per cent in Italy, 2.6 per cent in the US and 2.1 per cent in Japan – was obtained with higher productivity rather than added employment that it failed to reduce unemployment. In turn, a corporate choice to squeeze out more from the existing labour force rather than hire new employees is likely to be the consequence of high labour costs (especially inclusive of social security charges) and firing impediments. In spite of recent wage moderation, with an average hourly compensation inclusive of social security charges of $18.8 in the manufacturing sector in 1996, France remains a high labour-cost country, roughly on par with Japan ($20.4), although less expensive than neighbouring Germany ($30.3). Thus, rising labour productivity and the slow growth of employment are but two sides of the same coin: whereas the labour force grew by a cumulative 2.3 per cent over 1991–95, employment *shrank* by 0.7 per cent over the same period. As a result, France's unemployment rate stands in 1997 at 12.5 per cent, one of the highest levels in the OECD, and has been above the OECD average in every single year since 1983. On the other hand, the recovery of 1994–95 had a stronger 'job content' than previously, due in part to the development of part-time employment and to various government schemes reducing the burden of social-security charges on low wages. The slower productivity growth which also characterised this recovery was thus, from an employment point of view, good news.

As the unemployment rate is much higher for unskilled workers (23 per cent) than for skilled workers (10.7 per cent), and young people are more affected than the average, there is widespread suspicion that the minimum wage, punitive social security charges, and firing impediments, to which jobs for the young and the unskilled are particularly sensitive, are at the root of France's unemployment problem. However, rising labour costs cannot have been the sole reason for the net job destruction that has been taking place over the last few years. The highest rates of job destruction have in fact been observed not among salaried people, but among the self-employed, whose numbers shrank by 13 per cent over the 1991–95 period. For those people, labour costs can hardly have been the issue, and the puzzle of the disappearing self-employed can be explained instead by two factors independent of labour costs. One is simply the slow growth that has characterised the French economy over the last six years. The second has to do with the nature of that growth. The 1990s have been characterised, in France, by a consistently high savings rate and a stagnant consumption. As a result, whatever growth there was came, to a large extent, from booming exports. As individual firms, typically concentrated in the service sector, serve primarily the domestic market, they were hurt more than larger ones by a depressed domestic market.

Whereas depressed internal consumption has contributed to raise unemployment in spite of vigorous foreign demand, empirical studies have also suggested that France's high savings rate and depressed consumption are themselves largely attributable to the fear of unemployment. Thus, during the first half of the 1990s, the economy was trapped in a vicious circle whereby unemployment depresses consumption, and depressed consumption fuels unemployment. It was only with the sudden return of consumer confidence during 1997 that a ray of hope appeared. As household indebtedness reached a low point, consumers had accumulated a backlog of durable-good replacement needs, and a change of government triggered a turnaround in popular mood, favourable conditions were set for a recovery of consumption, which started to gather momentum towards the end of 1997. Can this still timid recovery do anything to dent the country's ever-rising unemployment rate? Although political leaders, loath of uttering again hollow promises, remain understandably cautious, there is reason to be moderately optimistic. The OECD estimates that France's structural rate of unemployment, given the present regulations affecting its labour markets, is around 9–10 per cent. A cyclical decrease from 12.5 per cent to 9.5 per cent would already be hailed by everyone in the country as a victory; such good news would further boost consumer confidence and provide a second-round impetus to consumption and investment growth. Would this be enough to set France's unemployment rate on a sustained downward path? There is reason to doubt this. A sustained reduction in the unemployment rate will require more than just a reversible recovery: it will require that the foundations be laid for long-run growth in the private sector.

CHALLENGES AHEAD

Whereas the reduction of France's unemployment rate is, and has been – to little avail, so far – at the top of the agenda of every single political party, there is in fact little that political leaders currently in power or in the mainstream opposition can do, or are willing to do, about it. Whether the recovery now under way will blossom depends primarily on exchange-rate developments and on the final outcome of the Asian crisis, both out of the reach of any European government. The best that France's current administration can do in the short term is probably to keep on resisting – as it has done so far – calls from its own left-wing to 'redistribute the dividends of growth' through further tax-and-spend schemes.

In the long term, however, in order to capitalise on its already deep and painful modernisation effort, France will need to remove three remaining obstacles to improved economic efficiency. First, it will have to free its labour markets from well-intended but counter-productive regulations. Secondly, it urgently needs to reform its welfare state and pension system. Thirdly, and perhaps most importantly – because this third element encompasses the previous two – it needs to shrink its state. But making these reforms politically palatable and getting their timing right will be no easy task. Labour-market deregulation is a case in point.

Few even among union leaders – except perhaps the most backward-looking – doubt that some degree of flexibility is needed in the country's labour markets. The growth of so-called 'interim agencies' which provide temporary workers to employers at a steep intermediation cost shows that there is a real need for hiring and firing flexibility, especially among small and medium-sized firms. The problem, of course, is to sell added flexibility to a restive opinion fearing that the immediate effect of looser firing regulations would be to trigger a flood of lay offs. Added flexibility against a background of high and chronic unemployment clearly means added precariousness, because in the short term, easier firing regulation will simply mean more lay offs, whereas the effect on hiring will be felt only over time. Comparisons between France – or continental Europe, for that matter – and the United States are, in this regard, of limited relevance. American-style labour-market flexibility is, of course, acceptable for workers against a backdrop of full employment, because easy lay offs are compensated by abundant job opportunities. But a generous welfare state *à la française* would be equally innocuous under full employment, because it would not cost much; indeed, France's welfare state did not seem to create more unemployment than in the United States until the 1980s. From then on, the two countries were clearly not on the same path, but they differed in (at least) two relevant economic variables. The first was of course the magnitude of the 'structural impediments' to hire. The second, no less important, was the macroeconomic-policy environment – the US has enjoyed a strong and almost uninterrupted boom since 1983, led by budget and current-account deficits that are, unfortunately, hardly sustainable in the long term. Thus, a better comparison of the effects of labour-market deregulation would be between the UK and continental Europe; but such a comparison would hardly suggest that labour-market reform works miracles overnight. In addition, given the magnitude of public resistance to such reform in France, however desirable in the long term, it would run a serious risk of further undermining consumer confidence; the extreme caution of French governments in this regard is thus quite understandable. All this does not mean, of course, that some degree of deregulation and added flexibility are not needed; rather, the point is that focusing on labour-market deregulation early on in the structural reform process might, quite unnecessarily, turn the whole thing into a scarecrow, jeopardising support for other, less contentious but equally urgent, aspects of the reform agenda.

For instance, France needs to rethink its welfare state. Without going into an in-depth discussion of welfare reform, a few elements of a widely shared diagnosis can be briefly laid out. The French welfare system suffers from many ailments, but two basic flaws stand out. First, the current system discourages work, because income-support measures for the poor are drastically reduced as soon as individuals obtain employment, thus implicitly taxing employment income at a prohibitive rate. Instead of alleviating poverty and exclusion, such a system actually *contributes* to the creation of a 'welfare trap'. Reform schemes loosely inspired of the American negative income tax concept are currently being considered (the negative income tax basically gives a lump-sum subsidy to every individual and taxes all income, so that people below a given income threshold *receive* money from the state; its key advantage is that an individual taking on a job is taxed at the normal rate, because employment income does not abruptly reduce the individual's subsidy entitlement). A full-blown negative income tax is unlikely to appear soon in France, but punitive effective tax rates for individuals who attempt to leave welfare status should be eliminated, and reform is, in this area, long overdue. The second looming large-scale problem is pensions. Under the present system, which is based on redistribution, active individuals pay for currently pensioned individuals. For demographic reasons, in France as elsewhere, the baby-boom generation must, so to speak, pay twice: it must pay for currently retired people, and it must also save money for itself, because tomorrow's active population will not be able to sustain the large numbers of retiring baby-boomers. Thus, in spite of partial reforms mitigating some of the present system's worst aberrations (such as reduced mandatory retirement age at a time of rising life expectancy) something more is urgently needed, namely a pension-fund system. But the fiscal incentives necessary to kick off such a system will necessarily hurt the financing of the redistribution system, because contributions to pension funds would entitle workers to deductions from social security taxes; hence opposition from the unions which manage the existing system. But in spite of predictable resistance from interested parties, reforms of this type are somewhat less contentious than labour-market deregulation; if presented in a reasonable way, they could certainly be sold to a public opinion that is, in many respects, more mature than an unimaginative political class seems to assume.

Finally, and perhaps most importantly, France can no longer afford a disproportionately costly bureaucracy which lives, to a large extent, on an outdated reputation of integrity and efficiency. An education minister recently struck a raw nerve when speaking of 'cutting in the mammoth's fat' – referring to a possible downsizing of the Ministry of Education itself. Cutting in the mammoth's fat is, as a matter of fact, overdue in virtually every sector of government bureaucracy in France. Whereas French officials in Brussels battle deregulation allegedly to preserve what they call 'a French model of public services', the reality is one of overpriced and obsolete services with little customer orientation and even less accountability. Part of the deep self-confidence crisis that affects today's France is due to the slow disintegration of a model in which an enlightened elite used to lead the country along the path of modernisation. That elite is now discredited, not only because it has not lived up to its own ethical standards – this would be serious enough in itself – but also because the model that it stood for (based on state-owned monopolies, industrial policy and a revolving door between the private and public sectors) has outlived its usefulness. France's 'enarchy', an expression designating the reigning *énarques*, or graduates of the Ecole Nationale d'Administration, is now a little like its chivalry after it had lost successively the battles of Poitiers, Crécy, and Agincourt to the English: costly given its limited prowess.

CONCLUSION

This brief overview of the French economy has tried to paint an optimistic yet uncomplacent picture of France's economic health. The country has transformed itself beyond recognition over the last 30 years, coping with 'decolonisation' and European integration outside, and with urbanisation and the disappearance of a still relatively large farmer class inside. Because these changes took place in a period of time that is short by historical standards (the shrinkage of the peasantry started much earlier in northern Europe), they imposed considerable stress on the country's social fabric and created a feeling of lost identity. But in retrospect, it is fair to say that France managed its transformation quite well, maintaining national consensus on a wide range of issues, preserving key aspects of a way of life to which the French remain deeply attached, and simultaneously acquiring a new drive for innovation and export. This capacity to look forward and tackle problems head on, which is not always perceptible from abroad, should make the French optimistic about their country's capacity to meet the next challenges and find a new 'French model'.

5

French Companies and the Euro

Jacques Creyssel, Conseil National du Patronat Français (CNPF)

From the outset, French companies have been among those most in favour of the single European currency. Today they are deeply immersed in concrete preparations for what is without doubt the most important economic event in the coming years.

OVERALL, FRENCH COMPANIES ARE IN FAVOUR OF THE EURO

The creation of the Euro on 1 January 1999 will represent a total revolution for all economic players and in particular for companies, their clients, their suppliers and their staff. These companies should derive significant advantages from the single currency which will be counterbalanced, in the early stages, by some considerable practical constraints.

Advantages for Companies

Overall, French companies should derive *five main advantages* from the introduction of the Euro (each company being more or less concerned by a specific point depending on its position or line of business):

- **An end to competitive devaluation**s Between 1992 and 1995 the successive devaluations of the lira, the pound, the peseta and the Scandinavian currencies were very expensive for

French companies in terms of exports, growth and employment, and seriously exposed them to the ravages of monetary crises.

Some studies have shown that through the cumulative results of these devaluations, between 1992 and 1995 France lost more than 130 billion fr in exports, the equivalent of 1.7 per cent of its GDP. Furthermore, calculations by the European Commission show that during these years the European economy as a whole lost the equivalent of at least half a point of growth per year, a figure which compares with 1 per cent annual growth in the French economy since 1990. Finally, a number of analyses by sector, particularly in textiles and footwear, showed the dramatic effects of these monetary variations on companies forced to lower their export prices, reduce their margins and then cut back sharply on their workforce.

For French companies, the Euro primarily means the end of competitive devaluations and the return to a more normalised competitive position based on prices and quality.

- **A reduction in financial costs**   Exporting companies should save significant sums in terms of exchange costs and exchange hedging. But, more important still, along with French business as a whole, they can expect an improvement in their financial profit due to greater stability in short-term interest rates.

  French companies today have two financial characteristics: a relatively low level of equity capital or quasi-equity capital and a high level of debt on a short-term index (around 50 per cent of current borrowing). They therefore suffered seriously from the sharp variations in short-term rates during the monetary crises in recent years, which has handicapped them compared to their competitors abroad, for no justifiable reason.

  For French companies, the Euro therefore means a single short-term interest rate for all European countries (in effect, there will only be one monetary market), by definition more stable than that at present, which will remove another factor distorting competition. It is therefore an essential element in security.

- **New market opportunities**   The use of a single currency in all European Union member states should consolidate the single market and enable companies to explore new markets without exchange rate risks.

  French companies will no doubt have assessed the competitive benefits on their own markets, but at the same time, they could seek out new clients in conditions equivalent to those of a domestic market. They will also be able to compare the prices from different European suppliers more easily and thereby improve, where possible, their purchasing position.

  For French companies, the Euro will therefore be a factor in increased competition on the European market but also the source of new opportunities, both in terms of clients and suppliers.

- **The consolidation of Europe's commercial and monetary weight** Just as Europe is stronger when it speaks with a single voice in GATT, the idea is that the Euro will carry greater weight than existing European currencies, and will therefore enable a rebalancing in worldwide economic relations.

  This is essential given that the dollar is involved in 83 per cent of transactions in exchange markets, and in 48 per cent of commercial transactions, while two-thirds of currency holdings are expressed in dollars. Now the Euro zone will have the same weight as the United States in international commerce. In addition, due to the amount of intra-Community trade, there will be considerably less exposure to the effects of monetary fluctuations in third party countries.

  For companies the Euro thus provides the opportunity to make 90 per cent of exchanges in a single currency.

- **Finally, a fantastic leverage to restore order to seriously run-down French public finances** This is essential given that strict adherence to the Maastricht criteria corresponds to a public deficit 20 per cent above the state's receipts or that the state debt now represents more than three years of these receipts.

Conditions for the Euro's success

French companies are among those in Europe which have the most to gain from the advent of the Euro. But the realisation of these advantages requires three conditions to be in harness:

- **Single currency for the maximum of members** The Euro's success clearly requires that the maximum number of countries, and particularly those whose currency has undergone competitive devaluation during recent years, join the singe currency as quickly as possible. Countries which do not enter the new mechanism in 1999 should make a definite commitment to convergence, enabling most of them to join by 2002. In this respect, the favourable evolution of the economic situation in Southern European countries (Italy, Spain and Portugal) is moving in the right direction.

- **Real economic stability** This requires countries becoming part of the single currency to be economically sound from the outset, and also to continue that way in subsequent years. Here again the project of the stability pact and the growth pact decided at the Amsterdam summit is going in the direction hoped for by companies, instituting a joint examination of economic policy and the possibility of very high sanctions for excessive public deficit.

- **'True' exchange parities** These will correct some of the unrealistic results of the monetary disorders of recent years. In this respect, one can only rejoice in the recent development which has seen the establishment of a virtuous link between the prospect of entering the single currency and the favourable evolution of exchange rates: the lire which was worth 1,270 lire to the DM has thus progressively come back down below 1,000 lire, since when the financial markets have believed in the possibility of Italy's rapid adherence to the single currency.

PRACTICAL CONSEQUENCES FOR FRENCH COMPANIES

The introduction of the Euro should have a number of practical repercussions on the evolutionary progress of French companies, often far more than imagined at the outset.

For a thorough analysis, a distinction must be made between constraints, technical problems, and the strategic issues.

Constraints for Companies

French companies are in danger of coming up against two serious constraints:

- The first fundamental constraint relates to the existence of a transition period between 1999 and 2002, during which two forms of the same money will legally co-exist, the Euro and the French franc.

  This stage, requested by the central banks for the manufacture of coins and banknotes, could give rise to significant costs for companies which are not used to working in several currencies and which have not sufficiently studied advance methods of minimising the cost of this additional complication with their usual partners (banks, advisers, and accountants). By contrast, for companies which have prepared themselves, depending on their situation, the transition period will offer a gradual changeover to the Euro and thus a spreading of the costs.
- The second constraint is a technical one, relating to the scale of the conversion works to be carried out on business computer systems. The age of the hardware and software could create a major difficulty here, and urgent thought should be given to it.

The Technical Problems

The Euro will directly affect:

- **Legal commitments overall, particularly contracts** The practical difficulties will nevertheless be relatively few due to the principle of contract continuity, adopted at the European level.

- **Accounting overall, from 1 January 1999,** and, if need be, until January 2002   Major problems that companies might come up against concern the choice of parity retained for closing the 1998 accounts, the treatment of the Euro flow in 1999, the methods for converting the opening balances for the first accounting period in Euros, the treatment of rounding up or down when converting, translation differentials, and the accounting of unresolved hedging operations at 1 January 1999.

  Each company can choose the date at which it will fully integrate its accounting in Euros, the choice is available to them from 1 January 1999.

- **Relations with the government**   Companies may pay their taxes and social security contributions in Euros from 1999, if they wish. Tax and social security declarations should also be in Euros, accounted in 1999 and 2000 respectively.

- **Relations with clients or suppliers,** according to the currency unit which will be used in the purchasing or billing chain   In order to forestall eventual difficulties, particularly between companies placing very large orders and the small and medium-sized enterprises (SMEs), regulations for good conduct have been established which should facilitate relations between partners.

- **Staff relations**   Modifying pay slips, company thresholds, training needs, etc.

- **Cash and exchange operations management**   Centralisation of cash management if necessary, reduction in hedging operations, short-term interest rates, etc.

- **Relations with banks**   Eventual opening of accounts in Euros, implementation of specific conversion services from French francs to Euros (and vice versa), eventual use of cheques in Euros, etc.

- **Daily life**   Notably including the range of problems posed by rounding up and down sums converted from Euro to French francs and vice versa (rounding on invoices, sales slips, pay slips, dividends paid to shareholders, conversion of company capital, etc).

On all these points, recommendations and regulations have been set out to facilitate the task for French companies by a mixed work group of professional administration organisations, financial companies and institutions, professionals in accounting and central banking, etc, commissioned to do this by the French government in order to put proposals to it, and positioned under the joint presidency of the Director-General of the French Association for Credit Institutions (Association Française des Etablissements de Crédit) and the Director-General of the Confederation of French Industry (Conseil National du Patronat Français – the 'Simon-Creyssel' group).

The Strategic Issues

Without any doubt, the resolution of all these technical problems will present an immense amount of work for French companies. The existence of numerous recommendations and rules of play for all participants (administrations, companies, banks, accountants) and recourse to the usual partners (banks, consultants, IT companies, chartered accountants) should, however, help the task significantly, if they set about it in time, but that is not yet certain.

Nevertheless, the greatest mistake by many companies at the moment is to focus on the technical consequences of the single currency's introduction, while forgetting the triple strategic issues that the Euro represents for the company.

The commercial issue

The introduction of the Euro will have extremely important consequences for the commercial policy of all French companies, whatever their field of activity:

- **The Euro will be a new business opportunity** The creation of a single currency and the elimination of exchange risks between many countries will enable the development of a lesser-risk export policy. The Euro thus provides the chance for many companies to totally review their business strategy.
- **The Euro will result in increased transparency of prices in Europe** It is expected that prices will be brought more into line, as will commercial practices, and this could lead to a substantial modification of pricing policies overall. Similarly, this new situation could lead many companies to change their buying policy, as they examine opportunities offered by new European suppliers.
- **The Euro will lead to conversion of all current prices:**
  - *current consumer price indexes will disappear:* new habits will be adopted or created, bearing in mind that the new prices in Euros will be seen to be about 6.5 times lower than the previous French franc prices. Many companies will therefore have to review their whole range of prices;
  - *'psychological' prices will also have to be modified:* the price of a pair of shoes marked at 199 French fr will in fact be 30.73 Euros,* which does not have the same interest in marketing terms;
  - *packaging will sometimes have to be changed:* either because of a new product policy (one pack of beers origin-

---

* For this example 1 Euro = 6.47551 French fr.

ally 19.99 French fr will become a pack at 3.09 Euros, a price which cannot be 'read' by consumers), or to minimise problems with rounding up or down (such as the production of small change coins with a unit value below 6 centimes, that is, one Euro cent).

● **The existence of a three-year transition period will also cause specific difficulties, especially concerning dual labelling**   In particular, companies will have to determine from what moment they will have to translate their prices and catalogues into Euros and define the psychological prices in Euros. In the commercial field, they will also have to implement an evolving strategy to inform their customers, with the aim of progressively accustoming them to future prices in Euros. Besides this, the emergence of the Euro will encourage the use of electronic or bank payment methods, which could necessitate adaptation for some companies.

The strategic issue of information technology

In many companies, the adaptation of IT systems to the Euro will create a heavy burden. Four additional difficulties will complicate matters:

● existing software or hardware which is obsolete or implementation is made difficult because the programme's author is no longer available;
● the importance of future technical developments, particularly in the marketing arena and electronic trading;
● the simultaneous problem of software and the year 2000;
● the impossibility of predicting, at the present time, the speed at which the Euro will spread in companies and among individuals during the transition period, and consequently the rhythm of tasks to be achieved between 1999 and 2002.

In many French companies, the implementation of the Euro should therefore be an opportunity to carry out a thorough strategic reflection on the company's medium-term IT requirements.

The strategic issue for the company

The division of salaries by 6.5 will represent a 'shock' for many workers. One of the main issues arising for companies when going over to the Euro will be to anticipate this difficulty:

● by communicating all the necessary information to employees about the consequences of introducing the Euro in each company to prevent it being seen in a negative way;

- by giving them information about their salary in Euros during the transition period;
- by training company staff in good time about the use of the new currency;
- by preparing thoroughly to mobilise executives about everything to do with this long-term company project;

The importance of the internal issue for the company should not be underestimated because it will generally be the same people who receive salaries in Euros, pay for goods in Euros and use the Euro within the company.

CONCLUSION: A NEW DEAL FOR COMPANIES IN EUROPE

The Euro will cause profound changes in Europe for at least three reasons:

- The heightened comparability between prices and wages will make different charges and taxes between countries more apparent than before. There will therefore be an irresistible pressure to harmonise systems, particularly in the taxation field. It is not surprising to note in this respect that two of the questions most frequently asked during discussions about the Euro concern the harmonisation of accounts and the harmonisation of tax.
- The consolidation of ECOFIN's consulting role will lead to the creation of a form of official European economic government (EURO-X), and thus to a consolidation of the economic interdependencies.
- Perhaps above all, it seems hard to imagine that the coexistence can last between a central bank, making decisions on its own, by majority, and a European economic authority, bogged down in the procedures of unanimous voting or in convoluted subsidiarity mechanisms. The pursuit of a genuine common economic policy thus requires quite a significant modification of the existing institutional mechanisms, in particular by extending the majority vote to all fiscal questions concerning the single market, but also perhaps by providing new powers on a European scale (for example concerning external fiscal policy). More fundamentally, the Euro is also bound to lead to a choice between consolidating the harmonisation of rules, particularly fiscal ones, and a more federal-type system with a heavier common budget.

In fewer than 200 working days, there will thus be a completely new world opening up for French businesses, not without some serious advantages, but doubtless full of pitfalls and fascinating discoveries.

6

The Structure of the SMEs

Jackie Vasseur and Jane Kassis, Joint Venture Research Centre, Ecole Européenne des Affaires de Paris (EAP)

THE FRENCH SME, AN ESSENTIAL PART OF THE ECONOMY

The Typical Profile of the French Small Enterprise: Young, Fragile and Tiny

Of the 2.3 million French companies, two-thirds are less than ten years old and almost 95 per cent have a turnover of under 5 million fr.* Most of them fall into the category of very small companies.† The small and medium-sized companies account for 7 per cent of the total; they consist for the most part of companies with fewer than 50 employees (see Table 6.1). Although the percentage of SMEs in the total number of companies is comparable with the European average, France lacks medium-sized companies in comparison with Germany in particular. 'Making the SME grow' is a constantly recurring theme.

French SMEs, are more oriented towards service industries than their European counterparts, which are more inclined to manufacturing,

---

* One pound sterling equals approximately 10 French fr.
† We will use the following abbreviations: VSEs – very small enterprises under 10 persons; SMEs – small and medium-sized enterprises between 10 and 499 persons; BEs – big enterprises over 500.
‡ 'Les nouvelles PMI', Ministère de l'Industrie, des Postes et des Télécommunications, DGSI-SESSI, 1997.

Table 6.1   Breakdown of companies by number of employees (except agricultural and financial companies)

VSEs – very small enterprises, 0 to 9 employees	SMEs – small and medium-sized enterprises 10 to 499 employees			BEs – big enterprises, >500 employees
	Small enterprises, 10 to 49 employees	Medium-sized enterprises, 50 to 199 employees	Medium-sized enterprises, 200 to 499 employees	
2,258,000	140,300	22,100	4,000	2,000
92.7%	6%	0.9%	0.2%	0.1%

Source: *Tableaux de l'Economie Française* 1996–1997, 1996 edn

particularly the German 'Mittelstand'. Only 40,000 SMEs‡ are concentrated in the different sectors of industry, more than half in traditional sectors such as clothing and metallurgy; in spite of this, the commonly held view of economists and politicians reflected by the media often associates SME and industry.

The SME: A Major Contribution to Economic Activity in France

Small and medium-sized enterprises are the biggest private employer in France with more than half the total number of jobs in the private sector (see Table 6.3). Over the last ten years the big companies have constantly reduced their payrolls whereas the SMEs, and particularly the smallest of them, have created new jobs. In 1995, according to their managing directors, French SMEs created nearly 40,000 jobs.* If France is to offer new employment opportunities, these will come from smaller companies.

SMEs Create Much of the Wealth in France

France's economic success owes a lot to SMEs. According to the *commissariat général au plan*† they account for half of the country's GDP‡ and for 45 per cent of the overall turnover generated in France. On average, they have a growth rate of domestic sales slightly higher (2 per cent per year from 1988 to 1997) than that of big enterprises

---

* UFB Locabail survey, December 1996.
† Administration in charge of the general planning of the French economy.
‡ 'La France, l'Europe, Xeme plan 1989–1992', Rapport de la sous-commisiion PME dans 'Europe technologique, industrielle et commerciale', Commissariat Général du Plan.

Table 6.2   Breakdown of companies by activity

No of employees	Industry	Public works	Trade	Transport	Services
0–9	10.2	13.5	27.7	3.8	44.8
10–499	28.4	13.6	26.0	5.8	26.2
>499	50.0	5.0	15.0	5.0	25.0
All companies	11.6	13.5	27.6	3.9	43.4

Source: Problèmes economique, 2531, 27 August 1997

(1.5 per cent) and if their profitability is lower due to the high financial costs they must bear, their economic result is higher. These general data hide considerable differences. Three-quarters of the most profitable companies listed each year by the monthly magazine *L'Expansion* are SMEs with growth rates reaching 25 to 30 per cent;* at the same time, the large majority of subcontractors have very low, almost non-existent, profit margins.

The SMEs and National and Regional Planning

Small and medium-sized enterprises play an important part in the local economy; three-quarters of them have been set up in *communes* (localities) of under 100,000 inhabitants, whereas big companies are situated in or near big towns.[†] The geographical location of SMEs varies according to their activity: those in manufacturing are mainly located in *communes* with fewer than 5,000 inhabitants; SMEs in the

Table 6.3   Percentage of SME added value and salaried employment in 1993

	VSE	SME		BE
		10–49 employees	50–499 employees	
Added value	32	24	27	17
Salaried employment	25	27	32	16

Source: B. Duchénéaut, 'Enquêtes sur les PME françaises', *Maxima Laurent du Mesnil Editeur,* 1995

---

* *L'Expansion* 556 du 11 au 24 Septembre 1997.
[†] B. Duchénéaut, 'Enquêtes sur les PME françaises', *Maxima Laurent de Mesnil Editeur,* 1995.

service sector are in the more populated localities. According to a survey carried out in 1994 by Rennes Business School, SMEs are generally associated with local development. In answer to the question: 'Will SMEs foster local development more than big companies in the future?', 89 per cent said yes, while only 9 per cent said no.

STRENGTHS AND WEAKNESSES

The success of French SMEs is due mainly, as in other European countries, to their family-owned managerial structure. This form of organisation led to a strong relationship between workers and owners and a flat hierarchical structure which, in turn, encouraged greater worker motivation and led to a high degree of flexibility and innovation with little bureaucracy. Their weaknesses are specific to the French situation: a lack of financial resources, an insufficient level in exports and great difficulty in developing long term strategic thinking (see Table 6.4).

Dominant Legal Form: SARL, Predominantly Family-owned

Many company founders opted for corporate status: SARL, 'anonymous company with limited liability' for the small enterprises, and SA, 'anonymous company' for the others. Small and medium-sized companies are mostly family-owned. Only very few of them are linked to a group financially. As they grow, some SMEs tend to lose their strategic and financial independence: whereas only 12 per cent of small companies are dependent on a parent company, this percentage goes

Table 6.4   Strengths and weaknesses of SMEs

Strong points	Weak points
• Rapid decision-making	• Lack of financial resources
• Proximity to the markets and clients	• Lack of human resources: limited staff, day-to-day pressure
• Strong competence in very specialised activities	• Lack of technical resources: production capacity, automation
• Responsibility given to teams	
• Adaptable to change	• Lack of competence in management

Source: J. Vasseur and J. Kassis

up to 39 per cent for medium-sized companies, and 57 per cent for medium-sized industrial companies.

Many Companies Flourish Despite Risks and Uncertainty, but a Lot of Companies Don't Grow: They Lack Financial Resources

Contrary to what one might expect after listening to people talking in the media about the difficulty of starting up new companies in France because of all the administrative complexities, setting up a new company has become commonplace, and is certainly no longer as difficult as it was 15 years ago. Each year, 300,000* new companies are registered, a lot of trading companies, a little agriculture and construction, and very little industry. The company renewal rate is about 13 per cent, almost the same as in the UK. One-third of all newly created entities disappear in the space of two to three years and half of them after five years. However, the situation is not as bad as in the USA.[†] To help entrepreneurs, many initiatives are being developed (see Box 6.1).

If creation is no longer a real problem, the lack of development of these new companies penalises the French economy and employment. Unlike the situation in the USA and in the UK, there is no exemplary success story in France comparable to that of Dell computers, Cisco System or Vodaphone. The number of French compa-

---

Starting up a business in France –   **Box 6.1**
a network of aid for business start-ups
independent of the public authorities

The French Chambers of Commerce and Industry and the French Banking Association have joined forces in order to help reduce business start-up failures. They have organised a national network of professionals to help the creation and the transmission of companies (banks, CCI, liberal professions, professional bodies, public bodies such as ANVAR (National Agency for Research Valorisation). All actors involved in company start-ups are represented at one desk, 'Espace Entreprendre' in the CCI. Their role is to offer expertise and a regular follow-up during a period of three to five years and to facilitate the administrative and financial side of start-ups. Only serious projects which respect a certain number of criteria are accepted. The creators of new companies are given a 'Passeport Entreprendre' which is a guarantee of credibility giving them privileged access to the different actors in the network. (1700 companies in 1997.)

---

* 'Les nouvelles PMI, beaucoup de créateurs malgré les risques', Ministère de l'Industrie, des Postes et des Télécommunications, DGSI-SESSI, 1996.
[†] 'Les plus belles PME françaises de la décennie', *L'Expansion*, 556 du 11 au 24 Septembre 1997.

nies generating a turnover of more than 50 million French francs ten years after starting up remains small: in 1996, only 29 could boast strong growth and profitability.

There are many reasons for these weaknesses:

- **The founders lack ambition** Three-quarters of new companies have no employees when they start up, only three out of ten opt for corporate status. Over time this behaviour has not changed: as the small number of medium-sized companies shows, SME managing directors fearful of losing control and autonomy, favour profitability over growth. During the last ten years they made on average one-third only of the total investments of French companies, whereas they created 50 per cent of added value. The nature of these investments also shows the desire not to grow: 67 per cent invest in order to renew their material; only 29 per cent see as their objective, increased capacity.*
- **SMEs lack long-term financial resources** Many analyses conclude that they are under-capitalised; the average equity/balance sheet ratio of SMEs is one-quarter lower than it is in big companies. Their financial debts are higher even if over the last ten years SMEs have been gaining financial autonomy; their debt ratio has decreased considerably from 65 per cent in 1985 to 33 per cent in 1996 (see Table 6.5), mainly because of their lack of investment; the structure of their debt has remained the same.†
- **Today, sources of finance for the development of the SME are still inadequate**‡ Access to the stock exchange for SMEs

Table 6.5   Breakdown of debt in 1996

	SME	BC
Bank loans and leasing	36.1%	16.2%
Current bank credits	29.2%	13.0%
Other loans	6.4%	6.5%
Commercial papers	0.24%	5.1%
Obligations	2.9%	14.8%
Parent co & partners contribution	24.9%	44.3%

Source: Bulletin de la Banque de France, 45, Septembre 1997

---

* J. Brisac, 'Un panorama des PME en France', Centre d'Information sur l'Epargne et le Crédit, 1997.
† *Banque*, 585, Octobre 1997.
‡ O. Esposito and F. Beuscart, 'Qui finance la croissance des PMI', *L'usine Nouvelle* 8 Février 1996.

is very limited: in 1995, only 18 companies were introduced on the *second market:* A new market based on the NASDAQ started on 14 February 1998; it will be reserved for service and high-tech companies with high growth rates.

Risk and development capital invest 3.5 to 4 billion francs a year; this concerns about one thousand SMEs which are either very young, innovative with a high development potential, or older SMEs with regular development projects (5 to 10 per cent growth per year).These funds are often criticised for wanting to have a rapid return on investment by getting their capital out quickly (four to five years).

The one and only source of finance for many SMEs is bankers; but many misunderstandings exist between SMEs and banks. The latter repeatedly claim that 'it is not money which is lacking but good candidates'; and they ask the SME for more guarantees and to cover the economic risk with more capital. Managing directors of SMEs have a different view; they reproach bankers for refusing to take risks and for having high rates in general one or two points above those granted to big companies: 'I work with four banks and I have tried to put them into competition with each other; but they ask for enormous deposits. They will lend you one million as long as you yourself put one million on the table', were the words of the director of Cash System, a company with an exemplary development record. He set up his company five years ago with 50,000 fr; his capital today amounts to 1.5 million fr earned through reinvestment of the profit generated by the company.

SMEs and Management of Human Resources

There is a very heavy legal framework regulating industrial relations in France. But the presence of trade unions in companies is very low (10 per cent of trade union membership); unionisation does not exist in SMEs: when there are personnel delegates they are usually not trade union members.

Two legal threshold levels have a strong influence on the behaviour of SME directors:

- The threshold of ten employees means the company must offer on-the-job training and introduce a system of representation for person-nel through elected delegates whose function is to ensure that labour law is enforced. Many directors refuse to let the company expand in order to avoid having to have delegates; many others have holdings in very small entities in order to achieve the same objective.
- the threshold of 50 employees means the company must set up a work's council and must accept negotiations (the *Lois Auroux*).

Some companies, known as the 49 club, deliberately keep their numbers below the 50 threshold so as to avoid having to meet these obligations.

Liberals want to abolish these thresholds which they think penalise SMEs by raising labour costs:

Small and medium-sized enterprises have a very positive image in France. According to popular belief, levels of motivation and loyalty are much higher among the personnel of small companies. The survey conducted by B. Ducheneaut,* gives three reasons which explain why employees find SMEs attractive: the conviviality, the absence of bureaucracy, and their specific cultural context. However, on close inspection, it appears that there are many disadvantages for employees in SMEs if the overall context is compared with that of big companies. Working hours are longer in all sectors when the size of a company is smaller. Salary levels are on average 15 per cent lower than those in big companies, whatever the level of qualification; on-the-job training is insufficient and of poor quality; there is little interest and participation on the part of the personnel in the profits of the company. All this leads to higher personnel turnover rates.

The situation of the *cadres* (managerial staff) is no better although many of them appreciate their autonomy and liberty to take initiatives. One feature of SMEs is their relatively light management structures. The *cadres* are often polyvalent and paid less than in big companies.

SME VITALITY

SMEs and Innovation

Many SME directors claim to be innovating by improving their products or services. An analysis of the figures leads to a different conclusion; in spite of the high level of public research in France, the ratio of the turnover generated by new products in relation to the total turnover of the company remains low, around 10 per cent for SMEs compared to 30 per cent for the big companies. Furthermore, a study has shown that innovation in SMEs is above all in products (40 per cent for the 86–90 period) rather than in procedures (16 per cent) or on commercial aspects (11 per cent). Little research has been developed: SMEs employ only 8 per cent of researchers in the industrial sector; the companies which invest in research tend rather to subcontract to big companies when they are part of a group, or to public laboratories.

---

* B. Duchénéaut, opus cité, 1995.

Here again the differences between the companies should not conceal the fact that there are very innovating start-ups in France, particularly in information technology, design, mechanical construction and metallurgy.

The government is helping SMEs to become more innovative through the creation of technology parks to increase technology cross-fertilisation between companies and laboratories and through an agency – the ANVAR (see Box 6.2).

Exports

The export results of French SMEs are altogether unsatisfactory. In 1996,* 300 big companies accounted for more than half of the external trade figure of 1,485 billion fr, a minority of SMEs (20,000) of interna-

---

ANVAR – an agency to promote and finance innovation   **Box 6.2**

In 1979 the French government entrusted ANVAR, a public agency, with the task of promoting and financing innovation. ANVAR provides support for innovative projects in any type of company regardless of its sector of activity. The only condition is that the project presents a technical and financial risk in relation to the company's resources and that this innovation assists the company in crossing a significant threshold with regard to development, particularly in market terms. ANVAR is involved both in the creation of technological enterprises as well as the development of more traditional companies. ANVAR also provides support for all of those participating in technology transfer and partnerships: public and private laboratories, technology centres, consultants or business companies. Finally, since 1990, ANVAR has made the international expansion of SMEs one of its priorities. It has developed tools suited to their needs, which enable them to position themselves both on foreign markets in Europe and throughout the world.

ANVAR offers an original financial product: innovation support. This takes the form of an interest-free loan, repayable if the project is successful, to help cover up to 40 per cent of the expenditure associated with an innovation programme or carrying out technology transfer.This support can also take the form of a grant to finance more selective operations (seeking partners, hiring researchers, preparing innovation programmes . . .).

Results:

Resources: 1.5 billion fr a year.

Staff: 365 people at headquarters and in 24 regional offices.

Grants (1993): 1,953 grants and loans to innovation projects, 371 grants for hiring researchers, 192 technology transfer grants, 70 grants for European technological partnership, 978 grants and loans to young people's projects.

---

* *Le Moci*, 1303, 18 Septembre 1997.

tional renown brought in 45 per cent and occasional exports of the other SMEs account for the remainder. Therefore for a relatively high proportion of French SMEs, exports represent a small part of the turnover. In some activities, however, SMEs are very strong: agricultural products (97 per cent), food products (35 per cent) and consumer goods (94 per cent). It is interesting to compare these figures with the results of German or Italian SMEs which register respectively 75 and 60 per cent of their sales abroad (see Table 6.6). Furthermore, unlike SMEs in other European countries, the French are also little inclined to look for export markets outside the European Union and their traditional markets in Africa. The lack of financial and human resources and of a clearly defined strategy are often given as explanations for this poor result.

The government is trying to change this situation through many different forms of support available for the international development of SMEs. For instance there is:

- financial aid for consultancy services to help build an export strategy: limited to 200,000 fr maximum, covers 50 per cent of the service;
- recruitment aid for export personnel. This form of aid is the most in demand, it is also limited to 200,000 fr to finance the first year of a new employee;
- aid for setting up businesses abroad: it is possible to obtain regional subsidies abroad, averaging 185,000 fr for investments on average lower than 1 million fr. To this can be added many forms of regional aid: for taking part in trade fairs and exhibitions, for training courses in international business, for employing young people in the company in the context of their national service;

Table 6.6   The external market of exporting SMEs (in per cent of replies)

	Destination of exports					
Country of origin	Other EU countries	Other countries in western Europe	Countries in eastern Europe and CIS	North America	Asia– Pacific	Other countries*
Germany	92	51	35	18	26	12
France	90	26	15	17	21	26
Italy	87	48	26	32	33	17
EU Average	86	40	26	24	28	20

* Africa and Latin America.
Source: Exco and Grant Thornton's Survey, Enquête 1996 sur les PME Européennes.

- the insurance policy 'Prospection Simplifiée' (Simplified Prospection) run by the COFACE (Compagnie Française d'Assurance du Commerce Extérieur) offers cover for the risks of business failure resulting from attempts to export.

Subcontracting

A great number of industrial SMIs are still subcontractors or very dependent on their clients; they are often in a vulnerable position; for nearly half of them, the first three clients account for 50 per cent of their turnover.[†] However, subcontracting in its traditional form is gradually being replaced by industrial partnerships in which SMIs intervene earlier in the development and production process by providing services in the conception stage. At the same time, the process of certification which gives the contractors a guarantee of the quality of its partners services is becoming a widespread practice. These certifications are mostly granted according to the ISO 9000 norms: 'quality of the product from conception to after-sales' and to a lesser extent 'production or installation operation' (see Box 6.3).

New rules of the game for the SME   **Box 6.3**
sub-contractors in the automobile industry[‡]

In the absence of a recovery in the automobile industry, manufacturers are having to compress their prices which is having an effect on the margins of the whole sector and particularly on the subcontractors. For instance the forks for gearboxes, manufactured by GF GARCONNET, an SME specialised in small metal parts, have been sold to Peugeot at the same price since 1987. These SMEs must improve their productivity in order to survive. In 1996, the turnover per employee was 800,000 fr for GARCONNET, whose objective is to reach 1 million fr.

The contractors purchasing conditions are becoming harder. To continue working for them, subcontractors must satisfy ever more stringent requirements, the selection criteria being:

- quality: the need to be certified
- logistics: just-in-time work
- a capacity to innovate
- a critical size: this is imposed by the automobile manufacturers who wish to deal with more powerful subcontractors. Rockwell puts it at a turnover of 500 million fr. In order to reach this level, the SMIs are grouping together.

---

* It is mainly manufacturing SMEs which are involved in subcontracting. We will use the term of SMIs – small and medium-sized industrialised companies.
† 'La sous-traitance industrielle en 1995', Ministère de l'Industrie, des Postes et des Télécommunications, DGSI-SESSI, 1996.
‡ J. Vasseur, 'PME et coopérations internationales', Joint Venture Research Centre, 1997.

Small and medium-sized industrial companies are more involved in partnerships than big companies; this represents more than a third of the turnover for SMIs of 20 to 50 employees. The partnership is based on production according to specification in many sub-sectors of intermediary goods (smelting, metal work, transforming plastics, etc). It involves the processes of conception and production in the case of capital goods (equipment for the car industry, material for railways, etc).

Alliances

In most sectors the constitution of the European market has meant that companies have to become both competitive in terms of cost and differentiated in terms of services and products in order to cater for the diversity of European consumers. The alliance is a form of development which can conciliate these contradictory requirements while at the same time being well adapted to the SME's specificity (directors' objective of independence, confusion between the company and the family heritage, lack of assets and of specialised competence, flexibility of structures, etc). For the SME, collaboration takes three forms:

- In innovating sectors (all activities linked to information technology for example), alliances developed by entrepreneur-directors lead to many collaboration agreements, through contracts or joint ventures along the value chain in R&D, production, distribution with partners of different status. In each situation there is a rigorous selection process based on a thorough analysis of potential targets to find the best partner. Development is based on synergy building and the result is star-shaped networks of companies radiating out from the SME. A good illustration of this is NOMAI (see Box 6.4).
- 'Mirror distributive agreements' between two or several SMEs are also common. This situation corresponds to SMEs specialised in international niches for technical products (precision instruments, tools, garage equipment, etc). The SMEs concerned are often leaders in a specific segment of the market, for example O1DB, which specialised in acoustic measures. Positioned in the mid- or up-market range because of their high level of quality guaranteed by an ISO 9000 certification, their development is based on crossed distributions of products in order to increase their range of products and services: O1DB commercialises its partner's products in France and in Norway, NORSONIC does the same. The forms of this distribution agreement are very open from the renewable annual contract to the setting up of an equity joint venture.

A company which owes its development   **Box 6.4**
to *the Esprit programme – NOMAI*

NOMAI, a new company set up in Avranches in 1992, produces mass memories to meet the needs of users of numerical data in the fields of information technology and multimedia. To produce its magnetic cartridge drive, NOMAI resorted to an ESPRIT programme which helped both with the development of the product as a whole and with the production of specific parts linked to certain technologies.

Cooperation was indispensable as the development of a drive required very different technologies which NOMAI does not master. The process is a risky and costly one.

The cooperation brought together NOMAI, Myrica, a Scottish laboratory specialised in hard disks, Accorn, an Olivetti subsidiary specialised in information technology for education, and two English universities who were associated with this programme because of their work in the very specialised field of coding systems.

Once the project was accepted by the EEC, a consortium was set up to carry it out. The project was a success: the objectives were met. NOMAI produced its drive in collaboration with an English firm Xeratex, a former subsidiary of IBM, and launched it on the market.

- The third situation is that of SME subcontractors, often long-established and strongly dependent on their contractors in spite of their specific competence and the ever more frequent development 'partnerships' with these 'clients'. They have no choice but to do as their 'client' requests: become bigger and follow them outside the country. However, some SMEs manage to turn the situation to their advantage by developing original forms of working together. One example is G.F. Garconnet, a company producing metal automotive components which set up, along with two other SMEs in the same market ERCE and GRADEL, a holding called GEC which enabled them to start up business in China through a local joint venture. The holding enables them to share costs and to appear united and stronger in the eyes of their local partners. It gives a degree of flexibility by making it possible for other SMEs to join the process by becoming members of the holding. It can also provide a development framework in other zones with another local partner as GEC did in Spain for example.

PROSPECTS FOR SMES: PROBLEMS AND OPPORTUNITIES

French SMEs are under threat from several different sources.

A problem that they have to face is stagnation in their domestic market. This situation is exacerbated by France's high labour costs, taxes, tight regulations and bureaucracy. One new measure is particularly controversial: in order to reduce the high unemployment figures, M. Jospin's government has decided to reduce the working week to 35 hours by introducing a law which requires companies to negotiate with the unions on the reduction of working hours. If no agreement is reached through negotiations 'the 35-hour week' will be imposed in the year 2000 for all companies, except for little SMEs which have until 2002. The introduction of the 35-hour week is considered for most companies whatever their size to be a useless and harmful additional constraint which will mean a loss of profitability. Yet beyond questions of principle, which are very important in France, some companies have already reduced working hours in order to reorganise their company and rethink their work methods. This has enabled them both to increase motivation and productivity and to manage the seasonal variations in activity more efficiently. 'The 35-hour week' can therefore be used to remedy some of the problems connected with the organisation of work in France.

A second potential threat is European economic and monetary union with the coming of the Euro. The introduction of the single currency, scheduled to begin in 1999, holds out the prospect of SMEs being outpaced by bigger companies who are better able to grasp the opportunity of expansion across Europe. Another problem for SMEs which export is that they will now have to sharply differentiate their goods in different countries if they want to continue to sell products at varying prices in separate markets. For all SMEs, the transition to the single currency will burden them with high costs because of the need to adapt their accounting systems to the Euro. Finally, competition will be tougher than ever and many of the less competitive SMEs will be in danger of immediate bankruptcy. For the most successful SMEs, the Euro will certainly provide new opportunities for expansion in Europe.

7

Infrastructure and Distribution

Séverine Deronzier, Freight Europe (UK)

The rail industry and therefore the rail freight industry in France is handled by a single public company, the SNCF (Sociéte Nationale des Chemins de Fer), which was created by the French government in 1937 through the nationalisation of six private companies. The SNCF's current status dates from 1983, when it was turned into an EPIC (Etablissement à caractère Industriel et Commercial).

As a public company the SNCF has a public service agreement with the government for which it receives financial subsidies. It is also commercially active and is subject to the same financial and commercial rules as any other company.

In 1994 the SNCF transported more than 800 million passengers and more than 130 million tons of diverse goods. Despite competition from other forms of transport, the SNCF-managed rail network carries an eighth of all passengers (and half of public transport), and handles nearly 30 per cent of internal and 45 per cent of international freight; figures that no other rail company in western Europe can emulate. Thus the SNCF has managed successfully to complete the mission assigned to it by the government, ie to become an essential element of the French transport system.

In terms of finance, the SNCF turnover of 54 billion fr ranks it as one of the leading French companies. However, this is not the only contribution the SNCF makes to the national economy; in 1994, it employed more than 185,000 people throughout the country – that in itself represents an annual salary bill of more than 31 billion fr of which 12.8 billion are social charges. Through their orders to the rail industry and building companies, they inject vitality into other sectors of the French economy.

For several years now productivity efficiency and technical progress inevitably have forced many companies to reduce the number of staff working for them. The SNCF, however, has succeeded in maintaining a significant level of recruitment, in particular, young graduates. Staff are also encouraged to improve their level of qualifications by attending regular training courses.

The SNCF is not limited to just managing the rail network; it is also active in numerous other fields such as tourism and road transport for goods and travellers. Most of these are merged within the SCETA Group, one of the major transport operators in Europe.

Fret SNCF, the freight division of SNCF, is able to offer numerous different options for freight:

- **Block train**   Programmed in advance or simply the day before, despatches goods directly to the consignee. Loading capacity varies from 500 to 2,400 tonnes. Heavy trains can handle up to 3,600 tons.
- **Isolated wagons**   These are adapted to lighter tonnage. Wagons are assembled in marshalling yards in order to make up trains.
- **Intermodal transport**   Managed by SNCF and combines advantages of both rail and road. The bulk of the journey is done by train, collection and delivery are managed by lorries. Goods are placed in mobile containers and transfers are executed in specialist terminals. Combined transport also encompasses sea transport.

Specialist services offered are as follows:

- **'Chronofroid'**   Transport of perishable goods under controlled temperature. Rail transport is extremely fast, pick-up and delivery of goods are done by tractors and the service guarantees goods will not thaw.
- **Transeurochem**   Transport of chemical goods by mobile tanks.
- **Fretcombi**   A service which combines door-to-door delivery, in association with operators, but managed by the SNCF.
- **Chronodis**   Transport of palettes in uninterrupted flows along the Ile-de-France/South West corridor. This very specialist service includes transport, storage, handling, and preparation of orders.
- **Maxifret**   Exceptional transport.

Fret SNCF also manages tailored-made logistics services such as:

- organisation of transport;
- creation of rail terminals connected to the rail network;
- warehousing;
- direct programmed deliveries;
- 'just in time' deliveries coupled with stock management administration support'
- IT support.

These are split into seven business units, all dedicated to specific activities:

- AGRI (agriculture);
- automotive;
- BPVM (wood, paper, glass);
- PCA (coal, steel);
- PCM (oil, chemicals, metals);
- PGC (consumer goods);
- TIM (intermodal).

Fret SNCF also has different commercial delegations and subsidiaries based throughout Europe: in Brussels, Utrecht, Bern, Zagreb, Vienna, Milan, Madrid, Mayence and London.

Through Freight Europe UK Ltd, its London-based subsidiary, Fret SNCF offers the UK market a single point of contact for the entire delivery process, and access to its immense resources.

With the opening of the Channel Tunnel, sea transport lost its monopoly on cross-channel freight, road transport still offers the possibility of moving goods to the continent without transhipment – but it is becoming less acceptable as motorway congestion has slowed down the distribution process. Now there is another genuine contender: rail. With a continuous rail link between the UK and the Continent, goods can travel uninterrupted for thousands of miles across Europe.

Rail is sometimes described as 'yesterday's transport'; nevertheless, increasingly, businesses are realising that it is in fact tomorrow's transport. Multinational companies are treating Europe – including the UK – as a single market, with large-volume manufacturing plants serving the entire continent. As volumes rise and factory-to-shop distances increase, the economic benefit of rail is likely to become even more apparent.

Besides purely commercial factors, there are socio-political considerations, and the EU is using its influence to create the circumstances whereby the bulk of EU freight will move away from road towards rail as the favoured mode of transport. This policy is likely to continue for the foreseeable future, since it is backed by the powerful environmental lobby, which has done much to swing public opinion towards the rail option.

The European single market challenges British industry in particular to reassess distribution methodologies. Freight Europe is ideally placed to support businesses as they take advantage of the new opportunities.

For more information, please contact Tony Clifford (see Appendix B for contact details).

8

Business Culture

Robin Walden, DTI Export Promoter,
Consumer Goods, France

If you are not already doing business with France, the prospect can be daunting. After all, is this not the country which is our natural enemy, with whom we have waged war from time immemorial, and where the waiters, ever mindful of our past national differences, have the magical ability to render us invisible when we are trying to catch their attention to order a coffee on the Champs Elysees for the price of a small end-terrace house?

Reader – fear ye not! When you get down to basics, the French are by and large not too different to ourselves. They get out of bed in the morning, put on their clothes, have breakfast, send the kids to school, go to work, come home, watch television, etc. In other words, they are a western European nation just like ourselves, in many respects. In fact over the years in dealing with the French, I have found many more similarities than differences, and can empathise with the average Lyonnais or Lilleois to a greater degree than with many of my own countrymen. But after all, I am a Scot, and take comfort in the knowledge that we have the Auld Alliance with France, which every Scot knows about – and no Frenchman does!

If you are intent on doing business with France and the French, the first thing you must do is to take them seriously. Observations made to me over the years by UK companies are that the French:

- never reply to your faxes and letters;
- are often rude;

- take forever to pay;
- insist on speaking their own language.

What we on this side of La Manche remain blissfully unaware of is that similar observations are made by the French about us.

LANGUAGE

In discussing a business relationship with France, language comes at the top of the pile as the 'mother' of non-tariff barriers in working with this market. This is despite the fact that generally speaking, we in the UK learn French as our first foreign language at school from a fairly early age. Why British companies have this problem is not for discussion here. Suffice to say, that generally speaking, in the rest of the world, we expect everyone else to speak English. Indeed if a German is negotiating with a Spaniard, odds on that the language of negotiation is English.

However, this is not necessarily the case in France.

The French are fiercely proud of their mother tongue and strongly resent any Anglo-Saxon encroachments. It is perhaps the defence of their language which fosters the view in their own minds that if you are going to deal with them, you will jolly well speak their language, like it or lump it. Make an effort and it will make a difference.

Speaking your French customer's language is not just about being polite, it makes sound commercial sense. It is very doubtful if your Dutch, German and Swedish competitors will be communicating in their own languages, so why should you? By communicating in English, your French customer perceives that you are the one creating the non-tariff barrier, not him!

COMMUNICATION STYLE

How often have you heard the French being described as rude and arrogant? This to me is an unfair criticism of a national character which in its own way is refreshingly direct compared to that with which we are familiar, on this side of the Channel.

Witnessing a French couple having an animated discussion on a subject, you would swear on oath that they were having a flaming row and divorce was only just around the corner. Not the case. What you are witnessing is the French love of animated discussion. It only looks rude and offensive because it is not our style and culture to be like that.

When we look at communication in the sphere of negotiation, we discover that the French and British way of arriving at a decision can be quite different.

Consider the meaning of 'yes' and 'no', and the meaning of '*oui*' and '*non*'. If you start with the supposition that they have the same meaning, you can be in for a surprise. In comparing the no in the UK with a *non* in France, you have to accept that the British no, which happens rarely, is not the beginning of a yes. In negotiating with the French, the answer *non* does not necessarily mean that the discussion is over.

The British tend to avoid saying no or even to place the other party in the position of having to say so. Yes is also the final result of a discussion for the British; for the French it might only be the beginning of discussions. This, in part, explains why there are often misunderstandings in Anglo–French negotiations.

OBSERVATIONS ON DIFFERENCES IN THE FRENCH AND BRITISH BUSINESS ENVIRONMENT

The French are a nation of *Grands Projets*. Consider the Pyramid at the Louvre, the Arc at La Defense, the Pompidou Centre. This aspect of French culture translates into their outlook in business.

The French tend to go quickly to the 'big picture' and plan. In the UK, we tend to build up considerable detail and have a slower, wait and see, approach. This leads to fewer big mistakes but fewer *Grands Projets* (with the possible recent exception of the Millennium Dome!).

In the UK we are the master of the understatement; the contrary is true in France.

An example of what I have said so far is of a commercial bank which recently needed to develop a computer system, and recognising that a combined UK and French team was unlikely to make progress, two teams were established to propose a solution. After a while the UK team complained that the French were full of grandiose ideas but not getting on with the work. The French team then complained that the Brits were getting bogged down in the detail. In the end, both teams produced perfectly workable solutions – but would they have done so if working together?

SOME SOCIAL NICETIES OR NOT NICETIES

Handshaking

Handshaking is a French national pastime and is both formal but at the same time, charming. Employees will greet each other every morning with a handshake and again when leaving at the end of the day. You may interrupt your negotiations with your French counterpart to go for a coffee. He may shake the hand of the bartender in the local cafe. You will normally be expected to do the same. It is a practice much more widely spread throughout French society than it is in the UK. Long may it continue.

Kissing

The practice of kissing on each cheek is normally reserved only for close friends outside the workplace.

Lunchtime

During the course of a business meeting in France, you may have the opportunity to break off for lunch with your French counterpart. You will find that lunchtime is an opportunity to discuss subjects other than business, so be prepared. Subjects may range from arts to politics and the business of the day will only reappear with the coffee. Be prepared for this and if you have had time prior to the meeting, take in a local exhibition which you can then discuss over lunch. Your French colleague will be impressed with your knowledge and interest in French things cultural.

Dinner Invitations

If you know about them in advance, bring a gift from the UK. If feeling magnanimous, a bottle of fine single malt. Best to stay clear of a bottle of wine as it may cause offence – it may not be as good as the one your host plans to serve and he will feel obliged to serve your offering. A bottle of good champagne is usually received with enthusiasm. Flowers for your hostess are always acceptable, but beware – yellow chrysanthemums are a flower of mourning in France. A rather smart British fashion shop opened its doors a number of years ago in the rue du Faubourg St Honoré with a flourish and a window full of these (to British eyes) inoffensive flowers, but looking to the average Parisian more like an upmarket funeral parlour than a fashion shop.

Follow-up Action after Meetings

It is essential to follow up a meeting with your French counterpart with a letter recording your understanding of the decisions taken at that meeting, and with a clear note of your understanding of the points to be actioned especially if the French side has undertaken to do some follow up. This is vital in order to avoid misunderstanding, and resultant confusion.

Timekeeping

There is a European North/South divide when it comes to national attitudes towards timekeeping. Northern Europeans tend to keep strictly to appointment times; the Swiss, for instance, can tend to rather overdo it and even take a dim view if you are early – although like any stereotypical national image, this is a trifle exaggerated.

The French are more southern than northern when it comes to keeping appointments. There is in my experience an unwritten rule that you are allowed to be up to 20 minutes late for an appointment in France. It is not a practice I would advocate you adopt yourself but be prepared to have it happen to you. You may have to wait even longer to keep an appointment with a busy buyer in a hypermarket or department store and it is worthwhile bearing in mind this 'flexible' attitude towards appointment keeping in order that you can take it into account when organising your own schedule.

A SUMMARY OF DOS AND DON'TS

- Do learn a little French history and culture.
- Do ask people how they spell their name if you're not sure.
- Do shake hands every time you meet a customer, not just once in a while.
- The guest of honour always sits to the right of the host.
- Don't drink your aperitif or wine before your host.
- If you find your phone calls are getting you nowhere, get the secretary's name, the correct title of your contact, and ask the secretary if you can forward your proposal so that it can be passed on to your prospective contact.
- Don't make an appointment more than five weeks ahead of your meeting; three weeks is about average.
- Resist asking personal questions about marriage and children.
- Verbal orders by phone should be taken seriously, and should be followed up immediately.
- Do discuss the latest football match or tennis tournament, especially the French Open.
- Don't assume that your potential customer knows nothing about your company.
- Always make sure you have your business cards to hand.

Part Two

Investment Issues

9

Management Education and the *Grandes Ecoles*

Ian Tovey, E.M.LYON

Anyone seeking to understand the typical culture of a given country would probably do well to look at its education system. The study of the institutions, the structures and the aims of such a system, far from simply providing a little local colour, can give people an insight into behaviours, attitudes, values and reflexes that have been forged during the period of secondary and higher education. This is also true for the business world and its culture, and a study of the respective management education institutions can help us to understand the origins of, say, the highly professional American manager or the gifted all-round amateur with personality, typical of the traditional British business system.

This approach is especially valid in the case of France, which, like a number of advanced countries, possesses an education system devoted to the training of professional managers for French and international firms but which, unlike other such countries, has developed a highly specific system outside the traditional university structures. If we also take into consideration the fact that French firms, to a large extent, are said to 'subcontract' the selection of their future managerial staff to these educational institutions (Bauer and Bertin-Mourot 1996), it is clear that an understanding of French management can be greatly enriched by a study of their breeding grounds.

This chapter will try to provide an insight into these French institutions. We shall begin with an overview of the *Grandes Ecoles*, in particular, those which contribute to producing a large proportion of the ranks of senior and middle management in French firms. We shall then go on to study one *Grande Ecole*, the Ecole Nationale d'Administration (or ENA as it is usually known), which plays a very specific role in the development of management resources for French firms. As such, ENA is not a centre for management education, and yet a study of its graduates' presence among the most senior management levels of French firms leaves no doubt as to its importance in the French business system.

THE FRENCH *GRANDES ECOLES*

When studying the French system of higher education one is immediately struck by one essential characteristic: the French system is a dual system which divides up the educational effort between, on the one hand, the universities and, on the other, the *Grandes Ecoles*. The creation of the latter goes back to the 18th century, ie a period when the French universities were in decline and when the French tradition of centralised management of the country totally held sway.* In order to respond to the growing need to develop scientific and technical knowhow, the kings of France were to create a number of elite schools specifically designed to produce highly qualified engineers who would serve the state and further its development (Magliulo, 1982). The names of the schools thus created give a clear indication of the specific areas in which the future engineers would contribute to France's power and prestige (Ecole des Ponts et des Chaussées, created in 1715; Ecole d'Artillerie, 1720; Ecoles des Mines, 1783).

Although these institutions suffered setbacks during the initial years of the French Revolution owing to their elitist character, the rise to power of Napoléon I was to bring them back to the fore and entail an important phase of expansion. One of the most notable creations during this period was the Ecole Polytechnique (which many French people commonly refer to as 'X'; thus one can say 'he is at X' or 'she is an X'), founded in 1794 with a view to giving a solid scientific training to students destined to enter the specialised public service schools mentioned above.

For Napoléon, the *Grandes Ecoles* were to provide the engineering, military and administrative resources necessary to build up the Empire and ensure France's domination of Europe. For this purpose, he also required that the institutions and the students being trained there

---

* This style of government is referred to as *Colbertiste*, after Jean-Baptiste Colbert, statesman and Controller General of Finances under King Louis XIV.

show total allegiance to the state (a quality not common in the universities of the time).

In comparison with the engineering schools, the *Ecoles de Commerce* (business schools) emerged at a later date. Although one of today's leading schools was founded in Paris in 1819 (ESCP), the creation of such schools did not really take off until approximately 1870 after a long period of industrial development. In particular, the Siegfied brothers, having fled their native Mulhouse after the annexation of Alsace by the Germans and having abandoned the school they had created there in 1869, helped finance the creation of a school in Le Havre in 1870 and gave an impulsion to the founding of other schools in cities such as Rouen, Lyon, Marseilles and Bordeaux in the ensuing years (Grelon, 1997).

In contrast to the engineering schools, which, from the beginning generally enjoyed the highest level of academic prestige, the *Ecoles de Commerce* were predominantly local institutions set up by the regional business community and financed by the local chambers of commerce. Often of undefined academic status, their main objective was to train the offspring of local merchants and businessmen with a view to guaranteeing the handing over of the firms and businesses to capable descendants. The 20th century, however, has borne witness to the efforts of these institutions to give themselves the same academic status as their elder cousins, and the *Grandes Ecoles de Management*, as they are officially known today, reveal the same academic structures, post the same academic requirements, and now enjoy a solid position in the traditional French system of higher education.

If one of the factors in the development of the management institutions was the emulation of the French engineering schools, the other predominant influence was certainly the American graduate business schools. The increasing economic power of the United States after the Second World War led France to reflect upon its own standing in the international economy during the 1960s and to conclude that, if it was to keep pace with America, it had to invest heavily in such resources as management education. Thus it was that a national foundation for the development of management education (FNEGE) provided the funding to enable many a talented young graduate to go and study on MBA and doctoral programmes in the United States, expecting them to come back to France and develop management teaching in France's own schools. Consequently, and in spite of differing structures, the typical programme of a *Grande Ecole de Management* bears a strong resemblance to that of a standard American MBA programme.

The schools which we have so far presented are not the only institutions that go to make up the French *Grandes Ecoles* system. Apart from the 140 engineering schools and the 28 management schools that are members of the *Conférence des Grandes Ecoles* (a professional association dedicated to defending standards and the interests of the institutions), there are a number of other institutions dedicated to turning out state administrators, magistrates, architects, librarians, and the higher ranks of the police, amongst others. Not all these institutions have the same status: some are public educational establishments under the administrative supervision of a government ministry, some are private but enjoy a 'consular' status in as much as they are affiliated to the local chambers of commerce, and some are funded by entirely private means. With this variety in mind, one can wonder to what extent these institutions form a sufficiently homogenous group.

The *Grandes Ecoles* reveal a number of common characteristics that define them as a separate group *vis-à-vis* the universities:

- their small size: *Grandes Ecoles* are generally small institutions with an average yearly output of 120 graduates each (ranging from 50 to 400 per year for most of the schools, with only a very few exceeding 400 per year). This enables them to be flexible and adaptable, and to develop a fairly entrepreneurial approach in responding to the needs of the business world;
- a high level of selectivity: after the *baccalauréat* (equivalent to British A levels), prospective candidates already have to submit an application in order to enter the *classes préparatoires*, a two-year period of intensive study of mathematics, sciences and languages for those pursuing a career in engineering, and mathematics, economic history and geography, general culture and languages for those pursuing a management career. The major objective of the *classes préparatoires* is to prepare students for the competitive entrance examinations into the various *Grandes Ecoles*. In spite of efforts to reduce the weight of the system, this huge selection machine, comprising both written and oral exams (lasting in all from the end of April until mid-July in some cases) is a long and arduous undertaking for candidates;
- strong links with the business community: this is, of course, particularly important for schools as major providers of managerial resources. Cooperation takes many forms: firms often visit campuses for job forums, conferences and round-tables discussion, and they finance research and teaching programmes on a large scale; most faculty members have professional experience and/or a consultancy, and participate in executive education; field research projects and internships are a highly developed and totally integrated element of the programme for all students.

Above and beyond these common characteristics, it is true that these schools are also very autonomous; no national body decides or even coordinates strategies, although the Conférence des Grandes Ecoles encourages cooperation and exchange and provides a system of accreditation. Competition between these institutions can be quite acute, as the recent reactions to a drop in the number of candidates from the *classes préparatoires* has shown. Nevertheless, as the main source of an institution's reputation has traditionally been its *Grande Ecole* programme, and owing to the fact that a common academic and even social reference has established itself over the years, the need to acquire prestige has generally led to a certain homogeneity in the programme offer of these schools. If they seek to distinguish themselves from other schools, then this battle will be played out in the arena of other programmes (MBA, specialised *Mastères*, or doctoral programmes) or other services to firms (research institutes, a large executive education branch). However, in the past, building up a strong reputation has generally implied conforming to a certain commonly recognised standard.

After two years of *classes préparatoires* and three years of study in a *Grande Ecole* students usually graduate with a *Diplôme de Grande Ecole* (bearing the name of the institution), ie a Masters-level degree (eg a Masters in Management). But what is the usual profile of the students who study within this system and the graduates/managers it produces?

As we have already seen, the *Grandes Ecoles* system is extremely demanding and intensely competitive, where issues of prestige and status are of the utmost importance, not only for the institutions, firms or the students, but also for many other 'stakeholders' such as the parents or the *classes préparatoires*. The enormous machinery and the pressure which the system thus creates tend to produce a certain conformism, particularly among the students who feel the need to master the rules of success and a certain culture in order to advance. A few schools have realised this and have, over the last ten years or so, made an effort to develop parallel systems of recruitment in order to bring more and more French and international university graduates into their programmes at the graduate level, and thus diversify the culture of their programme.

The strong mathematical and Cartesian analytical background also produces clear preferences and choices in terms of subjects and concentrations in as much as students typically tend to favour the technical or hard subjects within the programme. In management schools where a wide choice of hard and soft subjects is available, subjects such as financial management or accountancy and management control inevitably attract the large majority of students, with marketing usually coming in a clear third. It seems that such highly technical and analytical subjects conform to a noble image of high intellectual ability, whereas sales or human resource management enjoy little prestige and consequently attract only a small percentage of students in spite of the fact that more and more French companies are crying out for highly qualified salesmen. It comes as no surprise to learn that between 40 and 50 per cent of graduates regularly take up their first job in the fields of financial management, management control and audit.

Entrepreneurship as a management field enjoys a status that is far less clear in France. If France probably has its fair share of entrepreneurs creating or developing new companies, they do not traditionally have a *Grande Ecole* education behind them. It is true that the growing visibility of a number of high-profile American entrepreneurs has clearly inspired students in these institutions, but their traditional attraction to the control and analytical functions, and a certain conformism and aversion to risk-taking still tend to encourage many of them to seek a stable well-paid job in a large French firm. Entrepreneurship is certainly a field that is progressing in France, and a number of schools such as E.M.LYON and HEC are among the few that have built up large-scale entrepreneurial programmes for their degree-students and for would-be entrepreneurs from their local region, but few schools as yet offer more than an initiation into the field.

If the previous remarks have referred predominantly to the graduates of management schools, it should not be forgotten that France is also clearly marked by its long tradition of prestigious engineering *Grandes Ecoles* and graduates. This heritage has led to a strong production and technocratic culture and has clearly contributed to France's leadership in industrial fields such as energy and nuclear power, transportation and communications. The meticulous analytical skills of France's engineering graduates are an essential element in what is acknowledged as a dominant quality: their ability to plan, set up and manage long-term, large-scale engineering projects. The TGV, the Channel Tunnel, and the recent construction of a 17 km bridge across the mouth of the Tagus River in Portugal more than bear witness to such planning skills.

Common to both types of graduates is an ostensible analytical rigour, which sets great store by intellectual brio and which attaches as much importance to form as to content. French managers practically consider these qualities to be the foundation of their professionalism and they will have nothing but the utmost disdain for a badly presented project or a poorly structured argument.

As has already been stated, France has a strong technocratic tradition, and one of the most striking corollaries of this fact is that there is relatively little interest in the human aspects of management and the firm; it is not a subject area which attracts many students in school, either. It is true that their strong international orientation (most students must have a command of two foreign languages) has led more and more students to become interested in the cultural aspects of international management, but this rarely translates into a pragmatic approach to managing and motivating human beings.

It is not possible here to provide a more exhaustive overview of French management culture, but it should already be clear how the typical French manager is likely to differ (in more than one sense, perhaps) from his traditional British counterpart, the gentleman amateur for whom personal and leadership abilities often take priority over strong technical and intellectual skills. Further striking differences also appear if one considers another very specific institution within France's system of higher education.

ECOLE NATIONALE D'ADMINISTRATION

The Ecole Nationale d'Administration (ENA) was founded in 1945 as a specialised postgraduate school dedicated to training future high-ranking civil servants. Before this each ministry would organise its own competitive entrance exams, recruiting gifted young graduates from all areas of study. The newly founded school was designed to provide specific training for civil service functions and thus create a more homogenous profile and coherent turn of mind among those who would be called on to serve the French state.

The training lasts 27 months and includes 15 months of academic courses and 12 months of practical training in the field, generally meaning a 6-month period in a *préfecture* (the organ of French central administration in each *département*) and a 6-month period in an embassy or other international organisation. The programme is designed to provide students with an education in all the fundamental areas relevant to the state (law, economics, international and European affairs, etc), a command of all the necessary administrative skills and procedures, and a hands-on familiarity with state institutions.

At the end of the 27 months, the ranking of each student in the final graduation list is extremely important in that it will determine the position that each graduate will occupy. Those at the top of the list will accede to vacancies among the *Grands Corps*, the most prestigious ranks of senior civil servants such as the finance inspectorate

(*Inspection des Finances*), the council of state (*Conseil d'Etat*) and the court of auditors (*Cour des Comptes*), as well as the civil administration of the Ministry of Finance. Those who have not done so well might find themselves in a provincial branch of the social security or other such regional administrations.

The question here, however, is to know what impact such an institution has on the world of business. A recent study asked if ENA should not in fact be considered as a business school (Bauer, Bertin-Mourot 1997). The study itself shows that about 17 per cent of all living *énarques* (as graduates of ENA are called) have spent a substantial period in firms and that, at the present rate of increase, this could easily reach 20 per cent in the coming years. An earlier study by the same authors also revealed that more than 50 per cent of the top 200 French firms had already hired ENA graduates and that, among the top managers of these same firms in 1993, roughly 50 per cent had been through ENA or through the X-Mines route,[†] whereas only 7 per cent had come from HEC, one of France's leading business schools (Bauer and Bertin-Mourot, 1996).

Clearly ENA plays a role in the production of managerial resources for French firms. It also seems that many young *énarques* increasingly consider ENA as a springboard into the world of business in that they are going into French companies immediately after discharging their minimum duty to the state. One could imagine that this movement predominantly concerns those who are disappointed by their final ranking and the posts they have been attributed. On the contrary, those who go into the business world have in fact generally followed the traditional route for senior civil servants.

The typical *'pantoufleur'* (as *énarques* going into a French firm are referred to) will probably make this move around the age of 39 after having spent 11 years in the civil service. He (but not so frequently she) will have been nominated to one of the more prestigious *Grands Corps* mentioned above, and over 40 per cent will have spent the ensuing period in a ministerial (or presidential) cabinet as an adviser (Bauer and Bertin-Mourot, 1997).

The sectors which traditionally receive a large number of *énarques* are the industrial and the financial sectors with a much smaller but

---

† It should be noted that those who have entered the Ecole des Mines or the Ecole Nationale des Ponts et des Chaussées after having studied at the Ecole Polytechnique are generally being prepared to enter the *Grands Corps* of the ministries of Industry or of Equipment.

noteworthy proportion going into the cultural sector, services and insurance, professional associations or consultancies. They are rarely to be found in the recently expanded retailing and distribution sectors, and the number of *énarques* having left the civil service to set up their own business is infinitesimal.

The fact that 42 per cent of *pantoufleurs* are to found in firms that have always been in private hands seems to imply that the distinction between private and public ownership is of no great importance. What is more striking, when one considers the total number of firms in France, is that such a small number of firms employ the total number of *énarques* in the business world (a little over 660). As well as establishing a certain conformity, this also reveals that *pantoufleurs* have a tendency to follow in the footsteps of those that have gone before and go somewhere they already know will offer a satisfactory welcome. They also have a strong preference for large firms, which, for a number of observers, implies a desire to manage and control a large business that is already well established rather than invest in developing a growing concern. As for the *Grandes Ecoles* in general, there seems to be a general lack of entrepreneurs, not to mention adventurers.

Another striking feature is the high level at which most *pantoufleurs* enter the firm. Almost 50 per cent enter at the highest levels of most large and medium-sized firms or major subsidiaries of a large firm. A further 35 to 40 per cent, if they do not arrive immediately in a top management position, find themselves in posts in which they have been identified as future top management potential.

Given the situation as it has been presented above, one is obliged to wonder why French firms are so likely to put their fate in the hands of highly qualified state administrators coming from the civil service rather than seek more deliberately to groom top managers from within the ranks of the firm itself. This concern becomes particularly pressing when one considers how globalisation is fundamentally transforming the business environment thus causing traditional management logic to evolve and become increasingly distinct from the logic that governs civil service administration.

Many of the remarks made about *Grandes Ecoles* graduates in general are also valid here. We notice the same ability to analyse and master complex technical situations rapidly, as well as develop grand projects and implement them through carefully detailed plans. These intellectual skills together with an ability to build up a network of useful business and political contacts are all qualities that are both enhanced during the ENA programme and held in high esteem in French society as a whole.

At the same time, however, these very skills are held to be their major disadvantages in the managing of a firm. *Enarques* rarely enter top jobs after having come up through the ranks of the firm; their knowledge of the real workings of the firm is gained through annual reports, memos, and financial analyses, and is thus fairly conceptual. The charge of mismanagement, or, at least, of insufficient management ability for the specific competitive context of business has begun to stick in recent years, especially after the now notorious *Crédit Lyonnais* debacle in which the building up of an extensive banking empire through the taking of large stakes in such areas as real estate and the cinema industry was given priority over sound financial and business strategy. Low profitability, little strategic specialisation, and untimely investments also characterised the performance of UAP, a leading insurance giant, which for a long time was also in the hands of a well-known *énarque*.

For many the reassuring aspect of this system is the way in which it allows the logic of the state to prevail over most of the important sectors of the economy. The fact that *énarques* feel invested with the notion of public service underpins an *esprit de corps* that enables the state to enjoy a great deal of informal influence, if not necessarily direct control, over major French firms. This has surely been a major factor in ensuring that French firms have generally remained in French hands through such techniques as cross-shareholdings and the *noyaus durs* (hard cores of shareholders). It has also supported the phenomenon of long-term planning which is still highly favoured in France.

This system clearly has its weaknesses though. This closely-knit network of *énarques* and the quasi-incestuous relationship between the state and business has in many instances led to corruption and encourages those concerned to turn a blind eye to the actions of others. The intrinsic features of the system also create a kind of caste isolated from the realities of its environment, slow to grasp logics outside those it has been inculcated with, and allergic to reform. This became painfully clear when Jean-Yves Haberer, after having been forced to stand down from the top post at the *Crédit Lyonnais*, claimed that he could not understand how his successor would be able to run the bank successfully; after all, he had not been through ENA.

Above all, it is the system of social reproduction that has been stigmatised by such intellectuals as Pierre Bourdieu, one of France's eminent sociologists. In spite of claims to the contrary, studies have shown that ENA is recruiting an increasing proportion of its ranks from the sons and daughters of top-ranking civil servants, professionals and senior managers. The real danger is that the recruitment of top managers from such a narrow social base might deny French industry the necessary diversity in a world where internationalisation, deregulation and unpredictability are the key phenomena.

A CHANGING ENVIRONMENT

In this chapter, we have presented the long-established French system of producing managerial resources for firms. France itself, however, is also changing internally. Next to the *Grandes Ecoles*, some universities are now beginning to offer interesting postgraduate programmes in specialised management areas, while others are creating smaller more selective units within their own walls. As far as ENA is concerned, the system which has clearly served France through much of its postwar economic expansion is now being called into question, and is frequently denounced by politicians and businessmen alike. Clearly, there is some pressure to evolve. As France seeks to acquire a leading position in the new global business environment, it is possible that the system may need to be considerably overhauled or, at least, adapted to the new economic pressures. In view of the highly entrenched nature of the system, many may doubt that it is possible, but, in spite of its traditional image, the country has also shown in the past that it is quite capable of change when faced with such a critical issue.

BIBLIOGRAPHY

Bauer, M and Bertin-Mourot B, (1996) *Vers un Modèle Européen de Dirigeants? Ou trois modèles contrastés de production de l'autorité légitime au sommet des grandes entreprises*, Abacus, Paris

Bauer, M and Bertin-Mourot, B, (1997) *L'ENA: est-elle une Business School*, Harmattan, Paris

Bourdieu P, (1987) 'Variations et Invariants – éléments pour une histoire structurale du champ des Grandes Ecoles', *Actes de la Recherche en Sciences Sociales*, 70

Bourdieu P, (1989) *La Noblesse d'Etat: Grandes Ecoles et Esprit de Corps*, Editions de Minuit, Paris

Grelon, A, (1997) 'Ecoles de Commerce et Formations d'Ingénieurs', *Entreprises et Histoire*, 14–15, June

Magliulo, B, (1982) *Les Grandes Ecoles*, PUF, Paris

10

Vocational Training, On-the-Job Training, and Apprenticeships

Thérèse Brodu, Délégation Générale à l'Emploi et à la Formation Professionelle (DGEFP)

The French vocational training system is wholly original and is characterised by:

- The key role played by the social partners (in elaborating rules) and the state (which legislates, finances and controls).
- The obligation for enterprises to contribute to the financing of employee's vocational training.
- The historical distinction between initial vocational training (under the responsibility of the Ministry of National Education) and continuing vocational training (which comes under the responsibility of the Ministry of Employment and Social Affairs).
- The conditions of access to training, which depend on the status of individuals (employees, young people, job-seekers, etc).

Five dominant trends can be observed:

- New decentralisation, which gives the regions increasingly greater responsibilities in matters of vocational training.
- The determination to have a clear understanding and control of how different organisations finance vocational training.

- An attempt to individualise training (through tailor-made training paths).
- The development of alternating training.
- The integration of a European dimension in vocational training policies.

PLANNING VOCATIONAL TRAINING

Vocational training has been planned so that it can become:

- one of the levers for the economic development of enterprises and the mastery of technological developments;
- a means for social advancement and personal development;
- a tool for fighting unemployment, particularly among those sections of the population experiencing difficulty.

Economic and Technological Development

Vocational training answers the needs of the enterprise for a qualified workforce. It is considered as one of the main factors of productivity and economic development, progressively becoming both a necessary and a profitable investment.

Social Advancement and Personal Development

Opportunities for social advancement and personal development can be enhanced through training by allowing employees: individual training leave, 'training-time capital', skills assessment, new engineering training paths and accreditation of prior professional experience.

Individual training leave

Asserted by the social partners in 1970, individual training leave permits an employee, at his own initiative, to follow the training of his choice, independently of courses organised under a company training plan. This represents a genuine right to training for the employee (the employer can only refuse for very precise reasons).

The employee's request must be accepted by a certified organisation which then takes responsibility for the trainee's remuneration and the training cost.

Other procedures, such as skills assessment leave, training and research leave, examination leave, etc equally permit employees to receive training.

'Training-time capital'

A new path for training has emerged from 'training-time capital', a scheme which offers the possibility for interested employees to be trained through a company training plan. Different professions negotiate specific applications of this scheme.

Skills assessment

Any worker (employee, or self-employed person) or job-seeker is entitled to a skills assessment. Through the analysis of motivation, personal and professional skills, a 'skills evaluation'* reviews past experience, identifies acquisitions and permits the elaboration of a personal project which may or may not include training.

The results, recorded in a final document, are given to the beneficiary.

New engineering training paths

To enhance the opportunities for professional promotion and to encourage the engineering industry's higher technicians to move towards executive status, various arrangements have been implemented. The new training paths for engineers (*nouvelles bilières d'ingenieurs* or NFIs) permit employees to achieve status as engineers after a two- to three-year course, alternating periods of in-company training, with theoretical training.

Accreditation of prior professional experience

Thanks to accreditation of prior professional experience, a diploma can be obtained with the exemption of certain subjects, according to the skills the individual has acquired in the field.

The accreditation of prior learning encourages the mobility of workers.

Within the various professional branches, social partners may recognise qualifications acquired at work or through training. An increasingly large number of professional qualification certificates are being established by professional branches.

Unemployment

Employees threatened with dismissal or redundant workers are offered, in the framework of in-company retraining plans, various training possibilities by their company. These are particularly oriented towards skills assessment and the adaptation of their qualifications to the needs of the market.

---

* An analysis made by a specialist organisation, which determines what a person is good at and what type of training they need in order to improve.

Particular measures have been foreseen for the unemployed who are encountering difficulties re-entering working life (long-term or more elderly unemployed). They range from an initial contact with the world of the enterprise to the establishment of specific employment contracts which may also include training.

Summary

So, continuing vocational training, managed by a numerous diversity of actors is opened to young people, workers and job-seekers.

TRAINING FOR 16–25 YEAR-OLDS: A NECESSARY INVESTMENT

Training Paths Leading to Qualifications for Young People

On 1 July 1994, the state transferred and reinforced the responsibility of the regions concerning vocational training for young people by implementing the following:

- The regions now have legal powers in matters of training for youngsters. Regional programmes for their employment and training are being established.
- For those who have left school without qualifications, or who are finding it difficult to integrate into the world of work, the public authorities are undertaking a policy of global integration, through individualised training paths.
- An initial assessment leads to a personalised training programme during which the trainee is observed by a team of training professionals. At the end of training, the qualifications acquired can be accredited according to different methods.

The Development of Alternating Training

Occupational integration has developed, thanks to alternating training and its associated in-company application periods. The public authorities provide support to all types of training requiring an in-company application period, whether for alternating courses or work contracts requiring training actions.

There are two types of alternating training:

- an apprenticeship contract, which is the initial training channel and is the responsibility of the National Education body. It is a work contract financed by a tax levied on companies (0.5 per cent of their wage bill) by the state and by the regions, and provides a complete training package including an opportunity to gain qualifications up to engineer level. In 1997 342,000 young people were employed under this type of contract;

- an occupational (or alternating) training contract set up and managed by social partners. This is the channel for continuing vocational training and is financed by an additional levy chargeable to enterprises, by the unemployment insurance for the training of some job hunters and by the state. In 1997, occupational training contracts accounted for approximately 120,000 young people.

Apprenticeships and occupational training have traditionally been practised in the craftwork industry, but are now being extended to the service and industry sectors. (See Boxes 10.1 and 10.2).

Breakdown of apprenticeship   **Box 10.1**
contracts by sector in 1996

Sector	Percentage
Agriculture	2.2
Industry	19.6
Construction	22.6
Services	55.6
Total	100

Breakdown of occupational training   **Box 10.2**
contracts by sector in 1996

Sector	Percentage
Agriculture	1.3
Industry	18.0
Construction	8.1
Services	72.6
Total	100

Quality in-company training via a work contract

Whether through an apprenticeship contract or an occupational training contract with alternating training periods, apprentices or trainees are monitored by a more experienced employee in the enterprise (apprentice supervisor or company tutor).

Chosen from among volunteer qualified employees, the tutor is responsible for welcoming, informing and guiding throughout the length of the contract. The employer must give the tutor the necessary time to carry out these duties.

The tutor can take a role-related training course and cannot supervise more than three people at the same time. Again the employer must grant adequate time for these duties.

EMPLOYER FINANCING OF CONTINUING VOCATIONAL TRAINING: MAIN FEATURES AND CONSEQUENCES

The principle of employer participation and the forms it should take in the development of continuing vocational training are specified in the Labour Code. These clauses (law of the 16 July 1971) have been altered several times since but the general philosophy has remained the same: to urge enterprises to use continuing training as a tool for their own development and for the benefit of their employees.

The obligation for enterprises to spend a minimum percentage of their wage bill in order to develop vocational training is not considered a traditional tax, but as a way for them to invest in training. They can spend their obligatory contributions directly by financing employee training or by giving their contributions to specialised mutual fund organisations.

The resources managed by all these fund organisations total 16 billion fr, representing 40 per cent of the legal obligation which is evaluated at 45 billion fr. There are ninety-six collector organisations at both national and regional levels.

The level of obligation varies with the number of workers the enterprise employs:

- Enterprises which employ ten or more employees must spend at least 1.5 per cent of their annual wage bill.
- Enterprises which employ less than ten employees must spend at least 0.25 per cent of their annual wage bill.

(See Box 10.3 for a breakdown of the obligatory contributions made by both.)

Breakdown of obligatory contributions   **Box 10.3**

Training	Percentage of Annual Wage Bill	
	Ten or More Employees	**Less than Ten Employees**
Company training plan	0.9	0.15
Training of young people	0.4	0.10
Individual rights of employees	0.2	0
Total obligations	1.5	0.25

In fact, companies finance vocational training beyond the legal obligation level. In 1996, the average contribution devoted to vocational training by companies with ten or more employees was about 3.27 per cent of their annual wage bill (see Figure 10.1)

Continuing vocational training is now available in all major sectors of the economy, and many employees are taking advantage of what is on offer. Figures for 1995 are shown in Box 10.4.

The obligatory financial obligation imposed on enterprises has had positive consequences that contribute towards the development of continuing training:

- The responsibility for training is with the enterprise; for large enterprises this means offering in-house, direct training, for smaller enterprises, training through external bodies.
- Continuing training has become professional and its efficiency has increased, especially throughout the training market which was set up under the Labour Code.
- Social partners contribute towards refining the system.

    There has been a key relationship between negotiation and legislation since 1970, when the first national and interprofessional agreement was signed by the social partners. The agreement later became law and formed the basis of the present training system, although over the years the system has developed through a combination of efficient agreements and legislation.

    Generally, the national agreement precedes legislation, and the social partners are usually invited to negotiate on issues which may require legislation.

    There is also permanent consultation between the state and the social partners concerning the entire body of legislative control

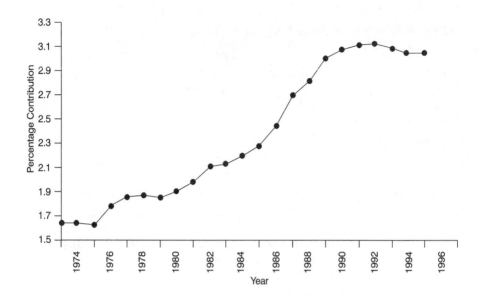

Figure 10.1 Average contribution percentage rates for companies with ten or more employees, 1974–96

Training in the major economic sectors in 1995			**Box 10.4**
Sector	Payroll Devoted to Training (%)	Employees Receiving Training (%)	Number of Employees (000s)
Electricity and gas	8.89	49.1	165
Land transport	5.12	43.4	497
Finance	5.05	63.4	389
Architecture and engineering	2.62	28.0	1030
Food industry	2.52	33.9	365
Wholesale trade	2.43	27.5	668
Metal work	3.28	41.7	271
Retail trade	2.40	33.4	738
Health	2.10	22.0	466
Construction	1.73	17.0	654

of specialist bodies within the vocational training sector. This plays a determining role in producing the framework for training.

As for the provision of training, the professional unions are called upon every five years to negotiate new agreements. In enterprises, workforce representatives are consulted every year about the training plan being offered by the employer. In many enterprises, training is the main subject for negotiation, so much so that a works council has the power to set up a special commission to study any issues relating to it.

VOCATIONAL TRAINING AS A HIGH PERFORMANCE ECONOMIC SECTOR

Training is a high performance economic sector whose importance is growing constantly. The vast sums spent on vocational training are generated by the state, enterprises, regions, UNEDIC* and individuals; in 1996 they amounted to 138 billion fr (see Box 10.5).

Financing by the state (43.5 per cent) and by enterprises (40 per cent) totalled 83.5 per cent of national training funding in 1996, compared to 99 per cent 20 years ago. However, during those 20 years, increasing financial support from the regions and UNEDIC has taken up any shortfall.

Nearly 59 per cent of funding is to provide training for the active workforce (employees, self-employed and civil servants), 20 per cent is for first-time occupational integration (16 to 25-year-olds), and 20.8 per cent is for training the unemployed.

Financing training costs in 1996	Box 10.5
Source	Amount Spent (in billions of fr)
State	60 (includes 28 billion fr for training civil servants)
Enterprises	55
Regions	15
UNEDIC	8
Total	138

* National Interprofessional Union for Employment in Industry and Trade. Represents those with jobs which are common to all areas of industry and trade, eg typists.

The training organisations

The training of the active workforce is carried out mainly by training centres within enterprises and administrations, then by private organisations and lastly by National Education establishments.

Training organisations fall into several categories:

- **Public organisations** These depend on different ministries, particularly the Ministry of National Education.
- **Semi-public organisations** Includes the AFPA (National Association for Adult Vocational Training), which depends on the Ministry of Labour, and the chambers of commerce, which depend on the Ministry of Industry.
- **Associations** Private non-profit-making organisations.
- **Private limited companies.**
- **Individuals.**

See Figure 10.2 for a breakdown of the market share each category obtained between 1990 and 1995.

The vocational training market is characterised by the presence of very many small training organisations with a low turnover. There are many more small entities than large ones, but it is the large organisations that concentrate 80 per cent of the activity.

In 1994, 83 per cent of training organisations declared a turnover of less than 1 billion fr; whereas 16 per cent of staff training organi-

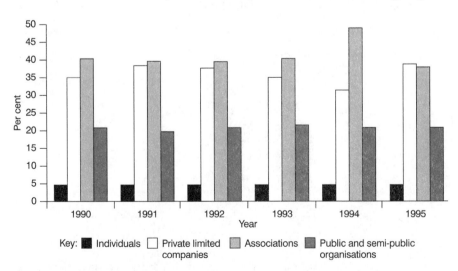

Figure 10.2 Market share of training organisations, 1990–95

sations accounted for 85 per cent of the total continous vocational training turnover (ie 30.3 billion fr). Also, the 35,360 staff trainers accounted for a total income of 35.6 billion fr. Nearly half of this came from agreements signed with companies and administrations for the training of their staff. One-third came from agreements signed with the state and regions, mainly for the training of job-seekers.

THE REGIONS: AN INCREASING ROLE

Since 1983 the regions have been responsible for instruction and vocational training. The need to adapt training policies to the needs of the regions has led to the reinforcement of their responsibilities and to the development of a partnership with the state.

The Act of 20 December 1993, which relates to work, employment and vocational training, transferred the responsibility for training of young people to the regions. It allows regions to have a more global outlook on training, thus giving them scope to present a coherent programme for the whole youth training system. Alternating training, the occupational integration of young job seekers and training associated with the Ministry of National Education are now all gathered into a regional development plan for youth training (PRDF).

The PRDF is produced under the responsibility of the regions and in agreement with the state and social partners. By taking into account their strong points, it is better able to define the types of training each region should offer.

The state has also drawn up planning agreements with the regions. Among the objectives that have been set concerning vocational training, the most important is the development of alternating training for young people (in accordance with the last planning agreement, which ran from 1994 to 1998).

THE STATE: A SPECIFIC ROLE

The state has specific duties in relation to vocational training:

- **It is responsible for the cohesion of the system**   It is the State's responsibility to fix the regulations applying to vocational training (laws, controls, texts). One principle always guides its actions: consensus seeking. Arrangements are not set up unilaterally, but call for concerted action and partnership with all the actors concerned (social partners, regions, economic actors, etc).

The principles negotiated by the social partners are incorporated in law, but legislators who wish to challenge them can intervene on their own initiative (as they did in 1993, 1994 and 1996).

- **It intervenes in regulating the system**   The state controls the market according to both economic and financial rules.

  To improve the quality of training and ensure greater financial clarity, controls have been reinforced, especially through the verification of the tax declarations of enterprises, the setting up of a single accounting plan for all training organisations and the creation of a new system for the collection of funds.

- **It promotes concerted action with institutional partners at local level**   Since the state has decentralised authority to the regions in matters of vocational training, it now has a form of partnership with local communities, but in particular with the regions. Its role is to ensure that synergy is introduced into the systems and procedures in order to develop employment.

11

The Role of the Trade Unions and Works Councils

*Professor Jean-Francois Amadieu,
Department of Management Studies, Paris
Panthéon Sorbonne University*

French Trade Unions cut an exceptional figure among the industrialised countries. On the one hand they represent only a very small number of workers, and on the other hand, they are extremely numerous and divided. These two factors weaken the unions' position. However, this weakness is partially offset by the unions' degree of institutionalisation which ensures their opportunity to establish themselves easily in a company, even where they have no members, and guarantees them financial means and personnel resources which do not depend on the number of members.

HISTORIC FRAGILITY

Although they are totally accepted by public opinion and have been legally recognised for a hundred years, French trade unions suffer from a fragile legitimacy. This is a result of their political, social and union history.

The legalisation of trade unions was slow to take place and it is significant that the French Revolution in 1789 was accompanied by the abolition of the old corporations. The unions were thus seen as non-democratic bodies conflicting with the republican ideal. As a result, political power prevailed over unions and management when defining employment conditions for the workforce, a situation which continues today. The unions therefore have to exercise influence over the political authorities. Nevertheless, it is worth noting that France has never had a 'labour party' like that in Britain; historically French unions are in competition with, and not in collaboration with, the political parties. At the present time, relations between political parties and unions are being questioned and the position varies for each group of affiliated unions. Different unions maintain links with different parties without being subordinated to them.

In other respects, through strikes, the unions succeeded in obtaining what traditional collective bargaining could not manage to achieve. The legal period of existence for unions began with workers' organisations being tolerated after the end of the Second Empire (1871), and subsequently fully recognised in 1884. Strikes were thus legal before trade unions which resulted in a tendency to give conflict greater weight than negotiation, reflecting the weakness of trade unionism. For a long time, conflict was the obligatory route because it enabled the position of political power and employers to be reoriented. Strikes were all the more prevalent because the low extent of the unions' membership was not a sufficient threat to avoid recourse to striking (in other words frequent short strikes were necessary as a reminder of the unions' ability to mobilise the workers).

THE DIFFERENT TRADE UNIONS

Divided Trade Unionism

French trade unionism is full of divisions and its long tradition of segmentation has accelerated in the 1990s. The history of French unions is marked by schism, exclusions and the setting up of new unions. Latterly this trend has resulted in numerous splits and the creation of new unions.

The SUD union, created from a split within the CFDT, made its mark in the union scene by scoring a number of successes, in particular at France Telecom and in the Postal Service. The FEN teachers' union also saw a split which gave birth to a rival teachers' union, the FSU, which became a force to be reckoned with after winning the occupational elections. The National Front has multiplied its efforts to gain a foothold in the unions. Other splits and regroupings are under way within the CGT-FO, the CFDT and the CGC.

Such union divisions give birth to new organisations which take away employee memberships, and this in turn adds further fuel – as if any were needed – to breakaway unions and new creations.

The industrial tribunal elections in December 1997 made it possible to assess the degree of segmentation in the French union movement. Never had the lists of competitors been so numerous (to the five main affiliated union groups were most notably added UNSA, FSU, SUD and CFNT).

Regroupings certainly take place among the unions, and these movements give birth to huge confederations. Thus, some autonomous unions regrouped themselves under UNSA, and the SUD unions formed a totally new association originally known as the 'Group of Ten'. Competition between the unions is exacerbated by these recompositions.

This splintering process is virtually unique among the industrialised countries.

The unions are in competition to represent workers and are weakened by this situation. They cannot prevent new competitors from developing as a result, and these new union organisations have every reason to multiply. In fact, there are considerable opportunities for development on the employee representation market because of the low number of members and the patchy establishment of unions in French businesses. The representation market is not very concentrated in France, a situation which is unique among industrialised countries, and corresponds to an extreme and unprecedented weakness in the level of union membership.

The number of unions competing to represent workers is a distinctive feature of the industrial relations system in France.

Nevertheless, the pluralist character of French trade unionism should not be exaggerated, because although the divisions are big at a national level and the number of competing unions high in the public sector and in large companies, the same is not true for the majority of SMEs. At confederate level, in the public sector and in the largest companies, French-style pluralism is highly complex and extensive.

Closer observation of the actual establishment of the unions in French companies, reveals that the number of unions present is in fact very limited, and so, therefore, is the real choice available to workers.

For elections to works councils, the average number of candidates listed in the elections was 1.4. Three-quarters of all ballots, involving 47 per cent of the electorate, were made with a single candidate listed. In only 3 per cent of elections (equating to 14 per cent of voters) were there more than four candidates, and more than three candidates were offered for worker selection in 7 per cent of cases (18 per cent of voters). Furthermore, 75 per cent of the cases where no competition was offered involved non-union candidates. Thus in half the elections, there was no competition between unions since, officially at least, there were no unions on the list.

Ultimately, while divisions in the unions cause little concern in small businesses they do pose problems elsewhere.

Extensive pluralism is in fact the result of a system of industrial relations which suffers major handicaps (weakness of union establishment and low membership levels, state control, lack of conventional activity, difficulty in cooling down before settling differences, and in regulating strikes, etc). Negotiation carries little weight, but this may well be due to the fact that the system sanctions a number of negotiators and single signatures (an agreement is valid even if it is signed by a very minor union).

The legitimacy, recognition, authority and ability of the trade unions suffer from their segmentation. This can deter the peaceful settlement of conflicts via negotiation and equal representation, something which has never been imposed. The chances of industrial conflicts developing are therefore considerably heightened.

The divided state of French trade unionism is a paradox. What can explain the regular increase in the number of unions at the same time as a sharp decrease in the number of members (or at best static membership in recent times), along with the interest of voters? In the context of union decline, and in the face of the powerful position of employers due to the current state of the labour market, a merger between unions and perhaps even serious *rapprochements* between confederations might be expected. By definition, such alignments could help create economies of scale and a better geographical and occupational coverage, give workers a sense of unity and power, and present a united front in times of industrial conflict and collective bargaining. However, nothing like this is forthcoming – on the contrary.

Pluralism among trade unions is deeply inscribed in French law, and union segmentation is clearly facilitated. The legal and contractual framework has a bearing on the recognition of trade union organisations and their methods of action. This relates to regulations governing trade union creation, laws concerning their representation within businesses and administrations, and rules dealing with the methods and powers of unions and the principle of freedom to join.

The French union movement has been carved up by ideological, political and religious divisions. Added to these reasons for discord there are practical motives like power struggles between unions and conflicts between companies, jobs and categories of workers.

The Main Stages in Trade Union History

Over the years, four trends have had an impact on French trade unionism with different degrees of intensity and they form its basis today: anarcho-unionism or revolutionary trade unionism, Marxism, reformist socialism and Catholic social doctrine. The various unions do not have a common consistency and whatever the organisation, the militants are always liable to react in a way which differs from their confederation's official line.

The CGT (Confédération Générale du Travail) is the largest and original union association. Despite a spectacular decline, it still occupies the foremost position in industrial elections. It has the advantage of a sound organisational base and a solid constituency in certain trades and professions. Its audience and influence are rather greater than that of the Communist Party, to which the union is closely aligned. The CGT seems to have curbed its decline and is now making renewed headway.

Parallel to the CGT, the CFTC (Confédération Française des Travailleurs Chrétiens), founded in 1919, had little importance until the Second World War, since when it has grown rapidly at the expense of the CGT, particularly during the 1950s.

In 1946 and 1947, the CGT broke up (there had been other splinter groups and recompositions). The anarchist wing left to set up the CNT (still very marginal), unions or federations left without rejoining or created other union associations: the RATP and SNCF for example, or the powerful FEN (Fédération de l'Education Nationale) which has no party affiliation. The reformist socialist minority joined the majority Marxist wing with its Communist Party links and set up the CGT-FO confederation.

The CGT-FO, for many years the employers' favoured partner, developed somewhat radically. Its less reformist and more protest-oriented approach was far from shared by the majority in the confederation. This is not surprising given that this union association saw the cohabitation of powerful far-Left militants at the head of the organisation with reformist socialists and less ideological or political elements that were very open to dialogue, forming its base legions.

Meanwhile, when France was liberated at the end of the war, the white-collar union CGC (Confédération Générale des Cadres) was created (ultimately becoming the CFE-CGC with CFE standing for Confédération Française de l'Encadrement). The CGC defines itself as a proposing not an opposing union and is now declining. The CFDT (to some extent friendly with the CGT) provides strong competition to the CGC's executive electorate. Whether it can survive as an autonomous organisation not integrated into a larger association is in question.

At the CFTC congress in 1964, a majority resolution abandoned the 'Christian' reference and changed its acronym to CFDT (Confédération Française Démocratique du Travail), the minority separated and created a competing confederation, CFTC (retained). The CFTC with its reformist attitude has remained weak and its influence is declining, particularly since the CFDT has also embraced reformist positions. The latter, self-governing, politicised and active in its demands, has experienced substantial development since 1979 and is now a favoured partner among state employers. This organisation has enhanced its constituency in the private sector but is declining in the public sector. In practical terms, the CFDT groups together Christian militants ready for social compromise as well as militant minorities who are more active in their demands, more politicised and more prepared to promote industrial conflict. The CFDT enjoys a good reputation particularly among executives and the better-qualified workers.

Other union confederations exist which were created in parallel. UNSA regroups moderate socialist unions and federations, mainly in the public sector. A new trade union association (formerly known as the Group of Ten) has been established from the far-Left unions (particularly the SUD) whose constituency is growing in the public sector. However, these new confederations have not found themselves recognised as fully representative, or having a recognised organisational quality which carries with it all the importance, rights and privileges of a trade union organisation.

At the confederate level, the French trade union scene currently offers five representative confederations: the CGT, CGT-FO, CFDT, CFTC and CGC. This situation which seems to have lasted for a long time, is developing rapidly for a number of reasons: the weakening of the CFTC and the CGC, the continuing progress of the left-wing autonomous unions, and foreseeable splits and recompositions within the large confederations (the FO, CGC, and CFDT). The trade union scene is therefore only stable in private sector companies which are dominated by the CGT and the CFDT.

The Ideology of the Trade Union Organisations

It is worth noting from the outset that a trade union is not a political party, and could not operate as one. On this basis, judges have proscribed the new trade unions linked to the National Front.

Furthermore, the great majority of union members in all confederations do not belong to any political party. Having said that, it is clear that the ideological character of French trade unionism is marked by, but not – contrary to many European trade unions – linked *institutionally* through any of its components to a political party. But as with all other unions, links nevertheless exist to a greater or lesser extent between some elements and some political and trade union movements, through people, sympathies, and orientation.

A number of leaders in CGT units at all levels operate as militants or activists, particularly within the French Communist Party but also, much less widely, in other parties. This is possible because, unlike other French union confederations, the CGT permits members to hold both political and union office so as not to 'politically disable' the militants. In the words of the former general secretary himself: 'As a union for the masses, it cannot be communist because it does not want to exclude any members, but it is certainly not anti-communist.'

Prohibiting members to hold both political and union office in the other confederations makes the links between union and party less tangible. However, it is clear that there is a convergence between part of the CFDT or UNSA and some sections in the Socialist Party. In the CGT-FO, several movements are present which are sympathetic to other trends in the Socialist Party but covering a range of areas from reformism to Trotskyism. In the CGT, as in the other confederations, more important than the complex, shifting and quite well-controlled links between union and party in France compared with what happens in other countries, is the establishment of an ideology specific to each confederation. As far as its own ideology is concerned, the CGT defines itself as a union of class and the masses, committed to the defence of the working class, the struggle against economic exploitation and the goal of socialism as the means of production and exchange. It is thus allied to Marxist ideology.

At its 1970 congress, the CFDT also defined itself as an organisation of class and of the masses, setting its objectives as worker control, the social take-over of the means of production and democratic planning. To the fight against economic exploitation, CGT's principal objective, it added the fight against the alienation and control of workers. The policy of 're-unionisation' which it had followed since the thirty-eighth congress in 1978, has, for the majority of the CFDT, pushed the ideological aspect to the background in favour of a return to concrete activity, qualified by 'refocusing' at the level of the problem – in other words, the expectations of workers on the ground, and particularly the most disadvantaged among them. Meanwhile, an active minority is contesting this modification of the objectives.

The CGT-FO defines its ideology as independence in relation to the Church (in opposition to the CFTC and even the CFDT), independence in relation to political parties, marked by a virulent anti-communism putting it in opposition to the CGT, and independence in relation to business which sets it in opposition to the ideas of worker control or joint management seen in the current CFDT, an ideology further qualified as union–party because of the extent of its objectives. It also recognises the inevitability of the class struggle but has opted for a gradual socialisation of capitalism: reformism by accumulation of the advantages for workers leading to economic democracy.

The CFTC holds to the social doctrine of the Catholic church, expressed in papal encyclicals, and the CGC, ie it is mandated to defend the interests of its workers.

These ideological positions are confederate positions which are not always found automatically at the grass roots, ie the same attitudes are not always found in union branches and among militants within companies.

The trade unions often follow doctrines or treatises which may seem to be revolutionary or at least very revengeful (the CGT, FO and SUD in particular). The CGT calls most often for strikes. Nevertheless, in practice, the unions have proved themselves able to conclude collective agreements at a company level. They sign between 80 per cent and 95 per cent of the documents put to them by companies. The CGT has shown itself to be very pragmatic. It is only in the very large companies and in industrial sections that some unions are reluctant to sign.

In smaller companies, particularly in the SMEs, there is generally one union (either a single or a dominant union). In such a context, there is less chance of overbidding between unions for what it might yield in elections. Dialogue is conducted through a works council or single personnel delegation (a new simplified authority which is based on the works council and staff representatives in firms of between 50 and 200 employees). In these companies the important areas are the management of company operations and questions of training, subjects not inherently conflict-based. Strikes are therefore rare.

STRUCTURE AND ORGANISATION

For historical reasons, French trade union organisations have relatively similar structures although there are major differences in their methods of appointment and the reciprocal powers of their bodies.

The language used is, however, a source of confusion since 'trade unions' as they are frequently called does not distinguish whether it concerns a federation, confederation, union branch, or even sometimes – exceptionally designated with their correct title – trade unions proper. At the core of the system is the trade union composed of workers in the same field (French trade unionism is dominated by a model of industrial organisation as opposed to the craft or task model which bands together all workers doing the same job whatever field they are working in). The trade union is the pivotal element and has its own internal structure (office, leaders, etc). It is often established on a local basis, bringing together workers from several local businesses in the same field. However, there are exceptions: national unions (for teachers and merchant seamen for example), or unions by department, the French administrative regions (for example, the PTT – post and telecommunication services), and sometimes by company (for example, the CGT). The trade union is the base structure for the union confederations, collecting members and enjoying the privilege of appointing union delegates within companies, who have the sole right to conclude collective agreements on the union's behalf.

Sometimes union workers belong to the union branch of a company which co-ordinates the union activity in each company but which does not, however, have the union's ethical personality or organisational importance. The union branch does not have the right to legal action, to negotiate collective agreements, or to formally appoint a union delegate.

Unions are grouped together according to two standpoints: on the one hand geographically, in local, departmental or even regional unions, where unions in the same areas, departments or regions join together, whatever field they are working in; and on the other hand industrially, in national industry federations which join together all the unions nationwide from one industrial branch or sub-branch (metallurgy, chemistry, banking, etc). These federations then join together in a confederation. The confederate bodies have a rather cumbersome structure (national committee or national confederate committee) which meets several times a year to ensure close links between the base and the leadership bodies, and other less weighty bodies (executive committee and confederate council) dealing with current problems and which meet more frequently, and finally the leadership body limited to a few members which manages daily business and directs the organisation (confederate board) in which the secretary general is the personality most widely known through the media. Major political decisions are made by Congress which meets every three years and is composed of the union delegates. Following sometimes complex procedures, in which the role of the intermediate bodies can be lively, Congress appoints or elects the members of the other bodies.

WORKFORCE AND INFLUENCE

For various reasons (historical, structural, lack of a union security clause, lack of additional advantages linked to unionisation, etc), the number of union members in France has always been among the lowest in western Europe. During the last 20 years, the situation has considerably worsened in this connection. In a European context where some union movements have lost members but where others have been stable or have even, in several cases, increased their membership, French trade unionism has experienced a damaging loss. In simple terms, from a membership base that was already low, the downward trend has continued since the end of the 1970s. This decline has affected all the union organisations to a greater or lesser degree.

In 1998, INSEE, the French Central Statistical Office, assessed the level of French union membership at 6.5 per cent of workers in the public and private sectors.

Union membership levels are even lower than this in the private sector because it is particularly in the public services and public companies that trade unionism is powerful. INSEE estimates that about 3.5 per cent of workers in the private sector belong to a trade union. Fewer than 2 per cent of employees in business are members, with levels at 5 per cent among white-collar workers. Put another way, the number of members in a business boils down to the elected personnel.

In addition, the level of average membership masks the fact that trade unionists are found mainly in big companies and in particular areas of business. In companies of fewer than 50 employees where the election of a works council is not obligatory, trade unions are usually absent. Staff representatives elected in these companies are not usually members of a trade union. To compensate for the steady disappearance of trade unions in SMEs, French law has opened up the possibility for trade unions to designate a representative in firms (a personnel delegate or an ordinary worker) to negotiate collective agreements in the company. Until this law was enacted, it was necessary for a union branch to have a union delegate in a firm so that an employer could make a valid agreement. There is no doubt that this new law will have increasing application.

A variety of explanations are frequently put forward to explain the low level of trade unionism in France: psychological characteristics such as 'Frenchmen are too individualistic to belong to groups'; or simplified sociological analysis such as 'French trade unions are too politicised' (thereby deterring potential recruits); or even, 'the employers' suppression of the militants is so ferocious that it is crushing the trade union movement, particularly in the SMEs'.

In reality, the low membership levels are explained by the absence of a financial incentive to join. Whether or not he or she is in the union, an employee benefits from all labour agreements signed between his or her employer and a trade union. The situation is different in many other countries where being in a union produces positive additional advantages. Also, French unions do not offer much in the way of services to members (no 'syndicated' pension schemes, sickness and unemployment benefit, etc) except in a partial way in the public sector. A strike pay fund is virtually non-existent. Furthermore, obligatory membership has always been forbidden by law.

In spite of the undeniable decline in numbers of French trade unionists, workers should not be confused between representation and power. A unique feature of the French trade union movement with its low membership is that it traditionally carries considerable influence among workers, especially in the institutions for staff representation, which are mainly composed of union members. Elections to these various institutions within the company (such as works councils and staff representatives) and outside the company (elections to industrial tribunals) provide a useful barometer of this influence. Traditionally, non-union members or members of unions other than those affiliated to the big, so-called representative, confederations, were in the minority in the internal elections, which was not explained solely by the union monopoly over presenting the first round candidates. As in the external elections which were open to all, with no monopoly on the presentation of candidates, the representative confederations retained a crushing superiority. Tables 11.1 and 11.2 show that the situation is changing. According to the workers, union influence is under threat.

Table 11.1   Elections to works councils (results in percentages of votes cast)

	1966–67	1976–77	1986–87	1988–89	1990–91	1992–93
Turnout	71.9	71.2	67.3	66.1	64.4	66.4
CGT	48.8	39.8	27.0	25.9	22.7	22.5
CFDT	18.6	19.6	21.3	20.9	20.2	20.7
CFTC	2.3	2.9	4.3	4.2	4.0	4.6
FO	7.9	9.2	12.8	12.5	12.2	11.9
CGC	4.1	5.4	6.7	6.1	6.5	5.7
Other unions	3.6	6.6	5.5	5.6	5.6	6.6
Non-unions	14.6	16.5	22.5	24.9	28.7	28.1

Table 11.2   Industrial tribunal elections (results in percentages of votes cast)

	1979	1982	1987	1992	1997
Registered voters	12.3	13.5	12.2	13.9	14.6
Abstentions	36.8	41.4	54.0	59.6	65.95
CGT	42.4	36.8	36.3	33.3	33.11
CFDT	23.1	23.5	23.0	23.8	25.34
FO	17.4	17.7	20.5	20.4	20.55
CFTC	6.9	8.5	8.3	8.6	7.52
CFE-CGC	5.2	9.6	7.4	6.9	5.92
Various	4.6	3.8	4.3	6.8	–
CSL					4.22
Others					3.34

The results shown in Tables 11.1 and 11.2 should certainly be interpreted with great care. On the one hand, the electorates are not comparable. For works councils, in businesses of more than 50 employees, between 2.5 and 3 million voters are registered, depending on the year, and for elections to industrial tribunals the figures are nearer 15 million blue-collar workers, across all businesses and branches. On the other hand, the voting frequency is different, every two years for works councils (which makes it impossible to compare one year with the next, so they are compared between even or odd years), and every five years for industrial tribunals. Finally, global data like this is bound to hide the considerable disparities between companies depending on branches, regions, and sizes (size alone has a significant effect, with small businesses being much more likely than others to have non-union representation).

There is evidence of a slow decline in the CGT, which is not offset by the small gains of the other representative unions, and a constant rise in non-union members and a smaller rise in other (non-representative) unions. These worrying elements are mitigated by an increase in abstention levels. Furthermore, the total number of union delegates in companies has decreased, as well as the number of institutions in which they were present.

A closer analysis of the figures shows that the union presence varies considerably according to sectors and retains its strongholds. It would be a mistake to draw any conclusions that a death notice has been served on trade unionism which, in the course of its history, has seen considerable fluctuations and transformations. It remains deeply rooted in the French structure and it would be even more dangerous for a manager to conclude that he could economise on his organisation's industrial relations policy.

Weak and divided trade unions losing ground in elections are not in fact totally denuded of power and resources. The weakness of union membership is partially offset by significant financing of trade union activity which comes from employers and public authorities (the state and local communities). In fact, employers have to ensure that staff representatives can carry out their duties (time and place for meetings, operating budgets for works councils, etc). The authorities also contribute to the financing of the trade union movement.

The low membership is not explained by the poor image of unions in the eyes of workers and public opinion in general. In fact, three-quarters of French people believe in the value of the trade unions even if the majority deplore the unions' politicisation. French people have also expressed hope for a consolidation of the unions. They have a high opinion of some of the union leaders like N. Notat (CFDT) and even M. Blondel (FO), despite his poor image in the media.

The trade unions have close relations with the political parties to the extent that their influence on public decisions (local and national) is not insignificant. In a country where political power plays an important role in the development of the law relating to business (laws on the reduction in working hours, for example) and where collective bargaining remains less important than political power, the influence of the unions at this level must be taken into account.

The French unions traditionally draw power from another source, their ability to conduct highly successful strikes. On this point, today even more than in the past, the ability of the French unions to trigger conflict is not to be ignored. This is, however, true only for the public sector and in some of the very large companies. Elsewhere, the number of strikes which has never been high in France, has continued to decline in the last 20 years. Thus, the ability to mobilise the unions which is tested periodically (in 1995 for example), in fact only affects the public sector. Nevertheless it should not be forgotten that the French judge some of these conflicts sympathetically. This can be seen in the opinion polls which underline the low reputation of the heads of major companies and a suspicion of employers (a distrust which is less evident for SME leaders).

French trade unionism is certainly exceptional. However, its increasing uniqueness is not as much as one might think, due to the politicisation or the revolutionary character of the unions. While these aspects are not absent, it should be remembered that there is no organic link between trade union and political party and that the militants are very pragmatic at company level (particularly in the SMEs). The truth is that the exceptional characteristic of the French lies more than ever in the segmentation of the unions (the competition between them) and the very low extent of their membership.

12

Employment Analysis

Christiane Pacotte, Union Nationale des Entreprises de Travail Temporaire (UNETT)

ANALYSIS OF THE WORKFORCE

The Working Population in France

In accordance with the norms set up by the ILO,* the INSEE[†] under-takes an annual *Employment Survey* in March with a random sample of 75,000 supposedly 'ordinary' households in metropolitan France.

In this survey the working population is broken down into two groups: the 'occupied working population', ie people of working age (between 16 and 65 years old) with a job, and the unemployed (as defined by the ILO).[‡] Results for 1997 indicated that the occupied working population numbered 22,430,000 (as against 22,022,000 in March 1993), with 19,554,000 of them in salaried jobs and 2,876,000 in non-salaried jobs, and the unemployed 3,151,586.[§]

The working population in France is growing by around 150,000 extra jobs a year. Depending on the period, there are three main factors

---

* Bureau international du travail [International Labour Office (ILO)].
[†] Institut National de la Statistique et des Etudes Economiques [National Institute of Statistics and Economic Research].
[‡] ILO's definition is based on a resolution adopted in October 1982, according to which a jobless person is one without employment, is immediately available for work and is looking for a job. This definition excludes every unemployed person who has been in part-time active employment.
[§] *Employment Survey*, March 1997, INSEE.

behind this phenomenon: immigration (above all between 1962 and 1968), the length of the working life of the population and crucially, the development of active employment amongst women.

Active employment amongst women has had an extremely diversified impact since the beginning of the 1950s. Up until the end of the 1960s, the combined effect of the reduction in the number of farms and small traders (where there were many mothers' helps) and the raising of the school leaving age brought about a reduction in the rates of active employment amongst the youngest women. However, since 1968 the growth phenomenon in adult women's active employment has been accelerating. Thus the percentage of women aged between 25 and 54 in professional employment has increased from 44.6 per cent in 1968 to 54 per cent in 1975, 63.7 per cent in 1982, 74.4 per cent in 1990 and 79.4 per cent in 1996. The combination of several factors may explain this phenomonen: progress in academic levels, the development of the service sector (with increasing numbers of women working in it), the reduction in fertility rates, the change in society's attitudes towards women working.

Nowadays, women are getting more of the quality jobs in the civil service and in business, but the development in female employment has also taken place in jobs requiring few skills, particularly in the service sector: sales agents and representatives or staff selling services direct to individuals.

Also, in so far as the length of the working life of the French population is concerned, two factors have helped to shorten it: students prolonging their education and the earlier retirement of the oldest salaried employees from the labour market. Increasingly, young people are continuing their studies up to the level of the baccalauréat (school-leaving certificate and qualification for university entrance) with the result that their entry into working life is postponed.

At the same time there is the trend towards early retirement, particularly as part of the FNE;* people retiring as part of the measures relat-

* National Fund for Employment. Within the framework of a planned redundancy scheme a business can conclude an agreement with the state enabling older salaried employees affected by a lay-off for economic reasons to benefit from their anticipated retirement from the labour market by receiving a specific pension valued up to the settlement of their retirement pensions and supported by credits from the FNE.

ing to the replacement pension for employment, the ARPE;* people retiring to indemnified unemployment; or other measures of this type. In 1968 the active employment rate of the over 65s was still 19.3 per cent; by 1996 it had fallen to less than 2 per cent. This phenomenon also affects the 55–59 age bracket, 82 per cent of whom were working in 1975 but only 70 per cent of whom were working in 1996.

The profound changes which the salaried population has experienced have brought about distinct transformations in the development of socio-professional categories: from the development of service sector jobs to an increase in white-collar workers and the executive class as well as the intellectual professions.

Socio-Professional Categories

The social structure of the salaried population never stops developing. According to the last INSEE surveys, from 1982 to 1994 the 'executives' – 'upper intellectual professions' – and the 'intermediate professions' have increased from 60 per cent and 17 per cent respectively. The *Business Panel* published by the Agency for Executive Employment (APEC) confirms this trend: in 1997, 37,900 executive jobs were created. On the other hand, the number of non-qualified workers has fallen from 30 per cent while the number of self-employed and employers has fallen from 20 per cent. The development of IT, the concerns of management which increasingly rationalise human resources and above all the strengthening of sales and techno-commercial functions within the business, help to explain the rise in socio-professional groups such as executives and intermediate professions, which when combined are now more numerous than white-collar workers (one-third of the working population) or manual workers (30.3 per cent of the working population in March 1997).

Distribution of Jobs by Sectors of Business Activity

The old distinction between the three sectors of business activity has undergone quantitative upheavals in the second half of the 20th century. While the number of jobs in the primary sector, farming, has fallen

---

* This system, which came into force in October 1995, allows salaried persons in private business aged 57½ to cease their active employment voluntarily in advance while at the same time receiving up to their sixtieth birthday a pension which is equal to 65 per cent of their former gross salary. The ARPE is granted on condition that the employer agrees, that the employee has contributed for more than 40 years and that on their departure a young person is taken on. The result of an agreement between labour and management, this measure has aroused very keen interest, leaving behind as it does public measures. At the end of February 1998 98,664 pensioners took advantage of the ARPE, and the ASSEDICs recorded 88,213 recruits being taken on (at 99 per cent in CDI and 15.5 per cent on ¾ time) as replacements for those salaried workers taking ARPE. The average age of those taken on was 30.

from more than 25 per cent to 4.5 per cent and the secondary sector, industry and BTP,* has seen its share decline from 42 per cent in 1975 to 34 per cent in 1985 and 27 per cent in 1996, the tertiary sector, services, starting in 1975, brought together half of all jobs and almost reached 70 per cent in 1996. These trends do not explain the progress which is particular to each sector. The following developments attempt to analyse the changes that have taken place.

Where farmers or farmworkers are concerned the heavy decline in the active farming population is a striking and well-known fact of the second half of the 20th century. The proportion of baccalauréat graduates and higher has increased from about one-third to almost a half. The trend in this sector has been towards integration and thus larger farms, but smallholdings have not completely disappeared (the latter still represent one-third of the total). Finally, the phenomenon of multi-activity is tending to increase: many farming households take part in occupations which are outside the farmer's world and this allows them to increase their incomes.

The secondary sector workforce, which on 31 December 1997 was estimated at 4,057,700 salaried employees for industry and 1,111,400 for the construction trade, has undergone two phases: a strong increase from 1955 to 1974, then a significant decline to date which varies according to the type of occupation. Some sectors have experienced a considerable reduction in jobs: coal-mining, the steel industry, basic chemicals, textiles-clothing. On the other hand, other industries have created jobs: pharmaceuticals and parachemicals, the press, meat and dairy products. This reduction of employment in industry has above all affected manual workers and white-collar workers; however, upper management has clearly moved forward. The share of small and medium-sized businesses (PME) has tended to increase in this sector. In reality, big companies do away with jobs, restructure themselves (break-up, hive-off as a subsidiary rather than merging), contract out or subcontract activities, or indeed disappear to the profit of small companies.

Since the end of 1997 the sector has taken advantage of dynamic exports and the increase in domestic demand, and has therefore seen its employment stabilise; job losses are lessening appreciably, particularly in capital goods, in consumer goods and in the energy industry. Similarly, the auto sector is stabilising its losses. The outlook for activity in the BTP remains good at the beginning of 1998, especially in so far as maintenance-improvement work and new housing are concerned.

---

* Bâtiment et Travaux Publics (BTP) [Construction and Public Works].

With a 68.6 per cent share of employment, the services sector is made up of very mixed sub-sectors: trade, transport, financial activities, property activities, business-to-business services, services to individuals, health, education, welfare, etc.

The pronounced spread in jobs in sales in the course of the 1980s stems from the development of new areas of activity such as consultancy and research for businesses. This rapid expansion in services to businesses is widely linked to the contracting-out of functions which before would have been carried out by production businesses, such as staff catering or ancillary services (cleaning, conditioning) and hiring temporary staff. Job creation in sales has also been accomplished in the areas of medicine and old people's care.

Non-sales services employed 6,300,000 people in 1996, amongst whom were 3,000,000 state employees, and around 40 per cent of whom are still in state education. Administrative activity where employment is concerned is not just taken up by state civil servants. To this must also be added the public sector workforces in health, social security and local government. Assisted jobs contribute widely to the growth of non-sales services employment. In its entirety the services sector remains the motor for growth.*

Movements in Labour

If in 1996 firms with ten salaried employees or more in the private sector took on staff representing 32.9 per cent of their workforce at the beginning of the year, they recorded an equal number of staff leaving (excluding temporary staff). Generally speaking, these flows are much more significant in services than in industry and construction: rates of staff turnover here are 42.2 per cent as against 19.8 per cent and 18.6 per cent respectively.

The rotation of staff in the services sector is slow in financial activities and in government services, moderate in transport, auto repair and trade, and research and development, but everywhere else staff turnover rates exceed 30 per cent (51 per cent in the retail trade and health and welfare, 62 per cent in staff and domestic services and more than 85 per cent in hotels and restaurants, and sporting, cultural and leisure activities).

Spread of Qualifications

Qualifications in this sense mean not only the level of training achieved by a worker, but also work experience.

---

* By way of example, 73,000 new jobs were created in the fourth quarter of 1997.

According to data from the Ministry of Education, 5 per cent of the population held the baccalauréat in 1950 and 63 per cent in 1995, and between 1962 and 1996, 2.7–21 per cent obtained a degree from higher education (post-baccalauréat). These figures illustrate the increasing emphasis placed on degree level education by the working population. The number of those leaving the education system at the lowest level (below the CAP [City & Guilds/vocational training] or the sixth form) fell from 25 per cent to 10 per cent between 1973 and 1993, but is unlikely to fall much further and a levelling off of young people unsuited to the current school system is anticipated.

Continuous training during a person's working life affects slightly more than 30 per cent of salaried workers. Companies' training strategies depend on their choices in terms of personal management; in fact, the more qualified workforce often benefits from further training.

Since 1973, the potential working population has increased by more than four million, whereas the number of jobs available has not kept pace; the obvious effect has been that unemployment has risen.

Unemployment*

France has experienced weak growth in employment for 25 years while at the same time the population who are of working age and the working population have developed quickly. This has been translated into a huge rise in unemployment and job losses. Nevertheless, after a period of stability, unemployment started to decline at the end of 1997. According to the ILO norms, unemployment in France reached 3.1 million at that time, or 12.1 per cent of the working population as against 0.5 million at the beginning of the 1970s, 1.5 million at the beginning of the 1980s and 2.2 million at the beginning of the 1990s.

The period has also been marked by the rise in long-term unemployment: according to the *Employment Survey* carried out in March 1997, the number of people who had been unemployed for more than a year was approaching 1,300,000. Long-term unemployment can be translated into significant losses in terms of human capital for the

---

* The two main agencies which measure unemployment in France are l'Agence National Pour l'Emploi (ANPE) [French National Employment Office] and INSEE, whose annual *Employment Survey* takes the norms set out by the ILO as its reference.

Non-commercial assisted jobs appeared only in the middle of the 1980s with community jobs (TUC) and nowadays with solidarity employment contracts. In February 1998, breakdown of non-commercial assisted jobs showed that there were 281,000 solidarity employment contracts, 92,000 funded jobs and 14,200 urban employment contracts.

people concerned, and this makes their later reintroduction into employment more difficult. Situations of recurrent unemployment are also appearing with the development in particular of fixed-term contracts leading to more frequent movements between employment and unemployment.

More specifically, the situation of young people is clearly improving by virtue of the particular attention which is being paid to them: priority is being given to hire them under certain systems, work and training contracts are being developed and the public authorities are creating opportunities which favour young people.*

Unemployment amongst young people in France is very typical, but is not as worrying as certain statistics suggest. In fact, the ILO's classic indicator of the unemployment rate (the number of jobless in the sense defined by the ILO in relation to the total working population) appears to be especially inappropriate for France, taking into account the weakness in the rate of jobs among young people linked to their school leaving ages. Indeed, raising the school leaving age is one of the most striking facts of the last 20 years: 49.9 per cent of the population in the 16–25 age group was receiving schooling in 1997 as against 24.1 per cent in 1975. So the process of introduction into employment now affects the 25–29 age group.

Even if it stays at a relatively low level, the unemployment rate among executives has increased strikingly during the first half of the 1990s. In March 1996, slightly over 140,000 executives were unemployed as against approximately 60,000 ten years earlier. The majority (76 per cent) were business executives: sales and administrative posts have been the most affected. But age seems also to have been a decisive factor: it is young people and the oldest who were the most affected from the end of the 1980s. Then, in the course of the early 1990s, unemployment spread to the entire executive class and applied to salaried employees of all ages equally.

---

* In effect, more than one young person's job in three benefits from employment assistance. The share of apprenticeships has tripled since 1975 to reach 12 per cent in 1996. Other forms of work and training contracts have been created starting in 1977 at the time of the job-creation schemes for young people, but replaced by contracts of qualification which have included more than 100,000 young people on average every year since 1990 and adjustment contracts which have affected 30,000 young people a year since 1993. Other assisted sales jobs developed from 1977 to 1982 with practical training courses with businesses and tax relief for hiring (SIVP, APEJ and relief for taking on the first salaried employee). More recently, many young people have benefited from the job initiative contract (CIE): in February 1998, 392,000 of them were listed.

A degree from higher education* has not always saved the executive class from the risk of unemployment, unless they have held degrees from the top schools. Even if a degree from higher education remains vital for young people to rise to the executive grades, the significant number of jobs created at executive level has proved to be insufficient during the past ten years to confront the flood of young degree holders presenting themselves on the jobs' market.

The economic upheavals and crises at the beginning of the 1970s have brought about the development of new forms of employment aimed at improving the economy's flexibility and challenging the traditional forms of employment during periods of growth, ie those on a full-time basis and contracts without a fixed length (CD1). Thus jobs have appeared which have been labelled 'untypical': part-time, temporary work, fixed-term contracts (CDD), work from home, etc.

Part-time Work†

The percentage of the working population doing part-time work, which was hardly developed in France in comparison to certain foreign countries up until the 1970s, has increased from 5.9 per cent in 1973 to 9.6 per cent in 1983 to 16.8 per cent in March 1997.

The term 'part-time' comes under two headings: part-time under constraint and part-time chosen. It is more often the former which prevails, above all with men and young people, since slightly under half of wage earners employed under this type of work stated in March 1997 that they wished to work full-time.

Women easily occupy the majority of this form of employment: out of 3,726,966 people working part-time in 1997 3,052,269 were women, or almost 82 per cent. Among men, part-time work remains marginal and corresponds to a transitional period, most often at the beginning or the end of their professional life. The proportion of those benefiting aged 50 and above is especially significant (23 per cent): in this case part-time work most frequently takes the form of progressive early retirement. Part-time work also affects the younger male population, ie a growing number of young men in insertion programmes.

By providing the opportunity to adapt the presence of staff to the volume of activity and to adapt according to periods in the day or in the

---

* Top schools, higher degrees.
† The law (article L. 212-4-2 of Labour Law) considers the following to be part-time work: where the hours are less than at least one-fifth of the legal duration of work or the duration fixed by agreement for the industrial sector or the business.

week, part-time work is now very largely directed (85 per cent) towards service sector professions, in particular to occupations which have to respond to client requirements, like for example, the cleaning sector or those of sales and distribution (by way of illustration more than half of check-out assistants today work part-time), or again the hotel–café–restaurant sector as well as those of health and welfare. On the other hand, it is less well developed in industry where it often takes the form of gradual early retirement.

In 1997, the usual average weekly duration of part-time work for a salaried employee was 22.6 hours and only 19.3 hours in services to individuals.

Greatly encouraged by the public authorities, the growth in part-time work for salaried employees has above all accelerated since 1992.

The first measure to encourage the development of part-time work, the law of 31 December 1992, introduced a standard deduction, currently fixed at 30 per cent, of employers' social security contributions in the event of recruitment under work contracts of indeterminate length, for part-time work or changing full-time jobs to part-time jobs under certain conditions.* To this special measure can be added the general measure of the reducing the cost of labour for low-paid jobs introduced since 1993.

Just as the norm of full-time salaried jobs has seriously diminished, so too has the number of indeterminate-length salaried employees considerably declined.

Temporary Work and the Fixed-term Contract (CDD)

In the French tradition, which rests on a 'command economy', the public authorities have widely intervened in the course of the last decades to regulate the recourse to salaried employees working for limited periods through temporary work or fixed-term contracts. This development aims to confront three types of situation: the replacement of an absent salaried employee, an exceptional increase in activity, and jobs considered to be customary (where it is not usual to resort to CDIs) or which have a seasonal character.

---

* In particular the range of a contract's period of work must be between 16 and 32 hours weekly, a floor which will be raised from 16 to 18 hours in accordance with the new law of 19 May 1998 on the reform and reduction of working hours.

These types of contractual practices tend to develop and respond economically to two additional requirements: regular offers of work by businesses on the one hand, requests for temporary jobs on the other. The temporary work contract and the CDD are currently used to adjust the volumes of employment to the variations in activity and can also result in indeterminate-length recruitment. It is therefore estimated that one temporary worker in five is recruited full-time at the end of his assignment.

One study carried out by the COFREMCA in 1997 showed that among businesses the recourse to temporary work increases significantly; 43 per cent of respondents consider that workers would definitely be hired six months to one year later. Temporary work is therefore both the means to acquire professional experience which is increasingly expected by businesses in addition to a qualification and to become known (and known again) by a possible future employer. This type of work today affects every sector of the economy at every level.

If the exercise of the CDD has for a long time had a relative importance almost three times greater than that of temporary work, it should be noted that in 1997 the number of temporary salaried employees in equivalent full-time work has increased from 21 per cent compared to 1996, whereas the CDDs have only increased by 7.5 per cent during the same period.

Considered as an advanced economic indicator capable of announcing the beginnings of a crisis or the chances of a recovery, temporary work today represents 1.9 per cent of the working population (in equivalent full-time work) as against 4.9 per cent for the CDDs.

The length of temporary assignments tends to grow smaller: 2 weeks on average in 1996 as against 3.8 in 1980. On the other hand, the average length of the CDDs is higher (3 months in 1996), even though it also remains very much lower than the maximum duration authorised by law (18 months).

As for the distribution of salaried employees linked to this type of contract, an almost equal division of men and women are in CDDs, in contrast to temporary work where the majority of jobs are occupied by men. For user sectors, temporary work is predominant in industry (54.6 per cent of business activity), whereas CDDs are used more in the services sector, and more particularly in commerce and services to business and to individuals.

Finally, it is appropriate to note that the social legislation applying to temporary workers is especially protective, whether it is a question of social protection (additional compensation for illness, accidents, maternity leave, death or disability), professional training (training contracts for young temporary workers, qualification contracts, individual training contracts), welfare, access to credit or housing.

ESSENTIAL RULES RELATING TO THE CONDITIONS OF EMPLOYMENT

SMIC

A significant limit has been imposed on free collective bargaining by the implementation of a minimum wage (SMIC). Since this is in the public domain, it is impossible to depart from it, even by collective agreement.

The first minimum wage was created by the law of 11 February 1950 in the form of a SMIC (minimum guaranteed interprofessional wage) and was determined according to the standard of living considered to be minimum at the time and indexed solely to prices. The SMIC guaranteed to maintain the most underprivileged of salaried employees' purchasing power, but in the long term it could not reflect the results of economic growth. Consequently, there developed a growing divergence between the average rise in wages and the SMIC.

As a result, the law of 2 January 1970 created a SMIC which from that point on is revised as of right according to two methods. Each rise of at least 2 per cent in the prices index is automatically followed by the same increase in the SMIC, and every year it is revised by decree with effect from 1 July according to the progress of the economy and the economic outlook. Furthermore, in the course of the year the government can decide by decree to raise the SMIC to a higher level than that which would result from the development of prices alone.

The SMIC is guaranteed to workers of both sexes, aged over 18 and physically normal, working in metropolitan France and the overseas departments.

On 1 July 1997 the SMIC was increased by 4 per cent and has been fixed at 39.43 fr per hour, ie for a basic of 39-hour week, the total amount of the SMIC per month is 6,663.67 fr gross.

Contracts and Collective Agreements

Contracts and collective work agreements can determine job classification, and for each job or category can fix the minimum remuneration.

The employer is obliged to comply with the minimum wage defined by the contract or the collective agreement. Without this, he incurs penalties.

Average Salaries

In October 1997, according to the results of the *Wage Earners' Earnings* survey published by the Ministry for Employment (DARES), average gross monthly earnings for full-time work in firms with ten or more salaried employees rose to 12,080 fr.

These results demonstrate that:

- The gap between men's and women's salaries remains fairly constant: in October 1997 a salaried man earned on average 22.5 per cent more than a woman. The gap had been closing with the increase in women's qualified jobs from 29.2 per cent in October 1991 to 22.2 per cent in October 1996. This is no longer the case.
- Large firms pay higher salaries than small ones: on average, wage earners from firms of 500 or more employees earn 21 per cent more than those from firms of 10 to 49 employees.
- Payments vary, but large firms can pay up to twice as much as small firms according to the sectors of activity: sectors which remunerate their employees the best (on average more than 15,000 fr) are those producing fuels (20,290 fr), certain services to businesses, such as research and development (17,980 fr) or consultancy (16,310 fr) as well as shipbuilding, the aircraft and rail industries (15,540 fr). At the other end of the scale, sectors employing a less qualified workforce with a less stable status and in general with more women working in them, such as the clothing sector, leather and shoes or the sales sector pay lower wages (less than 9,000 fr).

The hourly wage rate for workers increased by a yearly average of + 2.8 per cent in 1997. This rise in particular reflects the revaluation of the SMIC which took place in July (4 per cent) and which corresponds to assistance of 2.3 per cent in addition to the revaluation of 1.7 per cent which a strict application of the law would have led to.

SHARING THE PROFITS MADE BY THE BUSINESS

The French legal system can become most complicated when it comes to profit-sharing but it is also most interesting, since it offers a number of choices according to the needs determined by each business: the wish to motivate employees, to strengthen shareholders' equity, to exempt wages from taxation through three principal instruments, namely participation, profit-sharing and business savings plans.

Participation reflects the right of employees to benefit from a share in the earnings of the business. It is obligatory for firms with 50 or more employees and optional for the rest. The sums distributed between the employees who are benefiting come from the special participation reserve (RSP), and are calculated according to a legal formula which is the same for all businesses and is frozen for five years.

More widespread among small firms, profit-sharing allows the calculation formulas to be adapted to the specific requirements of each business. It therefore offers any business so wishing to allow its employees to benefit from its earnings or with increases in its productivity through a three-year agreement. It is both collective and random (it can change from one year to the next, and it can even be cancelled). The sums are immediately available or can be freely invested in a business savings plan (which would make it possible to benefit from tax and social advantages).

Finally, the business savings plan is a collective savings formula which can result either from an agreement or can be created on the employer's initiative. It enables employees to participate in the setting up of a portfolio of securities. Sums paid into these plans can be from profit-sharing, from money allocated as part of the participation, from voluntary payments by the employee which cannot exceed one-quarter of his annual remuneration, or finally from additional payments (lump sums) from the business, which also have upper limits set on them.

In 1995 more than one salaried employee in three, ie almost 5.3 million employees, was covered by a participation or profit-sharing agreement in 24,430 businesses. These profit-sharing schemes are above all a feature of big companies.

In 1996, 28.3 billion fr was allocated to more than 4 million employees: more than 3 million benefited from a participation bonus totalling 17.7 billion fr and 2.3 million received a profit-sharing bonus for a total amount of 10.7 billion fr.

Among the businesses that signed a participation agreement, the proportion of those which had sufficient earnings to be able to allocate them to their employees in 1996 increased with the size of the business: 70 per cent of firms had more than 2,000 salaried employees. The average participation bonus ranged from 2,300 fr in services to individuals to 8,470 fr in consumer goods industries.

Profit-sharing bonuses can vary. Since 1994 companies have no longer been able to award bonuses according to staff hierarchy, and as a result three-quarters of companies distribute bonuses using profit-share schemes.

Thus, in 1996 the average profit-sharing bonus paid to employees, technicians and lower management (ETAM) exceeded 5,000 fr per person, whereas for executives it approached 9,850 fr. On the other hand, bonuses allocated to workers were at least half those of executives.

Among businesses that signed a participation or profit-sharing agreement more than 7,100 (employing 2.8 million salaried employees) in 1995 chose to put a business savings plan (PEE) in place. Tax and social [security] reliefs encourage businesses to use profit sharing for savings purposes by means of the PEE.

More than one million employee-savers put a total of 10.5 billion fr into PEEs with an average total sum per saver of 9,750 fr.

DURATION AND MANAGEMENT OF TIME SPENT WORKING

The current foundations of jobs legislation go back to 1936, and certain founding principles still prevail today: the legal duration of jobs based on one week; a framework for the division and management of time [spent working] per week; the work schedule taking on a collective character.

Fixed at 39 hours per week* since the order of 16 January 1982, the legal duration of a job establishes the threshold which triggers overtime and short-time working. Firms have a quota of 130 additional hours a year which are not subject to authorisation, but according to how much is allocated to each employee, this additional time opens up the right to time off in lieu and is paid at time-and-a-quarter or time-and-a-half.

According to INSEE, in 1997 the average weekly hours, for salaried employees was 41 for full-time employees, the management worked longer hours per day than operatives (an average of 4 hours more a week) and men worked on average 1 hour 52 minutes more than women. These last two can be explained in particular by the predomi-

---

* New legislation, known as 'the 35-hour' law will be discussed in the second part of this chapter.

nance of men among executives. Certain professional categories are characterised by relatively long working days: thus, male executives in the private sector occupying administrative, technical or sales roles work approximately four hours more than all men. On the other hand, there is little difference between the hours worked per day by female executives and those worked by other salaried employees.

There are some dispensations from the legal work period. Certain professions are subject to what is called the system of equivalence whereby a part of the time is not counted as actual work. This is the case for employees in the hotel and restaurant trades, where full-time equals 43 hours, and for surveillance and security staff, where it equals 52 hours 40 minutes.

In addition, the legal work period can sometimes be revised downwards in some businesses as the result of an agreement with union organisations. Here one talks about 'the contractual length of the work period'. This expression also refers to industry-wide collective agreements which establish a reference period below the legal period, as for example in the chemicals business, where the agreed period is 38½ hours.

The order of 16 January 1982 opens the way for occasional alterations in the allocation and management of work periods on both an individual and a collective basis. The law provides for the implementation of a system of collective management of working hours through negotiation. This adjustment makes it possible for companies to adapt working hours to fluctuations in activity without paying for additional hours, on condition that the period does not exceed an average of 39 hours.*

Adapting the working period therefore is the same as designing schedules to make the control of the volume of work more flexible. The norm of a uniform 5-day week is losing popularity. Encouraged by the Auroux law of 1982 which makes the firm's annual negotiation over the actual working period and its organisation obligatory where there are union delegates, this development was accompanied by a decentralisation at the level of the negotiations, rendering the firm the

---

* There are three types of adjustment:
- Types I and II, dating from 1982 and 1987 respectively, consists in varying the weekly working period over all or part of the year, on condition that this period does not exceed an average of 39 hours per week worked.
- Type III, 'annualisation', in 1993 added the possibility of varying the working period within wider limits ((10 hours a day), 48 hours a week and 46 hours on average over 12 weeks) and of introducing this type or organisation over a period of less than a year. This type of adjustment is subordinate to a reduction in the working period.

favoured locus for these negotiations. From 900 agreements in 1982 there are now 4,000 agreements negotiated in relation to the management of working time at the level of the business.

The five-yearly law on work, jobs and professional training of 1993 unquestionably marks a change in the legislation, giving back a central place to the reduction in the working period, both to respond to the international requirements of ever stronger international competition, and to meet concerns to reduce unemployment.

The recent measures here have therefore made the conditions for implementing the collective reduction in the working period more flexible, and financial stimulation has been strengthened. The last laws, designed to combat the struggle for jobs, can only, as a consequence, contribute to reviving negotiations on the reduction of the working period as a counterpart to exemptions in costs.

The 'Robien' Law

The law of 11 June 1996 (the 'Robien' law) widens the measures encouraging the collective reduction in the working period. In fact, it gives companies more room for manoeuvre in searching for solutions which are suitable for each situation and in negotiations with union organisations.

The Robien law institutes a system for assisting businesses which are undertaking collective reductions in the working period, in order to further jobs. It takes the form of an agreement between the state and the firm or business which must as a matter of obligation be preceded by an agreement between workers and management at the level of the firm or business or industrial sector.

The measure contains two parts: the aggressive part which is aimed at creating jobs, and the defensive part which aims to avoid dismissals.

In both cases, the business which reduces the working period by at least 10 per cent for all of or some of its employees benefits from a remission in its employer's and social security contributions of 40 per cent in the first year and 30 per cent in the following six years. This reaches 50 per cent and 40 per cent within the framework of a reduction of 15 per cent in the working period. The level of employment must be maintained for at least two years.

Within the framework of the defensive part the same remissions are granted to businesses which implement a jobs plan to avoid dismissals and which undertake to maintain guaranteed workforces for a fixed period to be established by the agreement.

According to a study by the Ministry for Employment [and Solidarity] in 1997, 1,662 agreements, applying the 'Robien' law, were signed, two-thirds of which were 'aggressive' as against one-third 'defensive'. In total, the working period of 175,000 salaried employees was reduced.

As far as the distribution of agreements by sector is concerned, aggressive agreements can clearly be distinguished from defensive agreements, which are for the most part signed in services (61 per cent) by fairly small businesses (66 per cent have less than 50 salaried employees). Aggressive agreements, by contrast, are often signed by larger companies (31 per cent have at least 200 employees) which are part of industry (63 per cent of cases).

The provisions of this law were repealed by the '35-hour' law without cancelling the Robien agreements concluded previously.

The '35-hour' Law

On 19 May 1998, the French parliament passed a law 'the direction and purpose of which is to reduce the time spent working'. This reduced the legal weekly period of work to 35 hours from 1 January 2000 for companies and economic and social units (UES) with more than 20 employees and from 1 January 2002 for companies with less than 20 employees.

Up until these deadlines employers' union organisations, employers' groups or employers as well as union organisations for employees, acknowledged as representatives, are invited to negotiate the reduction in the time spent working by collective agreement.

This anticipated movement to 35 hours opens the way to support being granted to businesses which varies according to whether the business negotiates. These aids can be increased for various reasons as explained below. These increases can be awarded concurrently.

Basic financial support* will be offered to businesses which before 1 January 2000 (or 2002 for those with less than 20 employees) – and applying a collective agreement – reduce their working hours by at least 10 per cent to take them to 35 hours at the most, on condition that they increase their workforce by at least 6 per cent. Granted for five years, the total financial support is 9,000 fr per year per employee in the first year for the business (of more than 20 employees) which starts the system in the first half of 1998. It will be cut by 1,000 fr

---

* In the form of a tapering standard allowance in employers' social security contributions.

each year to be brought down to 5,000 fr in the fifth year. For companies starting the system in the first half of 1999 the basic support will be 8,000 fr in the first year, then it will be cut by 1,000 fr each year to end up at 5,000 fr in the fourth and fifth years. Finally, for businesses joining the system during the second half of 1999 the basic support will be 7,000 fr in the first year, 6,000 fr in the second year and 5,000 fr for the following three years.

The support will only be paid once the company has started to reduce its working hours and the companies or businesses affected must undertake to maintain their workforces for at least two years, with recruitment of staff being carried out within a period of one year as a matter of obligation.

The amount of basic support will be increased by 1,000 fr per year per employee (an increase maintained over five years) for businesses which make special efforts over recruitment (a quota above the minimum required, recruitment in the form of CDI, jobs for young people, for handicapped people or the long-term unemployed), once their situations have been taken into account. This subsidy will also benefit companies which take on a higher proportion of young people or handicapped people or the long-term unemployed.

When the reduction in working hours reaches at least 15 per cent and when the business undertakes to increase its workforce by at least 9 per cent, the state will grant an additional 4,000 fr per year per employee.

Finally, a reducing bonus of 4,000 fr per year per employee in the first year will be allocated to labour-intensive businesses which employ a high proportion of workers whose salaries are close to the SMIC.

Moreover, a similar measure has been put in place for businesses which as part of a collective laying-off procedure for economic reasons save jobs by reducing the time spent working. The assistance will then be given for an initial period of three years which may be extended by two years in the light of the firm's economic circumstances.

Having aroused keen debate, the law now gives a new definition of what must be understood by time actually spent working: it is the time during which the employee is available to the employer and must comply with his instructions without being able to attend freely to his own personal occupations. This extremely extended definition has been widely disputed. It permits the distinction to be made between actual work and obligations, during which employees can attend freely to their own occupations while at the same time being available, should the need arise, to carry out some task.

Moreover, according to this new law, all employees must benefit from daily rest lasting a minimum of 11 consecutive hours. Hitherto, this has been reserved for regulatory or contractual spheres.*

Also, the threshold after which a compulsory rest of 50% (of time worked) becomes compulsory in businesses with more than ten employees will have come down to 41 hours (instead of 42), starting from 1 January 1999 and the conditions for taking this rest period will be more strictly framed.

PAID HOLIDAYS

The organisation of paid holidays in a business (holiday period, order of departures, splitting, etc) is subject to a collection of legal rules which by virtue of their constricting and sometimes outdated nature (most of these provisions date from 1936) are very rarely complied with.

However, proper management of paid holidays means complying with legislation. Indeed, if this guarantees a 'sacred' right for employees, it confers on the head of the business control of its implementation which he or she will retain only in so far as he or she complies with the obligations which are his or her responsibility.

The law acknowledges the right of all workers or comparable categories of workers to an annual holiday to be paid for by the employer. It is up to the latter, in principle, to take the initiative for the holiday: in the final analysis the employer decides the holiday period and the order in which employees depart from the business.

In order to have the right to a legal paid holiday, one must have undertaken at least one month of actual work for the same employer during the 'reference' year, ie from 1 June of the previous year to 31 May of the year in progress.† The law determines the length of the paid holiday on the basis of two half-working days‡ per month of actual work without it being able to exceed a total of thirty working days, ie five

---

* Except for women and minors.
† So, for the 1999 holiday, one must have worked for at least one month between 1 June 1998 and 31 May 1999.
‡ Working days are said to be every day of the week, except for the day devoted to weekly rest (generally Sunday) and the days which are recognised as being holidays by the law and usually taken by the business. In contrast, days worked are the days normally worked.

weeks. However, contracts or collective agreements can provide for holidays which are longer than the legal holidays.

Between 1 May and 31 October* salaried employees have a right to a continuous holiday (called the main holiday) lasting a minimum of 12 working days and a maximum of 24 working days.

Not taking all of the main holiday continuously constitutes what is called 'splitting'. Splitting gives an entitlement to additional holidays, the number of which varies according to the number of days of holiday taken outside the legal period from the 1 May to 31 October.[†]

In the period during which the employee is on holiday, he or she receives a compensatory payment which is calculated on the basis either of $1/10$ of the wages he received between 1 June of the previous year and 31 May of the year in progress, or of the salary which he would have made if, instead of being on holiday, he had worked. The most favourable method of calculation is used for the employee.

In principle, holidays which have not been taken by the final date decided by the employer are lost, unless the employee 'capitalises' them, either for the purposes of a holiday (sabbatical or to start a business) or to pay into his savings-time-account,[‡] in so far as a collective agreement which is applicable to the business is signed to this end.

As has been indicated in this chapter's introduction, despite all the regulations relating to paid holidays, practices on the margins of the law have been established and endure because they satisfy both the employer and his employees (excessive splitting, change of date at the last moment, not actually taking holidays, etc).

COSTS ON SALARIES

The method of financing social security confers a special structure on the cost of wages in France, where the share of social costs is greater than in other industrialised countries.

---

* The legal period for taking holidays.
[†] Two additional working days if the employee takes at least six days between 1 November and 30 April, and one additional day if the employee takes between three and five days during this same period.
[‡] Put in place by the law of 25 July 1994 to benefit salaried workers so as to enable them to accumulate entitlements to paid holiday, the savings-time-account is fed in particular by the carrying forward of paid holidays (within a limit of ten days a year) or participation bonuses in time.

The share of social security contributions* for employees and employers merged together in an average cost is around 40 per cent. Unlike what happens in many neighbouring countries, in France income tax is not substituted for social security contributions. The rise in social security contributions has been relatively rapid since 1970 (high degree of social security cover).

Gross salaries include the share of wages for social security contributions. The employer's share as well as the taxes on wages[†] are added to the total amount of the gross salary. The entire gross salary and the employer's share of contributions make up the total cost of the salary.

Reading a pay slip is especially complicated, in particular because of the diversity of collection agencies, the tax bases and still more the reference ceilings. Wage slips are, according to the report by the Turbot Commission,[‡] the most difficult throughout Europe in so far as their presentation and methods of calculation are concerned.

Social security contributions are calculated on the total amount of the gross remuneration, whether this has an upper limit or not, according to the contribution items and include:

- social security contributions paid to the URSSAFs;
- unemployment insurance contributions paid to the ASSEDICs;
- additional pension contributions.

To these contributions other taxes and obligatory contributions are added.

Table 12.1 shows all of the social security and tax contributions relating to the wages paid to salaried employees in the social security system.

It is the payment of wages which constitutes paying contributions. The payment of the contribution falls to the employer, who is responsible just as much for the payment of the employer's social security contributions as for wage contributions deducted from the remunerations.

---

* Social security contributions from protected people or their employers to institutions granting social security benefits. They are the result of legal, regulatory and contractual obligations (collective agreements, business agreements, job contracts) or of voluntary individual choices (membership of mutual benefit societies).
[†] Parafiscal concepts (ie those lying alongside the fiscal system) are distinct from the social security system, which is fed by social security contributions.
[‡] Report developed to simplify wage slips at the request of Jacques Barrot, at the time the Minister of Employment and Social Affairs, in the third quarter of 1996.

Social Security Contributions Paid to the URSSAFs

The system

All workers and similar categories of workers in France are subject to the social security system whatever their age or nationality, the total amount and the nature of their remuneration, the form, nature or validity of their contract.

In principle, a foreign worker working on French territory is subject to the social security system whatever the nationality of the business which employs him. It is possible to escape this liability if the conditions of the worker's occupation correspond to a situation of secondment. The case of secondment is anticipated for citizens of member states of the European Union (cf the regulation of 14 June 1971) and through certain bilateral agreements.

The social security system for employees guarantees that the five risks to which the five contribution rates correspond, are covered: the illness–maternity–disablement–death insurance contribution, which is intended to finance payments in kind, such as reimbursements for medical expenses, hospital expenses, dental care, etc and cash payments (per diem allowances, death benefits, disablement pension); the widowhood insurance contribution, which finances widowhood pensions paid to the surviving spouse; the state pension contribution,* which finances pensions paid to member pensioners or their spouses; the contribution for family income support, exclusively payable by the employer, which is intended to finance the family allowances paid to members of the social security scheme, and the contributions for accidents at work and occupational illnesses, again exclusively payable by the employer, which finance health and safety at work. This latter contribution varies according to the firm's workforce. It can result either from an individual assessment which is based on the actual cost of dealing with health and safety at the company, or from a standard assessment stemming from national scales by sector of activity, or from a mixed assessment which combines the two previous ones.

Other deductions are also based on wages and collections by the URSSAFs.

Firstly, this concerns payments intended for public transport. This transport tax is payable by all businesses or companies employing more than 9 workers, and located in towns or built-up areas. Rates vary according to the localisation of the business.†

---

* These three contributions are also called national insurance contributions.
† By way of example it is 2.5 per cent in Paris and in the department of Hauts de Seine. Outside the Paris region the rate is fixed by the town council.

Table 12.1 Social security and tax contributions

Schemes	Total Rate (%)	Distribution Employer (%)	Employee (%)	Tax Base
URSSAF				
Health insurance illness, maternity, disablement, death	13.55	12.8	0.75	The entire salary
Widowhood insurance	0.1		0.1	
Family income support	5.4	5.4		
Housing aid	0.4	0.4		
State pensions	1.6	1.6		
Accidents at work	Rate varies according to the business	Rate varies according to the business		
General social security contribution (CSG)	7.5		7.5	The entire salary after deductions of 5% for professional expenses
Contribution to the repayment of the social security debt (CRDS)	0.5		0.5	
State pensions	14.75	8.2	6.55	Salary limited to the social security ceiling
Housing aid	0.1	0.1		
ASSEDIC				
Unemployment	6.18	3.97	2.21	Salary limited to the social security ceiling
ASF	1.96	1.16	0.8	
Unemployment	6.68	3.97	2.71	Salary between 1 and 4 times the social security ceiling
ASF	2.18	1.29	0.89	
AGS	0.25	0.25		Salary limited to the social security ceiling

Table 12.1 *continued*

Schemes	Total Rate (%)	Distribution Employer (%)	Employee (%)	Tax Base
Additional pension contributions				Salary limited to the social security ceiling
ARRCO*	6.875	4.125	2.75	Social security
Obligatory death insurance	1.5	1.5		
AGIRC*	18.75	11.875	6.875	Salary between 1 and 4
APEC	0.06	0.036	0.024	times the social security ceiling
Management AGIRC*	18.75	Free distribution	Free distribution	Salary between 4 and 8 times the social security ceiling
Exceptional temporary contribution (CET)	0.14	0.09	0.05	Up to 8 times the social security ceiling
Non-management ARRCO	6.875	4.125	2.75	Salary limited to 3 times the social security ceiling
Taxes and contributions				
Tax on salaries	4.25	4.24		The entire salary
Construction	0.45	0.45		
Apprenticeship	0.5	0.5		
Continuous training				
Firms with at least 10 salaried employees	1.5	1.5		
Firms with less than 10 salaried employees	0.15	0.15		

* Minimum rate.

Secondly, any employer who employs one or several employees is liable a contribution to the FNAL (National Housing Aid Fund).

Thirdly, again covered by the URSSAFs and introduced since 1 February 1991, a generalised social security payment (CSG) which has the characteristics of a tax deducted at source, is intended to finance social security. Its tax base is wider than those of the contributions since it is based on various revenues such as income from jobs and temping, income from property, gains and profits on capital, and certain investment products. Following the example of the CSG, the types of contributions to be made to repay the social [security] debt (CRDS) are presented in the order of 24 January 1996. The rules for collecting these two deductions are the same: wages and other affected items are paid gross after applying a specific standard deduction of 5 per cent for professional expenses.

In addition, on 1 January 1996 a tax aimed at financing additional provident payments was introduced. Payable at a rate of 8 per cent it is paid by employers on employers' contributions and by bodies (works councils) which represent staff.

Measures reducing social security contributions

Several measures exempting employers from making social security contributions exist. They aim to encourage employers to hire or to maintain employment by reducing costs on labour: relief when hiring a first employee; relief when hiring in certain disadvantaged areas. Other reliefs are granted within the framework of contracts of a particular type the purpose of which is training and professional insertion: the apprenticeship contract, the qualification contract, the adjustment contract, the vocational contract, employment initiative or employment support contracts, etc.

The following measure instituted from 1 September 1995 and modified several times since, endeavours to lower the wage costs of the least well-qualified staff by a total reduction on all of the employers' social security contributions. It is not subject to any conditions relating to the workforce or to hiring. For employers in the textile and clothing industries, the reduction applies according to particular and more advantageous forms.

According to the general system the rebate consists in a reduction in employers' social security contributions for wages paid during the calendar month and below 130 per cent of the SMIC over 169 hours.*

---

* ie 8,662.77 fr for a SMIC of 39.43 fr per hour.

The amount of the reduction varies according to whether the wages paid are less than or greater than 169 times the SMIC. In the case of jobs which are less than full-time over a month, the reduction is made pro rata according to the number of hours paid in the course of the month. Since 1 July 1997, the total amount of the reduction cannot exceed 1,212.79 fr.

The reliefs in social security costs on low salaries today affect almost five million employees. Sectors with a high proportion of employees who are paid low wages (hotels–cafés–restaurants, services to individuals, retail, etc) have been the main beneficiaries of this policy. Since the measure has come in only recently, it is still difficult to assess its effects on employment. However, it is generally agreed that it should lead to the creation of between 200,000 and 240,000 jobs over five years for exemptions of 40 billion fr (without taking into account the negative effects which the measure could have on jobs and employment).

Unemployment Insurance Contributions Paid to the ASSEDICs

The unemployment insurance system is financed by contributions from employers and from wage earners. The unemployment insurance contribution is based on gross earnings, giving rise to the payment of social security contributions within a limit of four times the social security ceiling. Furthermore, every employer is subject to the AGS (insurance for the management of wage earners' claims), the rate of which is 0.25 per cent.

Additional Pension Contributions

Additional pension schemes have been introduced to top up the pension paid by the general social security system. Two compulsory schemes exist: the AGIRC,* for management, and the ARRCO,† for every wage earner over 16. The contributions are calculated on wages paid in general during each quarter. Employers can apply for a higher rate of contribution than that of the compulsory scheme. For executives, an APEC contribution is compulsory as well as a contribution of 1.5 per cent into a contingency fund (death benefit).

In addition to these compulsory schemes there are supplementary schemes, which are optional.

---

* Association générale des institutions de retraite des cadres [General association of executive pension schemes].
† Association des régimes de retraite complémentaire [Association for additional pension schemes].

Parafiscal Costs

Besides those outlined above, employers must support 'parafiscal' costs, ie those costs which run alongside the main fiscal system. These include the tax on wages, the tax on apprenticeships, participation in continuous training and participation in the effort to regenerate the construction industry.

The tax on wages affects every employer in France who is not subject to VAT or partially subject to it for wages paid to staff, wherever the wage earner is domiciled and wherever his or her place of work is located. As for the tax on apprenticeships, this is a fiscal cost based on all of the sums paid by way of wages or other salaries which have been paid in the course of the previous calendar year. Fixed at 0.5 per cent of the gross annual wage bill, it finances initial technological and professional training [schemes] and must be paid to the public revenue department before 5 April each year (assistance for subsequent training comes under participation in continuous and professional training).

Furthermore, the law of 16 July 1971 introduced a minimum threshold of compulsory participation in the financing of continuous professional training. This participation is calculated on the wages paid in the course of the year in progress and its rate varies according to the workforce of the business (more or less than ten employees).

Finally, employers with at least ten employees must every year devote 0.45 per cent of wages paid in the course of the previous calendar year to financing their participation in the effort to regenerate the construction industry (acquisition and development of sites intended exclusively for the construction of local authority housing, the construction of housing, the renovation of old housing, etc).

M. Chadelat,* who was made responsible in December 1996 for examining the various routes modifications could take in the tax base of social security contributions, points out in his report that the drop in compulsory deductions which weigh on the economy is desirable. In relation to the slowdown in growth of the wage bill compared to national wealth, the weight of the social security costs which is bearing down on the income from labour, is disadvantageous to employment and justifies the idea that some of an employer's social security contri-

---

* The Chadelat report appears as an item in the file of the report which the government intends to put before parliament. It discusses the the 'consequences of a modification in the tax base of social security contributions payable by employers for the financing of social security and the situation of business'.

butions are based on things other than the wage bill. M. Chadelat's report also recommends the implementation of a new tax base which takes added value into account.

THE RELATIONSHIP BETWEEN FRENCH EMPLOYEES AND THEIR PROFESSIONAL ENVIRONMENT

A complete analysis of the French situation with regard to employment includes, besides a purely rational aspect, a fundamentally more subjective fact, based on the relationship of the French to employment. The economic presentation of employment in France might suggest that in a period of recovery, the French would currently be optimistic. Is this the case? Are the French happy in their work? Conscious of the threat of unemployment, do they appreciate it all the more? If certain polls confirm this judgement, other surveys reveal more surprising results.

There are numerous surveys on the attitude of the French to their work. As it would be impossible to provide an exhaustive description of them here, the following six points will suffice: What is the relationship between employees and their work? How in particular do executives judge their working conditions? Do the French change jobs frequently? What do the French think of employment policy in their country? How do the French spend their free time? Do the French believe that one has to work to be happy?

What is the Relationship between Employees and Their Work?

The motivation of French people in their professional life has been evaluated in two polls.

Asked what in their view was the point of work, CREDOC's* last survey, carried out in January 1997, showed that 65 per cent of employees considered that 'work primarily represents a source of revenue' while 19 per cent saw it above all as a means of personal fulfilment (particularly freelance workers), and 15 per cent as a means of fitting into and conforming with society.

---

* CREDOC, the research centre for the study and observation of living conditions, conducts an annual survey of attitudes to 'the living conditions and aspirations of French people'. The poll is carried out face to face among a sample of 2,005 people aged over 18, selected on a quota basis (age, sex, profession and urban area).

This question is also the subject of a bi-monthly* barometer, set up by the weekly human resources publication *Entreprises et Carrières* (*Companies and Careers*), which evaluates workers' attitudes towards their company. The most recent results† in this survey confirm the importance that employees attach to their work team and the satisfaction that this brings: in fact 91.8 per cent of employees questioned declared that they liked work because it offered the opportunity to be with colleagues. The second reason quoted with regard to their attitude towards the company, 'I work through economic necessity', was an opinion which jumped 13 points in one year, reinforcing the impression given in the first poll. Whereas in March 1997, 90.5 per cent of employees declared that they worked primarily because they found their work interesting, this reason moved from second position to fourth, and is now preceded by the need to have more free time.

The other purpose of the survey is to enable employees to judge the policy carried out by their human resources (HR) department. Overall, the results are quite positive: a large majority (more than 70 per cent) is satisfied with their daily work, followed by those who find their company situation and remuneration satisfactory. There is an 8-point decline (73 per cent in April–May 1997, to 65 per cent one year later) in the positive views held about their HR department's training policy. It is in companies of fewer than 50 employees and in industry where expectations in this respect are lower.

How in Particular do Executives Judge Their Working Conditions?

Every year since 1975, APEC‡ has questioned 3,000 executives to discover their opinion on their work and to define their working conditions better. According to the President of APEC in 1997, there was a noticeable deterioration in relations between executives and their companies. In fact, for the first time, executives explicitly admitted to experiencing difficult periods and pointed to an excessive work load.

---

* *Entreprises et Carrières*, No 435/436, 19 May–1 June 1998.
† A study conducted by the firm Epsy among a representative national sample of 400 employees, by telephone. Sex: women, 43.7 per cent, men, 56.3 per cent. Age: under 25, 15.9 per cent; 25 to 34, 29.8 per cent; 35 to 44, 22.3 per cent; 45 and over, 32 per cent. Professional status: executive, 12.6 per cent; management, 23.3 per cent; employee, 31.7 per cent; worker, 32.4 per cent. Size of company: up to 50 staff, 52.6 per cent; 50 to 199 staff, 22.7 per cent; 200 to 499 staff, 11.8 per cent; 500 or more, 52 per cent. Sector: industry 31.8 per cent; trade and distribution, 16 per cent; retail services, 29.4 per cent; non-retail services, 22.8 per cent.
‡ Association for executive work.

Although 85 per cent still declared themselves to be satisfied with their professional situation (interest in assignments entrusted to them and relations with work colleagues were mainly cited), motives for discontent were higher. First of all, executives found their work load excessive. Furthermore, almost one interviewee in two admitted to having experienced one or more difficult periods in their professional life in terms of working conditions.

Among the executives' chief preoccupations, 42 per cent were concerned about their lack of interest in the job, followed by the possibility of redundancy and salary increase.

Do the French Change Jobs Frequently?

Inter-company mobility

From a poll conducted to determine the attitude of employees towards their company,* it appears that 40 per cent, would, if they had the chance, change companies.

This showed that the average length of time during which an executive holds a post is six years. These are principally executives in the personnel–communication, IT, and research and development fields, who change companies more often than administrative, marketing or management executives.

Forming a specific survey in itself, executives under 35 declared that in their opinion, their priority for the next two years was first of all to change company, then role. Changes in role were particularly desired in personnel–communication and production–development among the 'bac plus 5'† and the under 30s. Engineers and doctors would prefer to work in a different profession. Finally, 10 per cent of the under-35s hoped to go abroad.

On the repercussions of this mobility at the level of salaries, a study by Véronique Simmonet‡ mentions that within the same business, changes in jobs are valued by men because they are assimilated in a build-up of specific human capital, whereas too great an internal mobility penalises women. In contrast, considerable mobility between companies is profitable for the latter, but not for men. The only efficient career pro-

---

* *Entreprises et Carrières*, No 435/436, 19 May–1 June 1998.
† The bac is the equivalent to three English A levels; bac plus 5 means an additional five years of study.
‡ On the occasion of the Expolangue trade show which took place from 28 January until 1 February 1998 in Paris.

file for both sexes is that of job matching: this consists in trying out the work in several businesses at the beginning of their working life before remaining with the one which most favours advances in salary.

Geographical mobility

A survey carried out by Ipsos* in December 1997 among 5,000 over-15s confirms the geographical mobility of French people compared with that of their European neighbours. To the question 'Would you personally be prepared to go to another country?' three-quarters of Germans interviewed said they would rather stay where they were, while more than half of French people who were questioned would not hesitate to leave their native land to go and live in another country. It is no great surprise that this mobility particularly applies to the young.

The main reason pushing young French people to live abroad was given as cultural curiosity or learning a foreign language (60 per cent), while 72 per cent of Spaniards would leave to find work or enhance their professional experience.

As far as the most popular destinations are concerned, the English-speaking countries come first, followed by Spain and Germany. Their capital cities in particular are favoured.

Finally, the latest information revealed by this survey is that 61 per cent of the French people know at least one foreign language, with 30 per cent of them speaking it fluently.

What Do the French Think of Employment Policy in Their Country?

This view is revealed every year in the already-mentioned CREDOC survey on 'the living conditions and aspirations of French people', thus enabling the attitudes of the French on employment policy and unemployment to be monitored.

Surveys carried out since 1985 testify to the French people's pessimism in the face of rising unemployment and their relative scepticism regarding the measures put in place to fight against it. Nearly 90 per cent of those interviewed by CREDOC considered that these measures were 'too few' or 'not at all' effective at the beginning of 1997. The French put unemployment at the top of their preoccupations (53 per cent), far ahead of serious illness, poverty, drugs or insecurity problems.

---

* 'Professional mobility and salary: differences between men and women', *Monthly Economic and Statistical Review 1996–9*, No 299, INSEE (French national statistics office).

According to public opinion, it is up to companies first of all to win the fight against unemployment. However, this specific role allotted to companies in relation to job creation does not exonerate the state from its responsibilities, which thus comes second in the fight against unemployment: in 1989, 77 per cent of interviewees said they were in favour of 'reducing social security contributions made by companies for the least skilled jobs'. In fact, more than three-quarters of the population (78 per cent) considered that the reason companies were not taking on more staff was because their contributions were too high. Senior executives and the liberal professions enjoyed better security from companies, while workers usually relied on the state. Similarly, the state is expected to play a greater role the older one gets.

French attitudes to the proposal to reduce working hours have changed. Whereas in 1993, 41 per cent of those interviewed by CREDOC considered that a reduction in weekly working hours from 35 to 32 would create jobs, now more than 60 per cent think so. The French are nevertheless much more reticent in accepting a reduction in salary to accompany this reduction in work: 22 per cent in 1993, to 14 per cent in 1996, a downswing which is just as strong among executives as among workers.

The opinion of the people interviewed by CREDOC on the effectiveness of developing part-time work to reduce unemployment has remained stable for four years, with a two-thirds positive response. However, those people who believe in the idea of part-time work reducing unemployment are not necessarily prepared to accept part-time employment for themselves.

How Do the French Spend Their Free Time?

According to the weekly *Entreprises et Carrières* scale, the change among interviewees on the question of free time is surprising concerning current legislation.

In fact, whereas in 1997 more than three-quarters of those questioned said that they would prefer more free time, now, at the very moment when the reduction in working hours has been presented by the French government as one of its priorities and when a large number of companies are working towards reduction in their hours, only two-thirds would 'prefer more free time'.

The question of ariloration between money and free time is also the subject of a survey conducted by CREDOC.*

---

* Telephone survey conducted in 1997 among a sample of 1,000 people, representative of the French population.

The French preference in general towards an increase in purchasing power is now greater than their requirements for free time: 60.1 per cent would prefer to have more money compared to 37.7 per cent who would opt for more free time. The responses vary between the sexes since women are much more interested in an increase in their purchasing power (66.5 per cent) compared with 53 per cent for men. The response also depends on the generation being questioned: among the 25–45 age group, the split between free time and money is more or less equal, whereas the tendency among the younger and older age groups, is for an increase in their purchasing power. The division finally gets wider according to socio-professional categories: the more that workers, employees and the retired want to see their purchasing power increase, the more executives are distinctly more inclined towards greater free time.

Do the French Believe that One has to Work to be Happy?

According to a survey by INSEE carried out on 6,000 people in January 1997, more than one French person in four says that work is essential to their happiness. In fact, to the question: 'What is the most important thing that makes you happy?', 27 per cent of those questioned mentioned work in their response. This proportion varies according to their social position. It was among those whose conditions of work are the most difficult, whose wages are the lowest and for whom the danger of unemployment is the greatest that work was given as one of the essential conditions of happiness. In fact, the word 'work' or one of its synonyms is cited by 43 per cent of workers compared to 27 per cent of company directors, executives and the liberal professions.

Marital status also has a bearing: if they live with a partner and especially if they have children, men cite work less as a component of happiness. On the other hand, among women, profession and qualifications have little or no bearing on their fulfilment. The value put on work decreases strongly among both professional women and those with qualifications as soon as they live with a partner and/or are over the age of 40.

According to INSEE, the explanation for this phenomenon supposes that the same is true for work as for all the other components of happiness: it is by its absence that its value can best be measured, and all the more so if it is under sufferance.

13

Property

Robert Lipscomb, Healey & Baker

PARIS

The Ile de France still dominates the market with an estimated 40,000,000 sq m of office stock of which about 15,000,000 sq m is within the city of Paris itself. While there are some 17th- and 18th-century properties converted into offices in the capital, most date back to the mid- and late 19th century when Baron Haussmann redeveloped large areas of Paris.

Typical examples would be six to eight storeys high, constructed from stone with ornate ironwork. Often a modern redevelopment is hidden behind the original Haussmannian façade.

The prime office district covers parts of the 8th, 16th and 17th *arrondissements* and contains the Golden Triangle, bordered by the Avenues of the Champs-Elysées, George V and Montaigne. In the business district there are a limited number of modern high-specification office schemes, such as Washington Plaza and Etoile Saint Honoré. Financial institutions, such as Crédit Lyonnais, BNP and Paribas, are concentrated in the 1st, 2nd and 9th *arrondissements*, although some have moved their headquarters to La Défense (eg Société Générale).

Other office locations such as the Fronts de Seine in the 15th *arrondissement*, the Montparnasse district in the 14th *arrondissement* and the Bercy district near Gare de Lyon and Gare d'Austerlitz in the 12th *arrondissement* offer larger more modern office space but are regarded as secondary areas.

The more sought-after suburban office markets are located to the western side of Paris in the arc formed by the districts of Levallois-Perret, Neuilly-sur-Seine, Boulogne-Billancourt and Issy-les-Moulineaux, known as the 'Golden Crescent'.

The most important office area outside central Paris is La Défense, with about 2.5 million sq m of office space. Designated as Paris's decentralised office zone at the end of the 1950s, its success is due largely to excellent road and rail links to the city centre. It also has a residential population of about 20,000 as well as retail, leisure and cultural facilities.

Lower-cost office space is to be found in the new towns of Cergy-Pontoise to the north-west, Saint-Quentin-en-Yvelines to the south-west, Evry to the south, Melun-Sénart to the south-east, and Marne-la-Vallée to the east. All have good links in to central Paris.

Around Roissy-Charles de Gaulle airport and, to a lesser extent Orly, large mixed-used business parks have sprung up, benefiting from rapid access to the French motorway network.

The area within the orbital road, the *périphérique*, is regarded as the city of Paris. About 2 million people live in the city itself with the western areas generally thought of as the most exclusive, particularly the 7th, 16th and southern parts of the 17th *arrondissements*.

Areas around Bastille and the Marais are fashionable gentrified districts, while the 15th *arrondissement* is another popular residential area. Residential accommodation is also sought after in the western suburbs of Neuilly-sur-Seine, Rueil-Malmaison, Boulogne-Billancourt and, further out, Meudon, Versailles and St Germain-en-Laye.

In contrast, the huge suburban estates built since the Second World War have serious social problems of high unemployment and crime rates which the French authorities are struggling to control.

Paris has a well-integrated transport system. There are three orbital motorways and a network of motorways radiating out from the *périphérique*. The 13 Metro lines are backed up by the RER rail system, taking commuters across Paris to the suburbs and new towns and also serves the main airports. New lines, the Eole and Meteor, are being constructed.

Planning policy is encouraging growth in eastern Paris. One area is the Seine–Rive-Gauche development zone near Gare d'Austerlitz, anchored by the new French National Library. Further out, Disneyland Paris has created a zone of activity to the east of Marne-La-Vallée.

An agency to attract inward investment into the capital, the Comité d'Expansion Economique de Paris, was recently set up.

THE REGIONS

Across Europe the competition to win corporate investment is fierce with France at the forefront. The system of aid packages and incentives is intended not only to bring in new investment but to keep established companies which may otherwise be tempted to relocate.

Poorer regions, particularly old industrial and agricultural regions, received special assistance from the European Union. A tax incentive, approved by the EU, is offered within privileged investment zones in France. Locating to one of these areas allows a company to cut corporate tax. Cash grants are also offered to reduce initial capital spending and start-up costs. The grant (PAT) varies by region but can amount to between 50,000 fr and 70,000 fr for each new job created. The EU fixes a maximum limit.

France has the advantage of possessing a significant land mass and the authorities will often sell serviced land at below market price or even give it away to attract inward investment because of the longer-term benefits it may bring to the local and national economy.

The regions likely to develop fastest in the near future are the Rhône-Alpes, Nord-Pas-de-Calais and Provence-Alpes-Côte d'Azur. Specific development includes:

- The south coast – the European sunbelt – is benefiting from technology, R&D and service sectors, bringing comparisons with Silicon Valley and the west coast of the United States.
- Marseille: three technopole sites, Château-Gombert, L'Arbois and Luminy, have been developed on the outskirts.
- Montpellier: similarly has technopole sites and a rapidly increasing population.
- Toulouse: Europe's aerospace centre has resulted in an impressive number of high technology and components firms in the area.
- The Rhône-Alpes region has a well-diversified economic base, particularly around Lyon and Grenoble.
- Lille: as northern Europe's transport crossroads it is benefiting from its close proximity to Paris, Brussels, London, Amsterdam and Cologne, plus relatively low office space costs. Recent developments include the huge distribution park at Lomme in the western suburbs and the Euralille city centre office and retail development built around the TGV station.

- Improved communications to the ports of Brest, Nantes and Bordeaux are bringing investment to the surrounding areas.

PLANNING CONTROLS

Responsibility for planning and zoning control is shared between central, regional, departmental and communal government officials with the *préfet* of each department being a key player. The Schéma Directeur is the structure plan, showing the strategic planning at a regional and departmental level. The Plan d'Occupation des Sols is a local land-use plan defining all zoning and developmental rights.

To discourage centralisation in the congested Paris region, developers face a higher regional tax and need to apply for an office development permit known as an *'agrément'*.

France has also introduced stricter planning controls on new out-of-town retail developments and extensions to existing shopping centres to protect existing town centres. There was a time when a retailer only had to apply for permission from the Commission Départmentale d'Equipment Commercial to develop a store over 1,500 sq m. Now it has been cut to 300 sq m.

But local authorities are keen to attract inward investment. They may designate a large serviced industrial or business zone, sell land at below market rates and offer incentives, such as tax breaks on new properties.

TRANSPORT

One area where France has excelled in recent years has been in developing a modern transport infrastructure. Its economy is now undoubtedly reaping the benefits of wise investment in high-speed rail and road systems over the past two decades.

The most obvious is the Train à Grande Vitesse (TGV) system which is opening up some of the poorer regional areas of France to the rest of Europe. The orbital Paris TGV route links Roissy-Charles de Gaulle airport, Disneyland Paris and Massy in the souther suburbs and plans to bring the La Défense office district in western Paris into the network by 2007.

Together with the obvious benefits of the Channel Tunnel has come the development of numerous multi-modal distribution parks, where suitable rail heads and motorway junctions exist, opening up prospects to the distribution sector.

The already impressive motorway system continues to expand with plans under way for a new Paris to Calais/Boulogne motorway, a coastal motorway from Le Havre to the Belgian border, a Geneva to Bordeaux highway and the completion of the motorway from Paris to the Spanish border.

Regional airports are being built or extended at Lille Lesquin, Nantes, Lyon Satolas, Mulhouse, Marseille and Nice. And planners always have regard to rail and road links from the airports with TGV stations already built within both Roissy-Charles de Gaulle and Lyon Satolas airports.

TAX, LEGAL, FINANCIAL AND ADMINISTRATIVE ISSUES

These need expert help to cope with. But the key elements include:

- Occupational taxes: the landlord is legally responsible for all property taxes although he often recovers them from tenants. There is an office tax; land tax; occupier's real estate tax; and business tax. The amount usually depends on location.
- Property transfer tax: this is one of the highest in Europe at around 19.5% on commercial property and affects market liquidity. In the Paris region, for example, with a notary's fees added in, it could be made up as follows:

Departmental tax	15.4%
Stamp Duty	0.385%
Commune tax	1.2%
Regional tax	1.6%
Conservator's salary	0.1%
Notary fees	0.825%
Total	19.510%

VAT (*taxe sur la valeur ajoutée*) may be added, but is recoverable, if a property is less than five years old or has recently been substantially refurbished.

Legal aspects when investing include:

- seeking permission from the Bank of France and Ministry of the Economy to bring in capital. They also check if the incoming investor will affect any French strategic interests. Exchange controls have been deregulated and capital can now flow freely in most cases;

- land tenure;
- the choice of corporate vehicle and level of tax transparency;
- choosing whether a foreign company operates directly through a branch, or forms a French subsidiary. The latter is usually preferred as it will reduce tax liability;
- commercial lease structure.

Following the property market crash of the 1990s, the remaining French banks handling real estate have introduced stricter lending criteria with 70 per cent normally seen as the maximum gearing. Emphasis is now put on the use of independent valuations, cashflow analysis and a thorough due diligence process. The latter involves a land registry search, town planning certificate (*certificat d'urbanisme*), pre-emption rights and a final agreement being drawn up by a notary.

There is no direct equivalent of the United Kingdom's Royal Institute of Chartered Surveyors. The main bodies are the FNAIM (Association of Estate Agents), IEIF (Institut d l'Epargne Immobilière et Fonciere) and IFEI (Institut Français de l'Expertise Immobilière).

WHO'S WHO IN THE PROPERTY MARKET

There are various types of player in the property market, the key ones being:

- Insurance companies. Their predominance has increased due to the small role played by pension funds. Major companies include UAP/AXA, GAN and AGF.
- SICOMI Companies (Sociétés Immobilières pour le Comerce et l'Industrie). They provide finance for commercial property through the credit-bail system of property leasing. Their role has much diminished since 1990 when their favourable tax status was abolished.
- SCPI Companies (Sociétés Civiles de Placements Immobiliers). They buy commercial and residential property for rental. Major fund managers are Crédit Agricole, Banque Paribas and Société Générale.
- Pension funds. They have historically concentrated on distribution rather than capitalisation and so their investment funds are limited and usually concerned with residential holdings.
- SII Companies (Sociétés Immobilieres d'Investissement). They mostly place their funds in residential property.

- Sociétés Foncières. They are property companies with no fiscal advantages. This group is increasing in importance as new *foncières* are created to house the property assets of the major financial groups. Former SICOMIs and SIIs tend to convert to Société Foncière status. Major examples include Sinico, Sefimeg, Unibail and Foncière Madeleine.
- Foreign investors/developers. Their involvement varies with market conditions. In recent years British, Dutch, Middle Eastern, Japanese, Swedish and American investors/developers have been active in the French market at different times.

Property developers fall into two categories – *promoteur* (developer) and *marchand de biens* (trader). The former is often owned by a major financial or construction group while the latter is frequently a private individual acting as a property trader in short-term transactions. Today there are relatively few private developers still active, most being controlled by larger groups.

RETAIL

In the late 1960s, France led the rest of Europe in developing big out-of-town shopping centres. Today most towns and cities have several, with Paris itself circled by more than 15 centres of more than 40,000 sq m. French and international multiples have been expanding into both out-of-town and prime town centre pitches.

The regional shopping centres ringing Paris are mostly close to the A86 inner surburban orbital motorway. Those measuring more than 70,000 sq m include Les Quatres Tempts at La Défense, Parly 2 and Vélizy 2 near Versailles, (south-west of Paris), and Rosny 2, Créteil Soleil and Belle Epine to the east and south-east.

Shopping centres have been highly popular among international investors in recent years. Planning restrictions have effectively halted new developments. This means that, with strong occupier demand from French and international retail chains, plus the chance to add value through refurbishment and marketing of existing centres, rental growth prospects look good.

PROPERTY OPPORTUNITIES

Foreign investment into commercial property began in Paris in the late 1960s and early 1970s until halted by the mid-1970s' recession. There was a second wave in the latter half of the 1980s when rental growth and capital values rose sharply, prompting generous bank lending and a large amount of office development.

The collapse in rental levels by 1991 left many developers, investors and banks with huge losses and unwilling to put their property assets on the market at much lower values. Only recently have the French banks and institutions started to make provision for the decrease in capital values of their property assets.

This is resulting in renewed interest from international investors and investment supply over the next few years should increase. However much of what will come onto the market will fail to meet institutional investment standards, while the high transaction costs may still deter some investors. This could bring the chance to develop modern quality space within prime areas of Paris.

Another opportunity is for developers or investors to take over the loss-making property assets of the various French financial institutions and add value through effective estate management and unravelling of the financial aspects. As the market bottoms out there will be a significant supply of recovery stock available.

Another result of planning restrictions on out-of-town shopping schemes will be good opportunities for both investors and retailers in town centre retail schemes which offer a good retail mix, car parking, a pleasant shopping environment and effective marketing.

Other areas of potential opportunity include:

- High specification office space meeting global business needs in Paris and other major cities.
- Leisure-related developments, such as multiplex cinemas, leisure parks, factory outlet shopping malls and tourist developments, where planning permission is obtainable.
- Conversion of surplus office stock into other uses, such as residential, although application is likely to be limited
- City/town centre retail and leisure schemes where development is possible and active town centre management takes place as part of local area regeneration.
- High specification industrial/distribution space to meet the needs of global business.
- Development of the property assets of French companies due to be restructured. For example, joint ventures with SNCF.
- The setting up of the Base des Données des Investissements Immobiliers (BD21), the property performance index, should improve transparency of the French property market. As a result,

liquid property investment vehicles, such as securitisation, unit trusts and tradeable property derivatives, could be developed.

This chapter has covered some of the main issues relating to real estate in France. Healey & Baker's Paris office has been in business for 25 years and is able to offer comprehensive advice on all aspects of commercial property.

14

Environmental Issues: Attitudes, Law and Implications

Corinne Lepage (Former Minister of Environment) and François Steinmetz, Huglo, Lepage & Associés Conseil

INTRODUCTION

From a practical point of view, French environmental legislation is principally passed at national level by means of laws (*lois*), decrees (*décrets*), orders (*arrêtés*) and circulars (*circulaires*), although the latter do not carry as much authority.

To control and apply these rules, there are several administrations which work at different levels. At national level, there is mainly the Environmental Ministry in addition to which there are independent councils: the National Council on Water (Conseil National de l'Eau), the National Council on Noise (Conseil National du Bruit), the General Council for Classified Installations (Conseil Supérieur des Installations Classées), the General Council for the Prevention of Technological Risks (Conseil Supérieur de la Prévention des Risques), and the General Council on Nuclear Safety and Information (Conseil Supérieur de la Sûreté et de l'Information Nucléaire).

Among all these independent agencies, one has to be distinguished. It is the Environment and Energy Control Agency (Agence de l'Environnement et de la Maîtrise de l'Energie – ADEME). This agency is the one most involved, after the Ministry, with environmental issues. It was created from the merger between the Air Quality Agency, the Energy Control Agency and the agency in charge of waste issues, and is responsible for collecting taxes regarding energy, waste and air pollution. It is also involved in negotiations between industries and state representatives. Eventually, the ADEME will also be responsible for regulating operators who run classified installations, making sure they comply with the regulations ordered by the prefect.

At the regional level, the main authority is the Regional Directorate for Industry, Research and the Environment (Direction Régionale de l'Industrie, de la Recherche et de l'Environnement). This body enforces legislation regarding water, protection of sites, nature, architecture, environmental impact assessments and advertisements, and, eventually, handles requests for permission for works within these categories.

At the departmental level, the prefect is the most important authority and is in charge of delivering authorisations when needed. More generally, he is principally involved in proceedings regarding noise, classified installations, mining of quarries, prevention of man-made and natural hazards, and with the protection of nature.

Still at the departmental level, the DDE (Direction Départementale de l'Equipement, which is the division in charge of departmental infrastructure), and the DDA (Direction Départementale de l'Agriculture, which is the division in charge of departmental agriculture and forestry), are concerned, in their respective fields, with environmental issues, but the real power of regulating control remains in the prefect's hands.

Finally, by application of Article L 132–2 of the Cities Code (Code des Communes), mayors are in charge of regulating some environmental matters (mainly prevention and repression of pollution) in their cities.

Regarding the laws themselves, it is possible to distinguish the laws of general application, the laws specially designed for classified installations and products and the laws protecting nature.

LAWS OF GENERAL APPLICATION

Although sources of environmental law are very diverse, environmental principles are essentially found in two laws: the Nature Law of 10 July 1976, and the Barrier Law of 2 February 1992.

The Nature Law (10 July 1976)

The most innovating notion of the Nature Law is the creation of an 'impact assessment' (*étude d'impact*) duty. This new notion is more precisely defined in the law's implementing decrees, the decree of 12 October 1977 and the decree of 25 February 1993. The later modified the former by implementing European Directive no 85.337 of 27 June 1985.

As a consequence, it is almost always necessary to include an impact assessment in all projects having an effect on the environment. This document is supposed to give an overview of the effect the installation will have on fauna, flora and human health. The administrative decision to authorise or forbid the project will be based mainly on this information.

There is actually two kinds of impact assessment. For some limited works, the administration will only require a notice. The notice on environment can be quite imprecise. Article 2 of the decree of 1977, as modified by the decree of 1993, just says that it has to state the project's potential effect on the environment and how the project complies with environmental concerns.

The assessment has to be much more detailed, and must include the following:

- an analysis of the initial state of the site and its environment;
- an analysis of the project's effect on the environment;
- the reasons why this specific project was chosen;
- the measures that the applicant intends to take, to preserve the environment, and an evaluation of the related expenses;
- the methods used and the difficulties met in this evaluation.

The Barrier Law (2 February 1992)

The law dated 2 February 1992 (also known as the Barrier Law) is especially remarkable because it established the following in relation to environmental law:

- The principle of precaution, ie there is no need to wait until damage actually occurs to take appropriate measures to protect the environment and the population.
- Preventive actions should have priority over repression, that is to say, over civil and criminal prosecutions.
- The notion of participation, ie the public has to be involved in any public inquiry regarding the environment.
- The rule under which the polluter pays.
- The right of everyone to a healthy environment.

The main feature of the environmental principles in France is that prevention and precaution are more important and essential than repression. The attitude of the administration and of the government is to give clear prescriptions to prevent, as opposed to cure, pollution. Of course, breaking the law will be punished and guilty operators will be sentenced to a fine or even to imprisonment. But the general philosophy is really to make it possible for everyone to develop all kind of activities, as long as it is in accordance with the law, and without major pollution.

LAWS DESIGNED SPECIFICALLY FOR INSTALLATIONS AND PRODUCTS

The Classified Installations Law (19 July 1976) and the Order of 2 February 1998

Classified installations could be defined as establishments officially listed because of the danger or the risk they pose to the environment.

Authorisation and declaration

The Classified Installation Law is dated 19 July 1976. Since it applies to any stationary installation operated or owned by any natural or legal person, public or private (Article 1), which threaten any danger or nuisance to the environment, it has a very wide application.

The criterion of nuisance, under the meaning of the law, includes both established and potential hazards. it poses, the law makes a critical distinction between installations needing an authorisation and installations just having to declare their activity.

Prior authorisations have to be authorised by the prefect. The application file must contain:

- an impact assessment;
- a risk assessment;
- an emergency plan;
- a paper on the workers security;
- the conclusions of the mandatory public inquiry which lasts at least one month (law of 12 July 1983).

If the operator just has to declare the company's activity, he or she must comply with mandatory conditions that he or she will receive when making the declaration. A non-compliance would be an offence.

Although authorisations are given for an unlimited time, a new one can be requested in case of significant modification to the activity. The Prefect decides whether a new authorisation is required.

The legislative framework is completed by specific rules regarding the most dangerous installations. Such installations are subject to a more stringent regime. Operators running such dangerous installations have to provide the administration with a specific safety assessment. In addition, more specifically, restrictive conditions of use can be imposed around such installations' sites at the request of the operator, the prefect or the mayor. The operator is liable to compensate owners and others with an interest in the property for direct and proven damages to their property.

Sanctions and liability

A special inspectorate is in charge of controlling classified installations: la police des installations classées. It has wide powers of control. Classified installation inspectors are allowed to demand any documents they consider necessary to aid their inspection; they can also carry out tests, and any costs incurred must be paid by the operator.

If one operator does not comply with the law, the prefect has to take administrative sanctions. After having served a formal notice to the operator, the prefect can order any relevant work to be undertaken, or order that any payments be made into an escrow account until the necessary modifications have been carried out, or even order the suspension of the operations. The final sanction is the closing down of the installation.

Beyond the administrative sanctions, the operator can also be sued for damages in a civil court. As official authorisations are granted without prejudice to the right of third parties, even if the operator received an authorisation, he or she is still responsible for the pollution or for unreasonably disturbing the quietness of the neighbourhood.

However, an action against the operator cannot be started if a claimant moved into the neighbourhood after the classified installation was authorised, and if the operator complies with the authorisation's prescriptions.

Of course, operators are criminally liable if they do not comply with administrative regulations or the applicable technical conditions. Operating without the requisite authorisation or declaration is punishable by 2 to 12 months' imprisonment, and/or a fine of 2,000–5,000 francs (Article 18, et seq).

The Order (Arrêté) of 2 February 1998

The Order of 2 February of 1998 covers activities of classified installations needing an authorisation. It is related to the taking of water, use of water and emission of all kinds.

The Order is divided into ten chapters, including prevention of accidents and accidental pollution, taking and use of water, effluents treatment, maximum emissions values, rejections and discharge conditions, emissions control, environmental balance and control of environmental effects.

It applies to air, surface and underground water, rainwater, waste, noise and vibrations.

The Waste Law (15 July 1975)

The legal framework

The main legislation concerning waste is the law of 15 July 1975. This establishes the essential principle under which operators who generate waste are responsible for the treatment and final disposal of that waste (Article 2 of the law).

It also states the obligation to provide information about the waste being generated but this was not a statutory obligation. As a consequence, this part of the 1975 law was reformed in 1992.

The law of 13 July 1992 reinforced the obligation to provide information. The purpose here was to facilitate the administrative control of waste treatment and disposal. But the 1992 law also intended to implement the European Directive which sought to limit the dumping of waste. As a result, the new law states that from 1 July 2002, disposal sites will be allowed to receive and stock only ultimate waste. All other kinds of waste will be reused one way or another (eg by being used as an energy source, by being recycled, by being incorporated in new materials, etc).

International Waste transportation

France is a party to the Convention of Basel, of 29 March 1989, which forbids international transportation of hazardous waste without bilateral agreements. But the Basel Convention only applies outside the European Union. Inside the European Union, waste transportation is not prohibited.

Actually, waste is considered to be like any other merchandise and thus benefits from the 'free movement of goods' inside the European Union. But the European Council allowed member states of the European Union to systematically refuse waste (Council Regulation dated 1 February 1993). As a result, the member states may choose to accept or refuse waste from other member states. The decision has to be global to be in accordance with the European Union's market rules.

If the administration is aware that waste is being unlawfully transported in France, the prefect can order the operator stocking the waste to return it to the country of origin (law of 30 December 1988).

Sanctions and liability

Once again, sanctions will be administrative. The 1975 law allows, after the serving of a formal notice, the prefect or the mayor, depending on the case, to take all necessary measures to make certain that waste is correctly treated. As for classified installations, the administrative authority can also order payment into an escrow account until the waste has been treated in accordance with the law.

Civil liability arises each time that someone falls victim to the wrongful treatment of waste, even if operators have complied with legal prescriptions.

There is also criminal liability when operators refuse to comply with a demand for information, with the legal and administrative prescriptions, or treat waste without authorisation, or more generally, do not comply with the 1975 law.

Fines and imprisonment depend on the gravity and the nature of the offence.

LAWS DIRECTLY PROTECTING NATURE

The Water Law (3 January 1992)

Actually, there are two water laws: the law of 12 December 1964, which is the ground for the legislation related to water, and the law of 3 January 1992, which completed and modernised the 1964 law.

The law of 1964

The purpose of the law is to organise the balanced use of water. For this, it created the financial basin agencies, which became, by application of the 1992 law the water agencies. Those agencies have had the foresight to apply the principle under which the polluter pays.

The water agencies receive a double tax. The first is based on the quantity of water used (*redevance de prélevement*), the second is proportional to the quality of water, after the operator used it (*redevance de pollution*).

The revenue collected finances loans and subsidies to improve water quality. Public or private sector companies may be contracted to carry out the improvement work.

The law of 1992

Basically, the 1992 law modernises the 1964 law. It also creates the General Planning for the Use and Management of Water (Schémas Directeur d'Aménagement et de Gestion des Eaux – SDAGE).

The essential consequence of this new document was to set up precise rules for the use of water. The prefect supervises the drafting of the SDAGE.

Obligations attached to water use

All activities or work having an effect on natural surface water or underground sources of water have to be declared or authorised. A decree of 29 March 1993 lists the activities needing an authorisation or a declaration. It also establishes the list of activities that are not controlled. Domestic use of water, and any equivalent use (less than 40 m^3 a day), do not require an authorisation.

The 1964 law (articles L20 and L21 C) establishes protection perimeters around the most sensitive and fragile areas. There, the use of water is completely forbidden.

The law also totally prohibits the discharging of specific substances (such as non-biodegradable detergents) into undesignated areas.

Sanctions

Water is one of the most protected resources. Usually, control of such resources will be based on the article L232–2 of the Rural Code (Code Rural). This article does not require an intention to harm (the intentional element – *l'élément intentionnel*) without which there is normally no criminal liability under French law. It is thus very easy for judges to fine operators. As soon as the pollution has an effect on the quality of water, operators are potentially guilty.

The other ground for control is the 1992 law. It created a new offence (*délit*) which applies to all kinds of water, and which is applicable each time that pollution has an effect on fauna or flora, or is a potential danger to human health. Moreover, there is no need for damage if the pollution is the result of waste rejection. In such a case, operators can be held criminally liable by just breaking the rules. As a consequence, they can be sentenced, even if there is no damage.

Operators can be sentenced to a fine ranging from 2,000 fr to 500,000 fr, and to two months' to two years' imprisonment. However, if operators comply with legal prescriptions, there is no liability under the 1992 law.

The Air Law (30 December 1996)

The law of 2 August 1961 was the first law related to the quality. It has been completely modified and modernised by the law of 30 December 1996.

The 1996 law

The law of 1996 totally transformed and reformed the former legislation. The new legislation is applicable to all products that could:

- be a risk to human health;
- debase biological resources or the ecosystem;
- influence climate change;
- damage goods;
- generate excessive olfactory problems.

It essentially affects four sectors:

- transportation;
- energy;
- health;
- air quality.

The law is very comprehensive, and thus does not address 'details'. It sets up the infrastructure of the new legislation concerning air protection. It should be completed by several implementing decrees.

The law opens with a statement: 'Everyone has the right to breathe air that does not damage one's health.' As a consequence, the 1996 law establishes the principle of pre-set air quality standards. The Environment Agency is responsible for controlling those standards.

In articles 12 and 13, the law establishes emergency procedures, for whenever a dangerous level of pollution is reached. The first rule authorises the administration to restrict or suspend activities contributing to the pollution. It can also reduce polluting emissions from fixed and mobile sources. This includes cars as a mobile source of polluting gases. If the population is not allowed to use cars for this reason, then public transport will be provided, free.

In the Ile de France region, prefects can also forbid the use of specific combustibles, or suspend or slow down specific activities. But this rule applies only when the substance polluting the air is SO_2 (arrêté interpréfectoral no 94–10504).

The 1996 law also intends to improve the air quality by a better and more rational use of energy. The main consequence for the industrial sector, with regard to this, is Article 21, which allows the government to regulate energy consumption through the implementation of technical criteria.

Sanctions and liability

For the classified installations, sanctions are mainly administrative. The prefect can, after serving a formal notice, order specific works to meet the required standards, order payment into an escrow account until the required modifications have been carried out, restrain or suspend the activities or the operations (Article 38 of the law).

There is also a criminal liability when operators pollute the air after having been served with a formal notice. In such cases, operators are fined 50,000 fr and sentenced to six months' imprisonment.

Companies, too, can be criminally liable for breaching the law. Usually, they would be sentenced to a fine.

The Noise Law (13 December 1992)

Most significant is the Classified Installations Law of 19 July 1976 and more specifically an Implementing Order of 20 August 1985, as amended by the Integrated Order of 1 March 1993; whereby such installations are compelled to meet certain pre-set noise standards. Failure to do so may result in sanctions.

In addition, on 31 December 1992, a law on noise abatement was adopted. It is subject to several implementing decrees, such as the decree introducing an airport tax to indemnify the residents of the surrounding district. It also adjusted the criminal sanctions and raised the sanctions to imprisonment for up to two years and/or a 200,000 fr fine.

The last important deposition regarding noise is the law of 29 March 1976 which forbids constructions in the proximity of highways and main roads.

PRINCIPLES RELATED TO INDUSTRIAL ACTIVITIES

The Duty of Disclosure

The duty of disclosure is the result of Article 8–1 of the Classified Installations Law. Since it is the ground for representations and warranties, it is one of the most important depositions.

The seller of an industrial site has to disclose all relevant information related to pollution of the site. Therefore, the vendee is completely aware of the risks. To balance this duty, it is possible for the seller to undertake representations and warranties, or warranties on liability. Such warranties may take several forms, depending on whether the transferor agrees to reimburse the vendee or directly reimburse his 'environmental' creditors.

Representations and warranties are potentially harmful to the seller's interests, and should thereby never be undertaken without having a full knowledge of the exact and accurate state of the site at the time of the purchase. Otherwise, the seller may be held responsible and could have to indemnify victims of any future pollution.

In consideration of this threat, it is highly recommended to proceed with an environmental audit before starting any new venture on the site. An independent audit will be the only way to determine which operator should be held responsible in case of a pollution occurring after the transfer (this is especially true when the new activity is similar to the old one, or when it induces the same kind of pollution).

Criminal Liability

In considering criminal liability it must be underlined that companies too can be held liable. The New Penal Code enacted in France in 1994 provides for moral entities, ie companies can be sentenced to fines five times higher than the fines applicable to individuals. The New Penal Code also establishes specific sentences for companies, such as the winding up of the company, placement under judicial scrutiny, exclusion from public procurement, the publication of a court's decisions, etc. Fines can also be added to these sentences.

Civil Liability

One of the most original aspects of environmental law is that even with an authorisation, someone carrying out an activity that pollutes can be held liable.

The two main grounds for civil liability in environmental suits, are pollution of private properties and excessive noise in quiet neighbourhood. In consideration of this risk, operators will have to pay careful attention to the location of their activities. Running an installation in a residential area might appear to be a mistake, although French courts are reluctant to award substantial damages.

Administrative Sanctions

French environmental law is grounded on administrative authorisations, prescriptions and control. Every activity involving pollution issues will induce an administrative proceeding.

It has been shown that prefects have important powers in their department, and that they can take serious, and even critical administrative sanctions (ie to interrupt the operation of installations). It is thus an obligation for operators to comply with administrative prescriptions.

CONCLUSION

Operators in France must keep in mind their environmental obligations. Once again, the government attitude is not hostile to pollution. But laws and regulations have been enacted to preserve nature and people from risks, and to make certain that industrial pollution will not create permanent damage.

To summarise the spirit of French environmental law, it could be said that it intends to establish the rules of a sustainable development. Operators going beyond those rules will be held civilly and criminally liable.

15

Incentives

Jean-Pierre Périer, Invest in France Agency

INTRODUCTION

A number of incentives have been introduced to answer the needs of companies wishing to invest in France. They vary according to the nature of the project and the company backing it.

Some types of financial assistance depend on the location chosen. They are granted by the state, local authorities or redevelopment corporations and have been introduced by the French government with the approval of the European Commission. The top incentive, the Regional Development Grant (PAT), which is decided upon directly by DATAR (the French government agency responsible for economic development and regional planning) is intended to encourage job creation. As well as this grant, local property subsidies and tax exemptions plus loans at special rates are also available.

Other types of assistance are linked to the operation of the company. For instance help is given to a company to improve its hiring procedure, training programmes, development of research programmes, investments in energy savings or in environmentally friendly production centres as well as export to far-flung markets.

Incentives for hiring and training of employees are extensive and cover the entire range of the company's activities: training prior to hiring to ensure that the new employee is qualified for the job, refresher courses on the use of new tools and technologies, hiring of young employees with no work experience or of people who have been unemployed for an extended period of time. All these operations qualify for subsidies or exemption from social charges.

Specific assistance has been introduced for research and innovation, a vital aspect in maintaining a company's competitive edge, to support the launching of innovative programmes and transfer technology. A special tax regime, the research tax credit, is applicable to small enterprises as well as large corporations.

INVESTING IN A BUSINESS ACTIVITY

Industrial projects or the creation of services in some priority zones may be eligible for aid from the state or local authorities. Such aid may translate into a direct subsidy or tax breaks.

Direct State Subsidies

Regional Development Grant (PAT)

The Regional Development Grant is an equipment subsidy granted by the state to companies whose investment will lead to job creation in listed regions.

The grant is available to companies planning operations in the industrial or service sector and can be used for the following:

- the creation of an establishment by a company which is already in existence or which is new, with a minimum of 20 permanent jobs over three years. The minimum number of jobs can be reduced to ten for top-flight service operations or for research programmes;
- the expansion of a business when this is of a substantial nature. The programme must entail an increase of at least 50 per cent of the total workforce over three years (with the creation of at least 20 jobs) or the creation of at least 50 jobs.

The project must involve an investment in excess of 20 million fr (exclusive of tax) whatsoever the nature of the operation.

The amount of the grant is dealt with on a case-by-case basis by the CIALA (Comité Interministériel des Aides à la Localisation des Activités) on the advice of DATAR. The points to be taken into consideration include the number of jobs to be created over three years, the amount of investment (pre-tax), the company's requirements, the site chosen and the extent to which the grant can prove to be an inducement to the investor.

For industrial concerns, two types of zone exist:

- Zones eligible for 70,000 fr maximum per job, up to a ceiling of 25 per cent pre-tax of the investment.
- Zones eligible for 50,000 fr maximum per job, up to a ceiling of 17 per cent pre-tax of the investment.

Companies involved in the service sector are eligible for a one-zone rating of 70,000 fr maximum per job created.

The Regional Development Grant is considered to be a taxable revenue as part of business profits. However, taxes on the grant can be alleviated to a considerable extent in two ways:

- The investor is allowed to impute the grant received to the company's earnings in proportion to current depreciation on the capital investment taken into account for the calculation of said grant.
- The fixed assets on which the grant was calculated may be depreciated on a basis equal to their cost plus half of the amount of the grant.

As for grants allocated to operations in the service sector where no capital investment has been made the beneficiaries are permitted to write-off grants to their taxable earnings over a period of ten years (the Regional Development Grant is always considered to be an equipment subsidy for the purposes of taxation, even when no capital investment is made).

Direct Subsidies Granted by Local Authorities

The Regional Employment Grant (PRE)

This grant is given according to the conditions set forth by the regions for any programme involving creation, expansion, company buyout or change in business activity. It is calculated according to the number of jobs created or maintained, up to and including 30 jobs.

The amount varies between 10,000 and 40,000 fr according to the area chosen. The Regional Employment Grant cannot be combined with the Regional Development Grant.

The Regional Grant for New Businesses (PRCE)

This grant is given by the French regions to encourage the creation of businesses, with no limitation on zoning. It may be combined with the PAT or the PRE. Application for this grant may be made only by companies which have been officially registered for less than 12 months at the time of application and which intend to create a minimum number of jobs stipulated by the Regional Council. The pre-tax ceiling amounts to 150,000 fr (200,000 fr for those areas which the regions deem to be priority zones).

It should be noted that the PRCE and the PRE are not granted in every region of France. They may be replaced by refundable loans, participation in equity capital or guarantees.

Assistance from the Redevelopment Agencies of Large Industrial Corporations.

Several large French corporations have created redevelopment agencies in order to find new jobs for employees they have been forced to make redundant, as well as the economic redevelopment of their production sites. In this regard, the range of financial aids offered by these redevelopment agencies is extensive. A free technical assessment is offered by them for each individual project.

The financial assistance offered varies in degree:

- Medium to long-term loans (five to ten years) at interest rates lower than the current market rates plus the possibility of deferred depreciation. These loans are not always subject to guarantee.
- Subsidies: companies hiring former employees of these corporations are eligible to receive direct cash grants or a supplement to the main loan from the redevelopment agencies.
- Participation in equity capital on the investor's project. Some redevelopment agencies may also participate in the financing of an investment project by contributing equity capital which usually takes the form of a minority or temporary interest. The agencies are not on the board and therefore not involved in the company's management. After a period ranging from three to seven years they sell their shares back to the investor.

Fiscal Exemptions and Tax Breaks

Companies choosing to either set up operations or expand or transfer to a priority development zone are eligible for fiscal breaks granted by the state.

The Tax Credit Break for Companies Located in Special Investment Areas (ZIP)

This tax credit is only available in the Nord-Pas-de-Calais region. Companies locating in a special investment area are eligible to receive

a tax credit break amounting to 22 per cent of the pre-tax manufacturing cost for industrial investment made over three years as of
incorporation.

The company must create at least ten jobs. This tax credit break is
applicable on the amount of company tax payable by the business
within ten years of its incorporation and is not refundable.

Exemption from the Business Tax (Five Years Maximum)

The business tax is a local tax on non-salaried business activities. The
rates applicable are subject to vote by the local authorities. In priority
development areas, a full or partial temporary exemption may be
granted by the relevant communes, departments and regions.

This exemption may or may not require the prior consent of tax
authorities:

- Official consent must be obtained to obtain exemption from the
  business tax in such cases as: buyout of production facilities
  belonging to industries experiencing difficulty, redevelopment of
  industrial installations associated with a sector of activity in
  decline, the creation and expansion of services involving management, survey reports, engineering or the computer industry.
- The creation or expansion of industrial or research establishments leading to a minimum number of jobs and a specific
  threshold of investment are eligible for exemption without the
  consent of the tax authorities.

The exemption is applicable for a maximum period of five years as of
the second year for new companies and as of the third year for business expansion.

Tax and Welfare Exemptions in Special Rural Zones (Rural Revitalisation Zones) and Cities (Urban Free Zones)

Exemptions are possible on corporate taxation, the business tax
and some other local taxes as well as on employer social security
contributions.

These exemptions can be granted for a maximum period of five years
in specific areas of French territory.

The regulations as regards eligibility will be dealt with on a case-by-
case basis, taking into account the size of the company involved as
well as the type of operation.

CONSTRUCTION OF INDUSTRIAL PREMISES

Most activity and industrial parks in France are managed by local authorities and chambers of commerce. They may offer the financing required for the premises, whether these already exist or need to be built.

Leasing Property

The construction or financing of industrial premises may be handled by third parties, notably real estate companies dealing with commercial and industrial property (SICOMI) as part of a real-estate leasing deal.

Rentals payable on premises are fully deductible from taxable profits with the exception of that portion which is not subject to depreciation (the land). When exercising the option to purchase, the lessee must reinstate in the taxable earnings for the year of purchase a portion of the rentals equal to the difference between the net accountable value of the premises and the purchase price, less the non-deductible portion (the land).

However, SMIs with premises leased between 1 January 1996 and 31 December 2000 located in regional development zones are exempt from reinstatement when purchasing the premises.

Assistance from Redevelopment Agencies of Large Industrial Corporations

Some of the larger French corporations sell or lease industrial land or premises at lower than market value. This means that recently built premises can be leased for as little as 25 or 30 fr per square metre per year.

Assistance from Local Authorities

Local authorities can buy up industrial premises for the purposes of selling or leasing them out, sometime after making the necessary repairs, thereby giving the purchasers/lessees the chance to benefit from the cut rates.

A 25 per cent maximum cut rate may be granted on sale or lease of premises located in those zones which are eligible for the Regional Development Grant. In other zones local authorities only assume responsibility for repairs to existing premises.

REDUCED LABOUR COSTS AND BETTER EMPLOYEE PERFORMANCE

Financial assistance from the French state to companies hiring and training employees may take the form of savings on salaries, total or partial exemptions on employer contributions, reimbursement of training expenses or a part thereof, and even a tax credit break on training.

The level of assistance available depends upon the skills and qualifications of the persons to be recruited, as well as their status and age.

Reduction on Employer Contributions for Employees in a Low Salary Range

Companies in the industrial, commercial or service sector who hire employees at a wage lower than 7,500 fr per month are eligible for a reduction in social security contributions (sickness, maternity leave, old age, invalidity, death, work-related, family allowances).

Hiring of Persons who have been Unemployed for an Extended Period of Time

'Employment initiation' contracts enable the employer hiring certain categories of applicants (especially those who have been unemployed for a prolonged period) to benefit from exemption on part of the employer social contributions as well as, depending on the case, a lump-sum payment of 2,000 fr over 24 months when the number of hours worked is at least equal to the legal requirement (30 hours weekly) or to that established by contract with the branch or company.

This assistance cannot be combined with other employment benefit schemes.

Hiring and Training of Youth Employees

Certain work/training contracts entitled 'qualification', 'apprenticeship' and 'orientation' contracts are open to companies hiring youth employees aged between 16 and 25 with no work experience on work/training contracts for a period which varies according to the type of contract (for instance a period of 6–24 months for a qualification contract, 6 months for an orientation contract, 12–36 months for an apprenticeship contract).

Work/training contracts mean that the employer is exempt from payment of social security contributions and can apply a lower salary as part of youth training while covering the cost of outside training.

Work Entry via Internship

The employer may benefit from taking on future employees as interns prior to hiring, for a period of anywhere between 40 and 500 hours. The state accepts responsibility for all remuneration and all or part of the expenses for professional training, according to the nature of the job on offer.

Training and Refresher Courses for Employees

The company may apply to the Department of Labour for a contract giving the right to train its workforce or to have the training carried out by an outside firm.

The state pays part of the salary and training costs. State assistance is available in the following cases: creation of a new company, conversion of company activities or subsidiary activities.

Tax Credit Break on Training

A company which undertakes to carry out a training programme over and beyond its legal obligation and the direct assistance mentioned in the previous section may be eligible for a tax credit break amounting to 25 per cent of the additional training expenses. This can be increased to 40 per cent for companies employing less than 50 people. Companies with over 50 employees can claim the 40 per cent rate on continuing vocational training only insofar as this only concerns employees doing jobs requiring minimum qualifications or who are aged 45 or more.

Any training eligible for such tax credit breaks may be set up by the company itself or contracted out to training centres. Courses are aimed at promotion and prevention of mishaps as well as the acquisition, updating or improvement of skills.

The ceiling on the tax break is 1 million fr (5 million fr for companies eligible for the 40 per cent rate).

The tax credit break on training is applicable on the income or corporate tax due for the year in which training expenses are declared.

If the tax credit break cannot be fully applied to taxes due, the latter being insufficient or non-existent, the surplus credit break is paid to the company.

RESEARCH PROGRAMMES

The Tax Credit Break for Research

Basic or applied research as well as experimental development programmes carried out by commercial or industrial firms may be eligible
for a tax credit break amounting to 50 per cent of research expenses
which have increased in comparison with the average for the previous
two years. New companies may apply for a tax credit break of 50 per
cent of R&D expenses during their first year of operation. The ceiling
is set at 40 million fr per company and is imputed to the corporate tax
for the fiscal year during which the expenses are undertaken and, if
need be, for the three subsequent fiscal years. This may be subject to
refund.

Expenses which may be liable for this research tax credit break are as
follows:

- depreciation of assets used in research;
- personnel costs related to technicians and research workers
  (manual workers and management are not included);
- operating costs (75 per cent of personnel expenses, 65 per cent
  in the Ile-de-France, 100 per cent in regional development);
- cost of R&D operations contracted out to organisations or experts
  whose credentials are recognised by the Ministry for Research;
- expenses relating to submission and registration of patents;
- depreciation on patents acquired to carry out experimental R&D;
- 50 per cent of the certification costs:
  - salaries and costs linked to time spent at official certification
    meetings
  - other costs relating to certification are inclusively deducted
    for up to 30 per cent of salaries and social contributions.

Special Depreciation on Expenses Involved in Software

Expenses involved in the acquisition of computer software may be
subject to accelerated depreciation over 12 months.

Reduced Rate of Taxation (19 per cent) on Transfer and Franchise of Patents

The yield resulting from the transfer or franchising of patents is taxed
according to taxation applicable on long-term capital gains at a rate of
19 per cent (+exceptional increase of 10 per cent).

Only the yield from patents, patented inventions or manufacturing processes considered to be incidental to patents or inventions (with the exception of all other intangible rights) may benefit from this preferential tariff, on condition that they have been part of the fixed assets for at least two years.

This chapter was first published by DATAR/Invest in France Agency in *A Guide to the Main Financial Incentives and Exemptions* (1997) and has reproduced with the permission of the publishers.

Part Three

Banking and Finance Systems

16

The Banking System

Robert de Bruin, Association Française des Banques (AFB)

THE NUMBER OF DIFFERENT INSTITUTIONS

On 31 December 1993, the banking system was reorganised under the Committee of Credit Institutions. The 1,611 institutions authorised included:

- 371 banks;
- 32 Banques Populaires;
- 74 regional Crédit Agricole banks;
- 28 Crédit Mutuel banks;
- 11 cooperative credit establishments;
- 1 cooperative society bank;
- 35 Caisses d'Epargne savings banks;
- 20 Crédit Municipal banks;
- 1,007 finance companies;
- 32 specialist finance institutions.

In addition to the 371 authorised banks there are 38 subsidiaries of community banks, which are subject – as of 1 January 1993 – to approval in their country of origin only, and the 16 Monacan banks.

The Crédit Agricole

The Crédit Agricole is structured on three levels:

- at the base level, local branches (3,000) collect deposits which they send to regional offices. They give advice on borrowing requests which they transmit to the regional office for decisions on the granting of credit;

- at the intermediate level, regional offices (74 at 31 December 1993) which have a cooperative banking statute manage the resources collected by their network of local branches. They send the surplus to the national office with some of the savings funds which are deposited in accounts (savings books, bonds, borrowings, etc);
- at the national level, two organisations:
  - the national office, Crédit Agricole's central body. Both a supervisory institution and a central finance organisation, ensures the network's development and manages all the subsidiaries and collective services. Originally created as a national public institution, it was privatised in 1988 as a limited company with 90 per cent of its capital held by the regional offices;
  - the Crédit Agricole's national federation. Adopts a representative role in dealing with the authorities and deals with the main company questions, particularly in negotiations with the unions.

Although it plays an essential role in financing agriculture, the Crédit Agricole has now spread its business to include domestic finance (housing) and rural professional activities (crafts, SMEs, liberal professions, trade). These additional services have not caused the loss of all the privileges from which it benefited (for example receipt of lawyers' deposits etc). On its balance sheet total, the Crédit Agricole mutual is the largest in the French banking network.

The Crédit Mutuel

The Crédit Mutuel has a three-level structure:

- 2,000 local branches which collect deposits and can give credit to their members;
- 18 regional groups or federations which have authority over the local branches and ensure their representation;
- federal offices which are credit institutions and manage surplus cash from the local branches, guarantee the settlements between them and finance major operations.

At the national level, the Confederation of the Crédit Mutuel is the network's central body. Crédit Mutuel's central office carries out financial operations (borrowing on various markets, and managing funds placed with it by the federal offices).

The Crédit Mutuel can undertake all banking operations, with the proviso that the credits it grants are only for the benefit of its members. This limitation is quite categorical.

On the other hand, the privileges it holds are considerable, particularly that of the blue savings book, which enables it to offer rewards to its savings customers on a par with those of the Caisse d'Epargne's savings books A, and like them, net of tax.

The Banques Populaires

Linked to the central body of the Federation of Banques Populaires, the network of Banques Populaires additionally comprises:

- 30 regional and cooperative popular banks;
- a popular bank, CASDEN, specialising in the specific customer base of staff and groups connected with the French Ministry for Education;
- a central banking office, the group's central credit institution.

For historical reasons the activity of the Banques Populaires is based mainly around craftsmen and small businesses, but they are subjected to the same risks as other banks. They can conduct the same operations as other banks, but for a number of years have tended to develop their business around individual customers.

The Crédit Coopératif

The Crédit Coopératif unites a group of credit cooperatives whose aim is to help non-agricultural socio-economic organisations: cooperatives, mutuals, associations, as well as the fisheries sector.

The central body of the Crédit Coopératif network is the Crédit Coopératif central office. This network comprises two categories of subsidiary:

- those managed by central office, ie four credit cooperative societies, one of which is an AFB bank and the Banque Française de Crédit Coopératif, the group's short-term credit and deposit organisation;
- those it does not manage (30), among which are the Crédit Maritime Mutuel establishments.

The network also includes several other specialised credit institutions (leasing, for example). The Crédit Coopératif can only finance its own companies.

The Caisses d'Epargne et de Prévoyance

This network of savings banks and provident companies comprises:

- a central body, CENEP, the national centre for Caisses d'Epargne et de Prévoyance;

- 35 regional offices;
- two national subsidiaries which carry out some specific activities.

Limited from the outset to savings book A investments, the Caisses d'Epargne have been progressively authorised to carry out the majority of bank operations for the benefit of all categories of customer: individuals, local government and community associations, entrepreneurs, SMEs/SMIs.

They have nevertheless held on (with the French Post Office) to the savings book A monopoly which constitutes a powerful and attractive product for them, while assuring a considerable return through commission on the proceeds which they receive from the Caisse des Dépôts et Consignations.

With more than 4,300 permanent branches, 35,200 employees, and more than 45 million accounts, the Caisses d'Epargne put their monopoly to good use by exercising strong competition which is bitterly resented by other credit institutions.

The Crédit Municipal

A continuation of the state-owned pawnbrokers' system, the Crédit Municipal offices are local public credit and social aid institutions, with a monopoly on the granting of loans for tangible security. There are currently 20 offices, of which the one in Paris is by far the largest.

In recent years, they have progressively diversified and developed their business towards individuals (particularly loans to clerical workers), to local government and to community associations.

The Finance Companies

This is the most diversified and numerically the largest category, since, including securities houses, at 31 December 1993, it grouped together 1,007 institutions.

They are defined by the common characteristic that they cannot receive short-term deposits from the public. They are differentiated primarily by the aim of their financing.

The different areas are:

- hire purchase finance companies
- leasehold with purchase option companies
- leasing companies

- mortgage companies
- guarantee companies
- factoring companies
- securities houses
- group finance companies.

To finance their operations, these companies have to use their own resources, call on money markets or financial markets, and for the very large number which are bank subsidiaries, seek support from their parent companies.

The finance companies are linked together in a professional organisation, the ASF (Association of Finance Companies).

The Specialist Finance Institutions

This category is evolving rapidly, since by law it can only include those credit institutions to which the state has granted a continuing public interest mission. These institutions cannot carry out banking business other than that relating to their mission except in a secondary capacity. So their development has often been fragmented, and even before the law of 1984, some of these institutions found their activity had dwindled. The State mission which justified their initial creation was modified, or disappeared altogether, and led them to find a rationale to develop their general banking activities, ie by distancing themselves from the spirit of their statute.

Currently 32 in number, with 12 institutions operating nationally and 20 regional development companies, the specialist finance institutions are represented in AFEC, the French Association for Credit Institutions, and by the professional organisation GIFS (Group of Specialist Finance Institutions).

Although every SFI, or every category of SFI, by definition has a specialist area of interest, the main institutions can be regrouped according to their field of operation:

- business support (credit, guarantees, share issues, aid, advice): the Crédit National, the CEPME (equipment leasing for SMEs), the regional development companies which are experiencing serious difficulties on account of the failures of many business in the last two years, and SOFARIS which guarantees the finance of SMEs;
- property financing: the main role falls to Crédit Foncier de France which, in addition to its traditional finance activities in construction, with state help participates in the distribution of loans, controls the enforcement of regulations and guarantees

supervision of the mortgage market. The Comptoir des Entrepreneurs and the Caisse de Garantie du Logement Social also participate in the distribution of social housing loans;
- local and regional community financing is the principal activity of the Crédit Local de France;
- financing French overseas departments and territories, particularly the Caisse Centrale de Coopération Economique, the Caisse Française de Développement, and SOCREDOM, the credit company for French departments overseas.

As regards the finance market, French law has conferred the IFS statute on the Société des Bourses Françaises which controls the operation of the French stock market MATIF SA, guaranteeing compensation on the futures market for financial instruments.

THE AFB BANKS

The number of AFB (French Banks' Association) institutions is still high but has varied considerably in recent years: 450 in 1946, 300 in 1967, 419 in 1980, 425 in 1993. Overall, this shows a slight decrease which does not, however, explain the movement towards concentration which has been under way for several years and is undoubtedly not yet complete. In reality, the increase in the number of banks under foreign control (179 at 31 December 1993 compared with 28 in 1946) has almost compensated in terms of statistics for the sharp reduction in the number of small and medium regional and local banks, of which more than 170 have disappeared.

Nevertheless, the AFB draws together a wide range of institutions:

- the 'big three' (BNP, Crédit Lyonnais, and Société Générale);
- the major general-activity banks (Parisbas, Indosuez, Crédit du Nord, CCF, CIC);
- approximately 60 regional and local banks;
- specialised finance banks.

Whatever their orientation, all the AFB banks have a full banking statute and can each conduct, without restriction, the full range of bank operations defined in French banking law.

Seven AFB banks figure among the ten major banks in France and three among the foremost 20 in the world.

OVERVIEW

In addition to the volumes of activity detailed elsewhere, the role and size of the French banking system as a whole and the different networks of the credit institutions can be assessed from other criteria taken from national accounting figures or documents produced by the supervisory authorities, relating to such items as the total workforce or the number of outlets.

According to national accounting data for 1991, the share of the French banking sector in GNP was more than 3.5 per cent, a share comparable to transport. By the end of 1993 the banking sector employed over 400,000 staff, that is almost as many as the energy sector and three times that of insurance (see Table 16.1).

While continuing to recruit young qualified staff, each year the banking sector devotes between 4 and 5 per cent of its wage bill to training.

If overall the workforce for the banking system has shown a net downward movement in recent years, chiefly due to productivity gains, analysis at the level of each network shows a different trend.

Based on 100 in 1987, according to the French Banking Commission, the workforce in 1992 stood at:

Table 16.1   Distribution of staff by network (1993)

Institution	No employed
AFB Banks	226,800
Banques Populaires	26,500
Crédit Agricole	69,100
Crédit Coopératif and Crédit Maritime Mutuel	1,975
Crédit Mutuel and Crédit Mutuel Agricole et Rural	22,100
Sociétés Coopératives de Banque	38
Caisses d'Epargne	35,250
Caisses de Crédit Municipal	1,280
Sociétés Financières	19,500
Institutions Financières Spécialisés	10,500
Total	413,043

Source: CEC

- 92.3 for the AFB Banks
- 92.6 for the Banques Populaires
- 98.8 for the Crédit Agricole
- 105 for the Crédit Mutuel
- 124 for the Caisses d'Epargne

It is hard not to attribute these development divergences to competitive distortions engendered by the maintenance of privileges in the only two networks in which the workforce has increased.

In the course of the last two years, the number of permanent bank outlets has increased sharply, from 15,037 in 1970 to 25,500 at the end of 1993 (see Table 16.2).

Regulation has strongly influenced this evolution. Until 1967, every new outlet opened had to be authorised by the French national credit council. In 1967, freedom to open unauthorised was recognised. This lasted until 1982, when quotas were restored, but followed by a return to 'unauthorised opening in 1987.

However, the most important factor determining the increase in the number of outlets, once freedom was attained, was the increased use of banks. The growth of the middle classes, the higher standard of living, urbanisation, the legal independent status of women, and of course, the necessity to pay for certain dealings by cheque, have brought new customers wanting to benefit from all the services that banks can offer.

As a result, the proportion of bank account holders is quite high in France, and the number of customers per branch is estimated at 1,331, compared with 1,070 in Germany, 752 in Belgium, 1,726 in Italy, 1,837 in Holland and 1,436 in the United Kingdom.

Table 16.2 Distribution of permant bank outlets by network (1993)

Institution	No of outlets
AFB Banks	10,442
Banques Populaires	1,625
Crédit Agricole	5,673
Crédit Mutuel	3,277
Caisses d'Epargne	4,254
Crédit Municipal	76
Crédit Coopératif	143
Total	25,500

Note that outside the European Union, bank account holders per branch stand at 2,419 in the United States (not including the Post Office), 2,045 in Canada, 1,793 in Japan, 1,747 in Sweden and 853 in Switzerland.

This chapter was first published by the AFB as 'Le Système Bancaire en France' (1995) and has been translated and reproduced with permission of the publishers.

17

Raising Finance for Corporate Investment

Marie-Annick Peninon, Association Française des Investisseurs en Capital (AFIC)

A business needs to raise finance at every stage in its life, and particularly to secure its development. Sometimes the usual resources which can be mobilised are inadequate and the business has to consolidate its equity by opening its capital and calling for financial investors.

The French capital investment industry is the second largest in Europe and annually enables around 1,500 businesses to benefit from substantial input. It is governed by clear regulations, in line with the standards employed in other countries.

OVERVIEW IN FIGURES

More than 200 investment funds provide 8 billion fr for 1,500 businesses. If bank finance (facilitated by the increase obtained in equity capital) is included, the total inflow is nearly 15 billion fr.

Nearly two-thirds of investments are made in businesses employing fewer than 100 staff. In recent years, finance invested in businesses with between 200 and 1,000 staff has increased by 30 per cent, with capital investment focused mainly on medium-sized expanding companies – the very businesses which are most susceptible to development and transfer problems.

Start-up and early stage finance represents 20 per cent of total investments, with the balance spread across development (33 per cent), LBO transfers (33 per cent) and minority take-overs (12 per cent).

The amount of investment and the type of activity invested in are as follows:

- The average investment is 4.5 million fr.
- The division of investments by sector has changed little over the long term, although there has been a tendency towards growth in the technology sector (comprising telecommunications, IT, electronics, biotechnology, health, energy and new materials). This sector now represents 26 per cent of the total (as against 18 per cent in 1993).

  Alongside this, consumer goods represent 24 per cent, industry 27 per cent, services 19 per cent and miscellaneous (from agriculture to public services) 4 per cent.

  Recent changes in the regulatory framework (see p 00) will strengthen the position of investments in sectors with a technological content.
- At 34 per cent, the main operations are no longer concentrated only on Paris and its environs of the Ile-de-France; the west at 18 per cent is meanwhile steadily increasing. The three other major zones (east and central France, Rhône-Alpes and the south) are showing little development, ranging between 12 per cent and 16 per cent, while the north is stable at 8 per cent.

COEXISTENCE OF DIFFERENT TYPES OF INVESTOR

The French market is composed of four types of investor:

- The independents (33 per cent) are investment funds or companies whose capital comes from a number of sources and which have no majority shareholder or stakeholder.
- The captives (36 per cent) are agencies specialising in capital investment, bank subsidiaries or divisions, financial institutions, insurance companies or industrial companies.
- The semi-captives (30 per cent) are subsidiaries of the same institutions as captives but they operate as independents and raise substantial capital from external investors.
- The public sector (1 per cent) is supplied wholly (or mainly), directly or indirectly, by public bodies.

Whatever their level of dependence in relation to their capital providers, French investors can be classified according to their activity: major or minor shareholdings; geographical involvement – regional or national, European or worldwide; sectoral specialisation (or none); start-up or LBO, early stage or development funding, etc. Each of these classifications can be combined with others.

RECENT AND CURRENT DEVELOPMENTS

French capital investment is a growth product which is becoming more consistent and more focused, and is developing in transparency and credibility.

The new equilibrium created since 1995, with a strong upsurge in investments and venture capital, is symptomatic of long-term structural changes, reinforced by recent legal provisions.

- Specialisation of start-up investment teams, more closely allied to the questions and demands of the business creators with whom they share a common technical language.
- Specialisation of financial teams in LBO–LBI operations, with national and transnational syndicates (respectively 40 per cent and 15 per cent of operations funded).
- Type and composition of financial cases which meet investors' criteria better, resulting from a better analysis by business leaders, a better understanding of investors' expectations and an approach which is less traditional and more commercially aware.
- Better reward for the risk undertaken due to improved liquidity of investments through the creation of the new French and European stock markets. From now on, these can provide a supplementary stage in the process of business financing.
- Greater flexibility in legal and fiscal statutes for investment structures. French venture capital investment trusts, the *Fonds Communs de Placements à Risque* (FCPR), were relaxed in 1997 and are now similar to limited partnerships.
- Creation of investment trusts focusing on the financing of innovative businesses – the *Fonds Communs de Placements dans l'Innovation* (FCPI) – which are open to subscription by private individuals and savers, and carry tax benefits.
- A number of articles in the 1998 Finance Law, of which the statutory instruments are awaited, should favour quasi-stock options and enable development of investments by business angels.
- The 1998 Finance Law also creates a new category of life assurance contracts which will benefit from considerable tax advantages if they allocate part of their funds to unlisted stocks, either directly or on the new market, or through capital investment structures, ensuring long-term resources and patient capital for capital investment dealers and businesses.

- A proportion of the funds collected through the privatisation of France Telecom are being made available for allocation to venture capital structures.
- There remain the main development areas of pension funds, stock-options, the status of researchers, business creators, etc.

HOW TO CHOOSE AN INVESTMENT FUND

Investment companies are increasingly specialising in their holdings: by sector of activity, by stage of investment, by geographical preference and by the amount of the investment.

AFIC (the French Association for Capital Investors) publishes a directory for most of these companies, providing all the necessary information on each of these criteria and the name of a contact person. Reference to some investments undertaken by these funds is also included.

This directory also lists associated members whose profession is closely related to capital investment and who are professional advisers helping with the choice of possible investors (accounting experts, lawyers, tax and company experts, etc).

The first stages in approaching an investor are standard, the idea being to contact three or four carefully targeted investors: approach the investor with a summary business plan, initial evaluations and preliminary negotiations which translate into an offer letter, audits prior to investment and final negotiations, and completion of the deal with draft agreement, shareholders' agreement, statutory modifications, and legal instrument.

The investor will then ensure the tracking of his investment, which may be more or less hands-on or hands-off, but he will always require receipt of regular management accounts, and to be a member or to receive the minutes of the meetings of the Board of Directors. Regional structures are often less involved than national structures.

Finally, after a satisfactory period of growth, between four and six years, the investor will hope to realise his investment, in agreement with the entrepreneur; either he will resell to the entrepreneur, or follow another possible exit route:

- sale to another company or another financier;
- LBO or LBI management buyout;
- introduction to the stock exchange.

It should not be forgotten during these stages that the essence of the investment is in the people and the teams. Alongside the business project and its market position, the experience, ability and personality of the team director who embraces it will be the determining element.

FINANCE PACKAGES

Whatever form the association takes, the capital is effectively increased, sometimes with the creation of a joint holding. In parallel with the issue of new shares, however, more complex packages can enable the opening of the capital base to be tailored to each case: priority dividend stock, shares carrying double voting rights, convertibles, subscription warrants, mezzanine debt, etc.

With some participation deals, the capital provider can insure part of his investment through Sofaris, a French government-funded insurance company which may guarantee up to 50 per cent of equity capital invested by capital development companies. The BDPME (Small and Medium-sized Enterprises Development Bank), controlled by the French state and Sofaris' parent company, the Caisse des Dépôts et Consignations, can provide co-financing with a bank.

ANVAR, the French national agency for research evaluation, can finance the preparation of business plans for innovative projects.

SOME USEFUL ADDRESSES

French Association for Capital Investors

AFIC, Association Française des Investisseurs en Capital
76 Avenue Marceau 75008 Paris
Tel: 00 331 47 20 99 09
Fax: 00 331 47 20 97 48

French National Audit Commission

Compagnie Nationale des Commissaires aux Comptes
6 Rue de l'Amiral de Coligny 75001 Paris
Tel: 00 331 44 77 81 25
Fax: 00 331 42 96 14 60

Council for Chartered and Certified Accountants

Conseil Supérieur de l'Ordre des Experts-Comptables et de Comptables
Agréés
153 Rue de Courcelles 75017 Paris
Tel: 00 331 44 15 60 00
Fax: 00 331 44 15 90 05

French National Bar Council

Conseil National des Barreaux (solicitors)
23 Rue de la Paix 75002 Paris
Tel: 00 331 53 30 85 60

Notary Public Chambers

Chambre des Notaires
12 Avenue Victoria 75001 Paris
Tel: 00 331 44 82 24 00
Fax: 00 331 44 82 24 10

18

Sourcing and Managing Start-up Finance Capital

Marie-Annick Peninon, AFIC

The French venture capital industry has seen strong development over the last three years. Start-up and early stage reached nearly 1 billion fr and has a share in the creation of 400 businesses per year. Financing innovative businesses is rising sharply, reinforced by a change in attitudes and helped by a favourable environment.

FINANCING BUSINESS CREATION – SOME FIGURES

Nearly 1 billion fr have been channelled to new businesses by public and private institutional investors. Funds invested directly by private individuals, business angels, are not currently measured.

At the end of 1997, business creation and post-creation represented 25 per cent of operations and 15 per cent of the amounts invested by French capital investment. The figures position France well above the European average.

Across 400 businesses, 90 per cent of these investments were focused towards sectors with a high-technology content (telecommunications, IT, electronics, biotechnology, health, energy and new materials).

Investors follow their target companies closely, guaranteeing several rounds of financing, and accompanying them in their development up until specialised stock exchange listing, or selling their holding to another investor specialising in development finance, or selling to a commercial company.

REASONS FOR THIS RECENT EVOLUTION AND EXTENSION

The specialisation of investment teams, the type and composition of business creations better suited to investors' criteria, offering better remuneration for the risk involved through an improvement in the provisional liquidity of investments, and the role of the authorities, are all factors resulting in positive long-term trends, and explain the recent growth.

- Venture capital teams are increasingly specialised. Composed of engineers, IT specialists, chemists, and doctors, they provide the business creator with a genuine professional and technical ear, capable of analysing and measuring the impact of products and markets.
- For their part, the business creators know how to respond better to investors' expectations by sufficiently preparing their business plan. The inclusion of SWOT analyses are elements in their success. The approach of French entrepreneurs is evolving and their analysis is becoming more commercially aware.
- Confidentiality in the distribution of the business plan is respected by professional members of AFIC (the French Association for Capital Investors) who are bound by their professional code of practice.
- The creation of stock markets in Europe designed for new innovative businesses has significantly improved the liquidity of investments and has therefore had a positive effect on the analysis of risks and the development of existing projects. The role of the new market in France (stock market capitalisation of 13 billion fr, 3 billion fr raised and 40 companies introduced at mid-March 1998) as well as the launch of EASDAQ (capitalisation $10 billion, $13 billion raised and 25 companies introduced in 23 months) open up possibilities for businesses to raise capital rapidly to ensure their growth. Nearly 70 per cent of businesses quoted on the French new market had a financial investor in their capital at the time of their introduction. The dynamics of the new market and its relationship with the other European markets through the Euro–NM alliance is a fundamental constituent of the French venture capital market.

- Two organisations play a significant role: ANVAR and Sofaris. ANVAR (the French national agency for the evaluation of research) allocates a range of repayable advances or grants which enable innovative businesses to seek advice from consultants, to carry out preliminary studies, to prepare business plans, to make use of technological distribution networks, to employ a European technological partnership, to recruit an R&D unit, and to acquire or sell technology, etc. ANVAR has 24 regional branches.

Sofaris is a company guaranteeing the financing of small and medium-sized businesses, whose parent company, the BDPME is majority-controlled by the French state and the Caisse des Dépôts et Consignations. It operates alongside banks and investment funds as guarantor (or in co-financing). The guarantee can cover up to 50 per cent of new finance, rising to 60 per cent if the company benefits from ANVAR aid and 70 per cent for new business creations. To accompany its significant investment programme, the BDPME can offer a 'development contract' which is an amortisable loan. A recent agreement made between the French government and the European Investment Bank allows Sofaris to guarantee new investments in venture capital for technology up to 2 billion fr.

- The authorities have played a significant role in boosting financing for innovation and new businesses by:
  - establishing the FCPI (investment trusts for financing innovative businesses). These investment funds are open to private individuals for a modest outlay, and allow them to benefit from reduced tax (25 per cent of outlay with a ceiling of 150,000 fr per couple). They must hold their shares for a minimum of five years and the FCPI must allocate at least 60 per cent of its investments to new innovative businesses. To date, in two months nearly 400 million fr have already been subscribed, and further FCPI issues are expected between now and the end of the year. FCPIs will make a significant contribution to new business creation
  - allocating 500 million fr, when France Telecom was privatised, to swell private investment funds specialising in venture capital for technology. In addition, 150 million fr have been dedicated to the establishment of priming funds, the poor relation in French operations. These funds will help to fill the void between researchers, entrepreneurs and financiers. These measures have only recently been decided and have not yet been put into practice; the market is expecting regulatory instructions before the summer.

- Still pending are important points like that of the researcher-creator, since the fiscal and social consequences of failure are nowadays too enormous for researchers to take the plunge and create their own business. Similarly, the French taxation system on stock-options must be reviewed. Subject to social security contributions and very strict operating rules, the system offers little interest, and in these conditions it is difficult to attract researchers or new business managers.
- Finally, the role of business angels is underestimated. There are few statistics available, but the potential from this source of finance is sufficiently significant for the 1998 Finance Law to make provision for taxes to be deferred on the capital gains made by a private investor when selling his shareholding in a business, if that capital gain is reinvested in a new young business.

THE MAIN FRENCH INVESTORS

About forty funds listed by AFIC, the French Association for Capital Investors, finance business creation, with 90 per cent of cases relating to technological investments: 14 funds specialise in telecommunications, 5 in the media, 15 in biotechnology and health, and 3 in defence.

Some funds take a more regional approach and band together in UNICer, the French national union for investors in regional business creation.

USEFUL ADDRESSES

French Association for Capital Investors

AFIC, Association Française des Investisseurs en Capital
76 Avenue Marceau 75008 Paris
Tel: 00 331 47 20 99 09
Fax: 00 331 47 20 97 48

French National Union for Investors in Regional Business Creation

UNICer, Union Nationale des Investisseurs en Création d'Entreprises en Région
c/o RTVL
445 Boulevard Gambetta – Immeuble Mercure 59200 Tourcoing
Tel: 00 333 20 24 97 87
Fax: 00 333 20 27 18 04

19

Stock Markets

Mike Geary and Didier Sidois,
Corporate Finance, PricewaterhouseCoopers

GOING PUBLIC

Presentation of the Different Markets

Securities listed in France are placed under one of four headings: the *Premier Marché* or *Cote Officielle* (the First Market or the Official List), the *Second Marché* (the Second Market), the *Nouveau Marché* (the New Market) and the *Marché Libre OTC* (the Over-the-Counter Market).

These markets together with the associated listing requirements are presented in Box 19.1.

Regulated market status is awarded to markets operating on a regular basis, with a set of rules defining listing requirements, offering transparency and announcing all transactions.

The *Premier Marché* is intended for large companies previously listed on the *Second Marché*, with the exception of large companies in the process of being privatised. The following pages concentrate on the *Second Marché* and the *Nouveau Marché*, created in 1996 to provide a fresh source of capital to young innovative companies.

Markets and listing requirements   Box 19.1

Financial Market	Type of Companies	Requirements	Listed Securities
Regulated markets			
Premier Marché	Large companies Turnover: around 800 million fr	Older than three years	At least 25% of capital or 600,000 shares and capital of at least 30 million fr
Second Marché	Medium-sized companies	Older than two years	At least 10% of equity
Nouveau Marché	Innovative companies with potential for high growth	At least FF 8 million of shareholders' equity	At least 100,000 shares and 10 million fr in market value
		No track record is needed	
Unregulated market			
Marché Libre OTC	Medium-sized companies	Older than two years	No requirements

Major Actors in the Flotation Process

Controlling authorities

The controlling authorities for the French stock markets are:

The *Commission des Opérations de Bourse* (COB), responsible for protecting investors and ensuring the information given to shareholders is accurate. Listing application files must be submitted to and agreed by the COB.

The *Conseil des Marchés Financiers* (CMF) is the professional regulatory authority which defines the rules under which the markets and brokerage firms operate.

Governing bodies

The *Société des Bourses Françaises* (SBF) is the stock market governing body. The SBF implements CMF decisions. Furthermore, it monitors the trading system, generates and disseminates up-to-the-second data on market conditions, provides a complete range of listing and issuing services, and acts as a clearing house for transactions between members, thus guaranteeing securities and cash will be available for clearing and settlement.

The SBF–Bourse de Paris has the major decision-making role in determining listing on the *Premier* and *Second Marché*.

The *Nouveau Marché* has a specific governing body: the *Société du Nouveau Marché* (SNM), a wholly owned subsidiary of the SBF–Bourse de Paris, responsible for the management of the *Nouveau Marché*, including market regulations, approval of members, approval of company listings through the admission committee and operation of the trading system.

Financial intermediaries

The listing candidate must choose at least one financial intermediary to manage the listing process and ensure a post-listing security follow-up.

On the *Second Marché*, these financial intermediaries are:

- a bank, which submits the listing application file to the market authorities and manages the listing process;
- a stockbroker, which carries out a company valuation and ensures security liquidity under a management contract and publishes financial analyses on a regular basis.

On the *Nouveau Marché*, listing candidates must appoint one or more member firms with the status of listing advisor/market-maker (*Intermédiaire Teneur de Marché* – ITM) to provide assistance with listing and to act as market-maker(s) for their securities thereafter.

Financial intermediaries offer investors the assurance that a company's prospects have been properly examined, and that there will be a secondary market in its securities.

Other actors

Companies often appoint a listing advisor who helps the company manage the listing process and deals with financial intermediaries.

The listing advisor should work closely with the financial intermediaries and the other advisors of the company namely:

- the statutory auditor(s) who guarantee(s) the quality of financial information;
- the communication agency, appointed by the company, which provides assistance in publishing documents and organising meetings with financial analysts and journalists.

Listing Requirements

The Second Marché

The company and its listing advisor(s) must submit an application file to the stock market authorities (COB and SBF) including the following documents pertaining to:

- the company: the corporate charter, modified to fulfil listing requirements (the corporate charter must not include any limitation which would restrict trading, such as a right of approval); the minutes of the annual shareholders' meetings and Board of Directors meetings for the past two years; the certified consolidated financial statements for the past two years, together with the board of directors' reports;
- the securities secondary market: a copy of the liquidity contract with the stockbroker;
- other documents to be disclosed are a draft prospectus drawn up in compliance with the regulations and instructions of the COB including legal, commercial and financial information; the letter of application by the company for listing of its securities, which gives undertakings concerning disclosure; a copy of the documents published by the company (if any).

The Nouveau Marché

The company and its listing advisor(s) must submit an application file to the SNM similar to the one for the *Second Marché* except for the following items:

- the *Nouveau Marché* offers real flexibility in terms of listing requirements. Very young companies may apply, as they are not required to produce previous years' accounts;
- the company must disclose a three-year business plan providing a detailed analysis covering technical, commercial and financing aspects, the company's strategy and the resources it intends to commit to achieve its growth target; since January 1997, management is no longer required to include financial forecasts in this business plan.

In addition, company founders and management must agree to retain 80 per cent of the equity held after the flotation for a period of three years (this rate is increased to 100 per cent for companies created less than two years before listing). The SNM principally encourages flotations to take place through a capital increase.

Timing and Costs

The costs of going public and the time necessary vary greatly depending on the company's needs and objectives.

Timing

Second Marché   The listing procedure begins once the company has fixed its listing strategy. The length of time required varies according to the complexity of the application file. If the process is well planned, it will normally take from six months to a year.

After deciding to go public, the company must firstly undertake some preliminary restructuring operations, regarding principally:

- the choice of the listing perimeter: reorganise the company/group in order to present an activity consistent group to the stock market. Furthermore, it may be important to modify the corporate charter;
- financial information: enforce the production, review and release of financial information. The first step may be to restate statutory and consolidated accounts in order to present two-year pro-forma accounts. Consolidated accounts are compulsory for companies listed on a regulated stock market.

The key event in the listing process is the submission of the listing application form at least three months before listing; once the first version of the application file has been submitted, a two-month period is usually taken by the COB and SBF to study and approve the file and the attached prospectus.

The listing decision takes place three weeks before flotation thus launching market information and subscription to shares.

Permanent admittance to quotation takes place after a three-year probationary period, as described hereafter.

Nouveau Marché   The timing on the *Nouveau Marché* is very similar to that of the *Second Marché*.

After preliminary restructuring, the company will need four months to prepare its listing, beginning with the choice of its listing advisor(s) (ITM) and communication agency. The company will prepare the listing application file with its ITM, including a three-year development project. After the file has been examined by the COB and the SNM, the final admittance decision is made by the admission committee. As soon as a positive answer has been received (three weeks before flotation), the marketing of shares may begin in France and abroad, as well as the final listing procedure.

Listing costs

Listing costs may be analysed as follows:

- preliminary costs regarding the necessary company restructuring prior to listing;
- flotation costs which comprise the listing advisor's fees; the information and communication costs; the COB and the SBF (or the SNM) admission fees;
- quotation costs which include the cost of shareholder information; the cost of the liquidity or the market making contract; the annual quotation fees.

Admission and listing costs are highly variable. Nevertheless, studies carried out by market authorities reveal that the total flotation cost is around 1 or 2 per cent of the company's market capitalisation.

It appears from recent flotations that listing costs range roughly between 3 and 7 per cent of the money raised, with a minimum of approximately 2 million fr. Costs linked to flotation on the *Nouveau Marché* are slightly higher than those incurred on the *Second Marché*, due to the very nature of this market (ie young and innovative companies, high-tech activities and associated higher risks).

Listing Obligations

Once a company is listed on the stock market, it has to inform its shareholders, the market and the regulatory bodies. The issuer has an obligation to disclose accurate, true and fair information necessary to enforce market efficiency. These requirements are very similar for both the *Second Marché* and the *Nouveau Marché*.

Financial information consists of three aspects:

- continuing information, ie the company must disclose any event or fact which may have a significant impact on the share value;
- legal information comprising all compulsory information releases due to be published in the *Bulletin des Annonces Légales Obligatoires* (BALO), ie accounting information (quarterly turnover, half-year income statement, annual statutory and consolidated accounts)and information linked to annual shareholders' meeting;

- information on certain operations: an information document, to be controlled by the COB, must be published in case of a share issuance, a take-over bid, a merger operation.

Furthermore, a listed company must have two statutory auditors.

On the *Second Marché*, admittance is made final after a three-year probationary period. The final admission decision is taken by the COB and the SBF on the basis of the following criteria being achieved:

- share liquidity;
- quality of information;
- quality of statutory and consolidated accounts, appreciated through a review of the auditors' files.

If the above quality standards are not met, the probationary period may be extended. De-listing remains exceptional.

STATISTICAL OVERVIEW

In order to complete our description of French stock markets, official SBF statistical data regarding listed companies and market evolution are presented below.

Listed Companies

At year-end 1996, 891 companies (see Box 19.2) were quoted on the French stock markets.

Number of companies quoted on the French stock market			**Box 19.2**
	Premier Marché	*Second Marché*	*Nouveau Marché*
Listed Companies	**590**	**283**	**18**
French	406	280	16
Foreign	184	3	2

These companies belong to 12 sectors. The market capitalisation by industry sector for French companies listed on the First and Second Markets as at 31 December 1996 is shown in Box 19.3.

Over the past few years, the market capitalisation for French companies listed on the First and Second Markets has increased significantly (see Box 19.4).

Market capitalisation by industry sector in billions of francs   Box 19.3

Sector	Number of Companies	Market Capitalisation	Transaction Volumes in % of Market Capitalisation
Energy	10	254	57
Raw Materials	39	177	47
Construction	21	164	51
Consumer Goods	67	221	53
Automobile	16	132	64
Other Consumer Goods	102	401	31
Food industry	46	281	42
Industrial Goods	**301**	**1,630**	**46**
Retail	58	330	41
Other Services	96	376	49
Services	**154**	**706**	**45**
Property	39	65	21
Financial Services	104	477	55
Investment Companies	88	195	32
Financial Companies	**231**	**736**	**46**
Total	**686**	**3,073**	**46**

Market capitalisation for French companies, 1992 to June 1997   Box 19.4

Year	Market Capitalisation (in billions of francs)
1992	1,932
1993	2,689
1994	2,412
1995	2,446
1996	3,073
June 1997	3,642

New Listings

The number of new listings over the last three years is divided as shown in Box 19.5.

Approximately two thirds of the companies listed on the *Second Marché* and on the *Nouveau Marché* in 1996 operated within the service sector.

Newly listed companies in 1996 had an average market capitalisation of 5,318 million fr on the *Premier Marché*, 343 million fr on the *Second Marché*, and 197 million fr on the *Nouveau Marché*. The average percentage of shares held by the public was 28 per cent on the *Premier Marché*, 17 per cent on the *Second Marché* and 31 per cent on the *Nouveau Marché*. The average amount subscribed by the public was 893 million fr for the *Premier Marché*, 96 million fr for the *Second Marché* and 87 million fr for the *Nouveau Marché*.

New listings 1994–1997				Box 19.5
	1994	**1995**	**1996**	**1997**[†]
Premier Marché	10	9	8	2
Second Marché	34	19	32	22
*Nouveau Marché**	–	–	18	9
Total	**44**	**28**	**58**	**33**

* Created in 1996
[†] First half

Volume of Transactions

During the first half of 1997, transactions for French companies quoted on the First and Second Markets amounted to 1,118.5 billion fr (see Box 19.6), representing approximately 80 per cent of the transactions for the whole of 1996 (a record year with transactions totalling 1,416 billion fr) representing an increase of 64.3 per cent compared to the first half of 1996.

The average daily volume of transactions on French companies listed on the First and Second Markets amounted to 9.1 billion fr compared to 5.5 billion fr during the first half of 1996 (a 65.4 per cent increase over the same period in 1995), and 5.67 billion fr for the whole year.

Volume of transactions in billions of francs			Box 19.6
	First half 1996	First half 1997	Variation (%)
Premier Marché			
French Companies	657.9	1,088.5	+65.5
Foreign Companies	14.0	26.4	+88.6
Second Marché			
French Companies	22.5	30.0	33.3
Nouveau Marché	0.7	2.1	200.0
Total	**695.1**	**1,147.0**	**+ 65.0**

During the same period, transaction volumes on foreign shares ranged from 16 billion fr in 1992 to 30 billion fr in 1996 (see Box 19.7).

Transaction volumes, 1992 to 1996 (billions of francs)				Box 19.7
	Premier Marché		*Second Marché*	
	Transactions	Market Capitalisation (%)	Transactions	Market Capitalisation (%)
1992	627	35	18	15
1993	930	37	26	17
1994	1,061	47	36	23
1995	1,005	44	28	19
1996	1,369	48	47	23

Indexes

There are four indexes managed by the SBF:

- CAC 40: calculated from a sample of 40 French stocks listed on the *Premier Marché* chosen from the 100 largest market capitalisations which also need liquidity;
- SBF 120: calculated from 120 French stocks substantial in size, offering more requirements diversity than the CAC 40 and designed to be a benchmark for funds invested in French stocks;

- SBF 250: represents the evolution of the market as a whole in order to offer a benchmark for long-term investments in French equity;
- MidCAC: made up of 100 French stocks from the First and Second Markets, excluding those companies with the 20 per cent highest and 20 per cent lowest market capitalisations, companies traded less than 175 days a year, property and financial companies. This index satisfies investors growing interest in the middle-sized companies.

Their index performance for the period 1994 to 1996 is shown in Box 19.8.

The rate of increase in 1996 of Wall Street was followed by all main indexes worldwide, with the exception of Japan's Nikkei. The increase in France continued from January to April 1997, remained steady until July and then increased again. In Paris, the most important rise came from companies in the service industry (+40 per cent), followed by industrial companies (+28 per cent), and finally financial companies (+15 per cent). During the first semester of 1997, the CAC 40 index increased by 23.4 per cent.

Index performance		**Box 19.8**
	1994–95 Variation (%)	**1995–96 Variation (%)**
CAC 40	– 0.5	23.7
SBF 120	– 0.3	26.1
SBF 250	– 1.4	26.7
MidCAC	– 16.8	35.7

Part Four

Auditing and Accounting Framework

20

Financial Reporting and Accounting

Pierre Riou and Christian Davoult,
Audit, PricewaterhouseCoopers

In spite of the existence of EU directives, International Accounting Standards (IAS) and the ever-increasing number of international business transactions, French accounting retains the reputation of being something of a mystery. Considerable attention has been devoted to gaining a better understanding of French accounting and this remains an important task for anyone engaged in or contemplating doing business with France. This chapter covers the most important rules regarding financial reporting and accounting in France and highlights some of the most frequently encountered differences from UK or international practice.

REPORTING

Source of Generally Accepted Accounting Principles

French accounting principles are derived predominantly from the French Commercial Code (*Code de Commerce*), the General Accounting Plan (*Plan Comptable Général*), and pronouncements and recommendations issued by the National Accounting Board (*Conseil National de la Comptabilité*).

In most respects, the accounting principles applicable to the statutory financial statements of individual companies also apply to consolidated financial statements of groups. However, in specific instances, groups are either required or permitted to apply valuation methods that are not acceptable for statutory reporting purposes. These consolidation adjustments are designed to enable French groups to present consolidated financial statements that are in accordance with international accounting standards, while individual statutory accounts are still driven, to a greater or lesser degree, by tax considerations.

Contents of Financial Statements

For the accounts of companies and groups which have not voluntarily decided to comply with international accounting standards, the following general rules apply:

- the financial statements include the balance sheet, the income statement and the notes shown as the *annexe*. Accounting regulations specify the information to be included in the notes, which varies depending on the size of the business. The balance sheet and income statement should include comparative figures for the prior year. It is also required that the opening balance sheet agrees with the closing balance sheet of the preceding year (thus, ruling out prior year restatements);
- a statement of retained earnings and a statement of cash flows or statement of changes in financial position are encouraged but not required;
- assets and liabilities are not segregated between current and non-current, but this classification is required in the notes. Balance sheet items are classified on the basis of their purpose or origin;
- the income statement is presented by type of income and expense. However, as a departure from this rule, the consolidated income statement can be presented by function, provided that certain minimum requirements concerning content are adhered to;
- there is no regulatory format for the statement of changes in financial position, which, as mentioned above, remains optional although its presentation is encouraged by the Stock Exchange Commission (COB). Professional institutes now recommend presentation of a cash flow statement in the international format;
- a full set of parent company financial statements must be separately published even when the presentation of consolidated financial statements is required. The parent company financial statements are generally included in the same document as the consolidated statements (annual report), although the use of a separate document is also allowed.

Audit and Public Company Requirements

All *Sociétés Anonymes* (SA) and *Sociétés en Commandite par Actions* (SCA) are required to appoint independent auditors who are responsible for ensuring that the annual financial statements have been properly prepared and comply with the 'true and fair view' principle. The same applies to *Sociétés à Responsabilité Limitée* (SARL), to *Sociétés en Commandite Simple (SCS), Sociétés en Nom Collectif* (SNC) and other legal entities that meet any two of the following three criteria at the year-end (see Chapter 26 for company definitions):

- total assets in excess of 10 million fr;
- total annual sales in excess of 20 million fr;
- average number of employees in excess of 50.

Companies required to publish consolidated financial statements must appoint two independent auditors. This requirement applies to groups headed by public companies and other corporations that meet, in aggregate, any two of the following criteria:

- total assets in excess of 100 million fr;
- total annual sales in excess of 200 million fr;
- average number of employees in excess of 500.

Subgroups that are controlled by another corporation and are included in that corporation's consolidated accounts are exempt from the requirement to publish consolidated accounts, provided that the controlling group's consolidated accounts are audited, published and made available to subgroup shareholders in French. Moreover, if the controlling group is from outside the European Community, the parent company of the French subgroup must supplement this information with certain disclosures concerning its own sub-consolidation.

The auditors are appointed by the shareholders for an initial term of six years. There is no limit on the number of times their appointment may be renewed. Statutory auditors may not be removed from office during the six-year term, except as a result of a court ruling in the case of serious professional misconduct or disqualification.

Public companies are defined as companies whose stock is traded on a recognised stock exchange or unlisted securities market, or companies that have offered to sell securities to the public (defined as representing at least 300 people).

Prospectuses issued by public companies in connection with public placings or public offers to acquire shares (take-over bids) must be submitted to the Stock Exchange Commission for prior approval. Listing requirements vary according to the market (*Premier Marché* for larger companies and *Second Marché* for medium-sized companies). As a general rule, audited consolidated financial statements covering the most recent two-year period are required to be presented in French (translation to be verified by a French auditor for foreign issuers). If the listing occurs more than nine months after the last audited balance sheet, audited consolidated interim financial statements must be presented for the most recent half-year. Public companies are also required to file copies of published financial information with the Commission.

The financial reporting requirements for public companies are more comprehensive than for unlisted corporations. These requirements, which vary depending on whether the company's stock is quoted on a recognised or an unlisted securities market, include the publication of annual, semi-annual and quarterly financial information.

ACCOUNTING

General Accounting Principles

The basic concepts underlying the selection of accounting policies and the preparation and presentation of financial information include:

- the going concern concept;
- the accruals concept;
- the historical cost convention;
- the principle of prudence;
- the principle of consistency in accounting methods from period to period.

Assets and liabilities may not be offset in the balance sheet, and income and expenses may not be offset in the income statement.

Two basic principles recognised by the International Accounting Standards Committee (IASC) but which are not explicitly included in French accounting law are:

- the principle of substance over form: certain transactions, such as leases, are accounted for in France in a manner that conveys their legal form, rather than their substance;
- the principle of materiality (relative importance): this principle is not explicitly mentioned in French accounting law, but is generally applied as regards the contents of the notes to financial statements.

ACCOUNTING PRINCIPLES

Principles of Consolidation

In general, all subsidiaries should be consolidated, except in the following cases:

- subsidiaries engaged in a business very dissimilar to that of the parent company (equity method used);
- if control by the parent company is seriously and permanently impaired (the cost method used);
- subsidiaries only temporarily controlled by the parent (cost method);
- subsidiaries not significant to the group (cost method used).

Companies jointly controlled by a limited number of shareholders are consolidated by the proportional method, that is, on the basis of the consolidating entity's percentage share of assets, liabilities, income and expenses.

Control is indicated by:

- ownership of a majority of the voting rights;
- the designation of a majority of the members of the board of directors (*Conseil d'Administration*) in two consecutive years (the investor is presumed to designate a majority of the members of the board if the investor holds more than 40 per cent of the voting rights and no other shareholder owns an equivalent or greater percentage);
- being in a position to dominate decision making by virtue of a contract or clauses in the investee's articles of incorporation.

Equity accounting (mise en équivalence)

Companies over which the consolidating entity exercises significant influence are accounted for by the equity method. Significant influence over the management and financial policies of the investee is usually presumed to exist when the investor holds 20 per cent or more of the voting shares.

Minority interests (intérêts minoritaires)

Minority interests are shown separately in the consolidated balance sheet and income statement to identify clearly the net assets and net income (or loss) attributable to the parent company. However, if a subsidiary has negative shareholders' equity, the interest of minority shareholders is shown as attributable to the parent company.

When a subsidiary is consolidated for the first time, minority interests in its shareholders' equity should be determined on the basis of the fair value resulting from the allocation of goodwill among identifiable assets and liabilities.

Goodwill (écart de première consolidation)

Goodwill, representing the difference between the purchase price of the investment and the acquiring company's interest in the underlying net assets at the date of acquisition, is allocated as far as possible among identifiable assets and liabilities acquired. The unallocated balance is recorded on a separate line of the balance sheet as goodwill or negative goodwill. In practice, goodwill is allocated primarily among non-current assets, including intangibles, and provisions or long-term debt. In no circumstances should the adjustments exceed the goodwill to be allocated.

Goodwill (and negative goodwill) is generally amortised over a period reflecting the assumptions and objectives prevailing at the time of the acquisition. If the original assumptions prove to be incorrect and the objectives for the acquired business are not met, resulting in a permanent, significant impairment in value, the amortisation period must be shortened accordingly. French law does not specify a maximum amortisation period.

The notes should contain all significant information required to enable the reader to understand and form an opinion on the consolidated financial statements, including details of the companies consolidated, the consolidation principles and methods applied, the content of and changes in certain balance sheet and income statement items, an analysis of consolidated sales by industry segment and geographical area and information on companies accounted for by the equity method (including summarised financial statements).

The notes should also include information on the amounts paid by consolidated companies to members of the board of directors of the parent company and on any commitments or loans given by consolidated companies in favour of board members.

Joint Ventures

French legislation acknowledges that joint ventures may be incorporated (*entreprises sous contrôle conjoint*) or unincorporated (*Sociétés en Participation*).

Companies jointly controlled by a limited number of shareholders are accounted for by the proportional consolidation method. Joint control could depend on an equal split of voting rights among venturers, but also on the existence of a contractual agreement providing that decisions in all areas essential to the accomplishment of the goals of the joint venture require consent of all the venturers.

Jointly controlled operations are conducted under a specific structure (*Société en Participation*) without legal existence. The venturers in charge of negotiating transactions with third parties are required to record such transactions as if they were achieved solely in their name. The net result of the joint venture is then allocated to the other venturers by use of specific accounts provided by the General Accounting Plan (*quote part de résultats sur opérations faites en commun*).

When venturers contribute assets to a joint venture without legal existence, they retain official ownership of those assets, which they must carry on their balance sheet at full historical cost. Conversely, assets that are undividedly owned by the venturers (for instance, assets purchased or created by the joint venture) are capitalised by each venturer according to its percentage interest in the joint venture.

The contribution of assets to a joint venture in exchange for an interest in the joint venture does not give rise to a gain or loss on disposal in the contributor's financial statements. Gains resulting from other transactions between the venturer and the joint venture should be recognised only to the extent of the interests of non-related venturers. However, losses should be recognised in their entirety.

Generally accepted accounting principles apply to incorporated joint ventures. Accounts of unincorporated joint ventures exist only for the use of venturers and for tax purposes.

For purposes of disclosure, jointly controlled entities included in consolidated accounts of the venturer must be identified, together with the method of consolidation used (normally the proportional consolidation method) and the percentage interest owned. Venturers in unincorporated joint ventures need only mention commitments with respect to the other venturers.

Principles for Specific Items

Property, plant and equipment (immobilisations corporelles)

In general, fixed assets are stated at historical cost less accumulated depreciation. Assets acquired for valuable consideration are stated at cost, including incidental purchasing costs. Self-constructed assets are stated at production cost, which may include capitalised interest, where applicable. Assets acquired in non-cash transactions to the company are stated at fair value at date of acquisition.

In 1945, 1959 and 1976 French corporations were permitted to perform a legal revaluation of assets, and the accounts of some companies may still include items carried at revalued amounts. Discretionary ('free') revaluations have been permitted since 1 January 1984, but only if all classes of property, plant and equipment and investments are revalued. The gain derived from the revaluation may not be credited to income but must be recorded as a separate component of shareholders' equity ('free revaluation reserve'). The reserve may be incorporated into capital stock but may not be written back to income at any time in the future. The reserve adjustment is subject to corporate income tax in the year in which the revaluation is performed. Upon sale of the revalued assets, a transfer to distributable reserves is not allowed.

Expenditure incurred to maintain assets in normal working condition until the end of their useful lives is expensed whilst expenditure that significantly increases the value of an asset or extends an asset's useful life is capitalised.

Two methods of calculating depreciation are used:

- **Book depreciation**   reflects the irreversible decline in value of an asset due to wear and tear, technological advances and so on. In practice, book depreciation involves writing down the value of an asset over its estimated useful life, until the asset is entirely depreciated or reduced to its residual value, depending on the asset, according to a predetermined depreciation schedule. Accumulated depreciation is shown in the balance sheet as a reduction of the carrying value of the asset, and the depreciation charge (*dotation aux amortissements*) for the year is included in the income statement. The asset's estimated useful life is determined by management, based on past experience and industry practice. No specific depreciation method is recommended or prohibited but, in practice, the most common methods are straight-line (*linéaire*) and reducing balance (*dégressif*);
- **Excess fiscal depreciation** (*amortissements dérogatoires*) charges depreciation solely to reduce the corporation's tax liability. Accumulated fiscal depreciation is included in shareholders' equity under the heading untaxed provisions (*provisions réglementées*), and the related charge for the year is classified as a non-recurring expense in the income statement.

Temporary impairments in the carrying value of a fixed asset may be recognised through a provision for depreciation, which is deducted from the asset value. Reversals are written back to income.

Intangible assets (immobilisations incorporelles)

In general the following items are recorded as intangible assets:

- start-up costs (ie incorporation expense and share capital issuance costs) that are essential to the existence, business or development of the entity but not attributable to the production of specific goods or services;
- internal and external research and development expenditures, which may be capitalised in certain cases;
- licences, patents, trade marks, manufacturing processes and similar items, consisting of costs incurred to obtain the benefit represented by the legal protection granted to the inventor, author or holder of the right to exploit a patent, licence and so on;
- leasehold rights (*droit au bail*), which are amounts paid or due to a previous tenant as consideration for the transfer of a lease under a private agreement or the terms of legislation governing business property;
- purchased goodwill (*fonds de commerce*), representing the intangible components of a business (eg clientele) that are not valued and accounted for separately in the balance sheet but that contribute to maintaining or developing the company's business;
- purchased and internally developed software (*logiciels*) for internal use.

Intangible assets are generally valued in accordance with the same principles as property, plant and equipment, that is, acquisition cost or production cost in the case of software and research and development expenditures. However, intangible assets may not be revalued, although internally generated goodwill could have been created under the 1976 legal revaluation.

In principle, intangible assets are amortised if they have a finite useful life or are legally protected for a specified period. Intangibles that are deemed to have an infinite useful life, such as trade marks and purchased goodwill, are not required to be amortised but any impairment in value should be recorded.

Leases (contrats de location)

Leases are classified differently in the statutory financial statements and the consolidated financial statements. In the statutory financial statements, all leases are treated as operating leases, whereas in the consolidated financial statements, finance leases may be capitalised.

French law does not define finance leases, but they are generally understood to represent leases under which ownership is transferred at the end of the lease term, leases containing a bargain purchase option, leases whose term is equivalent to the useful life of the leased property or leases of which the present value of the minimum lease payments is equal to the fair value of the leased property at inception of the lease.

The lease payments of operating leases are expensed by the lessee and credited to income by the lessor in the period to which they relate. As regards finance leases, the lessee records an asset and a debt, and the lease payments are allocated between interest expense and a reduction of debt. The lessor records a receivable, and the lease payments are allocated between interest income and a reduction of the receivable.

Investments (placements)

Investments, depending on their nature, are classified as current or non-current.

Current investments (marketable securities) are investments that management intends to dispose of within a short time. They are stated at whichever is lower: cost or probable transaction value. The latter is defined for quoted investments as the investment's average market value for the final month of the accounting period; for unquoted investments, it is determined judgementally. Provisions for declines in value are determined on an individual line-by-line basis. However, there are two situations where investments may be valued on an aggregate (portfolio) basis: firstly, if the investments are quoted and constitute a highly liquid portfolio and, secondly, if market values have fallen abnormally and this decline appears to be temporary.

Non-current investments are stated at cost or their useful value to the investor, whichever is lower. The latter is determined judgementally. Non-current investments are valued individually line by line and may not be valued on a portfolio basis. As explained above, a decline in the value of non-current investments is provided for, but unrealised gains are not recognised. Investments cannot be revalued upwardly. However, there is one exception to this principle; it concerns investments in companies under the control of a parent company that prepares consolidated financial statements. These investments can be valued in the parent company's individual financial statements on the basis of its share in the underlying net assets (equity method); the difference arising from an upward adjustment of the share in net assets is not credited to income (and therefore not tax-effected) but is recorded as a separate component of shareholders' equity. However, if the parent company's share in net assets is adjusted downwardly, the difference is first applied to any reserve relating to a previous upward adjustment of the same investment and then charged against income. Companies that elect to use this method must apply it to all investments in companies over which they exercise control.

Accounts receivable (créances)

Receivables are normally recorded net of trade discounts. Cash discounts are normally recorded at the time of payment.

No specific method is stipulated in determining a provision for doubtful accounts. General provisions are rare, and specific provisions tend to be calculated only in extreme cases. The reason for this lack of a consistent, general practice is the historical link in France between accounting treatment and treatment for tax purposes, which tended to permit a deduction only in cases of pending or proven receivership/liquidation. The position is evolving.

Under French law, factoring is an arrangement that leads to a real transfer of the risk of non-payment to the factor. Consequently, the trade receivables transferred are immediately removed from the accounts, and the related expenses and financing commission deducted by the factor are simultaneously charged against profit.

Inventories and work in progress (stocks et en-cours)

Inventories are carried at whichever is lower: cost or either realisable value or replacement cost. This comparison should be made on an item-by-item basis. Only two methods of determining cost are permitted for statutory financial statements: weighted average and FIFO (First In First Out). For certain consolidated financial statements the LIFO (Last In First Out) method can be used. If inventories are manufactured, costs are determined using absorption costing principles. If the actual level of activity for the period is less than the normal rate, costs are imputed as if production were at normal operating levels; the excess overhead is expensed.

Current liabilities (dettes à court terme)

Current liabilities are not shown separately in the balance sheet. However, in the notes, debts are disclosed separately by maturity under the headings, 'due beyond one year and within five years', and 'due beyond five years'.

In the statutory balance sheet, liabilities are separated into the following classes, which may be combined in the consolidated balance sheet:

- customer advances;
- accounts payable-trade (*dettes fournisseurs comptes rattachés*), including accruals for goods received but not yet invoiced and net of accruals for credit notes and discounts (representing debts arising in the normal course of business);
- accrued taxes, social security taxes and personnel costs;
- other debts;
- deferred income (*produits constatés d'avance*).

Long-term Debt (dettes à long terme)

As mentioned above, debts are not separated in the balance sheet between long and short term, but total current items and total non-current items are shown below the balance sheet total and a more detailed analysis is given in the notes. Similarly, bank overdrafts and short-term borrowings (*concours bancaires courants*) are included in bank borrowings (*emprunts et dettes auprès des établissements de crédit*) in the balance sheet, but the total is also indicated under the balance sheet total.

Debts are shown in the balance sheet by type (although certain items may be combined in the consolidated balance sheet) as follows: convertible bonds (*emprunts obligataires convertibles*), other bonds (*autres emprunts obligataires*), bank borrowings, and other debts. Interest accrued at the period-end is included under the above headings.

Loans are always carried in the balance sheet at their outstanding principal amount. Bond redemption premiums (*primes de remboursement des obligations*) are included in assets and amortised pro rata to accrued interest or by the straight-line method over the life of the loan.

There are no specific accounting principles related to debt restructuring. Normal practice consists of recording the resulting gains or losses in income at the time of the restructuring.

For accounting purposes, a debt is considered extinguished when it has been repaid in full or has been subject to an in-substance defeasance. An in-substance defeasance must meet two conditions to be recorded: the transfer of the debt to the trustee must be irrevocable, and the securities transferred must be used solely to service the debt. The latter must be denominated in the same currency as the debt and the due dates for principal and interest payments must match those of the debt.

Commissions paid in connection with an in-substance defeasance and the difference between the value of the securities and the amount of the debt on the defeasance date are included in non-recurring items.

Contingencies (éventualités)

Contingent losses are provided for when the specific exposure or loss is clearly identifiable, or when the probability of the exposure or loss occurring results from events in progress at the year-end or are known by management at the time of the year-end closing. If the loss or exposure is not certain, general provisions for contingencies or provisions based on past experience may be set up.

Contingent gains are not recognised in the financial statements.

Capital and reserves (capitaux propres)

Shareholders' equity is generally divided between share capital (*capital social*), premiums (*primes*), revaluation reserves (*réserves de réévaluation*) and other reserves.

The share capital (number of shares and par value) must be indicated in the company's articles of incorporation. At least one-quarter of the par value of the shares must be paid up for the shares to be considered subscribed. The share capital included in equity always corresponds to the subscribed capital; any uncalled (ie unpaid) fraction is shown on the asset side of the balance sheet. A company may acquire its own shares to cancel them or to stabilise the price quoted on the stock market or for allocation to employees, for example, under stock option plans.

Premiums represent the difference between the par value of shares and the price at which they are issued. The issue price must be at least equal to the par value. When a company acquires its own shares to cancel them, the difference between the price paid and the par value of the shares is charged to premiums first and to reserves for the excess. The proceeds derived from the issue of unattached warrants (*bons autonomes de souscription*) are also included in premiums. However, if the warrants are attached to bonds, the proceeds are included in debt.

Revaluation reserves result from the revaluation of fixed assets or investments as described above.

Other reserves include:

- the legal reserve (*réserve légale*) – each year, 5 per cent of net income must be appropriated to the legal reserve until the reserve equals 10 per cent of share capital;

- untaxed reserves (*réserves réglementées*) – untaxed reserves primarily include income taxed at a reduced rate; if the reserves are distributed, additional tax becomes payable;
- other reserves-appropriations to other reserves are decided by the shareholders;
- special translation reserve (*écarts de conversion*) in the consolidated balance sheet, which is created only on consolidation, includes differences arising on translation of the financial statements of consolidated foreign subsidiaries.

Investment subsidies (*subventions d'investissement*) and untaxed provisions (excess fiscal depreciation and special provisions for tax purposes) are included in shareholders' equity in the statutory financial statements. In the consolidated financial statements, these items are restated. This restatement involves reclassifying the investment subsidies and any deferred taxes connected with untaxed provisions as liabilities.

Permanent capital raised on the money markets and repayable at the discretion of the company is classified as near equity (*autres fonds propres*). Near equity is shown on a separate line on the liability side of the balance sheet, between debt and shareholders' equity, if the company does not intend to effect repayment in the foreseeable future. However, in the consolidated balance sheet near equity may be included in shareholders' equity if no interest is payable because the issuer does not report adequate income.

Revenue recognition (constatation des produits)

Revenue is recognised when services have been provided or goods have been delivered. The notion of delivery is generally considered to be the relinquishing of the item sold to the protection and possession of the purchaser. At this point, title to the goods normally transfers to the purchaser, and the vendor recognises the sale as complete.

For long-term contracts (*contrats de longue durée*), revenue may be recognised by either the completed contract method (*méthode de l'achèvement*) or the percentage of completion method (*méthode du pourcentage d'avancement*). For the percentage of completion method to be acceptable, four conditions must be fulfilled: 1) the accounting system must be capable of determining the exact status of work in progress, 2) the purchaser must agree as to the extent of the work carried out, 3) reliable forecast figures concerning the contract must exist, and 4) it must be possible to calculate the overall profit with some degree of certainty. Progress billings are not deducted from work-in-progress in the balance sheet. Losses expected at contract completion should be fully provided for when they become probable.

Instalment sales (*ventes tempérament*) are generally recognised as outright sales when the goods are delivered to the purchaser.

Recognition of revenue from sales where the right of return exists depends largely on the nature of the transaction or industry practice. If the likelihood of return is considered minimal, there would be no reason not to recognise the sale on delivery of the goods. However, it may be considered advisable to set up a provision for returns if prior experience shows that some goods are likely to be returned.

Sales with reservation of title (*ventes avec clause de réserve de propriété*), that is, where the seller retains title to the goods, should be recognised based on commercial substance over legal form. Revenue should be recognised when the goods are delivered, with appropriate disclosure.

Product financing arrangements, which are agreements to sell a product and to buy it back at a later date, are not specifically dealt with in French standards. However, in this case legal form would take precedence over substance, and the transaction would be treated as a sale and not as a financing transaction.

Government grants and assistance (subventions et aides publiques)

Government grants and assistance are classified into two categories and the accounting treatment is different for each.

Operating subsidies (*subventions d'exploitation*), which are grants to promote the creation of new employment and to promote research, are included in operating revenues when received; however, recognition may be deferred if the funds are used to finance capitalised research expenditures.

Investment subsidies (*subventions d'investissement*), which are used to finance part of the cost of additions to fixed assets, may be either included in non-recurring income when received or recorded as a separate component of shareholders' equity in the statutory accounts or as a non-current liability in the consolidated accounts and written back to income to match the depreciation charged on the corresponding fixed assets.

Research and development (frais de recherche et développement)

Research and development expenditures are defined as expenditures for work carried out by a company on its own behalf in the areas of basic and applied research and experimental development. This definition excludes expenses incorporated in the production cost of products ordered by third parties, which are normally expensed or included in work in progress.

Research and development expenditures are normally expensed as incurred. However, as mentioned previously in this chapter, research and development expenditures may be capitalised as intangible assets if the project is clearly defined and the costs attributed to it can be identified, and the technical or commercial feasibility of the product or process has been established.

Capitalised research and development expenditures must normally be amortised over a maximum of five years. There are no clearly established rules concerning the starting date for amortization; consequently, amortization may be charged either from the date on which the expenditure is capitalised or from the date on which the product or process is first marketed or used.

If the project subsequently proves to be unsuccessful, the unamortised capitalised costs are written off immediately as a non-recurring expense. Once written off, expenditures should not be reinstated, even if the situation reverses.

Capitalised interest costs (incorporation de charges financières à des éléments d'actif)

Inventory   If the production cycle exceeds 12 months (this specific condition does not apply to consolidated financial statements), the interest cost on funds borrowed to finance production may be included in the value of inventory. In practice, this principle applies only to a very limited number of industry segments (such as construction).

Property, plant and equipment   Interest costs incurred during the construction period of self-constructed assets and assets manufactured by subcontractors may be capitalised. However, the capitalised interest cost may not exceed the total interest expense incurred by the company during the period.

Extraordinary or unusual items (éléments exceptionnels ou inhabituels)

Under French accounting standards, all events that do not relate to the day-to-day operation of the business are classified as exceptional or non-recurring (*résultat exceptionnel*). This definition is very broad and includes both non-recurring items and extraordinary or unusual items outside the ordinary operations of the reporting entity. In particular, non-recurring income and expense includes all forms of penalties paid or received, gains and losses on disposals of fixed assets, and subsidies granted.

Whatever the amount involved, non-recurring items are reported in the non-recurring income and expense section of the income statement. No distinction is made in the income statement between tax on non-recurring items and tax on continuing operations.

Foreign currency translation (conversion monétaire)

Foreign currency denominated transactions are translated at the transaction date exchange rate, and foreign currency monetary items outstanding at the balance sheet date are revalued at the balance sheet date spot rate.

In the statutory financial statements, unrealised losses are generally charged against income; unrealised gains are deferred. If a loan is taken out in a foreign currency to finance the acquisition of property, plant and equipment or an equity investment, any unrealised loss can be written off over the life of the loan. Unrealised gains may be netted against unrealised losses on foreign currency transactions in comparable currencies with comparable due dates.

In consolidated financial statements, companies may choose to include unrealised gains in income immediately, together with unrealised losses.

With regard to foreign operations, if a foreign operation is autonomous, its assets and liabilities are translated at the year-end exchange rate, and income and expenses are translated at either the year-end rate or the average rate for the year, whichever is more appropriate. The resulting translation differences are recorded as a separate component of shareholders' equity.

If a foreign operation is not autonomous and is influenced by the reporting company or if it is located in a hyper-inflationary country, the monetary items in its balance sheet are translated at the year-end exchange rate and non-monetary items are translated at the historical rate. Income and expense items are translated at the average exchange rate for the year. The resulting translation differences are recorded directly in income.

A transaction is classified as a hedge of a foreign currency exposure only if there is a firm, clearly identified commitment and the transaction effectively eliminates any exchange risk. The hedged debt or receivable is translated at the forward exchange rate, and the difference between this rate and the historical rate is recorded directly in income.

With regard to disclosure, the notes should include the following information on open hedging positions at the year-end: type of transaction hedged (asset, liability, off balance sheet item), type of market on which the position has been taken (organised market, over-the-counter market) and impact on income of positions taken during the year. Details concerning the method used to translate the financial statements of foreign subsidiaries should also be given in the notes to the consolidated financial statements.

Income taxes (impôts sur les bénéfices)

Income taxes are treated differently in the statutory financial statements and the consolidated financial statements:

- **Statutory financial statements** Present French accounting principles require only current taxes (ie the amount currently payable) to be recorded. In particular, the only tax losses that may give rise to the recognition of a deferred tax asset are those effectively eligible for carry-back under French tax rules. In such cases, the tax credit is accounted for in the year in which the loss in incurred.
- **Consolidated financial statements** Deferred taxes are recorded in the consolidated financial statements. Companies may choose between the deferral method (*méthode du report fixe*) and the liability method (*méthode du report variable*) and between partial and full recognition of timing differences.

The future tax benefits attributable to tax loss carry forwards may be recognised if it is probable that they will be realised. Reasonable probability is deemed to exist if:

- the losses can be offset against deferred tax liabilities; or
- the losses correspond to an exceptional, non-recurring loss and there is a strong probability that the company will earn profits in the future.

Post-retirement benefits (prestations de retraite)

Two types of pension plan exist in France: defined contribution plans which are always externally funded (may be compulsory – government-sponsored plans – or voluntary – initiated by the employer); and defined benefit plans which may be funded internally or externally (provide for the payment of either a life annuity or a lump sum upon retirement).

Defined contribution plans are funded by contributions made by both employees and employers based on current salaries. Employers' contributions are expensed when paid. Substantially all pension costs incurred by French companies are for defined contribution plans that are government sponsored.

In the absence of specific rules for defined benefit plans, common practice is to distinguish between liabilities relating to retired employees, which are provided for, and commitments for employees who have not yet reached retirement age, which may or may not be provided for, at the discretion of the company. Provisions for pensions are calculated based on actuarial assumptions. The most common method used to provide for commitments for employees who have not yet reached retirement age is the accrued benefit method, pro-rated based on years of service.

The effect of changes in actuarial assumptions and the adoption of new plans on past service costs can be deferred and amortised over the expected average remaining service life of the employee group concerned.

Changes in accounting policies and other items affecting prior years (changements de principes comptables)

The effects of an event which impacts prior year results should be recorded in the profit and loss account for the year in which the event arises as an exceptional item (in accordance with the principle that the opening balance sheet must agree with the closing balance sheet at the end of the previous period). The only changes whose effects on opening balances can be shown as an adjustment to opening stockholders' equity (retroactive restatement) are those changes made compulsory by a change in the accounting regulations, or a limited number of changes which result in an improved presentation of the accounts.

With regard to disclosure, changes in accounting principles should be described and explained in a note. The effect of the change on income should be shown as a non-recurring (exceptional) item and explained in the notes, if necessary. The effect of changes in accounting estimates should be included in operating income.

With regard to the timing of events, for conditions existing at the balance sheet date, the financial statements must be adjusted if the amount of the risk or loss can be reasonably estimated. For conditions arising after the balance sheet date, the financial statements should not be adjusted.

For conditions existing at the balance sheet date, if the financial statements have not been adjusted, a note should indicate the type of event and the reason a reasonable estimate of the risk or the amount of the loss cannot be made; if the financial statements have been adjusted, disclosure is not compulsory, but material adjustments are normally described in a note.

Conditions arising after the balance sheet date that are likely to affect the company's ability to continue to operate as a going concern must be disclosed in a note; otherwise, disclosure is recommended but not compulsory.

Discontinued operations (arrêts d'activité)

There is no prescribed accounting method for discontinued operations in France. However, in practice the total net cost resulting from a business closure or the reorganisation of a business segment is normally recognised when the decision to discontinue operations is made. The net cost includes probable losses on the sale or scrapping of fixed assets (net of related gains), operating expenses up to the date of closure or reorganisation and the cost of any planned lay-offs.

Earnings per share (résultats par action)

There is no formal accounting standard prescribing the disclosure of earnings per share in the financial statements. However, this information must be given in the schedule included in the report of the board of directors summarising the company's business results for the past five years. Earnings per share are generally computed by dividing net income by the number of shares outstanding.

If a company has issued warrants, diluted earnings per share must be disclosed in a note. There is no prescribed method for calculating diluted earnings per share. At present, earnings per share information is not disclosed by all French corporations.

Related party transactions (opérations entre parties liées)

The Business Code and the Fourth and Seventh EC Directives define related parties as:

- the dominant entity (parent company);
- dependent entities – that is, entities controlled, either directly or indirectly, by the parent company; or
- associated companies, over which the parent company exercises significant influence, either directly or indirectly.

For directors and board members, the following specific disclosures are required:

- total remuneration;
- loans and credit commitments.

French accounting law does not include any provisions concerning the accounting treatment of related party transactions. However, it is recommended that balances deriving from transactions with related parties be shown on a separate line of the balance sheet. Where it is considered essential, the following information should also be disclosed:

- proportion of investments, debts, receivables, interest income and expense concerning related parties;
- amount of financial commitments given to or received from related parties.

Segmental information (informations sectorielles)

French companies are required to disclose net sales by industry and geographical segment. If a company does not wish to disclose certain segmental information on the grounds that it would be damaging to its business interests, the relevant note should stipulate the reason for which the information is not provided. In addition, public companies must publish quarterly consolidated sales by industry segment.

French accounting law does not define industry or geographical segments. Corporations should therefore use judgement in deciding the basis to be used in presenting the information. However, the General Accounting Plan stipulates that the disclosure is necessary only if the company operates in several very dissimilar industries or markets. A segment may be considered to be sufficiently important to require disclosure if it represents more than 10 per cent of sales, operating income or total assets.

SIGNIFICANT DIFFERENCES IN BASIC ACCOUNTING PRINCIPLES

The accounting principles discussed differ significantly from those in the UK or under international practice. Table 21.1 summarises the differences.

Table 21.1 Summary of significant differences in basic accounting principles

	France	UK	IAS
Intangible fixed assets			
Capitalisation	Licences, patents and trade marks covered by legal protection, leasehold rights, purchased goodwill, purchased and internally developed software for internal use can be capitalised. Internal and external R&D costs can be capitalised under specific conditions.	It is permissible to capitalise concessions, patents, licences, trade marks and similar rights and assets, if they are created by the company as intangible fixed assets and the historical cost can be determined. Expenditure on pure and applied research costs should be written off. Development costs may be capitalised, provided that specific conditions are met.	Generally conforms with UK GAAP (Generally Accepted Accounting Principles). However capitalisation of development expenses is *required* when specific conditions are met.
Expenses incurred in starting up or expanding a business	Start up expenses and business expansion may be capitalised if they are essential to the existence of the entity.	Expenses incurred in starting up or expanding a business may not be capitalised.	Generally in conformity with UK GAAP.
Goodwill	In statutory accounts, goodwill is not required to be amortised but any impairment in value should be recorded. On consolidation, goodwill is amortised over its useful life.	Normally immediately written off against reserves but, if capitalised, goodwill should be amortised systematically through the profit and loss account, over its useful economic life. A new accounting standard, FRS 10, will become effective from 1998 which requires capitalisation and amortisation of goodwill and prohibits immediate write off to reserves.	Goodwill amortised over its useful economic life.
Tangible fixed assets			
Cost	Historical cost concept. Legal revaluation was permitted in 1945, 1959 and 1976.	Revaluation possible (particularly for land buildings).	Historical cost concept alternatively revaluation permitted.

Depreciation	All depreciation claimed for tax purposes (including reducing balance and accelerated depreciation) must be reflected in the commercial financial statements. Excess fiscal depreciation is included in the shareholders' equity.	Reducing balance method permitted but not widely used. Accelerated depreciation for tax purposes not permitted in the financial statements.	Depreciation for tax purposes not permitted.
Finance leases	*Statutory accounts* Leases treated as operating leases (charged in the profit and loss account). *Consolidated accounts* Finance leases may be capitalised.	Capitalisation by the economic owner based on a series of tests.	Similar, but test criteria differ significantly from UK GAAP.
Investments	Historical cost concept. It is generally not permitted to revalue fixed asset investments above cost – they should be carried at cost less provision for diminution in value compared to market value or equity/share value. Unrealised gains are not recognised.	Alternatively investments may be stated at revalued amounts (market value/current cost).	Alternatively investments may be stated at revalued amounts; for investments associates, equity accounting should be used.

Current assets

Inventories *Purchase or manufacturing cost*	Average cost and FIFO are allowed for statutory accounts. LIFO is permitted only in consolidated accounts.	LIFO not usually acceptable.	LIFO method is permitted but average method and FIFO are preferred.
Revaluation	Stocks may not be valued above cost (alternative accounting rules not permitted).	Where a company adopts alternative accounting rules, stocks may be included at current cost.	Historical cost concept
Lower of cost or market value	At the lower of cost or either realisable value or replacement cost.	Net realisable value test only uses the selling price as the basis for market value.	Generally in conformity with UK GAAP.
Long-term contracts	Either the completed contract method, or the percentage of completion method, provided that specific conditions are met.	Use of the percentage of completion method unless information as to cost or progress is unreliable, in which case the completed contract method may used.	Percentage of completion method is used. Where outcome cannot be estimated reliably, revenue should be recognised equal to the contract costs expended.

Table 21.1 *continued*

	France	UK	IAS
Liabilities			
Accruals for future repairs and maintenance	Certain accruals must be set up and others can be set up depending on various conditions.	Generally not permitted.	Generally not permitted.
Pension accruals	Pension costs may, on occasions, be recognised only when benefits are effectively paid, with the corresponding commitments explained in the notes to the financial statements.	Funded system: actuarial expertise is required to determine an appropriate level of contributions to fund the obligations.	Generally similar to GAAP.
Deferred taxes	*Statutory accounts* Only current taxes. *Consolidated accounts* Possible choice between the deferral method and the liability method, and between partial and full recognition of time differences. Future tax benefits attributable to tax loss carry forwards may be recognized in cases of reasonable probability of occurrence.	A deferred tax asset should be recognised unless recovery is not assured. Partial liability method (it must be probable that a tax asset or liability will materialise in the foreseeable future).	Full liability method only.

Part Five

Mergers and Acquisitions

21

Acquiring in France

John Hadley and Sabine Durand,
Corporate Finance, PricewaterhouseCoopers

INTRODUCTION

Surveys have indicated many reasons why companies choose the acquisition route to expansion. Where the parties involved are of differing nationalities, access to new markets is often the key factor.

Anglo-Saxon investors have long viewed France as the prime continental European location for acquisitions, due to its key economic role in Europe. The USA and the UK have made the most acquisitions in France over the last few years. Data for 1996 is set out in Table 21.1. Overall, the number of acquisitions by foreign acquirors has increased significantly since 1993 following the general trend in mergers and acquisitions over the period, as shown in Table 21.2.

In this chapter, we provide an overview of the acquisition process. Certain aspects are handled in greater detail in other chapters of this section.

We do not seek to describe the different steps involved in the acquisition of a French company as these are to a large extent similar to those in the rest of the world. We seek, however, to highlight matters which, from our experience in France, foreign purchasers have found different from their own country practice and contrary to their expectations. As many foreign purchasers establish an initial presence in France by way of a minority participation in an existing business, as a prelude to taking control, we also set out some of the key considera-

Table 21.1 Acquisitions by foreign acquirors in 1996

Country	Total Value (millions of francs)	Number	Average Value (millions of francs)
USA	30,452	63	483
UK	28,872	41	704
Switzerland	24,370	15	1,625
Belgium	22,538	18	1,252
Germany	14,340	34	422
Acquirors from several countries	10,272	15	685
Italy	5,935	20	297
Netherlands	4,217	22	192
Canada	3,400	14	243
Japan	3,313	9	368
Other	8,556	52	165
	156,265	303	516

Source: *Fusions & Acquisitions,* January 1997

tions to be borne in mind when purchasing less than 100 per cent of a French company's share capital.

At the outset it is useful to understand that the French attitude to company acquisitions and disposals has traditionally been different from that in Anglo-Saxon countries. Deals used to be concluded quickly, with little investigation or due diligence on targets, and with brief sale and purchase contracts restricted to the essentials of the transaction. This practice could be commercially justified when the particular market or sector was small, the parties knew each other well (particularly where there was a French vendor and purchaser) and any dispute could be easily settled.

This is now changing. More and more foreign purchasers, particularly British and American, have been entering the French market by way of acquisition, resulting in not only an increase in the number of acquisitions, but also in the gradual introduction of 'Anglo-Saxon' perceptions and methods of acquisition. As a result the practices mentioned above, although still present, have become increasingly difficult for French vendors to justify successfully to their foreign purchasers.

We have chosen to compare and contrast the following aspects of acquiring in France with Anglo-Saxon practice:

Table 21.2 Number of acquisitions by foreign acquirors 1993 to 1996

Year	Total Value (millions of francs)	Number	Average Value (millions of francs)
1996	156,265	303	516
1995	84,871	247	344
1994	106,912	215	497
1993	40,934	140	292

Source: *Fusions & Acquisitions,* January 1997

- available public information;
- acquisition process;
- acquisition price;
- due diligence procedures;
- financial and accounting information;
- acquisition structure: purchase of shares vs assets, merger;
- form and content of contracts;
- labour legislation;
- cultural differences.

AVAILABLE PUBLIC INFORMATION

Gathering key information concerning the target company is an essential part of the acquisition process. Such information includes the target's competitive position (products, markets, principal customers, etc), the names of its directors and managers, key financial data and ownership structure. The majority of this information is publicly available in France and Anglo-Saxon countries. It is derived from company accounts submitted to the authorities (such as the Trade and Companies Registry, the Land Registry and the National Institute for Intellectual Property), reports and articles published in the press, and market surveys and other research conducted by industry specialists.

It should be noted, however, that data available in Anglo-Saxon countries is generally more comprehensive and reliable than it is in France. There appear to be three major factors behind this:

- quoted companies are more numerous in Anglo-Saxon countries and have to provide much more information to investors on their performance, business environment and the markets that they serve than do unquoted companies;
- in Anglo-Saxon countries, the provision to investors of information on quoted companies is a business in its own right, with teams of financial analysts churning out volumes of reports;

- equally, there are many more Anglo-Saxon companies involved in the provision of market research.

As a result, a potential French acquiror can gain more insight into a foreign target than an Anglo-Saxon acquiror can in France. This gap, however, is gradually narrowing.

ACQUISITION PROCESS

Anglo-Saxon and French companies involved in a major acquisition will probably use the advisory services of an investment bank.The acquisition process in France nevertheless differs markedly from the approach adopted in Anglo-Saxon countries, particularly in respect of the role of advisors in acquisitions involving small- and medium-sized enterprises (SMEs).

Anglo-Saxon SMEs tend to use their own accountants/auditors to advise them throughout the acquisition process. Where this is the case, their role may include valuing the target company, handling the related negotiations, drafting the offer letter and performing due diligence procedures. Anglo-Saxon clients often seek the advice of their accountants/auditors at each stage of the process, not limiting their role to the provision of financial data. For example, in the UK and the USA, the corporate finance departments of the 'big six' audit and consulting firms are involved in more than 100 transactions each, per annum.

On the other hand, French acquirors tend to seek external advice only for the specific aspects of the transaction that they cannot cover themselves (for example, the review of the financial accounts, the drafting of the legal contracts).

This Anglo-Saxon approach to working with advisors has begun to be increasingly used by the French in recent years resulting in a similar development of corporate finance activities by some of the 'big six' firms in France. For example, due to the development of 'lead advisory' services in our firm, specialised sector teams now exist in London, Paris and New York, covering financial services, the pharmaceutical industry, retail, computer services, and the automobile industry.

An example of the role of the accountants/auditors for a foreign acquiror in France that we encountered, illustrates this point. We initially provided information limited to French accounting rules, but were then required by the foreign acquiror to give advice on the acquisition contract and subsequently on the structure of the offer. The

French vendor was later surprised to learn that the structure of the offer had been suggested by the foreign investor's accountants/auditors, while its own accountants/auditors' role had been confined to the provision of financial information.

ACQUISITION PRICE

One of the key issues in any acquisition is arriving at a price that is acceptable to both the acquiror and seller. We have observed that in transactions between French and Anglo-Saxon players, differences between the valuation methods used by the two parties can often lead to problems.

An Anglo-Saxon acquiror generally values the target company using the latter's forecast profits. If the acquiror is a quoted company, it is often unwilling to pay a price which would dilute its own earnings. Unquoted companies likewise are often not prepared to pay a price corresponding to an earnings multiple higher than that paid for comparable companies.

The quality of the target company's net assets is treated as a secondary consideration, unless the acquiror has to inject new capital. This view partly reflects the fact that goodwill is usually not a major issue for Anglo-saxon acquirors. This used to be particularly the case for UKacquirors who could write off goodwill in full against reserves, without any impact on the profit and loss account.

In comparison, French acquirors often pay particular attention to the net asset value of the proposed acquiree, and particularly to the difference between the acquisition cost and the target's net book value, as French GAAP stipulates that goodwill arising on an acquisition must be written off against future profits over its estimated life. French acquirors can, therefore, be reluctant to pay amounts significantly higher than the target's net asset value, even if the proposed acquiree is expected to realise substantial profits.

This difference in approach may be reduced in the future as UK accounting rules have changed recently and goodwill has now to be amortised against future profits over its estimated life as is the case in France. The International Accounting Standard Committee (IASC) is presently preparing an accounting standard concerning the treatment of goodwill on acquisition to be published by June 1999.

DUE DILIGENCE PROCEDURES

Another important difference between Anglo-Saxon and French investors can be the nature and scope of work performed to investigate the proposed target.

The need for adequate due diligence procedures, an Anglo-Saxon concept, is rapidly being accepted in continental Europe. It is impossible, however, to establish precise limits for the nature and scope of a due diligence because these depend on factors such as the transaction risks to which the acquiror is exposed and a wide range of other factors.

In practice, however, Anglo-Saxon acquirors tend to initiate broader due diligence procedures than their French counterparts in a transaction with similar risks. The procedures generally include research into the target's markets, customers and products, an assessment of the target's manufacturing plant, environmental issues, employee and management issues, and, of course, an analysis of the target's financial, tax and legal position.

Another difference in the acquisition culture is that Anglo-Saxon acquirors generally initiate the major portion of due diligence procedures before entering into a contractual undertaking to acquire the proposed target. Furthermore, the acquiror may seek to revise its purchase offer based on the findings of the due diligence and will usually wish to negotiate appropriate cover to be incorporated in the seller's warranty in the sale agreement, where appropriate.

For French companies, the nature and purpose of due diligence procedures are not always clear. For the typical French company, due diligence procedures often comprise an audit, traditionally limited to an analysis of the target's financial, tax and legal position. While the Anglo-Saxon investor expects to be given a great deal of information and to have access to the target company's management before the sale agreement has been signed, the French seller often wishes due diligence procedures to be implemented only after a contractual undertaking or binding offer has been made to purchase his company.

This differing interpretation of the due diligence concept is often a source of problems when an Anglo-Saxon company seeks to acquire a French company. At the same time, a French investor wishing to acquire an Anglo-Saxon company often benefits from the vast pool of data usually provided to potential investors by Anglo-Saxon enterprises.

It is therefore advisable at the outset of the transaction (in the letter of intent for instance) to set out clearly the nature of the information and documents which the purchaser wishes to be supplied with or have access to for the purposes of his due diligence. This may help to avoid subsequent problems as French vendors are not always aware of the degree of disclosure expected by a foreign purchaser.

FINANCIAL AND ACCOUNTING INFORMATION

A review of the extent and relevance of the financial information produced by the target company is usually a significant feature of a due diligence.

In Anglo-Saxon countries, the periodic publication of reliable financial information has long been given high priority, reflecting the key role played by finance directors in most Anglo-Saxon companies and the importance of external sources of funds (shareholders other than senior management, banks and other financial institutions). Anglo-Saxon companies are therefore accustomed to producing monthly financial statements within tight deadlines, together with annual budgets and other long-term projections.

On the other hand, French accounting rules and, more particularly, the prescribed format for the presentation of financial statements, are traditionally determined by laws and ministerial decrees. In addition, French accounting practice has long been strongly influenced by corporation tax rules, the primary consequence of which has been that provisions are often recorded up to the maximum amount deductible for tax purposes. Similarly, tangible fixed assets are generally depreciated over a shorter period than their economic lives in order to derive maximum tax benefits.

The presentation of monthly management accounts and annual budgets, with a distinction being made between information produced for the management accounts and that produced for the tax accounts, is now widespread in France. The Anglo-Saxon acquiror can nevertheless still expect to be given less extensive and up-to-date management information concerning a French company than a French investor acquiring an Anglo-Saxon country.

ACQUISITION STRUCTURE: PURCHASE OF SHARES VS ASSETS, MERGER

Companies are generally acquired through the purchase of their shares, possibly followed by a merger, which is a simpler way to acquire control of a business than through the purchase of assets. The latter route may be taken, however, if, for example the target is involved in serious litigation and the acquiror does not wish to be associated with this liability.

The choice between acquiring a company's shares or assets is likewise influenced by the treatment of such transactions for tax purposes. Generally the French tax regime can be said to discourage the acquisition of corporate assets in that the related registration duties are higher than for the purchase of shares. For example, registration duties may be as much as 11.4 per cent for the majority of asset categories if the agreed sale price of the assets (or their market value, if it is higher) exceeds 700,000 fr. In comparison, registration duties on the transfer of the shares of a *Société Anonyme* (Limited Liability Company) are 1 per cent, up to a maximum limit of 20,000 fr.

If considering the acquisition of less than 100 per cent of a French company, a foreign acquiror should be aware of the importance of the various levels of shareholdings in French companies.

The decision-making procedures of a *Société Anonyme* (SA) are divided between shareholders' meetings, the board of directors and the *Président-Directeur Général* (CEO or managing director). A holding of shares in an SA carrying more than 50 per cent of the voting rights enables the shareholder to pass ordinary resolutions, so giving effective control of the company (mainly approval of the accounts, nomination of the Board of Directors, etc). To pass resolutions proposed at extraordinary general meetings of an SA, however, French law requires the favourable vote of at least two-thirds of the shares. The modification of a company's statutes (articles), for example, requires a vote by a two-thirds majority at an annual general meeting). Accordingly, to be a 'blocking minority' of an SA, a shareholding of more than a third of the capital is required. This is not the case of a *Société à Responsabilité Limitée* (SARL) where the majority required to pass resolutions at an extraordinary general meeting is 75 per cent, so that a blocking minority is constituted by a holding of 25 per cent.

French law does not permit these prescribed majorities for shareholder resolutions to be altered; accordingly, for example, the shareholders cannot agree that ordinary resolutions which normally require simple majorities will require, say, the approval of 75 per cent of shareholders.

FORM AND CONTENT OF CONTRACTS

Agreements governing the acquisition of companies differ significantly from one transaction to another, in both their form and content. Two key documents, however, are generally used to set out the key aspects of the deal, namely:

- the memorandum of understanding or letter of intent;
- the acquisition contract.

Although French and Anglo-Saxon companies are both familiar with these documents, the many differences in their form and structure can lead to misunderstandings in cross-border transactions.

In Anglo-Saxon countries, memoranda of understanding are rarely drawn up to link the parties contractually. Their purpose is rather to obtain a moral undertaking, from both parties, to perform the transaction. If a final contract is subsequently signed, it usually follows very closely the terms and conditions defined in the memorandum of understanding. In France, however, letters of intent have traditionally been used to obtain an irrevocable undertaking by the contracting parties.

Additionally, the use of such letters in the context of acquisitions in France must be considered carefully as the 'subject to contract' – 'escape route' does not afford the same protection in France as it may in the UK for instance. If the letter is subject to French law and states the number of shares to be purchased and their price, a French court is likely to consider the letter as a binding offer which, once accepted, will form a definitive purchase agreement between the parties. It is therefore advisable to present the letter as purely a memorandum of understanding and clearly indicate that the suggested terms are intended to be the framework for future negotiations.

The principal terms and conditions of the proposed transaction should always be clearly spelt out in the letter of intent, ie that the offer or the price is subject to due diligence/audit, administrative authorisations before completion, etc. This is because the form of final agreement in France is usually not very different from the letter of intent and a French negotiator is likely to resist any significant new terms or conditions raised during the negotiation of the purchase agreement.

It should also be noted that the letter of intent, even if not a binding purchase agreement, will involve, under French law, an obligation to negotiate in good faith: any party withdrawing from the negotiations may be liable to pay damages if a loss has been suffered by the other party, if negotiations were broken off without prior warning and/or without good reason.

One of the main differences between French and Anglo-Saxon acquisition contracts is that the latter are generally more detailed and therefore longer than French contracts. This is because Anglo-Saxon agreements are designed to record not only the substance of the transaction, but also all the information provided by the parties on which the transaction is based. Any dispute which may arise is therefore resolved by reference to the conditions set forth in the acquisition contract.

French-style contracts, however, tend to be more concise because of the wide body of commercial and civil legislation, which can be referred to. In the event of a dispute between the parties, reference is made not only to the acquisition contract, but also to the various legislative provisions. In practice, however, acquisition contracts between French and Anglo-Saxon parties tend to follow the Anglo-Saxon model, reflecting the fact that the Anglo-Saxon lawyer and his client are not usually conversant with French commercial and civil law.

The approach of a French vendor (and indeed a French purchaser) as regards warranties to be given on the sale of a company remains different from Anglo-Saxon practice. In comparison, French-style warranties are usually much shorter and less comprehensive. However, French vendors often agree to give a general indemnity, called a *garantie de passif*, which is (in concept) extremely favourable for the purchaser and would, therefore, normally be unacceptable to Anglo-Saxon vendors.

Briefly, under a *garantie de passif*, the French vendor undertakes to pay the purchaser an amount equal (or calculated by reference) to any increase in liabilities or any reduction in assets not identified in the relevant balance sheet, and originating prior to the 'balance sheet date'. The vendor will be liable even if the target company did not (or even could not) know at the time of preparing the accounts of the existence of the fact giving rise to the increase of liability or decrease of assets.

When accepted, the *garantie de passif* has such a wide effect that a number of the 'usual' Anglo-Saxon warranties could seem redundant and this point is often raised by French vendors. This is generally countered by arguing that a *garantie de passif* relates to the target company's accounts only and does not cover other matters (ie employees, intellectual property etc) contained in warranties whose purpose is to obtain better knowledge of the target company.

As noted previously, the fact that Anglo-Saxon style warranties call for information and disclosure and that such disclosures can be used to limit the vendor's liability needs also to be explained carefully to French vendors, as this practice is not common in France.

The impact of the acquisition on competition at both a French and an EU level may also be relevant. In France, the monopolies and mergers regulations will apply if, as a result of the acquisition, the parties realise more than 25 per cent of the sales, purchases, or other transactions in the French market (or a substantial part of it) for the products or services concerned. The regulations are also applicable if the combined businesses (including those of companies which have long-term economic links with the parties to the merger) have an aggregate turnover before tax in France in excess of 7 billion fr provided that two of the businesses which are party to the merger each have a turnover of at least 2 billion fr in France. If applicable, approval of the acquisition can be sought from the Ministry of Economy (*Direction Générale de la Concurrence et de la Consommation*). Although there is no obligation to do so, it is advisable to obtain the necessary approval before completing the merger to avoid any difficulties afterwards. In addition, it is also possible to have prior consultation and discussions if clarification or guidance are necessary.

Furthermore, the consent of other relevant competent authorities may also be necessary if the target company carries on certain activities such as banking, insurance, or publishing newspapers.

LABOUR LEGISLATION

One of the key criteria for success in most acquisitions is the ease and speed with which the target's management and employees are integrated into the acquiring group. The integration process is often complicated by differences in work practices, management/employee relations and varying salaries and benefits. Although most acquirors strive to smooth out these differences, such action is often more difficult in cross-border transactions.

There are striking differences between labour legislation, employment practices and benefits in kind in France and Anglo-Saxon countries. France has extremely strict labour laws and most employees, whether members of a trade union or not, are covered by collective bargaining agreements. In Anglo-Saxon countries, labour laws are less stringent and have relatively little impact on the job market. In addition, employees covered by collective bargaining agreements are in the minority, their working conditions being determined by individual employment contracts. For example, most Anglo-Saxon acquirors are astonished to discover that senior managers' conditions of employment in France are also covered by national collective bargaining agreements, as opposed to the Anglo-Saxon norm of negotiating senior managers' working conditions on an individual basis.

If the target company employs more than 50 people and the directors of this company are aware of the acquisition, the managing director is obliged to consult a works committee, *comité d'entreprise*. 'Consult' means being informed in advance of and being able to voice opinions as to the conditions surrounding the acquisition. However, it is not necessary to obtain the 'approval' of the works committee, but everyone should be satisfied with the consultation procedure before any contract is signed – non-observance is a criminal offence. There is clearly a conflict between this and the confidentiality obligations of the parties as well as any obligation of the purchaser, if listed, *vis-à-vis* its own shareholders. Therefore the timing and content of any announcement to the works committee needs to be carefully considered.

In general, French labour and social legislation is a minefield for the Anglo-Saxon investor. Potential acquirors therefore need to seek expert guidance, which may not be essential in the less stringently regulated and less pro-employee Anglo-Saxon context.

The conditions of employment of senior management, especially perks, can be a further source of contention in the acquisition context if not handled skilfully. An acquiror wishing to make changes must tread carefully, mindful that perks are a sensitive issue for most senior managers.

CULTURAL DIFFERENCES

Most research into the reasons for the outcomes of acquisitions carried out by major groups indicates that in many cases success is largely due to the effective post-acquisition melding of the two entities. There is a broad consensus that the design and swift implementation of a suitable integration strategy greatly enhances the likelihood of future success.

In the case of a cross-border acquisition, the integration process is even more complex as a result of the need to reconcile cultural differences. There is no magic recipe, but adroit acquirors are generally those who anticipate difficulties likely to result from cultural differences during the integration process and move swiftly to pre-empt them. Cross-border acquisitions are often more difficult to execute than those between two companies located in the same country and pose greater risks. These difficulties notwithstanding, acquisitions continue to abound and 'marriages' between French and Anglo-Saxon companies account for a substantial portion of foreign direct investment in France. Anglo-Saxon and foreign acquirors in general need to gain insight into the mechanism of acquisitions and doing business generally in the target countries, in order to clinch acquisition deals and go on to manage their new French subsidiaries with brio.

22

Leveraged Management Buy-outs and Buy-ins

John Hadley and Sabine Durand,
Corporate Finance, PricewaterhouseCoopers

OVERVIEW

Introduction

Leveraged management buy-out (LMBO) and leveraged management buy-in (LMBI) are acquisition techniques first created in the USA in the 1970s that were extensively used in the early 1980s in the USA and the UK, and subsequently in the rest of Europe.

Their development in France was facilitated by a law regarding management buy-outs (law of 9 July 1984 concerning *Reprise d'Entreprise par les Salariés* – RES), which granted tax advantages to the managers and the holding company performing the acquisition, and by the subsequent 1988 law on tax consolidation.

The tax advantages created in 1984 were only partially continued in the 1991 law and buyers had to comply with tax consolidation requirements to benefit from these tax advantages. Since 1996, specific tax advantages are no longer granted to RES.

The number of LMBO/LMBI transactions significantly increased in France up to 1990, but decreased up to 1995 (see Table 22.1) for the following reasons:

Table 22.1 LMBO/LMBI transactions, 1987–96

Year	Number	Total Value (millions of francs)	Average Value (millions of francs)
1996	103	8,597	83
1995	101	7,266	72
1994	116	9,220	79
1993	99	7,719	78
1992	110	9,200	84
1991	120	11,988	100
1990	150	17,514	117
1989	130	9,414	72
1988	100	n/a	n/a
1987	50	n/a	n/a

Source: *Fusions & Acquisitions,* July–August 1997

- general economic recession;
- the partial abandonment of the favourable tax regime for RES companies in 1991;
- effect on investors of the failure of some significant transactions (Pier Import, Eminence, Jeanneau, Goupil, etc) often due to too little financial headroom being available or to excessively complicated transaction structures.

There are two main categories of companies performing LMBO/LMBI transactions:

- subsidiaries or divisions of large groups, sold off by their holding companies following group reorganisations (mainly French groups in recent years);
- family enterprises, as a way of solving succession problems for small companies. These represent an increasing portion of the total number of LMBO/LMBI transactions (see Table 22.2).

Although comprehensive statistics have not yet been published for 1997, the information available so far indicates that record levels of transactions were carried out in 1997. As shown in Table 22.3, nine deals in 1997 had a value of 500 million fr or more, three of which were greater than 4 billion fr, while in 1996 only one deal had a value in excess of 1 billion fr (MGE – UPS taken over by funds managed by Lbo France).

Another important feature is the growing importance of cross-border investments, especially from the UK, where funds are seeking to diversify abroad because of lower prices. France appears to be one of

Table 22.2 Sources of LMBO/LMBI

Type of Company	Total (1980–90)	Total (1991–96)
Family Enterprises	40.1%	49.9%
Subsidiaries of a Group	40.0%	40.8%
– French group	*22.7%*	*30.1%*
– Foreign group	*17.3%*	*10.7%*
Quoted Companies	9.0%	2.1%
Companies in Receivership	4.3%	6.2%
Other (Privatisation)	6.6%	1.0%
Total	100%	100%

Source: *Fusions & Acquisitions,* July–August 1997; PricewaterhouseCoopers

the most attractive European markets for several reasons: low inter-est rates, a strong stock exchange and a large number of family-owned small- and medium-sized companies in the process of restructuring their capital. The recent opening by Advent International, Legal & General Ventures, and Candover of offices in Paris mirrors the changing landscape of the French leveraged buy-out (LBO) market.

What are LMBOs/LMBIs?

LMBOs/LMBIs consist of an acquisition by a holding company of a tar-get company (with at least 95 per cent of the capital controlled by the holding company in order to benefit from the tax consolidation regime in France) and which is financed by a mixture of equity and debt (senior debt, mezzanine debt). Commonly a significant proportion of the equity capital is provided by financial investors (banks, venture capital funds, etc).

The equity investment is rewarded by way of dividends distributed by the target company, and the debt attracts interest which is charged against pre-tax earnings.

The target company may under certain conditions (section 217-9 of the Companies Act 1966), indirectly contribute to part of the financ-ing of its own acquisition (distribution of reserves, disposal of assets, etc).

Purchase negotiations, due diligence requirements, exchange of con-tracts and post integration issues are the same as for other types of acquisitions, as described in more detail in Chapter 21.

Table 22.3 Transactions over 500 million fr in 1997

Rank	Target	Total Value (millions of francs)	Equity (millions of francs)	Debt (millions of francs)	Lead Equity Financiers	Lead Debt Financiers
1	Elis	>5,000	n/a	n/a	BC Partners	Goldman Sachs
2	Cie Générale de Santé	4,300	1,300	3,000	Cinven/ ABN-Amro Invest.	Bankers Trust/ Société Générale
3	Panzalim	4,200	1,400	2,800	PAI	Citibank/ Bankers Trust
4	Bercy Management	3,420	1,850	1,570	BC Partners	Crédit Lyonnais
5	Néopost	3,050	500	2,500	BC Partners	Morgan Stanley
6	Elico	2,800	1,000	1,800	Advent International	HSBC
7	Alain Afflelou	> 700	n/a	n/a	Alpha	Société Générale
8	Manoir Industries	635	n/a n/a	n/a n/a	Acland/ HSBC PE	UE de CIC Finance
9	Domo-services	578	205	373	Schroder Partners	Citibank/D. Kleinwort Benson

Source: *Capital Finance*

What is an LMBO?

An LMBO is a form of LBO where the managers buy the company, business or undertaking that they manage from its owners. This is usually achieved with the help of financial institutions which put up most of the money in the form of debt and equity. An LBO is any form of acquisition which is 'leveraged', ie financed to a large extent by borrowings to be repaid out of the cash flows of the business.

Normally the management team will consist of the key executive managers of the business concerned. However, there are several variations on this basic theme, one of which is the management–employee-led buy-out (MEBO) known in France as RES (*Reprise d'Entreprise par les Salariés*) where a large number of employees also subscribe to equity in the bought-out business. MEBOs are popular where it is perceived to be desirable to retain and motivate large numbers of highly skilled employees or where it is desirable to see share ownership being widely spread amongst the employees.

In order to qualify as a RES under the legal sense of the term the following conditions have to be satisfied:

- employees must own at least one third of the votes of the holding company;
- 5 to 10 per cent of the employees must be part of the acquisition.

What is an LMBI?

An LMBI is a form of LBO where a team of experienced managers are supported by financial institutions to acquire a company or business to which they consider they can add value through their management expertise. The LMBI team may consist of experienced managers in the same industry as the target company or it may include managers experienced at turning around underperforming companies.

The growth in LMBIs in recent years has been substantial, reflecting the increasing number of opportunities for managers willing to take risks.

The risks associated with an LMBI are traditionally greater than those of an LMBO, for the following reasons:

- an LMBI team does not have the level of detailed 'inside knowledge' of the target company that an LMBO team does. There is, therefore, a greater risk that the LMBI plans might go wrong;
- the vendor of an LMBI target is likely to be less favourably disposed to an LMBI team than to an LMBO team. The chances of an LMBI team acquiring the business on favourable terms are reduced;
- an LMBI may require more work at an early stage in identifying a suitable target, putting together an appropriate team and raising finance, which in turn means that achieving a successful deal is less likely.

When Might an LMBO/LMBI be Appropriate?

Successful LMBOs/LMBIs have been carried out in every type of industry from traditional engineering and manufacturing through to retail, leisure and financial services. There is no limit to the size of deal. The success of the project will depend not on the industry in which the business operates, but on the ability of the management team and on several key characteristics of the LMBO company:

- it should be able to generate predictable positive cash flows which will normally be used to repay acquisition debt as rapidly as possible to de-gear the company. These cash flows will typically be generated from operating profits and working capital improvements;

- it should be able to support significant borrowings to enable it to gear up. The more of the purchase price that can be borrowed without risking the stability of the business, the less the equity investors will need to finance, which means that management will be able to own a larger share of the company;
- it should ideally have a strong position in its market and have an established product range.

Institutional investors in France prefer LMBO/LMBI targets to be in industries with established technologies and strong surplus cash flows as it is difficult to predict the timing and extent of the cash benefits to flow from developing technology. Experience has made the venture capital industry in France very wary of start-up finance.

For an LMBO/LMBI to be successful, not only must the business have the characteristics outlined above, but it must also be available for sale at the right price.

Suitable targets are more likely to be available for sale if they fit one of the following categories:

- non-core businesses of a group;
- profitable, or potentially profitable, subsidiaries of a cash-starved group;
- businesses which do not generate sufficient returns on capital employed;
- family-owned businesses with succession problems.

The Management Team

A critical feature in the success of an LMBO/LMBI is the quality of the management team. Institutional investors must be convinced that the team is sufficiently experienced, entrepreneurial and committed to the buy-out before investing their funds.

An LMBO/LMBI involves a degree of risk for the management team. The managers need not be wealthy, but they will be expected to make a commitment to the funding of the buy-out and be prepared to lose it if the business fails.

A successful LMBO/LMBI management team is likely to be one which can answer 'Yes' to all of the following questions:

- is there a strong team leader? A strong team leader is essential to see through to fruition what can be a complex and difficult transaction;

- does the team include managers experienced in all the functions essential to the business (eg marketing, production and corporate development)?;
- is the team used to 'getting its hands dirty'? A management team used to the support and decision-making process of a large corporate organisation may not be best suited to a 'stand alone' LMBO/LMBI environment;
- does the team have a well-thought-out and achievable strategic plan for the company which is consistent with the constraints of high leverage? As well as implementing its plans after the LMBO/LMBI, the team will have to sell its plans to prospective investors in a clear and convincing way.

FINANCING THE BUY-OUT

The Role of the Lead Advisor

It is essential that before approaching financial institutions for debt and equity finance the managers appoint skilled advisors who have in-depth experience of management buy-outs. Their knowledge and experience will help them achieve:

- the best possible deal from debt and equity providers;
- the maximisation of management's shareholding.

For much of the LMBO/LMBI process, management and their advisors will have common interests, particularly when negotiating with the vendor. To achieve the best deal for themselves, management need specialist expert advice from someone independent of any source of finance.

The lead advisor will:

- review the business plan;
- assist management in preparing an approach to the vendor;
- make introductions to appropriate sources of finance;
- advise management on the presentation of the plan to financiers;
- advise on deal structure and financial modelling;
- review and negotiate the terms of financing offers received;
- provide corporate and personal tax advice;
- advise on management (and employee) shareholdings;
- advise on human resource issues; and
- negotiate the deal with the vendor.

In addition, the lead advisor will assist the buyers in selecting and appointing lawyers experienced in LMBOs/LMBIs.

The Business Plan

The business plan is an essential tool for any LMBO/LMBI management team, not only as part of the finance raising process, but as an aid to management in focusing on where the business is going, how it will get there, what steps are needed to ensure success and their financial implications. A clear, concise, well-presented business plan to be included as part of an information memorandum is an important factor in securing investors' confidence in the management team and the LMBO/LMBI proposal.

Written by the management team as early as possible in the finance raising process, the plan should portray the business in a positive manner, capturing its essential characteristics but not attempting to hide any weaknesses or threats to the business or its strategy. The plan should address and dispose of any significant problems in a reasoned and logical manner.

The business plan will be read by people who know very little about the company or its industry, therefore jargon and excessive technical detail should be avoided.

There are no hard and fast rules as to the contents of a business plan. As a general rule, LMBO managers have access to much more detailed information on the business than managers in an LMBI team. However, an LMBI team should still be able to present a clear assessment of the target business and the markets in which it operates, as well as a statement of its objectives and intentions.

Management Involvement

An LMBO/LMBI will always require some investment from the management team. This may not be significant in the context of the acquisition price, but is normally enough to ensure management's commitment to the project.

At an early stage in the finance raising process, managers and institutions need to agree on how much of the equity each will get. This stage in the negotiations can cause considerable friction in what otherwise should be a harmonious relationship, making the advice of financial advisors crucial.

Debt or Equity?

The cheapest form of institutional finance normally available to the management team is bank borrowings secured on the assets of the company. This is generally know as senior debt and may typically take the form of a medium-term loan with a fixed repayment schedule (quarterly or monthly) together with an overdraft to meet the working capital requirements of the business.

The more senior debt that can be raised, the less equity finance needs to be raised and the easier it will be to achieve the returns required by the institutional equity investors. However, there is a limit to how much debt can be supported by the cash flow of the company and its asset base. It is important that the level of debt and its servicing costs do not impair the viability of the business, particularly in the event of an increase in interest rates or a downturn in trading against that projected at the time of the buy-out.

The interest rates attributed to senior debt will normally depend on a number of factors, including the size of the business, the level of gearing, the asset cover and the perceived risks.

A more 'expensive' type of debt which is an increasingly common feature of the larger buy-outs, is subordinated borrowing, known as mezzanine finance. Mezzanine finance generally attracts a higher rate of interest than that attached to senior debt to reflect the greater risks to mezzanine providers. A mezzanine loan may also provide the opportunity for a higher return to the holder via a premium on redemption or 'an equity kicker' through *bons de souscription d'action* (the right to acquire shares for a nominal amount on sale or flotation of the company). Mezzanine finance is normally appropriate where there is inadequate security to support further senior debt but where there is sufficient cash flow to fund additional interest costs. Mezzanine loans generally take a similar form to senior debt except that the security is subordinated and repayment is often made on sale or flotation of the company making it more risky. The level of interest required by mezzanine lenders is, however, higher.

The most 'expensive' type of finance available is institutional equity. Institutional investors require returns substantially in excess of the cost of borrowing to reflect the risks of investing in a highly geared, unquoted private company. They will, however, be prepared to take a substantial proportion of their return in the form of capital appreciation. For this reason, the exit route for the equity investor is extremely important.

The institutional investors will measure their potential and actual success on an investment by reference to the internal rate of return (IRR) which is the rate of return on their total investment represented by the discounted value of future income and capital cash flows.

The types of equity taken by institutional investors are varied and depend as much on investor preferences as on the structure of the business. Equity investors normally subscribe for some form of ordinary shares (or preferred shares convertible into ordinary shares at a later date), preference shares with a fixed or variable ('participating') dividend, loan stock or a combination of the above. The precise terms vary from deal to deal.

LMBO/LMBI Structure

There is no such thing as a standard LMBO/LMBI structure. Deals are structured by lead advisors, investors and management to take account of a host of different factors, including the required investor returns, the debt capacity of the company and its projected cash flows.

However, taking a hypothetical example of an LMBO of a manufacturing company for 200 million fr, the financing of the LMBO might be structured as Table 22.4. The associated structure, cash flows and exchange of legal contracts schedule are presented in Figure 22.1.

Performance Ratchets (*intéressement*)

Ratchets have become a common feature of LMBOs/LMBIs in recent years. A ratchet is an arrangement whereby the managers own a greater proportion of the shares if the company does well and a smaller proportion if it does badly. The philosophy behind a ratchet is that it encourages management and reduces the institutional investors' risk.

Table 22.4 Financing an LMBO

Funding Required	Francs (mn)	Funds Raised	Francs (mn)
Acquisition cost of the business	200	Management team: Ordinary shares (20%)	2.5
Working capital financed required for the first year after the LMBO	15	Institutional equity: – Ordinary shares (80%) – 8% Preference shares	10.0 95.0
Fees and expenses	15		
		Total equity funding	107.5
		Senior debt: – 7-year term loan – Revolving overdraft – Cash*	102.5 10.0 10.0
Total funds required	230	Total funds raised	230.0

* Dividend distributed by the target, free of any equalisation tax (*franchise de précompte*)

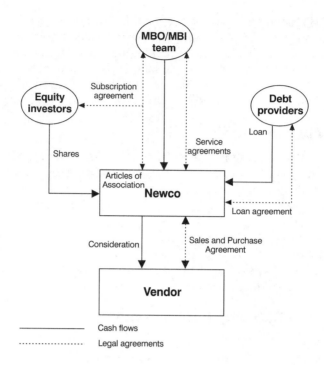

Figure 22.1 Associated structure, cash flows and exchange of legal contracts schedule

Management should not forget that it may also reduce in time the institutional investors' interest in the share capital of the target.

There has been much debate on the advantages and disadvantages of performance ratchets. In summary, these are:

- advantages

    - encourages management to do better;
    - reduces the risk for institutional investors if projected performance is not achieved;

- disadvantages

    - can distract management's attention from the long-term objectives of the business;
    - complicates the transaction;
    - can cause conflicts of objectives between management and institutional investors;
    - variations to ratchets can be highly problematic from a tax perspective.

TAXATION

Taxation Issues for the Management Team

The three main areas of taxation and tax planning for the buyers are:

- the extent to which tax relief may be available on any loan interest associated with finance obtained to purchase shares;
- the avoidance of income tax on managers either on their acquisition of shares or thereafter;
- the sheltering of future capital gains tax liabilities that will arise from a successful exit.

Tax relief for loan interest

Tax relief is available for interest on a loan obtained in order to acquire ordinary shares in a 'close' company, provided certain conditions are met. 'Close' means that the company is either controlled by its directors or by five or fewer 'participators', broadly shareholders and their associates.

Acquisition of shares

Income tax charges on acquisition of shares or thereafter   If directors or employees are permitted, by reason of their employment, to purchase or subscribe for shares at a discount, then the discount is a taxable benefit on which they will be liable to income tax in the year in which they acquire the shares. Early and detailed advice on appropriate structures is, therefore, required.

Growth in value   Whether or not the management team acquires shares at a discount, an income tax liability may arise on the growth in value of the shares if they are acquired by reason of employment rather than by management acting as entrepreneurs. The legislation governing growth in value is complex. It may be triggered by the removal or variation of restrictions on shares or the creation of variation of rights. Moreover, if the company created to shelter the LMBO/ LMBI (Newco) is, or is likely to become, a subsidiary of another company, early advice must be taken.

The operation of a performance ratchet should not, in itself, create a growth in value subject to income tax provided the governing provisions in the Articles of Association or Shareholders' Agreement have been appropriately drafted. Generally, there is no income tax on the growth in value if the shares were acquired under a French Tax Administration approved employee share scheme.

Capital gains tax   If successful, the management team will realise substantial gains which, except for certain reliefs, will be fully chargeable to capital gains tax (CGT) when their Newco shares are disposed of. Expert advice has to be sought in order to draw up specific tax efficient schemes to take advantage of any reliefs currently available.

Taxation Issues for Newco

The main areas where tax considerations are crucial are:

- the form of the consideration used to purchase the company;
- the extent to which the company may have potential tax liabilities, tax losses to carry forward or capital gains tax liabilities;
- the financing of the transaction.

Form of consideration

The vendor may wish to reduce the potential capital gain that may be realised on the sale of the company's shares, by, for example, taking part of the consideration in the form of a dividend from the company. Newco and the management team may wish to assist the seller but should be aware of the following:

- the reserves of the company must be sufficient to pay the dividend;
- depending upon the origin of the profit distributed, a dividend distribution may attract an equalisation tax (*précompte*) liability.

Potential tax liabilities, tax losses carried forward and potential capital gains

The management team and its professional advisors should consider whether:

- all potential taxation liabilities arising from the company's past performance are covered by tax warranties and indemnities;
- tax losses carried forward may be lost if there is a 'major change' in the nature or conduct of the company's business. This point is invariably subject to close scrutiny by the French Tax Administration;
- the company was a member of a group of companies prior to the LMBO/LMBI, implying that additional capital gain liabilities may accrue to the company if it owns assets which were transferred to it by a member of the vendor group.

Financing the transaction

Care needs to be taken that taxation does not impose additional costs on the financing, for example:

- interest charges incurred by Newco may be funded by dividends from the operating company and tax relief may be obtained for the interest by group relief surrendered to the operating company. However, the position needs to be reviewed as early as possible to ensure that full tax relief is obtained on interest paid by Newco;
- it is important that an LMBO/LMBI is carefully structured to minimise the tax liabilities of Newco and its subsidiaries. Tax planning for companies being acquired or disposed of is a complicated area and expert advice should always be sought at an early stage of negotiations.

OTHER ISSUES

Pensions: Management and Employees

Pension schemes have grown to become a major social and financial force, impacting both on employee relations and corporate profitability. The key issues in an LMBO/LMBI are:

- ensuring that the nature of the pension liabilities and risks are fully understood and that 'true' pensions costs are properly identified;
- ensuring that any bulk transfer of pension fund monies from the vendor's pension scheme to Newco's pension scheme is at least sufficient to cover the accrued benefits and expectations of the transferring membership;
- ensuring that the format of future pension provision fully reflects corporate post-acquisition objectives, in terms of both costs and management and staff incentives. Effective employee communication is often the key to the success of a company's pension scheme.

Most French companies have no pension plan for their employees and retirement benefits are reduced to a lump sum payment on retirement date, depending on the last salary, age and seniority in the company. An accurate estimation of the potential liability taken over by the acquiror needs, however, to be undertaken.

Share Option Schemes and Employee Involvement

An LMBO/LMBI success can depend on the motivation of management and employees. Effective incentive structures are key to this.

For the management who form the LMBO/LMBI team, this is achieved through the shares in Newco that they have acquired. In order to motivate employees involved in the LMBO/LMBI, and to attract new key employees of sufficient calibre to help the venture succeed, many management teams seek to extend employee share ownership. This may be limited to key management and employees or extended to all group employees.

In order to avoid potential tax liabilities on the growth in value of the shares (see 'Taxation Issues for the Management Team' above) and to enable shareholdings to be acquired in a tax efficient manner, many companies achieve employee participation through French Tax Administration approved schemes. There are three types of approved scheme:

- executive share option schemes;
- profit sharing schemes;
- savings-related share option schemes.

Share option schemes are always a very complex area. Detailed advice on the implications and administration of any proposed scheme should always be sought.

Many LMBOs/LMBIs use Employee Benefit Trusts (EBTs) or Employees Share Option Plan (ESOPs) as part of their internal market arrangements, the EBT acting as market makers for departing employees for example. ESOPs may be a good solution to management's and employees' motivation and incentive issues but their use and financing should be carefully examined.

Where there is a large workforce, it may be more appropriate to provide incentives with bonuses or through a French Tax Administration registered profit related pay scheme.

Art. 217-9 of the law of 24 July 1966 and Financial Assistance

All limited companies are prohibited by law from giving financial assistance for the purchase of their shares under Art. 217-9 of the law of 24 July 1966.

Financial assistance is widely defined by the Companies Act 1966 and includes 'gift, guarantee, security, indemnities, release or waiver, loan or similar transactions'. There is also a 'sweep-up' category of 'any other financial assistance' which materially reduces net assets.

In an LMBO/LMBI, the most common form of financial assistance is where the target company allows its assets to be used as security for a loan to Newco to enable it to finance the purchase price.

Legal advice must be taken as soon as possible to establish whether the Art. 217-9 of the Law of 24 July 1966 applies, as the provisions are complex and carry both civil and criminal penalties if breached.

23

Joint Ventures

John Hadley and Sabine Durand, Corporate Finance, PricewaterhouseCoopers

For most of the last 50 years, international business has been dominated by the rise of multinational companies whose corporate style has been characterised by self-reliance and strong control mechanisms. Joint ventures (specific, project-based alliances) have been seen simply as means of gaining entry to difficult foreign markets where national laws or commercial conditions required partnerships with local firms. From the multinational partner's point of view the partnership was essentially a way of enabling the company to establish a foothold in a foreign market. The situation has changed dramatically in recent years for three major reasons:

- growing internationalisation of world markets necessitating local marketing expertise and distribution and sales networks with, possibly, the acquisition of a local brand name;
- increasing complexity and speed of technology requiring huge and continuing investment in research and development;
- increasing size of investments and corresponding financing needs; with large projects involving a level of risk that one company may be unwilling to bear on its own.

If organic growth alone is not a realistic option for a company facing these challenges, there are two possible strategies:

- achieve growth by acquisition;
- form joint ventures.

Historically in Anglo-Saxon countries, companies have tended to see the acquisition strategy as the best route for growth, whereas in mainland Europe, particularly France and Italy, strategic alliances have been popular. However, although traditionally the favoured route, Anglo-Saxon companies have found that acquisitions may be risky, especially when a cross-border transaction is involved. In such cases companies may encounter a number of significant problems, chiefly:

- a lack of reliable financial information with which to assess potential targets;
- a lack of listed companies available for acquisition by public offer;
- a prevalence of defensive shareholding structures;
- a lack of knowledge of the local environment;
- difficulties arising from differing corporate cultures which act as a barrier to effective integration within the group.

The purchase of a company as a way of accessing new markets or new technologies can prove therefore to be an expensive and risky process. In addition, the alternative procedure of entering a new market by establishing a subsidiary or branch can prove to be a long and costly process if the investor has little knowledge or prior contacts in the market.

As a result, companies are increasingly turning to joint ventures as an alternative to aquisition, especially if the company operates in a technology or capital intensive industry. A study by INSEAD showed that approximately 85 per cent of joint ventures entered into by European industrial companies in the 1980s concerned one of the following five sectors: aerospace, electronics, automobiles, information technology and telecommunications. In more recent years, joint ventures in the defence industry have been particularly important.

As a consequence, a significant number of joint ventures have been created in France. Some of them have been created as a basis for long-term co-operation and are still operating succesfully. Some of them have been created for a shorter period in order to meet particular short-term requirements such as access to markets and technologies or to carry out common research and development projects. Some of the better examples are set out in Box 23.1.

Joint ventures can take a number of different forms, but essentially they are the formation of a company or partnership by two or more parties with the aim of broadening the activities of each partner.

Advantages of Joint Ventures

The main advantages of joint ventures are:

Joint ventures   Box 23.1

Activity	Joint Venture	Partners
Aircraft	Airbus	Aerospatiale, Dasa, Daimler-Benz, Aerospace, British Aerospace and Casa
Engineering	GEC Alshom	GEC and Alsthom
Missiles	Matra BAe Dynamics	Lagardère and British Aerospace
Helicopters	Eurocopter	Aerospatiale and Daimler-Benz Aerospace
Factoring	Elysées Factor	CCF and SFF
Life insurance	Antarius	Cardif and Crédit du Nord
Automobile	Douai plant	Delphi (GM) and Calsonic
Automobile	Sevel Nord	Fiat and PSA
Animal health	Merial	Merck and Mérieux

- limitation of investment;
- limitation and sharing of risks;
- overcoming national prejudice;
- merging of skills and strengths based on respect for corporate individuality;
- capacity to manage a project with a single operator, with separate financing by the various partners and, in the majority of cases, fiscal transparency.

Disadvantages of Joint Ventures

There are, however, significant disadvantages to entering a joint venture, the two principal ones being:

- lack of total control resulting in difficult decision-making processes and possible conflicts of interest. Such difficulties may be avoided, however, by the introduction of majority decision making or by the designation of one of the partners as the operational partner;
- major adverse consequences in the event of failure. Perhaps the biggest problem affecting a joint venture is to assess the consequences of possible failure. Apart from financial problems and those associated with intellectual property rights, the image (eg of the foreign party) may be severely damaged in the country in which its joint venture failed. However, if the joint venture is transparent for tax purposes, losses can be deducted directly from partners' profits, whereas in the case of a limited company,

for example, the carrying up of losses to shareholders may be difficult and costly from a fiscal viewpoint.

TYPES OF JOINT VENTURE

Joint ventures may be categorised by their purpose or their structure. They may be established for a single project or type of business, or for a group of similar projects, but typically they will be established for one of the following:

- tendering for and executing a particular contract or contracts. This is probably the most common case, especially when the parties are from the same country;
- opening up a new territorial market. In these cases a foreign company will often link up with a locally established business to overcome import restrictions and gain entry to the market place;
- developing and exploiting a new product;
- merging related activities;
- reorganising existing activities. This may be the natural conclusion of a previously close relationship between companies who have co-operated on an informal basis.

This idea of sharing risks and rewards is a key motivating factor behind the formation of a joint venture. Essentially, there are four main types of joint venture structures:

- supply agreements;
- strategic investments;
- equity joint ventures or partnerships;
- partial mergers.

CHOICE OF STRUCTURE

Structuring the joint venture effectively in both management and financial terms is critical to its success.

As described above there are several different types of joint ventures available. Selection of the most appropriate may permit companies to gain the use of resources which are not for sale, such as management skills or access to a distribution network.

The timing and amount of investment finance must be phased in accordance with expansion plans and the scheduling of new products to meet market demands and need not necessarily be contributed immediately.

The structure adopted must cater adequately for a smooth exit route on expiry of the projected life of the venture, and must define the conditions and any penalty which would be applied in the event of early termination. Liquidation on expiry of the project is one possible exit, but other possibilities could include exercise of pre-emption rights, a trade sale, or flotation.

In considering the structure of an alliance, it is therefore crucial to determine exactly what the objectives of the venture are and where the project fits into the company's overall strategy. In order to do this, the company must determine the stage of development of the markets in which it operates. The type of alliance that the company may wish to form is usually closely related to the maturity of the market. The product/market life-cycle model (Figure 23.1) helps to illustrate this. The greatest potential for change in competitive position occurs during the shaded phases and it is in these phases where alliances are most useful.

STAGES IN FORMING A JOINT VENTURE

There are a number of stages involved in the preparation of a joint venture. The usual path to a joint venture will involve the following:

- considering the alternatives;
- choosing the partner;
- initial contact;

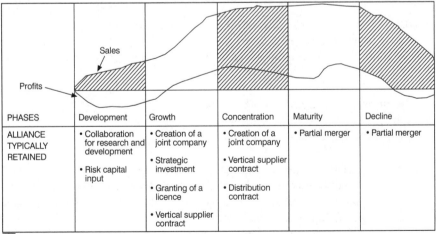

PHASES	Development	Growth	Concentration	Maturity	Decline
ALLIANCE TYPICALLY RETAINED	• Collaboration for research and development • Risk capital input	• Creation of a joint company • Strategic investment • Granting of a licence • Vertical supplier contract	• Creation of a joint company • Vertical supplier contract • Distribution contract	• Partial merger	• Partial merger

Strong potential for major change in the competitive position

Figure 23.1 Product/market life-cycle model

- exchange of information;
- negotiations;
- letter of intent;
- joint venture agreement.

Senior management should be involved in all stages of the joint venture process, but particular attention must be paid to the following to improve the chances of success:

- decision to form a joint venture;
- choice of partner;
- planned management of the joint venture.

The exchange of information, negotiations and letter of intent are very similar to other types of acquisitions, as previously described.

Think Ahead and Set Clear and, Whenever Possible, Quantify Objectives

Agreeing to enter a joint venture in principle is only the first step in the process. For a joint venture to be successful, prior consideration of the objectives to be achieved is essential, for example target turnover and earnings. Other issues to bear in mind include resources to be deployed (personnel, assets and finances), structuring operations and the optimal management system for the joint venture. It is also advisable to assess the impact of the proposed solution on the company's other businesses and its advantages over other strategic options.

Trust cannot be underestimated as a factor in a successful joint venture. If forward planning is the *sine qua non* of a fruitful partnership, it is mutual trust that is necessary for success. There are three elements crucial to genuine trust:

- understanding one another's business;
- appreciating one another's objectives;
- establishing good personal relationships.

Trust will ensure that the 'managerial chemistry' is right, that each partner is receptive to the other's needs and that any potential difficulties that may arise can be discussed in an atmosphere of mutual self-interest rather than confrontation.

It is important for companies entering strategic partnerships to identify potential sources of conflicts and to second-guess any hidden agendas that a partner might have. A partner might secretly be trying to use a combination of alliances as a springboard to build up in-house capabilities and mount a competitive attack on the other partner's business.

These potential risks may be reduced in a number of ways, depending upon the purpose and structure of the venture. These include:

- allocating geographical markets – although companies must be wary of the anti-trust implications of such an action;
- defining the scope of the business – it is important to ensure that the potential for competition with the parent companies is effectively managed;
- reducing the seepage of technology – there is a danger that technology and expertise may flow, via the venture, from the technologically stronger partner to the weaker. This may be negated by dividing the project into carefully defined components, so as to make the collaboration as vertical as possible. In any event it is important that staff understand clearly the limits of the relationship and the information which can and cannot be shared.

Assign Responsibilities Clearly

Clear definition of responsibilities is essential in any business or project, and one of the most important aspects of structuring a joint venture is choosing the right leader. There are two ways to create strategic leadership:

- create an independent leadership structure;
- nominate one of the parent companies to take on the role of project management.

Adapt to Circumstances

In joint ventures, where objectives may differ between partners as well as diverge over time, a different approach to business building is required. At best, plans and budgets might be negotiated; at worst, total control over them may have to be given to a management team over which there is no formal supervision.

Under these circumstances, a company may not be able to direct the venture in a conventional sense and may even be unable to obtain adequate information about its performance. Companies involved in strategic partnerships must therefore learn how to manage without the kind of control to which they are accustomed.

Cultural Issues

Cultural differences between joint venture partners pose potentially the greatest hazard to the success of the venture. Such conflict may arise in a number of areas, typically from:

- differences between large and small company management structures;
- differences in national business cultures;
- differences between the management styles and business approach of individual corporations: decision-making processes, particularly when the corporations are based in different countries.

Seize Learning Opportunities

Every company has a different way of doing things and joint venture partnerships offer the opportunity for one company to observe how another operates. There is considerable scope for management to acquire exposure to different styles of operating in areas such as managing R&D programmes, organising business development programmes, controlling foreign subsidiaries and even determining remuneration packages.

It is, however, important to establish a clearly defined group of people to monitor the venture on behalf of the parent, and who are able to assess the venture's technical work and identify possible commercial applications. It is most often necessary to set up specialised subgroups (technical, commercial, financial, legal, etc).

FINANCING A JOINT VENTURE

In addition to strategic and management considerations, financing and tax issues are key factors to address in structuring a profitable venture. Joint ventures have traditionally been funded by equity, but at present, especially in respect of large projects, capital investment required has been such that partners are unable or unwilling to provide finance on a pure equity basis from their own resources and have looked in part to debt finance. However, there are frequently too many joint ventures chasing too little money from banks, which are unwilling to grant loans for certain activities considered to be risky. Joint ventures must therefore ensure that the financial packages and partial guarantees offered reduce risks to an acceptable level.

The typical sources of funding for joint ventures are:

- partners' contributions (in cash or assets);
- if the joint venture must arrange its own borrowings with minimal external guarantees, an adequate level of equity and quasi-equity

must be provided as security for lenders. The terms and conditions of quasi-equity (mezzanine debt) must also be defined on the basis of the company's capacity to bear the related financial expense over the life of the project;

- retained profits (a method of financing which in virtually every case will have to be combined with one or more of the alternative ways of funding joint ventures). It is generally the most advantageous method from a tax viewpoint and, therefore, is the principal method used to finance projects beyond the initial launch/construction phase;
- domestic currency loans as when revenues are denominated in local currency, local currency financing must be maximised.

For the purpose of financing joint ventures, banks have taken to using 'limited recourse' project finance techniques (ie without a guarantee outside the project). However, this option is possible only for projects with a forecasted cash flow which, based on prudent calculations, will suffice to repay the debt over the projected term, with an adequate safety margin.

Security over earnings may take the form of a charge on the bank account of the joint venture. In addition, banks may well require partial guarantees from partners or other third parties so as to reduce their risk. In this case, corporate lending is used alongside limited recourse financing.

The Appropriate Form of Funding

Some issues to consider when determining the appropriate form of funding for a joint venture are:

- gearing;
- currency of funding;
- repatriation of profits;
- repayment profile;
- project phase financing/refinancing;
- leasing;
- security required by lenders;
- taxation and accounting.

TAXATION AND ACCOUNTING

Tax planning for international joint ventures is an extremely complex area, requiring careful consideration of the objectives and the tax status of each partner. In addition, accounting considerations such as the desire to hold the joint venture off the balance sheet may be relevant.

If, as is likely, the venture is financed by large borrowings, a partner may well be unwilling to consolidate the venture in its accounts due to the detrimental effect consolidation would have on the parents' own balance sheet and gearing ratios.

Some of the most significant tax issues to be considered are:

- selection of the entity to carry out the joint venture;
- contribution of assets;
- financing of the joint venture;
- exit routes.

Selection of the Entity to Carry out the Joint Venture

The entity to carry out the joint venture will be either a partnership, a company (eg *Société par Actions Simplifiée* – SAS) or a grouping of companies (eg Economic Interest Grouping – EIG).

If a partnership is used, it may be fiscally transparent and the joint venture parties will be taxed on the income of the partnership.

If a company is used, it is the taxable entity and the joint venture partner will be subject to tax only when the profit from the joint venture company is distributed. Dividends from the joint venture will be subject to tax based on the tax laws prevailing in the parent companies' countries and any existing tax treaties.

The *Société par Action Simplifiée* (SAS) was created by the 3 January 1994 Act as a more flexible corporate structure than *Sociétés Anonymes* (SA), in order to foster co-operation between companies. The SAS is a limited company, the management and administration of which are defined by the articles of association. It is governed by the same legal provisions as an SA, with the exception of those concerning the company management (board of directors, management board and supervisory board) and shareholders' meetings.

An SAS cannot be quoted on the stock exchange. It must have a minimum share capital of 250,000 fr, and must have at least two shareholders, whose own share capital must be not less than 1,500,000 fr or the equivalent in the relevant foreign currency.

If a grouping of companies is used, the partner companies will benefit from the tax transparency of the grouping and each partner will be deemed to have assumed a portion of the tax charge and received a portion of the grouping's revenues.

This transparency for tax purposes is often considered to be an important advantage of a flexible joint venture structure. However, it renders impossible the deconsolidation of financing used to fund each partner's share of investments.

An Economic Interest Grouping (EIG) is a legal entity whose members pool their efforts in order to facilitate or develop economic activities in common. It is totally independent of its members' own businesses and offers a high degree of organisational and operational flexibility.

European Economic Interest Grouping (EEIG), a similarly flexible structure, was created under EU Regulation no 2137/85 to facilitate cross-border development and co-operation between companies operating in the EU.

Contribution of Assets

Where new companies are being formed, a major issue will be how to transfer assets to the joint venture entity without triggering a capital gains tax charge in the contributing companies. The disposal of an asset will result in a potential tax charge if the asset is sold to a French company which is outside the vendor's tax group.

In this case, the creation of a grouping rather than a new company will also limit transfer duties, as each partner retains ownership of the assets made available to the grouping.

Financing

Tax planning will have a significant role to play in determining the optimum funding structure for the new joint venture.

Essentially there are two forms of finance, equity or debt. Convertible bonds are treated as loans until they are converted into shares. Other quasi-equity instruments are subject to more complex tax rules, which should be studied carefully prior to using such instruments.

Dividends received by a French company from another French company are not subject to tax due to the mechanism of a tax credit (*avoir fiscal*) and the application of the tax grouping regime (*régime des sociétés mères et filles*). However, as noted above, dividends received from foreign companies may be subject to tax in France and dividends paid by a French company to a foreign parent may similarly be subject to tax in the parent company's country.

In the case of an EIG, it is treated as a transparent entity for income tax purposes, as with a partnership. The EIG partners are then taxed on the basis of their share of earnings. With regard to other taxes, EIGs are taxed in the same manner as other companies, even though their purpose is not to make profits for themselves. In France, they are also liable for business tax (*taxe professionnelle*) and for VAT on their operations.

Interest, whether received from a French company or from abroad will be subject to tax in France. It may also be subject to withholding tax, which can be set off against the tax due by the receiving company. In normal circumstances, the joint venture company should be able to claim a tax deduction for interest payments. Dividend payments are not tax deductible, however.

Therefore, when determining the funding structure of the joint venture, the following factors need to be considered:

- corporation tax: rates differ between countries;
- tax losses: if the venture is expected to make losses at first, consideration should be given on how to utilise such losses as early as possible. If start-up losses are expected to be significant and to exceed the amounts that can be carried forward and set off against future profits (as tax loss carry forwards) they could be reduced, for example, by considering the possibility of spreading the investments over a longer period;
- debt location: it is essential that the structuring of debt finance is considered from a tax perspective. If a venture has operations in more than one location, it is better to locate debt in high-tax jurisdictions;
- undercapitalisation: certain rules may disallow an interest deduction on debt above a specified level;
- transfer pricing: provisions exist to prevent the export of profits to other countries through artificial inter-company pricing arrangements or through excessive interest, royalties or management charges and to ensure that all goods or services provided to (or acquired from) foreign affiliates are not undercharged or overcharged.

Exit Routes

A capital gains tax liability may occur on the termination of the joint venture agreement. Methods of avoiding or mitigating such a potential liability include:

- dividend stripping: this involves the target company paying as large a dividend as it is legally entitled to declare to the vendor company. The dividend will reduce the value of the shares in the target company and the chargeable gains arising on the sale of those shares. However, the dividend may represent taxable income;

- share for share exchange: tax provisions may state that no disposal for capital gains tax purposes arises where a third party issues shares in exchange for shares in the target company;
- capital gains company: the vendor company interposes a foreign holding company resident in a country which treats chargeable gains favourably, for instance the Netherlands. The affiliate resident abroad can then be sold by the foreign holding company without any liability in respect of any gains realised. Planning well in advance of the ultimate disposal is required.

24

Tax and Legal Considerations

Jean-Eric Boiron and Xavier Rohmer,
Coopers & Lybrand CLC Juridique et Fiscal

INTRODUCTION

In principle, foreign investors are free to acquire businesses in France, except in a limited number of economic sectors.

There are two main routes for acquiring a business in France, namely the purchase of assets and the acquisition of shares in a company (see Chapter 21). In most cases, the acquisition of assets concerns the purchase of the company's business and, if necessary, the premises where the business is located. It is possible to acquire all or only some of a company's assets (eg business goodwill). Alternatively, the majority of the company's issued share capital may be acquired. Tax and legal treatment varies according to the chosen acquisition route.

French law distinguishes between a company selling all or some of its assets, following which the purchaser is the direct and immediate owner of the acquired assets, and the transfer by shareholders of all or some of their shares in a company, following which the purchaser acquires a right to the share capital of the company concerned. In principle, the acquisition of assets does not include liabilities related to those assets, while a company whose shares have been transferred keeps all of its assets and liabilities.

From a tax standpoint, both the acquisition of assets and the acquisition of shares are subject to registration duties, although the applicable rate varies according to which method is used.

Briefly, the sale of a business is subject to complex and stringent legal formalities (compulsory disclosures in the related deed, without which the transaction can be avoided, objection period open to creditors, and sale price retention by the purchaser, etc), as well as high registration duties. The seller of the business assets is not expected to provide the purchaser with extensive representations and warranties, however. In comparison, the acquisition of shares is less regulated, but the seller is more often expected to provide the purchaser with extensive representations and warranties.

Like mergers, acquisitions of assets and shares must comply with other regulations, including labour law, competition and anti-trust law and, if necessary, environmental regulations related to polluted sites. Both the acquisition of assets and the acquisition of shares are subject to European Union and French competition and anti-trust rules. Consequently, mergers and acquisitions are referred to the administrative authorities when certain legal thresholds are reached and where there is a risk that the operation will directly or indirectly threaten competition in the national market (see Chapter 31).

ACQUISITION OF ASSETS

Legal Aspects

The acquisition of assets usually corresponds to the acquisition of either a going concern, or all the assets of a company, ie business and other assets.

Definition of a business (fonds de commerce)

A business is composed of intangible assets (clientele, goodwill, contracts, trade marks, patents, leasehold rights where business premises are leased, intellectual property rights, etc) and tangible assets (equipment, furniture, tools, inventories, work-in-progress, etc). A business is commonly defined as an activity's clientele, as business and customers are indivisible under French law, although other assets, such as leasehold rights, may be the principal and more valuable business components. In addition to the business itself, the other assets which may be transferred are property and related rights, and receivables.

Assignment of contracts

In principle, the sale of a business is only a transfer of assets and consequently does not include the assignment of contracts entered into by the seller with third parties in the normal course of business. French law nevertheless provides for the continuation of some contracts in the event of the sale of a business. Eligible contracts are automatically assigned with the business, while other contracts may be transferred only with the consent of the co-contracting party.

Contracts automatically transferred with the business   These include employment contracts, lease agreements and insurance policies.

Pursuant to Article L. 122-12 of the French Labour Code, in the case of a change of control, all employment contracts in force as of the date of the sale are automatically transferred to the business's new owner. This requirement is stringently applied and any employee can claim the benefit of such transfer if he can demonstrate that his job is directly related to the transferred activity.

Pursuant to Article L. 121-10 of the French Insurance Code, all insurance policies related to the business remain in full effect in favour of the purchaser of the business, although this issue is generally negotiated between the parties.

As the commercial lease for the premises where the business is carried out is generally essential for the operation of the business, French law (Decree of 30 September 1953) prohibits contractual provisions which prevent assignment of the lease to the acquiror. The lease agreement may impose a number of formalities, however, such as the lessor's involvement in the sale and purchase negotiations.

Contracts not automatically transferred with the business   All contracts other than those mentioned above are not transferred with the business, whether concluded *intuitu personae* or not. Indeed, French law equates the transfer of contracts to the transfer of both rights and obligations, with the result that renewal of contracts with the assignee is subject to the acceptance of the contracting parties. Contracts concluded *intuitu personae* are those for which the identity of the co-contracting party was an essential motivation for entering into an agreement (eg franchises, licences, financial agreements, supply agreements, leases).

Furthermore, if the business is a regulated activity, such as banking and insurance, industrial operations and tourism, it is important to verify that the assignee will be able to run the purchased business effectively. An administrative authorisation, granted *intuitu personae* or to the business itself, may be required. In practice, a condition precedent concerning the granting or maintaining of the administrative authorisation is included in the sale and purchase agreement.

Absence of warranties

The sale of a business is in principle only a straight sale of assets, with related liabilities excluded. The seller is expected to pay the existing liabilities, as those liabilities are borne by the company or the individual acting as the seller. The contracting parties may nevertheless negotiate the transfer of all or some liabilities at the same time as the business transfer. From a tax standpoint, the cost of the transfer of liabilities should be added to the sale price and subjected to registration duties.

Agreements concerning the sale and purchase of a business do not usually include specific warranties from the seller in favour of the purchaser. The only warranties are those prescribed by French law, ie the seller's warranty covering potential undisclosed liabilities, and a warranty assuring that the seller will not compete with the purchaser and that the seller's creditors will not sue the purchaser.

Transfer of property and employees

As stated above, employment contracts are automatically transferred with the business.

The premises in which the business is run may be leased or owned by the seller. In the first case, the lease is transferred with the business. If the property is owned by the seller, the seller may either sell or lease the premises to the purchaser of the business. It is usual for two distinct purchase agreements to be signed when premises are to be sold.

Rules governing business sales and property sales are different. Property sales must be carried out by way of a deed of conveyancing drawn up by a notary. The deed is then made public in order for the sale to be valid against claims from third parties. The sale and purchase agreement does not need to be notarised, but must be registered with the tax authorities.

Tax Aspects

Territoriality rules

Registration duties are due whenever French assets are transferred, irrespective of whether the related contracts are signed in France or not. Transfers of foreign assets for valuable consideration are liable to registration duties only if the related contracts are signed in France.

For the purposes of registration duties, business assets are considered to be French assets when located or operated in France, as is property located in France.

Principles of taxation

Purchasing a business as a whole (which presupposes that the related clientele is transferred at the same time) through the acquisition of its assets, involves heavy registration duties, calculated on the following progressive basis:

- 0 per cent on the first 150,000 fr;
- 7 per cent between 150,000 fr and 700,000 fr;
- 11.40 per cent beyond 700,000 fr.

The transfer duty is assessed on the higher of the price stipulated for all tangible and intangible property transferred, including any charges, or the market value of the business assets concerned. Registration duties are not levied on receivables and inventories transferred with the business assets, however.

Transfers of property attract special taxation. Where the sale of a building occurs less than five years after the completion of that building and is the first sale since completion, it is subject to VAT at 20.6 per cent. The sale of a building completed more than five years earlier is subject to registration duties at a rate of approximately 18.20 per cent.

It is important to bear in mind that registration duties applicable to the transfer of business assets also apply to any agreement for valuable consideration enabling someone to exercise a profession, function or occupation engaged in by his predecessor, even where the said agreement does not involve a transfer of clientele. Such agreements are called successor agreements.

The scope of successor agreements (Article 720 of the French Tax Code) is broad, extending to any transaction whereby an activity is transferred other than by the sale of business assets or clientele. For example, it has been held in court that the assignment of contracts in progress falls within the scope of Article 720.

As a result, registration duties may be quite significant, as they are levied on all amounts due by the 'successor' under the agreement, whatever the term used to describe them.

ACQUISITION OF SHARES

Legal Aspects

The acquisition of a majority stake in a company's share capital is the most common method used to acquire control of a business. As a company may issue different classes of shares, control over it may be achieved without a majority interest in the issued share capital.

Share categories

The two main corporate forms affording limited liability in France are the *Société Anonyme* (SA) and the *Société à Responsabilité Limitée* (SARL) (see Chapter 26).

A distinction is made between shares; the issued shares of an SA (and of simplified companies, such as the *Société par Actions Simplifiée* – SAS) are called *actions*, whereas the issued shares of an SARL are called *parts sociales*. The transfer of each of these types of shares is subject to different rates of registration duties and different legal formalities.

Classes/categories of shares   French law allows the shares of SAs and SASs to be divided into different categories. Specific shares may be created for a number of reasons (eg to ensure effective control over the company by a shareholder or a group of shareholders, to grant additional dividends to certain shareholders, etc). Apart from ordinary shares, preference shares (granting, for instance, preferred rights to profits) or double-vote shares may be granted to some shareholders. Similarly, non-voting shares carrying a preference dividend may be created to maintain control over the company. Specific legal conditions govern and limit the creation of all these types of shares.

Transfer of shares to third parties and between shareholders In principle, there are no restrictions to transfers of *actions*, except where the company by-laws provide for a prior approval clause requiring the consent of the existing shareholders for the transfer of shares to non-shareholders. Under the French Companies Act of 24 July 1966, the transfer of *parts sociales* to non-shareholders must be notified to the company and approved by half of the shareholders representing at least three-quarters of the issued shares. Transfer of *actions* or *parts sociales* between shareholders is not restricted, however.

Prior approval covenants, pre-emptive rights, change of control clauses

As stated above, the French Companies Act restricts only the transfer of *parts sociales* to non-shareholders. Restrictions over the free transfer of other shares may be stipulated in the company by-laws or shareholders' agreements. The related clauses mainly establish prior approval (*clause d'agrément*), pre-emptive rights (*clause de préemption*) and change of control (*clause de changement de contrôle*).

Prior approval covenants   Prior approval covenants restrict the freedom to transfer shares to non-shareholders. The purpose is to control share transfers and thereby prevent certain individuals or legal entities (eg competitors) from acquiring an interest in the share capital. As explained above, this protection is automatic in the case of SARLs. With regard to SAs, commercial law upholds freedom of transfer, but allows shareholders to include in the company by-laws the same restrictions governing the transfer of *parts sociales*.

Pre-emptive rights   Pre-emptive rights concern share transfers between shareholders. They entitle shareholders to pre-empt shares in the event that a shareholder intends to dispose of all or some of his shares. The underlying motivation for such a clause is generally to secure equilibrium between shareholdings.

Pre-emptive rights may be provided for in shareholders' agreements, which are often concluded between a limited group of shareholders. In practice, the only legal remedy in the event of a breach of pre-emptive rights is the granting of damages, as French courts refuse to order compulsory enforcement of the violated agreement and nullify the disposal of the shares. However, the by-laws of an SAS may provide for shareholders' pre-emptive rights, with non-compliance resulting in the nullity of the share transfer. In practice, both a pre-emptive subscription rights clause and prior approval clause are provided.

Change of control clauses   Change of control clauses are also a means of securing a stable ownership structure and voting rights. In practice, this type of clause provides for either the compulsory purchase of the shares of the other shareholders, or for the compulsory sale of the shares of a corporate shareholder which has undergone a change of control. In addition, voting rights may be suspended and/or the shareholder which has undergone a change of control excluded. Under French company law, this type of clause may be inserted in the by-laws of SASs.

Share transfer agreements

The transfer of *actions* is not subject to registration duties if a share transfer agreement is not signed by the parties in France. In practice, however, written agreements are drawn up for a number of important reasons, particularly the provision of representations and warranties in favour of the purchaser. Under company law, the assignment of *parts sociales* must be recorded in a written deed (ie a share transfer agreement).

Earn-out clauses

Earn-out clauses included in share transfer agreements provide that the sale price, or a portion of the price, be adjusted during one or several years following completion of the sale in light of future events (profits, business turnover/gross income).

Seller's warranty

In order to guarantee the purchaser against any increase in liabilities or reduction of assets after completion of the sale, seller's warranties are used to protect the purchaser against any undisclosed liabilities not taken into account in the purchase price (see Chapter 21).

By means of such warranties, the seller guarantees, for a certain period of time and up to a certain amount (some thresholds may be fixed), payment to the purchaser of any and all undisclosed debts (eg debts resulting from a tax reassessment) originating prior to the date of the share transfer agreement which were unknown to the purchaser as of that date. Warranties may cover only a limited amount of debt stipulated in the share transfer agreement, or both an increase in debt and a decrease in net worth. Profitability warranties guarantee minimum profits over a specified period (eg three months). Sale price revision clauses provide for the revision of the sale price itself based on any debts which come to light after the share transfer.

Legal formalities and company requirements

Legal formalities differ for *actions* and *parts sociales*. The share transfer procedure is conditional upon specific provisions in the by-laws (eg a right of first refusal may be provided for).

Parts sociales   The *parts sociales* transfer agreement must be registered with the tax authorities and registration duties paid. Notification of the agreement is then made to the company by a bailiff (or delivered to the registered office of the company in exchange for a receipt), so that the transfer is binding upon the company. It is then also filed with the local Companies Registry in order to be valid against claims from third parties.

Actions   The transfer of *actions* is realised by a simple transfer from one shareholder account to another. Commercial law requires only the signature of the seller on a share transfer form stating the names of the parties and the number of shares assigned, and the company's transfer register is updated accordingly. Unlike the procedure for *parts sociales*, there is no requirement to file with the local Companies Registry or make notification. If the deed is signed in France, registration formalities must be fulfilled and registration duties paid.

Tax Aspects

Registration duties

A transfer of negotiable shares issued by a company which has its registered office in France is not subject to registration tax unless such transfer is evidenced by a written instrument signed in France. In this case, transfer duty is levied at a rate of 1 per cent up to a maximum of 20,000 fr per transaction.

As a general rule, for tax purposes, limited companies (eg SAs, SASs and *Sociétés en Commandite par Actions* – SCAs) issue negotiable shares. However, entities such as *Sociétés en Nom Collectif* (SNCs), *Sociétés en Commandite Simple* (SCSs), *Sociétés Civiles* (SCs) and *Sociétés à Responsabilité Limitée* (SARLs) issue non-negotiable shares.

The transfer of the non-negotiable shares of a company attracts registration duties at a rate of 4.80 per cent. Even when no instrument is prepared, registration tax is always assessed and the parties to the transfer must file a tax return within one month of the date of transfer.

In both cases (negotiable and non-negotiable shares), where the transfer duty is due, it is assessed on the higher of the contract price or the market value of the shares transferred.

Tax consolidation

French tax law allows the aggregation of the tax profits and losses of a 'parent company' and its 95 per cent-owned subsidiaries during a renewable five-year period. In order to be eligible for this option, the parent and its subsidiaries must be French entities subject to corporate income tax at the standard rate and must have the same 12-month financial year and the same financial year-end. A French branch of a foreign company is also eligible to be the head of a tax group.

The head entity of a tax group must hold directly or indirectly at least 95 per cent of the share capital of the subsidiaries. The head of a tax group may not be a 95 per cent-owned (directly or indirectly) subsidiary of another French company. It may be a wholly owned subsidiary of a foreign company, however, provided that the latter is not owned at 95 per cent or more directly or indirectly by a French company. The scope of the tax group is freely determined by the parent company, which may select from among its eligible subsidiaries those for which group relief will be elected.

Since group relief is optional, an election must be made by the head of the group prior to the beginning of the first projected consolidated fiscal year. As the purpose of group relief is to consider a tax group as a single entity subject to corporate income tax, the group's taxable income is determined by combining the tax results of each member of the group and eliminating inter-company transactions.

MERGERS AND BUSINESS CONTRIBUTIONS

Legal Aspects

A merger may be realised either by the absorption of a company by another, or by the contribution of all the assets and liabilities of two or more companies to a new company. In both cases, the original companies are wound up. The absorption process is more frequent.

Absorption may follow a normal or simplified procedure. The simplified procedure may be applied if all the shares of the absorbed company are held by the absorbing company at the time that the draft merger agreement is filed with the commercial court and until the merger operations are completed.

The simplified procedure does away with the need to fulfil certain legal requirements, such as the appointment of a merger auditor. The main characteristics of a merger are the universal assignment of the absorbed company's assets and liabilities and the winding-up of the latter.

Universal assignment of assets and liabilities

A merger entails a comprehensive transfer of all the assets and liabilities of the absorbed company to the absorbing company, with the liabilities of the absorbed company thus borne by the absorbing company. A merger also entails the automatic transfer of the absorbed company's business lease, together with the employment contracts of its employees. Specific regulations governing the traditional assignment of debts and contribution (transfer in consideration for shares) of business do not apply.

Some legal formalities must nevertheless be fulfilled if property is included in the transfer. If the absorbed company is party to any *intu-*

itu personae agreements, or has been granted administrative licences, or has entered into administrative contracts, assignments are subject to the approval of the other contracting parties. In remuneration for the assets transferred made by the absorbed company, the absorbing company must issue new shares in favour of the absorbed company's shareholders.

In the case of the contribution of some assets representing a complete activity sector under the merger procedure, all the assets and liabilities of the transferred activity are likewise assigned.

Winding-up of the transferor

The consequence of the transfer of all the assets and liabilities to the absorbing company is the winding-up of the absorbed company, without any official liquidation or appointed liquidator.

Conversely, in the event of the contribution of some assets representing a complete activity sector, the contributing company is not wound up, as it contributes only a portion of its assets to another company.

Tax Aspects

Special merger relief regime

In the absence of election for any favourable regime, merger between companies results in the total cessation of the absorbed company's business, leading to immediate taxation of reserves and capital gains, the assets of which are deemed disposal at market value.

Pursuant to a special merger relief regime, however, the merger of two or more companies subject to corporate income tax may be exempted from tax. Similar rules apply to demergers and business contributions (subject to the contributor's commitment to keep the newly received shares for a minimum of five years).

French domestic tax rules stipulate that any capital gains realised in the course of a merger are not taxed at the time of the transaction. The relief consists of a deferral of tax, but not an absolute exemption from tax.

The special merger relief regime has the following characteristics:

- deferred taxation of the capital gains realised on the transfer of non-depreciable fixed assets (goodwill, trade marks, etc) at the level of the absorbed company. These capital gains are preserved for subsequent taxation by shifting the tax liability to the absorbing company;

- deferred taxation of capital gains arising from the exchange of shares representing the capital of the absorbed company for shares in the absorbing company, in the hands of the shareholders. Any cash payment (up to 10 per cent of the nominal value of the shares) received by the shareholders in connection with the merger may be subject to tax, however. The taxation of the capital gain resulting from the exchange of shares is deferred until the subsequent disposal of the shares received in exchange.

Under the special merger relief regime, the tax deferral for corporate income tax purposes is granted provided that the absorbing company makes the following commitments in the merger agreement:

- to add back to its profits taxable at the full rate over a 5-year period (or a 15-year period for real estate and real estate rights) any capital gains realised on depreciable assets exempted in the hands of the absorbed company;
- to record in its own books and in an identical amount the tax provisions previously set up by the merged company;
- to record on the liabilities side of its balance sheet the special long-term capital gains reserve set up by the absorbed company;
- to compute any future gain or loss on the sale of non-depreciable contributed assets by reference to the fiscal value of these assets, as per the absorbed company's own books;
- to recognise assets, other than fixed assets, at their fiscal value as per the merged company's books. Otherwise, the profit corresponding to the difference between the new value and the previous fiscal value is included in the taxable income for the merger year.

Furthermore, losses incurred by the absorbed company prior to the merger may not be deducted from the future profits of the absorbing company, unless a special approval to transfer them to the absorbing company is obtained from the Minister of Economy. This approval is seldom granted, in practice.

Losses incurred by the absorbing company may still be carried forward for a maximum of five years, provided that the merger does not result in a substantial change in the absorbing company's activity.

Evergreen losses incurred by the absorbing company are converted into ordinary losses, which may be carried forward for a maximum of five years from the financial year in which the excess tax depreciation was computed.

A flat registration duty (1,500 fr) is due where two companies subject to corporate income tax are involved, without any requirement to fulfil specific conditions.

Accounting Aspects

Merger auditor

Court-appointed merger auditor   An *ex parte* application to the president of the commercial court must be made in order for a merger auditor to be appointed. The merger auditor must draft two reports dealing with the financial terms and conditions (particularly the share exchange parity) of the merger and the value of the contributions in-kind, and certifying that the net equity contributed is at least equal to the increase of capital of the absorbing company.

Court-appointed contribution auditor   A contribution auditor is appointed by the president of the commercial court under the simplified merger procedure or in the case of partial asset contributions. The auditor is required to assess the value of the contributions in-kind.

Date of Effect

In principle, the date of effect of a merger is the date of the last shareholders' meeting approving the merger. It is possible, however, for the merger agreement to provide for a retroactive date of effect, for tax and accounting purposes. From a legal standpoint, retroactive effect may not precede the absorbed company's last financial year-end, and from a tax standpoint, it may not precede the date on which results were declared by the two companies to the tax authorities, ie the beginning of the absorbing company's financial year during which the merger is approved.

Losses or profits realised by the absorbed company after the date of effect of the merger may be included in the absorbing company's results. Taxable income realised by the absorbed company will be taxed in the hands of the absorbing company. The absorbing company may offset against its own profits any tax losses realised by the absorbed company as from the date of effect of the merger.

JOINT VENTURES

In addition to the usual types of company, there are two other types of legal entity which are often adopted in setting up a joint venture vehicle: SASs and Economic Interest Groupings (EIGs).

Société Anonyme Simplifiée (SAS)

The SAS may be used as a joint venture vehicle. This new type of legal entity was introduced into French law in 1994 and is more flexible than the other existing legal structures such as SA and SARL.

The SAS must have at least two shareholders, which may be companies only, including partnerships, but not individuals or economic interest groupings. Shareholders may be either French or foreign companies. Each shareholder's share capital must be at least 1,500,000 fr (or foreign currency equivalent). If the 1,500,000 fr threshold ceases to be met, the shareholder in question must remedy the situation within a six-month period or sell its shares to a new shareholder. If the situation is not remedied, the SAS must either be dissolved or change its legal form. An SAS must have a minimum share capital of 250,000 fr, which must be fully paid-up at the time of inception.

The SAS's shareholders are free to include in the company's by-laws many provisions that are prohibited in an SARL or SA, such as:

- the non-assignment of shares for a maximum period of ten years;
- restrictions concerning the transfer of shares between shareholders;
- suspension of voting rights and exclusion of a corporate shareholder in the event that it undergoes a change of control;
- the exclusion of a shareholder.

Shareholders are free to choose management mode and conditions (collective management, management by a single person, etc). The sole legal constraint is the appointment of a chairman, who may be either an individual or a legal entity, to represent the SAS in its dealings with third parties. No board of directors is needed, as the chairman alone may exercise management powers. Shareholders are further free to set the conditions (quorum, majority) and procedure (written consultations, conference calls, etc) related to shareholders' decisions. Decisions having consequences regarding shareholders' individual rights must be unanimously approved, however, for example the exclusion of shareholders.

Despite the great flexibility afforded, SASs are subject to certain legal requirements. Shareholders are required to vote in a general meeting on the following matters: approval of the annual accounts, appointment of the statutory auditor, capital increases and reductions, amortisation of capital, merger, dissolution.

If the SAS's net equity falls below one-half of its share capital, the company must be recapitalised in accordance with the same requirements as for SAs.

Economic Interest Grouping (EIG)

The EIG may also be used as a joint venture. This corporate vehicle, which has legal status, must have a minimum of two members, but does not require any minimum equity. French law does not treat EIGs as companies.

The EIG's activity must be linked to its members' activities, its purpose being to facilitate or develop its respective members' businesses and to improve overall results. Functioning and management rules are established freely by the members in the by-laws. Members' liability for the EIG's debts is not limited, but joint and several. In practice, EIGs are often used for research and development ventures, joint sales, or as a distribution agent for members. From a tax standpoint, any profits realised by an EIG are taxed in the hands of its members.

Société en Participation (SEP)

SEPs may also be used for joint ventures. This vehicle has no legal status. A partnership structure is generally adopted in the case of major construction contracts abroad, for local tax reasons. The transfer of its shares is subject to a 4.8 per cent registration duty.

Shareholders' Agreements

Shareholders' agreements are used to establish rights and liabilities between shareholders which are not, or cannot be, provided by company by-laws. Such agreements may be concluded only by the shareholders concerned and may be kept confidential. The terms of shareholders' agreements mainly concern two aspects, which are the company's management (for example agreements may grant to minority shareholders a greater control over management than that provided under commercial law) and shareholder buy-outs, ie minority shareholders may be assured that in the event of any share transfer, the transferor will guarantee the purchase of minority interests.

The purpose of agreements may only be to grant minority shareholders specific rights (eg a minimum dividend), or to set rights in order to maintain the ownership structure (standstill agreements) and control the transfer of shareholdings (pre-emptive rights or exclusion rights, in the case of a change of control of a shareholder).

Violation of shareholders' agreements is punished only by payment of damages and, possibly, the cancellation of the contract by the court. For example, if a share transfer does not observe the pre-emptive rights conferred by a shareholders' agreement, the share transfer cannot be cancelled by the court. In addition to damages ordered by the courts, contractual penalties may be imposed if such a penalty is provided for in the agreement.

Ancillary Contractual Documentation

Generally the shareholders' agreement provides for some additional contracts to be entered into between the joint-venture company and one of the partners. These contracts are distinct from the main contract but are essential to the operating of the joint venture. They relate to services, supplies, transfer of know-how, management, and sales of products.

Part Six

Tax and Legal Issues

25

The Legal System

Sylvie Le Damany and Monique Bandrac,
Coopers & Lybrand CLC Juridique et Fiscal

Historically, French law is derived from Roman laws and Frankish customs. Following the French Revolution of 1789, the legal practices of the old regime were merged with the new revolutionary philosophy to form the Napoleonic Codes. The laws of France subsequently underwent major changes, particularly as industrialisation gained momentum in the 20th century.

SOURCES OF FRENCH LAW

The majority of French legal provisions are voted in parliament or result from regulations established by the executive, with little deference to common practice, apart from labour law which draws on it significantly. In France, case law is used primarily as a reference; judges do not establish rules, but merely interpret the texts which embody legislative or regulatory will. This approach leaves French judges free to resolve creatively issues not covered in legal texts, a situation which may often result in the provisions of the law being distorted.

French laws are based on the Constitution of 4 October 1958. The Constitution Committee ensures that laws comply with the Constitution, while the lawfulness of regulatory provisions is primarily the province of the Council of State.

Treaties and international agreements ratified by France have a higher authority than national law, provided that the ratification process is properly conducted (ie conforming to the French Constitution), and subject to the sole requirement of reciprocity.* France is therefore subject to European Union law and the European Convention on Human Rights. The Council of State has recently upheld the supremacy of European Union law over national legislation.

FRENCH LAWS

Form

French laws are embodied in written statutes.

Parliamentary laws are published in the Official Journal, but regulatory provisions are not always published. Decrees, ie regulations issued by the President of the Republic or the Prime Minister, are published; however, orders issued by other administrative agencies are generally not published.

It is necessary not only to have precise knowledge of a statute, but also of its interpretation in case law. Accordingly, supreme court decisions (*Tribunal des Conflits, Cour de Cassation, Conseil d'Etat*) are published officially, but the decisions of lower courts are made known to the public only if published in a private compendium. However, as justice is considered to be a public matter in France, copies of all court judgments may be obtained from the clerk of the appropriate court.

French laws are largely codified. The Civil Code, Code of Civil Procedure, Commercial Code, Penal Code and Code of Criminal Procedure (current penal procedure), referred to collectively as the Napoleonic Codes, were formulated between 1804 and 1810 at the behest of Napoleon. Their content has obviously undergone major transformations since that time and some of the many new texts have not yet been codified.

In addition to family law, the Civil Code contains the fundamental principles of French private law, ie contract law and civil liability. The Commercial Code embodies rules specifically applicable to businessmen and commercial dealings.

The Napoleonic Codes, designed to serve as legal systems and approved in this capacity, have been elaborated on a global approach basis by parliamentary assemblies. The Civil Code in par-

---

* Article 55 of the Constitution of 4 October 1958.

ticular reflects the philosophy of the French Revolution, while criminal procedure, inspired more by politics and pragmatism than by philosophy, has been more substantially amended, as has been civil procedure.

Other regulatory rules of the French legal system are codified by the administrative authorities. Codification in this case is not the work of a legislator and does not modify already existing laws; it is an administrative task concerned simply with completing all legislative and regulatory texts applicable to a given area and placing them in a particular order.

The Administrative Code, Administrative Tribunals and Administrative Appeals Tribunals Code, General Tax Code, Labour Code, Rural Code, Public Health Code, and so on are administrative codes.

Substance

In substance, French law distinguishes sharply between public and private law.

Public authorities are largely governed by rules and subject to jurisdictions different from those applicable to private individuals and their relevant courts.

Administrative laws confer a number of advantages on public authorities. Ownership of state assets or those of public authorities is governed by a special regime establishing inalienability and indefeasibility with regard to public property. The property of public authorities may not be seized, while the state has the right to recover what is due to it without having to take legal action. Contracts entered into by public authorities confer upon said bodies exclusive privileges under common law which are:

- the right of government to amend the clauses of a contract, subject to payment of compensation to the other party;
- the right of government to impose its own penalties (eg state control) on a contracting party in the event of default.

The liability of administrative agencies and government employees, too, is subject to special rules. The number of rules reflects the growing trend towards a state-controlled economy, with the public sector expanding relentlessly at the expense of private enterprise. Up until 1986, the State increased its control over production and distribution of wealth, thereby becoming an increasingly active player in the economy. The past ten years have seen a reversal of this trend as privatisation* and deregulation have gained momentum, without, however, disturbing the traditional line between public and private law.

French private law bears the hallmarks of 18th-century revolutionary philosophy. The liberalism and individualism which inspired it contrasts with the principles underlying 20th-century legislation and case law.

In principle, contracts are entered into at the discretion of the parties involved,[†] but the parties are bound by an ever-increasing number of statutory laws. These laws are either state-controlled legislative provisions, the number of which is declining as European Union legislation gains ground, or, much more broadly, laws aimed at protecting social categories perceived as weak and accordingly favoured (protection of consumers,[‡] tenants, etc).

With regard to torts, civil liability under common law is now only partially based on fault. In the case of damage caused by objects,[§] the obligation to make reparation lies automatically with the person having the use, control and management of the object in question. Similarly, in light of recent case law,[**] the obligation to repair damage caused by persons in custody lies automatically with the custodian. Special rules apply to damage caused under particular circumstances, for example traffic accidents[††] involving land motor vehicles, or by certain persons, for example a principal's liability for the actions of his agent.[‡‡]

In France, private ownership is in principle an absolute right.[§§] That right is nevertheless considered to be open to abuse and its exercise by the owner is therefore subject to imperative regulations that are extremely cumbersome and pervasive. Property is particularly prone to public interest regulations: zoning regulations, agricultural applications, town and country planning, protection of sites, mountains, water, the environment generally, and so on.

Transfer of ownership for valuable consideration is carried out under French law by a mere exchange of consent.[***] However, the related agreement will be binding upon third parties only if it has been drawn up in a certified form, ie by a notary. In France, announcements concerning the legal status of buildings[†††] are made through the mortgage

---

* Law of 2 July 1986.
[†] Article 1134 of the Civil Code.
[‡] Consumer law was codified within a law dated 26 July 1993.
[§] Article 1384, § 1 of the Civil Code, as interpreted by case law.
[**] Interpretation of article 1384, § 1 of the Civil Code.
[††] Law of 5 July 1985.
[‡‡] Article 1384, § 5 of the Civil Code.
[§§] Article 544 of the Civil Code.
[***] Articles 1138 and 1583 of the Civil Code.
[†††] Decree of 4 January and 14 October 1955.

registry, a purely administrative, and not legal, agency attached to the Ministry of Finance. The act of registration does not, however, cancel any defects contained in the deed of sale or mortgage agreement. Special arrangements exist for Alsace-Moselle.

Under French law, a person's total estate, without any exceptions, may be used to pay off that person's debts.* French law does not allow a debtor to shield any part of his assets from the creditor and stipulates that the allocation of certain assets to certain debts incurred in the performance of an activity is subject to the set up of a legal entity whose purpose will be the intended activity. French law likewise does not permit the assignment of debt without the consent of the creditor.

A debtor's assets may be seized, then sold by a creditor, who uses the sale proceeds to settle the debt. Creditors may therefore compete for a debtor's estate, with the exception of collateralised assets, such as mortgaged property. This procedure is, in principle, conducted at the initiative of each creditor individually, ie a single creditor may seize all the debtor's assets, have them sold and be allocated all the proceeds if the other creditors do not act swiftly to join him. If a debtor operates a company (commercial, craft, agricultural, professional) however, creditors must act collectively. All creditors are invited to make themselves known and are ranked equally, except where debts have been secured. Today, collective action by creditors is preceded by endeavours to restore the company's financial situation,† in the interest of employment protection.

Like all other aspects of private law, commercial law strongly reflects the repercussions of the development of economic public order. Commercial activities are now heavily regulated and company law, previously contract-based, is now enshrined in statutes. Laws dealing with business crimes, including the liability of management and the criminal liability of corporations, are growing steadily in number.

The Registry of Trade and Companies is the central body in charge of official commercial announcements, comprising local records kept by commercial courts and a national register kept by the *Institut National de la Propriété Industrielle* (INPI: French industrial property institute) in Paris.

---

* Article 2093 of the Civil Code.
† Law of 25 January 1985.

ORGANISATION OF GOVERNMENT SERVICES IN FRANCE

In France, government is administered by legally distinct entities, each of which has its own management structure, employees, services and assets. In addition to the State, which performs both political and administrative functions, there are the State-run institutions which oversee districts, departments, regions and overseas territories, as well as specialised institutions.

The State

For administrative purposes, the state is divided into a central administration and a territorial administration.

At its highest level, the central administration is inseparable from State politics and government, ie the President of the Republic, Prime Minister and other members of government who direct the nation's political life.* The members of government are also administrative authorities. They appoint government employees and exercise a general regulatory influence, issuing decrees and orders to establish general standards.

The central administration is divided into a number of ministries, each headed by a minister. Some services are accountable to the Prime Minister.

In recent times, an increasing number of independent administrative authorities have been established within the central administration. Such authorities hold individual or general decision-making power implying that their decisions may not be referred to or censored by a higher authority. They operate outside the central administration and are not accountable to a minister; their decisions are controlled by judiciary authorities alone. Their activity is related to highly sensitive sectors such as: *Commission Nationale de l'Informatique et des Libertés* (National Data Protection Commission),† *Conseil Supérieur de l'Audiovisuel* (National Broadcasting Board),‡ *Commission des Opérations de Bourse* (Stock Exchange Committee),§ *Conseil de la Concurrence* (Competition Council)** and so forth.

---

* Article 20, § 1 of the Constitution of 4 October 1958.
† Law of 6 January 1978.
‡ Law of 17 January 1989.
§ Order of 28 September 1967.
** Order of 1 December 1986.

Each ministry provides external services, which make up the territorial administration. They are overseen by a prefect in each *département*; the prefect of the *département* in which the region's principal town is located is also the prefect of the region. He represents the state's executive and accordingly has supervisory authority over the services at a regional level, in addition to police powers.

Local Authorities

Local authorities are autonomous, administrative, but not political, units charged with managing districts, departments, regions and overseas territories. They have their own budgets and have jurisdiction for dealing with local matters such as: zoning regulations, protection of national heritage and sites, housing, town and country planning, vocational training and apprenticeships,* state benefits and health support, national education and school transport, environmental protection, cultural activities, ports and waterways.† The state, however, retains the power to intervene and supervises the local authorities' management decisions through the prefects.

Specialised Institutions

Although attached to public authorities (ie the state and local authorities), specialised institutions have a distinct legal status. Included in this category are the major specialised national education establishments *Ecole Nationale de l'Administration,* (senior public administration), *Ecole Nationale de la Magistrature* (magistracy) and *Ecole Polytechnique* (sciences). Other specialised institutions include public companies (both local and national) which are involved in commercial and industrial activities. Also classed in this category are chambers of commerce and industry, which offer industrial, commercial and administrative functions. Public companies are managed by the state or local authorities, but their management and relations with third parties are governed by private law.

THE FRENCH JURISDICTIONAL SYSTEM

The overriding principle of the French jurisdictional system since the Revolution has been the separation of administrative and judicial functions, in accordance with the law of 16 and 24 August 1790.

As a result, a separate jurisdictional system has been set up alongside the judiciary, to handle disputes involving the administration. The sep-

---

* Law of 7 January 1983.
† Law of 22 July 1983.

aration of administrative and judicial functions is reflected in the concurrent existence of these two jurisdictional procedures – judicial and administrative.

A supreme court, *Tribunal des Conflits*, has been set up in order to resolve disputes relating to the respective jurisdiction of judiciary and administrative courts.

The *Conseil Constitutionnel* is the body responsible for checking that French laws conform to the French Constitutional Code. It is obligatory for certain laws involving constitutional issues or the internal regulation of parliament to be submitted to the *Conseil* for review. Other than these, the only way a claim can be brought before the *Conseil* for review is if either the French president or the prime minister or the president of both chambers of parliament or members of parliament (if more than 60) demand it prior to promulgation.

The Judiciary

The courts system uses a pyramid organisational structure. At the top is the *Cour de Cassation*, the highest court of judiciary, whose fundamental purpose is to ensure the consistency of the interpretation of the law.

The *Cour de Cassation* is the highest court of the judiciary and hears recourses against judgments made by all lower courts. Its role is to ensure that the decisions of lower courts conform with the law but not to re-examine the facts and evidence.

In accordance with the right-to-appeal principle (which does not apply for minor cases), litigants have the option to lodge an appeal against the judgment made by the lower courts with a higher court in the hierarchical network, the *Cours d'Appel* (Courts of Appeal). There are 37 *Cours d'Appel* on French territory, which have jurisdiction over several lower courts.

Like the *Cour de Cassation*, the C*ours d'Appel* are divided into specialised divisions which mirror the jurisdiction of the lower courts.

As regards lower courts, a distinction should be drawn between the civil, commercial and labour courts, which settle disputes relating to private interests, and the criminal or penal courts, which have the right to sentence offenders to fines or imprisonment.

Civil matters are in first instance heard before *tribunaux de grande instance* or for minor cases by *tribunaux d'instance*, commercial matters before *tribunaux de commerce* (commercial courts) and labour law issues before *conseil de prud'hommes* (labour courts).

There is at least one *tribunal de grande instance* in each administrative *département* (the primary geographic division under French administrative organisation) and in general there are also one or more commercial courts and labour courts in each district.

For criminal matters, the courts of first instance are the *tribunaux de police* (criminal branch of *tribunaux d'instance*) for minor offences and the *tribunal correctionnel* (criminal branch of the *tribunaux de grande instance*) for more serious offences.

Serious crimes are dealt with by the *cours d'assises* (jury courts) whose judgments cannot be appealed against.

Under French law, the jury court is the only court entitled to a jury of nine jurors in addition to a bench of three magistrates. Jurors are French citizens over the age of 23 chosen at random from a list based on the list of registered voters.

Administrative Courts

The administrative courts have jurisdiction over disputes related to public law between governmental agencies and those under their authority. The French administrative courts have jurisdiction over disputes and conflicts subject to public law, which mainly governs the relations between public bodies or agencies, and between those bodies or agencies and individuals, including some tax issues.

Moreover, the administrative courts have the power to cancel regulatory or individual acts entered into by the national or local public bodies, by means of *ultra vires* recourse (judicial review). Thus, decrees, government regulatory acts or unratified ordinances are subject to cancellation by the administrative courts, when they are inconsistent with the laws, constitutional principles or international treaties (such as European regulations).

The supreme court of the administrative courts is the *Conseil d'Etat* (highest administrative court), which is also the legal counsellor of the government.

The right-to-appeal principle is also found in French administrative proceedings. Administrative tribunals are the courts of first instance and administrative courts of appeal represent a higher level of the administrative hierarchy.

Specialised Jurisdiction

The increasing complexity of the global economic landscape and the subsequent regulatory issues it raises have necessitated the establishment of administrative authorities with jurisdictional powers in addition to their consultative or regulatory roles, such as the *Conseil de la Concurrence* or the *Commission des Opérations de Bourse* (COB).

Under competition law, the *Conseil de la Concurrence* is empowered to impose fines for anti-competitive collusion and abuse of dominant market position as well as for the enforcement of French anti-trust regulation. Appeals against the Council's decisions must be lodged with the Paris Court of Appeal, then possibly with the Cour de Cassation.

The *Commission des Opérations de Bourse* (COB) is an independent administrative authority responsible for the protection of savings invested in financial instruments and all other publicly-funded financial transactions.

The COB has the authority to grant an injunction against or fine any party which contravenes its rules. Appeals against the COB's decisions are heard by the Paris Court of Appeal.

26

Company Formation: Taxation and Legal Implications for Foreign Investors

Gilles Semadeni, Xavier Rohmer and Nicolas Granier, Coopers & Lybrand CLC Juridique et Fiscal

LEGAL IMPLICATIONS FOR FOREIGN INVESTORS

Introduction: Operating as a Branch or as a Company

Companies wishing to do business in France may do so directly through a branch, or by setting up a separate legal entity, usually a company. Should the setting up of a legal entity be retained, investors will select the structure most suited to their requirements from the various corporate forms allowed under French law. Their choice will depend primarily on the nature of the activities (civil or commercial), the size of the operations to be performed, the investor's liability and desired degree of control over the entity.

Unlike a company, a branch is merely an operations centre, without a distinct legal identity. Accordingly, the company which opens the branch is directly responsible for the transactions performed by it and must ensure that the branch is registered at the Trade and Companies Registry. The company's legal representative or an employee of the company is generally appointed to manage the branch.

Foreign companies setting up a branch in France are further required to submit their annual accounts, translated into French, to the clerk of the commercial court in the district in which the branch is registered.

The branch structure offers the advantage of flexibility and simplicity from a legal viewpoint and is generally used by foreign investors, either as an initial gateway into the French market, or for tax reasons.

Foreign corporations may also decide to open a simple representative office for the exclusive purpose of making contacts, advertising the parent company and gathering information. Although they have no commercial activity, representative offices must be registered at the Trade and Companies Registry.

Setting Up a Company

What types of companies can be chosen?

Under French corporate law, a distinction is made between companies engaged in civil or commercial activities, the civil option being restricted mainly to professional or property activities. The distinction between the various types of companies will also be made on the following bases:

- companies which are legal entities (all companies registered at the Trade and Companies Registry) vs companies which are not (eg *Sociétés en Participation*);
- companies in which the shareholders' liability is limited (eg *Sociétés Anonymes, Sociétés à Responsabilité Limitée, Sociétés par Actions Simplifiées* – see below) vs unlimited liability companies (eg *Sociétés en Nom Collectif*);
- companies the shares of which may be transferred simply by means of a transfer from one shareholder account to another (eg *Sociétés Anonymes* and *Sociétés par Actions Simplifiées*) vs companies for which the transfer of shares entails certain formalities (eg *Sociétés à Responsabilité Limitée, Sociétés en Nom Collectif* and *Sociétés Civiles*).

A further possible structure is an Economic Interest Grouping (EIG), which is a legal entity, but is not deemed to be an investment vehicle. The EIG is a legal structure which enables its members to pool their efforts in order to facilitate or develop their respective economic activities. It remains totally independent of its members' own businesses and offers a high degree of organisational and operational flexibility. The EIG structure is commonly used to carry out joint operations which would be difficult to perform on an individual basis, such as research and development services, marketing studies, advertising campaigns or purchasing groups.

The European Economic Interest Grouping (EEIG), a similarly flexible structure, was created under EU Regulation no 2137/85 to facilitate cross-border development and co-operation between companies operating in the EU.

Finally, a company may be transformed into another type of company without a new legal entity having to be created, unless its form is changed to that of a non-profit making organisation (*association*) or Economic Interest Grouping (EIG).

In all cases, transformation requires that the conditions applicable to the new company form, are fulfilled before the decision to transform the company is taken by the shareholders. For example, to be transformed into an SA, an SNC must have at least seven partners and a minimum share capital of 250,000 fr. In addition, the SNC's net assets must be declared to be at least equal to the share capital by an independent auditor.

Below is an outline of the main types of French companies suitable as investment vehicles in France:

- *Société Anonyme* (SA);
- *Société par Actions Simplifiée* (SAS);
- *Société à Responsabilité Limitée* (SARL);
- *Société en Commandite par Actions* (SCA);
- *Société en Nom Collectif* (SNC);
- *Société Civile* (SC);
- *Société en Participation* (SEP).

Company name

A company may choose any name, provided that this name is not held by an existing company or business, or is not a registered trade mark. A company's name does not have to be registered as a trade mark.

The company's name must be preceded or followed by an indication of the company's legal form (SA, SARL, SNC, etc) and must appear on all corporate stationery together with the registration number of the company and other corporate details, such as the share capital and head office.

Head office

The head office in France must be provided for in the articles of association. The company should have a formal right to occupy the head office premises, whether as owner, lessee or sub-lessee. Alternatively, the company may simply be domiciled at the premises of another group company or, under specific conditions, of its legal representative.

Accounts and audit requirements

All commercial companies are required to present a balance sheet, and an income statement at each financial year-end. In most cases, the financial statements must be filed with the clerk of the local commercial court and made available for inspection by the public at the Trade and Companies Registry. A report providing details of the company's activities is also required.

For certain forms of company, such as the SA, SAS and SCA, at least one statutory auditor must be appointed, together with a substitute statutory auditor. The statutory auditors' function is to ensure the protection of shareholders and report on the annual financial statements. For other companies and groupings (SARL, SNC, SCS, EIG), the requirement to appoint a statutory auditor depends on the size of the company's operations (turnover, total assets, number of employees).

Statutory auditors are distinct from the accountants who assist companies with the preparation of their annual accounts, who may be either internal or external professionals.

Authorisations, permits and licences

The establishment of a company in France may require an appropriate licence to be issued by the French authorities, if the business to be conducted by the French subsidiary is a 'regulated activity' (eg insurance, banking, armaments, transport, telecommunications, etc).

Immigration considerations

Depending on the type of company concerned, the company's officers (chairman and managing directors) must require a resident permit or a foreign trader's permit (*carte de commerçant étranger*) if he is not a French national or a national of another EU member state. Certain university degrees and/or professional qualifications may also be required, depending on the company's activity.

Registration

The setting up of the company will be effective as soon as the members have signed the articles of association and registered the company at the Trade and Companies Registry. Only then can the company be considered a legal entity. However, any acts taken on behalf of the company by its founders before such registration may be taken over by the company after it has been registered if the articles of association provide for it or by special resolution of the general meeting.

In some types of companies (SA, SARL), the share capital has to be paid into a bank account opened in the name of the company before the articles of association can be signed.

Outline of Various Types of Companies

Société Anonyme (limited liability company)

The *Société Anonyme* (SA) is the form most commonly used by large corporations when capital requirements cannot be met by a limited number of shareholders. As the SA may be quoted on a stock exchange and as its shares may be traded publicly, raising capital is easier. SA and SCA (*Société en Commandite par Actions* – see below) are the only companies eligible for quotation on a stock exchange.

Shareholders and share capital   An SA must have a minimum of seven shareholders, either private individuals or legal entities, whose liability for company debts is limited to their contribution to the share capital.

An SA's share capital must be at least 250,000 fr if the company is privately owned, and at least 1,500,000 fr if the company's shares are publicly traded. Only half of the share capital needs to be paid at the time of incorporation, the remainder being due within five years after the company's registration.

Shares are freely negotiable (by simple transfer from the transferor's shareholder account to the transferee's) and the transfer of ownership does not give rise to any registration duties, unless the transfer of the shares and the price are evidenced by a legal document signed in France, in which case registration duties of 1 per cent are payable, up to a limit of 20,000 fr per transaction.

In addition to ordinary shares, an SA may issue various types of securities, such as preferred shares (*actions de priorité*), preferred non-voting shares (*actions à dividende prioritaire sans droit de vote*), investment certificates (*certificats d'investissement*), bonds with equity warrants (*obligations avec bons de souscription d'actions*) and equity notes (*titres participatifs*).

Management and administration   An SA may be managed either by a board of directors and a chairman, which is the most common structure, or by a management board and a supervisory board.

Board of directors (*Conseil d'Administration*):

- The board of directors must have between three and twenty-four members elected from among the shareholders. Directors may be private individuals or legal entities. Legal entities must appoint a person of their choice to represent them at the board meetings. Directors may be removed from office at any time without any requirement to prove valid grounds.

- A director may not add to his duties as a director by having a separate employment contract with the company unless, at the time of his appointment to the board, he has previously been granted an employment contract by the company for a separate activity.
- The company is represented by the chairman of the board of directors, who is appointed by the board from among its members. The chairman is fully empowered to enter into contracts with third parties on behalf of the company. The company will be bound towards *bona fide* third parties by the chairman's actions, even if they are outside the corporate objective.
- The chairman of the board of directors may be assisted by managing directors, appointed by the board. Managing directors have the same powers as the chairman of the board *vis-à-vis* third parties.
- Any limitation of the chairman's or the managing director's powers, either contained in the articles of association or in a board decision, is not binding on third parties.

Management board (*Directoire*) and supervisory board (*Conseil de Surveillance*):

- The supervisory board must be composed of between 3 and 24 members, elected from among the shareholders, who then elect a chairman. The task of the supervisory board is to supervise the management of the company by the management board. The management board is elected by the supervisory board. Its members, usually numbering between one and five, may only be removed from office by decision of the shareholders. Members of the management board unfairly dismissed may claim damages. The members of the management board may be chosen from among or outside the shareholders, but may not be members of the supervisory board. They may be granted an employment contract with the company.
- The company is represented by the president of the management board (or the sole managing director), and, if any by the managing directors, who are fully empowered to enter into contracts with third parties on behalf of the company.

Shareholders meetings   At general meetings, shareholders elect, replace and remove from office members of the board of directors or of the supervisory board; appoint the statutory auditors; approve or reject the accounts and decide the appropriation of the company's net income. Furthermore, they have sole power to amend the company's articles of association.

At ordinary shareholders' meetings, decisions are made which do not call for amendments to the company's articles of association (as opposed to extraordinary shareholders' meetings). The two types of meetings have different quorum and majority voting requirements.

Shareholders must meet at least once a year at an annual ordinary general meeting to vote on the accounts of the previous financial year, on the basis of a report prepared by the statutory auditor(s).

Société par Actions Simplifiées (simplified limited liability company)

The 3 January 1994 Act created a flexible corporate structure, the *Société par Actions Simplifiée* (SAS), in order to foster co-operation between companies.

The SAS is a limited company, the management and administration of which are organised in the articles of association. They are governed by the same legal provisions as SAS, with the exception of those concerning company management (board of directors, management board and supervisory board) and shareholders' meetings.

Shareholders and share capital   An SAS must have a minimum share capital of 250,000 fr, which must be paid in full when the company is formed. The SAS's shares may be freely transferred, ie by simple transfer from one shareholder's account to another's, without any need for a deed of sale or other formalities. An SAS may not, however, be quoted on the stock exchange.

An SAS must have at least two corporate shareholders whose own individual share capital must remain at no less than 1,500,000 fr or the equivalent in the relevant foreign currency.

Management and administration   An SAS is represented in dealings with third parties by its chairman, who may be a private individual or a legal entity.

The administration and management of an SAS are established in the articles of association.

Shareholders' meetings   Conditions governing decisions taken by shareholders are freely established in the articles of association and may therefore be much less formal than in an SA.

Société à Responsabilitée Limitée (closely-held limited liability company)

The *Société à Responsabilité Limitée* (SARL) is the most appropriate legal form for small and medium-sized companies with limited capital requirements.

The SARL is the only form of company which can be set up with only one shareholder. In such a case, the company is called an *Entreprise Unipersonnelle à Responsabilité Limitée* (EURL).

Shareholders and share capital   An SARL can have up to a maximum of 50 shareholders, who may be either private individuals or legal entities and whose liability for company debts is limited to their contribution to the share capital. The share capital must be at least 50,000 fr and must be paid up in full at the time of the company's formation.

The shares of an SARL are not negotiable, ie their transfer is restricted both by law and by the company's articles of association, and must be formalised in a written agreement. Share transfers give rise to registration duties of 4.8 per cent of the purchase price or of the market value of the transferred shares, whichever is the highest, and involves a number of formalities.

Management and administration   An SARL is managed by one or several managers (*Gérants*) appointed in the articles of association or by an ordinary shareholders' meeting. They must be private individuals, but need not be shareholders.

The manager represents the company and is fully empowered to commit it *vis-à-vis* third parties. The company will be bound towards *bona fide* third parties even if the chairman has acted outside the company's objectives. He may be dismissed at any time by the ordinary shareholders' meeting. However, unfair dismissal of a manager may entitle him to receive damages.

He may also be an employee of the company if he holds, either singly or in conjunction with his spouse and children, less than 50 per cent of the company's shares and if his work as a company employee is clearly distinguishable from his management duties.

The manager is covered by a specific social security and tax regime:

- if he is a minority shareholder, his remuneration qualifies as a salary for both tax and social security purposes (except unemployment benefit, which may nevertheless be covered by private insurance policies);

- If he is a majority shareholder, for social security purposes, he must contribute to the special regime applicable to self-employed persons. For tax purposes, his remuneration qualifies as a salary.

Shareholders' meetings At ordinary shareholders' meetings, decisions are made which do not involve any amendments to the company's articles of association and are passed by a majority vote from shareholders representing more than half of the share capital on first call (on second call, decisions are adopted by a simple majority of shareholders in attendance and voting).

The articles of association may only be amended at extraordinary shareholders' meetings, subject to a majority vote of shareholders representing three-quarters of the share capital. Shareholders' decisions can be passed without the need for a meeting if shareholders consent unanimously to the same minutes or other document in question.

Société en Commandite par Actions (equity partnership)

The *Société en Commandite par Actions* (SCA) is a commercial structure that is very useful for businesses seeking investors and desiring a clear separation between investors and management.

Like an SA, an SCA can be quoted on the stock exchange and its shares are freely negotiable. The company has two kinds of members: limited members (*commanditaires*), whose status is identical to that of the shareholders of an SA, and general members (*commandités*), whose status mirrors that of the partners in a *Société en Nom Collectif* (general partnership).

Even if the limited members hold 100 per cent of the share capital, they have neither the right nor the power to participate in the management of the company. Instead, the company is managed by a manager, who may never be chosen from among the limited members.

In the event of a transfer of shares, an SCA provides protection to the management. For a quoted company, the SCA option offers protection against hostile take-over bids.

Finally, it is worth mentioning the existence of the *Société en Commandite Simple* (SCS – limited partnership) although this type of company is not very common. It is subject to most of the rules applying to SNCs (see below) and its limited members have the same status as shareholders in an SARL.

Members and share capital   The minimum number of members required for an SCA is four (one general member and three limited members), who may be private individuals or legal entities.

The SCA must have a minimum share capital of 250,000 fr (or 1,500,000 fr, in the case of a quoted company), half of which must be paid when the SCA is formed.

Unlike general members' shares, limited members' shares are freely negotiable. Like an SA, an SCA may issue various types of securities.

Management and administration   The SCA is managed by one or several managers, who are appointed by the limited members subject to the approval of all the general members, unless otherwise stipulated in the articles of association.

Managers may be private individuals or legal entities and may be chosen from among the general members or third parties, but not from among the limited members. They have full powers to represent the company in all its dealings with third parties. For tax purposes, they are governed by the same regime as that applying to the managers of SARLs (see p 000). Managers who are general members are excluded from the general social security regime applicable to employees (ie they must contribute to a special regime applicable to self-employed persons). Managers who are not general members, however, benefit from the general social security regime applicable to employees. They may be dismissed under the conditions set forth in the articles of association or by a decision of a court of law.

General meeting of members   An annual general meeting must be held to approve the annual accounts.

Separate meetings are held for general members and limited members. To be valid, decisions must be taken with the agreement of both sets of members. The limited members' meeting must satisfy the same quorum and majority requirements as those of an SA, while general members must take decisions unanimously, as in the case of SNC members (see below).

Control over management   A supervisory board (*Conseil de Surveillance*) representing the limited members assures the ongoing supervision and review of the SCA's management. The board submits a report on the financial statements and the activities of the manager to the annual limited members' meeting.

Société en Nom Collectif (general partnership)

The *Société en Nom Collectif* (SNC) is an appropriate form of commercial company for enterprises with a limited number of partners having a strong *intuitu personae* (personal understanding) for setting up the company together.

Partners and share capital   The minimum requirement is two partners, either private individuals or legal entities, who have unlimited joint and several liability for the company's debts. The clear and precise definition of the SNC's legal purpose is imperative. This alone provides a safeguard against unlimited partner liability towards third parties arising from the manager's actions.

There is no minimum capital requirement for an SNC and there are no rules specifying the amount that must be paid at the company's incorporation.

The shares of an SNC are not negotiable. Their transfer, even between partners, requires the unanimous consent of the partners and must be evidenced by a written agreement. Registration duties of 4.8 per cent of the highest of the purchase price or market value of the transferred shares are due on share transfers.

Management and administration   The SNC is managed by one or several managers, who may be private individuals or legal entities, but are not necessarily partners. A manager may be dismissed, but may claim damages for unfair dismissal under certain circumstances.

Vis-à-vis the partners, the manager has full powers to act in the company's interest, unless his powers are restricted in the articles of association. *Vis-à-vis* third parties, the manager may act and enter into contracts on behalf of the company within the scope of the corporate objectives.

With respect to its tax status, if the manager is a private individual, and is not a partner, his remuneration qualifies as a salary. If he is a partner, he is taxed at a rate appropriate to his income category which is determined according to the company's activity (trading profits, income from professional activities, property income, etc). If the manager is a company, its remuneration constitutes part of its taxable profit. These rules will apply only if the company does not elect the direct taxation regime.

With respect to its social status, the manager who is not a partner may contribute to the general social security regime applicable to employees in cases where his rights are limited in the articles of association. If he is a partner, he must contribute to the special social security regime applicable to self-employed persons.

General partners' meetings   The partners must meet to approve the annual accounts when requested to do so by any of the partners. Decisions must be taken unanimously when the articles of association do not stipulate otherwise or for important decisions defined by law.

Société Civile (civil company)

The *Société Civile* (SC) is a form of legal entity enabling its shareholders who have a strong *intuitu personae* between them to perform a civil (as opposed to commercial) activity within a very flexible structure. *Sociétés Civiles* are set up for purposes such as property transactions, agricultural activities, professional activities.

The distribution of powers and control within an SC may be organised on terms and conditions which are simpler than those encountered in commercial companies, with the exception of SASs.

Shareholders and share capital   The SC must be set up with a minimum of two shareholders, either private individuals or legal entities, who are liable for the company's debts in proportion to their contribution to the share capital. However, there is no minimum capital requirement.

The shares of a *Société Civile* are not negotiable. Their transfer must be evidenced by a written agreement and the prior unanimous consent of the shareholders is required, unless the by-laws stipulate otherwise. Share transfers are stampable in accordance with the rules applicable to the shares of SARLs and SNCs (see above).

Management and administration   The *Société Civile* is managed by one or several managers, who may be either private individuals or legal entities, but who need not be shareholders. Managers are appointed either by the articles of association or by a shareholders' meeting and may be dismissed by a simple majority vote of the shareholders. A Manager may claim damages in the event of unfair dismissal.

The powers of the manager are similar to those of managers in an SNC.

The manager of a *Société Civile* also has the same tax status as those of an SNC.

Shareholders' meetings   The terms and conditions governing the shareholders' decision-making process must be defined in the company's articles of association.

Société en Participation (unincorporated joint ventures)

A *Société en Participation* (SEP) is not a legal entity and therefore has no corporate assets separate from that of its partners. The SEP is generally used by partners who do not wish to disclose their specific project to third parties and joint ventures. It must be set up with at least two partners.

There is no minimum capital requirement. If shares are issued, they are not negotiable and their transfer must be evidenced by a written agreement and approved unanimously by the partners, unless otherwise stipulated in the articles of association.

The SEP may be undisclosed in which case each partner is deemed to act in its own name in dealings with third parties, with no liability falling to the other partners. If the SEP is disclosed to third parties, the partners are jointly and severally liable for the debts incurred by any single partner.

The SEP is run by one or more managers appointed from among or outside the partners, who are normally responsible for dealings with third parties. In the absence of any indication in the articles of association, all partners are deemed to be managers.

The conditions of appointment, remuneration and termination of the managers are stipulated in the articles of association.

TAX IMPLICATIONS FOR FOREIGN VISITORS

Branches vs Subsidiaries

Local branch of a foreign company

A branch may be defined as a permanent place of business having a certain degree of independence in its operations and dealings with third parties. It does not have either a separate legal or tax existence from the parent company.

However, from a French tax perspective, when the company creating the branch is a foreign entity, its French branch is normally deemed to be a 'permanent establishment' for tax purposes (ie the branch is treated as a company taxable in France on the activity performed in the French territory) by virtue of most tax treaties concluded with

France, and is subject to all tax obligations like a French incorporated company (eg corporate income tax, VAT, taxes assessed on wages and local taxes). In the absence of a tax treaty, a French branch of a foreign company must pay branch withholding tax on all of its net after-tax income (see below).

Locally incorporated subsidiary of a foreign company

Large business enterprises, where the capital needs cannot be insured by a limited number of shareholders, commonly choose to operate as an SA. Most small- and medium-sized enterprises choose to operate as an SARL.

From a tax perspective, a subsidiary is subject to the same tax obligations as any company incorporated in France (eg corporate income tax, VAT, taxes assessed on wages and local taxes). However, it is possible for a parent company and its branches or subsidiaries to be considered as a single entity liable for corporate tax (see Chapter 24, under 'Acquisition of Shares'.).

Profit Repatriation Considerations
Branch

Net after-tax profits realised by a French permanent establishment (whether a branch or not) of a foreign company are deemed remitted at the end of each fiscal year to shareholders of the foreign company. These shareholders are either individuals domiciled outside France or non-French companies. As a general rule profits remitted to such shareholders are subject to a 25 per cent branch tax.

Pursuant to the provisions of most tax treaties, the rate of branch tax imposed on profits deemed distributed by a permanent establishment of a foreign company is often reduced or eliminated. Foreign companies may, however, avoid reassessment by proving that the profits made in France by their permanent establishments are, in fact, either not distributed outside France or distributed to shareholders having their tax domiciles in France. In addition, further to a statement of the EU commission dated 5 August 1997, net profit from a domestic branch, which are passed on to a head office in the EU, are no longer liable to French branch tax.

Subsidiaries

French withholding tax/mechanism of tax treaty reduction
When profits derived by a French company subject to corporate income tax (*Société Anonyme, Société par Action Simplifiée*, or *Société à Responsabilité Limitée*) are repatriated to persons not hav-

ing an effective domicile or registered office in France, domestic law provides for a 25 per cent dividend withholding tax which can be reduced by a tax treaty and/or by the EU parent/subsidiaries directive.

In most treaties concluded by France, the dividend tax withheld at source from dividends paid to qualifying corporate shareholders is reduced to either 5 or 10 per cent of the gross dividend. For instance, the double tax treaty between France and the United States which entered into force in August 1994 provides that the distribution of dividends is liable to the payment of a withholding tax at a rate which cannot exceed:

- 5 per cent of the gross amount of dividends, where the effective beneficiary of the dividend is a company which owns directly or indirectly 10 per cent of the share capital of the company distributing dividends;
- 10 per cent of the gross amount of dividends in all other cases.

However, under the parent/subsidiaries EU directive, dividends paid by French subsidiaries to qualifying European parent companies may be exempt from withholding tax provided certain conditions are met. Such qualifying parent companies must own at least 25 per cent of the share capital in the distributing French subsidiary for not less than two years, or make the commitment to own such shareholding for an uninterrupted period of two years.

Précompte (tax equalisation) and credit tax   Where the distribution of dividends is paid out of profits which have never been subject to corporate tax at full rate (eg dividends from other subsidiaries), the French distributing company shall withhold a *précompte* at a rate of 33⅓ per cent. This is further developed in Chapter 27 under 'Taxation of Distributions'.

Tax treaty refund of the *avoir fiscal* and *précompte*   Certain double tax treaties allow non-residents to use the tax credit (*avoir fiscal*) which is made available to the recipient of French source dividends, established or having its registered office in France, in order to avoid double taxation (see Chapter 27 under 'Taxation of Distributions').

Transfer of this tax credit is generally restricted to individuals or legal entities which are not considered as parent companies for the double tax treaty purposes (in most cases, this means that the corporate recipient does not hold more than 10 per cent of the shares in the distributing company).

Where the recipient of the dividend is not entitled to the *avoir fiscal*, it may benefit from a reimbursement of the *précompte* due from the

French distributing company – where appropriate – if it is resident of a country with which France has concluded a double tax treaty.

Interest Paid to Foreign Shareholders

Thin capitalisation rules

Under French tax law, the deduction of interest paid by a French company to its direct shareholders, whether resident in France or not, is restricted.

- interest is not deductible if the share capital of the French company is not paid in full;
- the maximum rate for deductible interest is equal to the yearly average of the gross yield on bonds at issuance of private company bonds. This rate, which varies regularly, was 5.75 per cent for the 1997 calendar year;
- where the shareholders are considered to be managing the French company or owning over 50 per cent of the financial rights or voting rights in this company, interest is deductible only on loans from all of the shareholders concerned, up to a maximum of one and a half times the amount of the French company's share capital. This threshold is not applicable, however, to interest payments made by a subsidiary to its French parent company when the latter fulfils the conditions provided by the affiliation privilege regime.

It should be noted that the French Revenue also attempts to apply these rules in context of indirect share ownership.

French withholding tax

In principle, interest in respect of bonds held by non-residents is paid gross.

Interest paid by a French company in connection with a loan concluded abroad is subject to withholding tax at a rate of 15 per cent. This withholding tax may be avoided provided the following conditions are met:

- a loan agreement is concluded prior to the effective cash transfer;
- the lender must be a non-resident;
- the borrower is a French-registered legal person;
- the French Ministry of Finance must have prior notification of loans granted by non-EU controlling shareholders.

This domestic exemption applies to loan agreements but not to intra-group short-term credit facilities.

Start-Business Issues

Pre-operating losses and start-up/constructions costs

Start-up expenses, such as lawyer's or notary's fees, that are incurred for the creation and organisation of a company must either be amortised over five years or expensed in the first year. Tangible assets, such as network equipment, can be amortised. However, in principle, intangible assets, such as licenses, cannot be amortised.

Pre-operating expenses, such as those incurred through the installation of network equipment or the construction of a building, are capitalised.

The two principal methods used to depreciate such expenses are the straight-line method, which is used for commercial property, patents and industrial know-how, and the declining-balance method, which is used for industrial buildings, plant, equipment and vehicles. In general, the starting date for depreciation is the date on which an asset is put into service. When an asset is depreciated under the straight-line method, this date is the date on which it was acquired; when an asset is depreciated under the declining-balance method, this date is the date on which it was built. For example, if the construction of a cellular station begins during the 1997 tax year and takes two years to complete, the company will depreciate construction costs in 1999.

Tax loss carry-overs

Loss carry overs may not normally be transferred to another taxpayer. In other words, only the taxpayer who actually incurs the tax loss may benefit from it and only if the taxpayer does not change its corporate purpose or activity. Accordingly, in the case of a merger or a partial transfer of the taxpayer's business activity, loss carry forwards in the nature of unused depreciation deductions may no longer be carried forward indefinitely but are assimilated to ordinary loss carry forwards and utilisation is thus limited to five years. When a taxpayer sells a going concern or substantially changes the nature of its business activity or its corporate purpose, it also loses its losses.

Transfer Pricing Rules

Introduction

Statutory rules on transfer pricing adopt the arm's-length principle for related party transactions. In addition, there are a considerable number of court cases on issues pertaining to transfer pricing which aid in the interpretation and application of legislation. Despite limitations on available government resources, recent legislative developments emphasise the interest of the French tax administration in transfer pricing issues.

Statutory rules

There are two main statutory rules which address transfer pricing:

- Section 57 of the French Tax Code (*Code Général des impôts*);
- the concept of *acte anormal de gestion* (abnormal act of management). The courts decide whether this concept applies by comparing the commercial practices of the company under review with what they judge to be 'normal' acts of management.

In theory, the tax authorities can choose whether to apply Section 57 or the concept of *acte anormal de gestion* when questioning a transfer pricing policy. In reality however, this element of choice is likely to be removed by the limitations of each regulation.

Section 57   Introduced into the French tax code on 31 May 1933 and since then regularly updated, the most recent being on 13 April 1996, Section 57 can be applied only in relation to cross-border transfer pricing issues. Enforcement of Section 57 requires the tax authorities to prove that a dependent relationship existed between the parties involved in the transaction under review and that a transfer of profits occurred. It is not, however, necessary to prove dependency when applying Section 57 to transfers between entities in France and related entities operating from tax havens.

Dependency can either be 'legal' or 'de facto'. Legal dependency is relatively easy for the tax authorities to prove. It is defined as direct control by a foreign entity of the share capital or voting rights of the French entity under review. It can also mean dependency through indirect control, such as through common management. De facto control results from the commercial relationship that exists between two or more enterprises. For example, where the prices of goods sold by A are fixed by B, or where A and B use the same trade names or produce the same product, there does not have to be any direct common ownership. However, the fact that a large proportion of two or more companies' turnover results from transactions made between themselves does not necessarily mean that there is de facto dependency.

A transfer of profits can be inferred if, for example, transactions occur at prices higher or lower than prevailing market prices. This includes all types of transactions, including commodities, services, royalties, management services or financing.

Acte anormal de gestion   This concept was developed by the *Conseil d'Etat*, the supreme French tax court in charge of corporate income tax issues (including customs and excise).

For an *acte anormal de gestion* to be applicable it is necessary to prove that a transfer of profits has actually taken place and that there was a deliberate intention to move profits or losses from one taxpayer to another. It can be applied to both domestic and international transfer prices.

Under the *acte anormal de gestion* principle, a tax deduction can be refused for charges not incurred for the benefit of the business or not arising from normal commercial operations.

Other regulations

In addition to the legislation specific to transfer pricing, the following regulations are also relevant to the issue:

- the terms of various tax treaties;
- sections of the French Tax Code which deal with related issues such as transactions with entities in tax havens (Section 238(A) limits the deduction in France of commissions paid to entities located in tax havens, Section 209(B) requires consolidation in France of profits and losses realised through enterprises located in low-tax jurisdictions);
- a first regulation was issued on 4 May 1973 in the form of a 'note' (this regulation is the principal element of the tax administration doctrine and in April 1983 the tax authorities finalised and published this commentary on their interpretation of the transfer pricing legislation, once the Section 57 was amended to cover transactions with tax havens);
- a regulation published on 4 March 1986 on competent authority procedures;
- the tax authorities' commentary on legal cases involving transfer pricing, which has been issued over the years in the form of 'directives' (a directive is an indication of how the tax authorities will interpret and apply legal decisions).

Advance pricing agreements (APAs)

French tax regulations do not provide for APA procedures. The tax authorities' interpretation of the provisions in the French Constitution is that an APA procedure would be a breach of the principle of equality.

Despite this basic principle, however, there are areas in which de facto APAs are granted. For example in relation to 'headquarters' companies and, in the near future, also for distribution centres.

The US–France Tax Treaty also provides a form of APA procedure. Section 26(3)(d) states that the competent authorities shall endeavour to resolve difficulties or doubts 'concerning matters described in sub-paragraphs (a), (b) and (c) of this paragraph (which refer to attribution of profits, allocation of income, and determination of the source of particular items of income) with respect to past or future years'.

The French tax administration has not yet issued a commentary on this new treaty, but it is expected that it will confirm that this subparagraph refers to an APA procedure.

Miscellaneous

Annual tax of 3 per cent

Any legal entity, whether resident in France or not, owning property in France or real rights thereon, directly or through intermediaries, is subject to an annual tax of 3 per cent of the fair market value of this property or these rights.

A legal entity is considered to own property in France through interposed persons where it has a stake, in any form whatsoever, in a legal entity which owns property in France directly or through a third body corporate or is interposed in the chain of participations.

Yet, some exemptions are available to legal entities in the following cases:

- the property represents less than 50 per cent of all French assets of the body corporate involved (property used for industrial or commercial purposes does have to be taken into account);
- the legal entity, having its head office in a country which has concluded a tax treaty with France containing an exchange of information clause (Germany, Luxembourg, Japan, Sweden) reports each year to the French authorities on the property it owns in France and the name and address of its shareholders;
- French resident legal entities and those benefiting from a non-discrimination clause (eg Netherlands, Switzerland, United Kingdom) either disclose their shareholders or commit themselves to do so upon request by the French tax authorities.

If the legal entity is exempt on the basis of the second or third exemption (disclosure of its shareholders), its shareholders could become subject to the following French taxes:

- if such a shareholder is itself a foreign legal entity, it may be subject to the 3 per cent tax, unless one of the exemptions apply;
- if such a shareholder is a physical person, French net-wealth tax and French gift or inheritance taxes may become due;
- in case of a sale the capital gain may be subject to French (corporate) income tax.

Specific rules applicable to taxation of property capital gains

Subject to the application of double tax treaties, non resident individuals and companies are subject to a withholding tax of $33^{1}/_{3}$ per cent on capital gains on the disposal of property in France, other than construction and trading profits. This withholding tax exempts the capital gain from further French income tax. A special tax return is to be filed by the vendor who is required to appoint a fiscal representative in France (liable for payment of the tax).

Where considered as professional trading profits, gains realised on the disposal of property by non-resident individuals or companies (which do not perform their activity through a permanent establishment in France) are subject to 50 per cent withholding tax. This tax also exempts profits from further French income tax.

27

Business Taxation

Xavier Rohmer and Catherine Cruveilher,
Coopers & Lybrand CLC Juridique et Fiscal

CORPORATE INCOME TAX

The profits of certain corporate entities (principally *Société Anonyme, Société par Actions Simplifiées, Société à Responsabilité Limitée* and *Société en Commandite par Actions*) are subject to corporate income tax (*impôt sur les sociétés*), irrespective of their nature. Other entities which normally have no income tax liability at the corporate level, their income being taxed in the hands of their shareholders or members, may elect to be subject to this tax.

Income generated by professional or commercial activities is subject to personal income tax (*impôt sur le revenu*), calculated at a graduated rate on income from all sources earned by individuals resident in France.

TAXES ON BUSINESS

The following taxes apply:

- corporate income tax/personal income tax;
- VAT;
- business licence tax;
- other taxes.

DETERMINATION OF TAXABLE INCOME

Territoriality Principle

As a general rule, corporate income tax is assessed on profits derived from business conducted in France and on profits taxable in France under a tax treaty.

Consequently, a foreign company is liable to French corporate income tax on profits derived from:

- an establishment in France;
- activities performed by a dependent representative in France;
- a 'complete' cycle of transactions carried out in France.

If a tax treaty applies, taxable income is that attributable to a 'permanent establishment' (P/E) located in France, which is defined in the commentary of the 1992 OECD model treaty as a fixed place of business through which the business of a company is wholly or partly carried out.

Examples of places of business classed as P/E are a place of management, a branch or a factory. A liaison or representative office which carries out an activity of a preparatory or auxiliary nature does not constitute a P/E for tax treaty purposes.

As a result of this territoriality principle, French companies cannot set off losses incurred abroad against domestic profits and vice versa.

DETERMINATION OF NET TAXABLE INCOME

Net taxable income corresponds to the increase in a company's net worth from one year to the next. Net worth must be determined in accordance with accounting rules in force.

To determine net taxable income, it is first necessary to calculate the current year's gross income, whether related to the company's main businesses or not, including capital gains, income from property and securities, and interest on loans.

The next step is to set off deductible expenses against gross income. As a general rule, deductible expenses are those that are incurred in the company's interest, or are necessary for normal business operations.

Loss carry forwards are then set off against the amount thus derived to arrive at final net taxable income (see below).

Valuation of assets

For valuation purposes, assets are divided into two classes:

- current assets (*capitaux circulants*), such as inventories, account receivables and cash;
- fixed assets (*immobilisations*), such as goodwill, buildings and machinery.

Inventories should be valued at the lower of cost (*prix de revient*) or market value (*cours du jour*). For tax purposes, if the market value is lower than the book value, a provision should be recorded in the company's accounts.

Account receivables should be recorded at nominal value, with doubtful accounts and bad debts provided for.

Fixed assets may be treated in three different ways for tax purposes, depending on the type of asset. As a rule, tangible fixed assets, such as buildings, machinery and equipment, may be depreciated, while land and goodwill may not (save in certain circumstances and conditions). Securities likewise are non-depreciable, although a special provision may be set up for permanent impairment in value, where necessary.

Deductible expenses

The main deductible expenses are as follows:

Purchases of raw materials and other supplies   Certain taxes are deductible, mainly registration duties, property taxes, business licence tax and payroll-based taxes. The main non-deductible taxes are corporate income tax, withholding tax and tax equalisation (*précompte*).

Deductible labour costs include salaries, fringe benefits, reimbursed expenses and social security contributions and contributions made by the employer to employee benefit plans, such as profit-sharing plans (*intéressement*) and corporate savings plans (*Plans d'Epargne Entreprise*).

NB: a limit is specified for the deduction of directors' fees (*jetons de présence*).

Interest payments and other financial charges   Accrued interest on debt financing is deductible. However, the deduction of interest paid by a corporation to its shareholders is subject to certain restrictions (see Chapter 26 under 'Thin capitalisation rules').

Business expenses Restrictions on the deduction of business expenses are as follows:

- 'specific' expenses (cars, boats, etc) are either not tax-deductible, or their deduction is limited;
- company cars may be depreciated up to a maximum amount of 120,000 fr, without, however, exceeding the purchase price.

Depreciation See below.

Reserves As a general rule, reserves which cover deductible charges or losses are deductible if these charges or losses are likely to occur at the year-end. The reserves must also have been recorded in the company's books.

Depreciation

Depreciation recorded in a company's accounts is tax-deductible up to the limit normally prescribed for the business sector concerned. Companies may apply rates higher than those normally used, however, if they are able to demonstrate that their specific operating conditions warrant a higher level of depreciation.

Straight-line method The straight-line method is the standard depreciation method used and may be applied to all depreciable fixed assets. The depreciation rate is obtained by dividing 100 by the estimated useful life of the asset concerned. Straight-line depreciation rates range from 2 per cent for buildings to 25 per cent for trucks. Rates are applied to the original cost of assets on an annual basis, with the depreciation charge for the first and last years adjusted on a pro rata basis.

Declining-balance depreciation The declining-balance method is an optional method, used to achieve an accelerated write-off of cost in the initial years. It is expressly authorised by the French Tax Code for specific assets, including manufacturing and processing equipment. Only assets that are new or reconditioned and have a normal useful life of at least three years qualify for declining-balance depreciation.

In the case of purchased software, the related cost may be amortised in full over 12 months. However, this option does *not* apply to internally developed software.

The depreciation charge is calculated by multiplying the rate under the straight-line method by a ratio based on the asset's useful life as prescribed by law. The rate thus derived is applied to the net book value of the asset annually for each year of the asset's useful life. The year of acquisition is counted as a full year.

Exceptional depreciation Companies which make eligible investments (eg anti-noise and anti-pollution equipment) are entitled to record depreciation corresponding to 50 per cent of the cost of the qualifying asset, within 12 months following purchase or construction.

Expensing or capitalisation of software production and R&D costs

Companies subject to corporate income tax may choose between treating software development and R&D costs as operating expenses fully deductible in the year in which they are incurred, or costs can be capitalised and amortised over a maximum period of five years. For accounting purposes, R&D costs may be capitalised and amortised only when the technological feasibility of the related products has been established.

Purchased software may be amortised over 12 months. Losses arising from this method of amortisation may be carried forward for a maximum period of five years.

Loss carry forwards and carry backs, evergreen losses

As a general rule, losses incurred as a result of the operation of the taxpayer's business, or attributable to certain events occurring in the normal course of business are deductible in the tax year during which they arose if they affect the taxpayer's assets (eg bad debt losses).

Under French tax law, net operating losses may be carried forward or backward. If the taxpayer does not elect to carry back losses, the amount of the losses will generally be deducted from ordinary taxable income for the following tax year. A net tax loss may be carried forward for a maximum period of five years following the year in which it was incurred. When a taxpayer realises a net loss and the deduction of fixed asset depreciation is consequently disallowed during the loss period, the unused deduction may be carried forward indefinitely as an evergreen loss until it can be set off against net taxable income.

French companies may elect to carry back the losses of a given year and set them off against the profits of the three prior years. This does not give rise to an immediate refund, but to a tax credit receivable, calculated by multiplying the deficit actually written off by the normal corporate income tax rate applicable to the fiscal year in which the deficit was recorded. This tax credit receivable may be set off against corporate income tax (but not against the 10 and 15 per cent sur-taxes) for the next five years and any excess is reimbursed in cash thereafter. Another option would be to discount the tax credit receivable with a bank.

SPECIFIC RULES OF ASSESSMENT OF CORPORATE INCOME TAX

Corporate Income Tax Rates

To improve French companies' competitiveness and promote investment in France, the standard rate of corporate income tax was gradually reduced between 1988 and 1993 from 42 per cent to its current level of $33^{1/3}$ per cent.

However, due to the necessity to reduce budget deficit, companies have been required to pay a 10 per cent surcharge on their annual corporate income tax liability since 1 January 1995. Furthermore, for financial years ended on or after 1 January 1997, companies* are subject to an additional, temporary contribution equal to 15 per cent of their corporate income tax liability for 1997 and 1998, and 10 per cent for 1999. This means that the effective corporate income tax rate is $41^{2/3}$ per cent for fiscal years ending in 1997 and 1998, and 40 per cent for 1999.

Instalments Payable

Corporate income tax is paid in four instalments during the relevant financial or fiscal year, the total representing $33^{1/3}$ per cent of taxable income for the prior financial year. Any balance remaining must be paid no later than the fifteenth day of the fourth month following the year-end. Any excess paid should be set off against the next corporate income tax instalment due.

Companies with financial year-ends between 1 March and 31 December are required to pay an instalment on the 10 per cent surtax at the same time as their fourth corporate income tax instalment. Similar rules apply to the 15 per cent contribution.

---

* This additional contribution of 15% does not concern companies satisfying the following criteria:
- a turnover below 50 million fr; and,
- a share capital at least at 75 per cent owned by individuals or by one or several companies, 75 per cent of whose shares are controlled by individuals.

CAPITAL GAINS TAX

Before 1997, specific rules existed concerning the determination and taxation of capital gains and losses realised by companies subject to French corporate income tax. The rules applied to the sale, exchange, transfer or disposal of all fixed assets, both tangible (eg property and equipment) and intangible (eg securities and income generated by the sale or licensing of patents).

From 1 January 1997, application of these rules was restricted to the following assets:

- capital gains and losses on the disposal of securities held as long-term investments (*titres de participation*), certain mutual fund units and the shares of venture capital companies (SCR) held for at least five years;
- income generated by the licensing of patents.

Gains and losses on the disposal of the securities or shares referred to above that are held for at least two years are classified as long-term capital gains.

Short-term capital gains and losses on the disposal of qualifying securities and shares are netted off at each fiscal year-end. Net short-term gains are taxed at the standard rate. Net short-term losses are deducted from ordinary taxable income.

Long-term capital gains and losses on the disposal of qualifying securities and shares are likewise netted off at each fiscal year-end. Net long-term gains may be taxed at the reduced rate of 19 per cent, provided that the after-tax gain is posted to a special long-term capital gains reserve and is not distributed. Long-term capital gains realised in fiscal years starting 1 January 1997 are in addition subject to the 10 and 15 per cent surtaxes, resulting in an effective tax rate of 23.75 per cent.

Gains on the disposal of assets other than the qualifying assets, such as purchased goodwill (*fonds de commerce*), are all subject to corporate income tax at the rate of $41\frac{2}{3}$ per cent, whether the assets are held for less than two years or not, if they are realised by companies subject to the 15 per cent additional tax contribution.

Moreover, only a portion of long-term capital losses realised on disposals of assets excluded from the special long-term capital gains regime and carried forward to financial years beginning 1 January 1997 may be set off against long-term capital gains on disposals of similar assets.

TAXATION OF DIVIDEND INCOME

General Rule: Dividend Tax Credit (*Avoir Fiscal*)

To limit double taxation of distributed profits (at the level of both the French distributing company and the beneficiary), the recipient shareholder is entitled to a tax credit (*avoir fiscal*) equal to one-half of the dividend received.

The *avoir fiscal* is included in the taxable income of the shareholder (whether an individual or a corporation). In the case of individual shareholders, the *avoir fiscal* may be set off against their personal income tax liability, or refunded in part in the event of a surplus. Corporate shareholders which do not have the status of parent company (affiliation privilege) may use the *avoir fiscal* to reduce their income tax liability, but may not set it off against the 10 or 15 per cent surtax. Tax credit surpluses are not refunded.

Foreign shareholders resident in France are not entitled to receive the *avoir fiscal* unless a tax treaty provides otherwise.

Affiliation Privilege

Under this regime, dividends paid by a subsidiary, whether resident in France or not, to a parent company are exempt from corporate income tax, provided that certain criteria are met. The main qualifying criteria are that:

- both the parent and the subsidiary must be subject, by law or election, to French corporate income tax or a similar foreign tax, at the standard rate. It is not a requirement, however, that the parent company be governed by French law. The parent may thus be the French P/E of a foreign company;
- the parent company must hold a minimum interest of 10 per cent of the subsidiary's share capital, unless the amount of the investment exceeds 150 million fr. Furthermore, the parent must undertake to keep its interest in the subsidiary for a minimum of two years unless this interest has been susbscribed (instead of having been acquired).

TAXATION OF DISTRIBUTIONS

General Rules

Except for dividend withholding tax levied on distributions made to foreign residents, companies' dividend distributions do not give rise to any taxation when they are paid out of profits earned within the past five years which have been taxed at the standard rate.

Principles of Dividend Tax Equalisation (Précompte Mobilier)

Dividends distributed out of profits earned within the past five years, from which corporate income tax at the standard rate has not been deducted, are subject to dividend tax equalisation at the rate of $33\frac{1}{3}$ per cent of the gross amount distributed (or 50 per cent of the net amount). For example, tax equalisation is levied on distributions paid out of:

- dividends received by a parent company from subsidiaries;
- profits earned through permanent establishments located outside France;
- profits arising from periods older than the last five years (whether subject or not to corporate income tax at the standard rate).

However, the *précompte* is normally refunded to corporate sharehold-ers residing in a country with which France has signed a tax treaty, if said shareholders are not entitled to the refund of an underlying *avoir fiscal*.

OTHER TAXES

VAT

Intra-European Union VAT transactions

Pursuant to the EU Council Directive of16 December 1991, fiscal fron-tiers between member states were abolished as of 1 January 1993.

Intra-community supplies of goods from France to a taxable person established in another EU member state are in principle exempt from VAT.

Intra-community acquisitions of goods are taxable if the French acquiror is a taxable person. If the French acquiror is an exempt per-son or a non-taxable legal person or an individual, specific VAT regimes may apply, for example distance sales regime.

Payment and filing requirements

VAT is payable to the tax authorities:

- for goods: during the month in which delivery takes place;
- for services: during the month in which the services are paid for, unless the VAT payer has elected to pay at the time when the invoice is issued (*option pour les débits*).

VAT effectively due is determined by deducting input VAT from output VAT. If the input tax suffered exceeds the output tax, the taxable person is entitled to a refund. There is no VAT group regime available in France.

A VAT return must be completed and filed monthly with the tax authorities. Small businesses may elect to file on a quarterly basis.

VAT recovery procedure

Input VAT may be recovered during the month in which the goods, whether fixed assets or other goods, are delivered, or services are paid for.

Where some of the operations carried out by the company are not subject to VAT, the right to recover VAT will be limited by the following ratio:

income from transactions subject to VAT/income
from all company transactions

Specific rules applicable to non-French residents

Companies resident, but not incorporated in France which perform operations that are subject to French VAT must appoint a tax representative to fulfil VAT requirements and pay the tax in France.

Foreign entities which do not conduct transactions subject to VAT may follow a special procedure to claim refund of any French VAT invoiced by a French supplier.

VAT rates

Rates of VAT applicable are:

- 2.1 per cent on some medicines;
- 5.5 per cent on most foods, books, water and other listed products;
- 20.6 per cent in all other cases (standard rate).

Payroll-Based Taxes

Employment tax (taxe sur les salaires)

Employers liable to VAT on at least 90 per cent of their transactions are exempt from employment tax. Where it is due, however, the effective employment tax liability is determined using a specific ratio.

Employment tax is assessed on gross salaries paid during a calendar year at the rate of 4.25 per cent on each employee's compensation up to 41,230 fr, 8.5 per cent between 41,230 fr and 82,390 fr and 13.6 per cent above 82,390 fr.

Apprenticeship and training taxes (taxe d'apprentissage, participation des employeurs à la formation profession-nelle continue)

Apprenticeship and training taxes are assessed on salaries. Apprenticeship tax is levied at the rate of 0.5 per cent and training tax at the rate of 1.5 per cent for businesses with at least ten employees.

New housing construction tax (investissement obligatoire dans la construction)

All companies with at least ten employees are required to allocate an amount equal to 0.45 per cent of their total payroll to a programme of construction.

Business Licence Tax

Business licence tax is a local tax levied annually on individuals or corporations engaging in gainful, unsalaried activities on a regular basis. Tax rates are determined by local authorities.

The tax is calculated based on the rental value of the tangible assets necessary for the conduct of the activity and on 18 per cent of total wages paid. A distinction is made between property and equipment, depreciable over a period exceeding 30 years, which are included at 8 per cent of their historical cost in the tax base, and other equipment, which is included at 16 per cent of historical cost.

28

Employment Law

Antonio Sardinha Marques and Francis Collin, Coopers & Lybrand CLC Juridique et Fiscal

In France, individual and collective work relations are determined by mandatory rules that mainly apply to the protection of employees. However, labour law acknowledges the legality of the employers' powers and allows a certain amount of flexibility to companies (especially in terms of work duration and remuneration).

Despite the low rate of union membership (less than 10 per cent of employees), trade unions play an important part, especially in the negotiation of collective bargaining agreements (*conventions collectives*), the elections for employee representatives or the organisation of strikes.

The amount of social contributions on salaries is particularly high in France, in comparison with the other member states of the European Union. Nevertheless, the lower than average level of direct salaries offsets the higher social contribution and reduces the total cost of the workforce.

FEATURES AND SOURCES OF LABOUR LAW

Individual and Collective Relations between Employers and Employees

- An employee is a person who works for and reports to another party in exchange for remuneration under a contract of employment.

- The employment contracts of executive directors remain in force after they have taken up their seat on the board (eg a managing director who is both a *salarié* and a *mandataire social*) if certain conditions are met.
- Labour laws do not apply to civil servants, whose status is determined by administrative law and civil service law, or to the self-employed.

State-Imposed and Industry-Specific Rules

There are a growing number of international labour law sources, including international treaties, the ILO convention and EU treaties and directives.

At national level, the rules are based on a variety of laws and regulations, most of which are reproduced in the Labour Code (*code du travail*). However, many rules are derived from case law, because of difficulties in interpreting labour legislation.

Companies are also subject to the provisions of collective bargaining agreements (*conventions collectives*) generally entered into at national level and applicable to specific industries. The Ministry of Labour has extended the scope of application of most collective bargaining agreements so that they apply to all companies in the industry concerned, even those that have not signed the agreement.

Other Rules Set Up within Specific Companies

A company may enter into a separate collective bargaining agreement (*convention collective d'entreprise*) with one or several representative trade unions. Other agreements may also be entered into without any union involvement (*accords atypiques*) or the company may consistently follow certain practices over a long period of time, giving rise to a de facto obligation to continue to apply the terms of the agreement or to pursue the practice, although in principle the company can unilaterally decide otherwise.

Health, safety and disciplinary rules within the company are laid down in 'internal rules' (*règlement intérieur*) drawn up by the employer. All companies with at least 20 employees are required to issue a set of internal rules.

Selecting the Option that is Most Favourable to Employees

Companies have a basic obligation to comply with labour laws and regulations but they may opt to apply the provisions of a convention or contract, provided that these are more favourable to employees (known as the *ordre public social relatif* principle). However, certain legal rules must either be strictly adhered to (*ordre public social absolu* principle) or can, on the contrary, be ignored in favour of a collective bargaining agreement which is better suited to the company's business needs (*ordre public négociable* principle) covering, for example, working hours.

Labour Law: Complex and Constantly Changing

State-imposed rules focus primarily on protecting employees but they also allow a certain amount of leeway in some areas which may be helpful to employers. Collective bargaining is a widespread practice and helps to adapt labour law more closely to the needs and constraints of the various professions and businesses.

The trend is towards a reduction in state-imposed rules, giving social partners greater freedom to set their own terms and conditions provided that the legitimate claims of all concerned are respected.

LABOUR AUTHORITIES

Unemployment Office and Labour Inspectors

The *Agence Nationale de l'Emploi* (ANPE) is a government agency responsible for helping the unemployed to find jobs or training courses and helping companies to fill vacation positions or implement outplacement plans.

Companies are required to notify the ANPE of all job vacancies but are generally free to choose how they go about finding candidates (advertisements, other employment agencies, etc).

The *Inspection du Travail* is a government department responsible for ensuring that employers comply with the provisions of labour laws and regulations and the various collective bargaining agreements. The department's terms of reference cover all aspects of labour law and its inspectors have the right to visit a company's premises at any time and demand copies of all the documents that employers are legally required to keep. Breaches of certain labour laws may, in some cases, expose the employer to the risk of criminal proceedings. The *Inspection du Travail* also provides advice to companies on employee-related issues and can act as a conciliator in industrial disputes. In addition, it reviews proposals to adapt working hours and measures (*plan social*) proposed by companies in connection with downsizing programmes in order to limit the number of outright redundancies.

Structures to Deal with Employee Litigation

The *conseil des prud'hommes* is a labour court responsible for dealing with disputes relating to employment contracts (existence, signature, implementation and termination). Half of the magistrates sitting on the tribunal are elected by employers, and the other half by employees. Elections are held every five years.

The procedure begins with a conciliation hearing and if the parties still fail to agree, the case is heard by the tribunal. The length of the process varies depending on the jurisdiction. A fast-track procedure can be followed in certain exceptional cases, enabling a claimant to obtain an injunction preserving the status quo or temporarily suspending a measure.

Collective disputes and disputes that do not relate to an employment contract are dealt with by other jurisdictions. The *tribunal d'instance* deals with disputes concerning elections of employee representatives, the *tribunal de grande instance* hears collective claims relating to downsizing programmes (*plans sociaux*) and the *tribunal administratif* deals with appeals against decisions by labour inspectors.

EMPLOYERS' RIGHTS AND DUTIES

Employers' Rights: Recognised in and Restricted by Labour Law

Broadly speaking, an employer has the right to take any measures that he considers essential to run the business efficiently. However, labour laws and the collective bargaining agreements contain very strict rules governing the extent to which this right may be exercised in certain circumstances, especially with regard to downsizing programmes.

Employers also have the right to take disciplinary action against employees. This right is heavily regulated by legislation defining: the statute of limitations for professional misconduct (two months) and the related disciplinary measures (three years); the procedures to be followed (in principle, these consist of an initial meeting with the employee, followed by a period of reflection and then notification of the disciplinary measure, indicating the reasons); and illegal disciplinary measures (pecuniary or discriminatory measures). The disciplinary measures applicable depending on the seriousness of the misconduct must be indicated in the company's internal rules (*règlement intérieur*).

Employee Representation

All companies with at least 11 employees are required to have employee representatives (*délégués du personnel*), who are elected by the workforce for a two-year term. The main role of employee representatives is to submit individual or collective employee claims to management; however, employees may still submit their claims directly, if they wish to do so.

Companies with at least 50 employees are required to have a work council (*comité d'entreprise*). The council is chaired by the chief executive and is made up of members elected for two years by the workforce and union representatives. The members elected by the workforce take part in the vote but the union representatives attend meetings in a consultative capacity only.

The work council must be informed and consulted prior to any major decision concerning the company's organisation or management. In principle, however, the company is not required to take the work council's opinion into account.

The work council is also responsible for managing the company's welfare and cultural programmes (eg canteens, leisure activities, summer camps for employees' children, etc).

A health, safety and working conditions committee (*Comité d'Hygiène, de Sécurité et des Conditions de Travail* – CHSCT) must be set up at each facility with at least 50 employees. The committee is chaired by the chief executive and is made up of members of the workforce. It must be informed and consulted prior to any major decision concerning health and safety issues or working conditions.

In companies with at least 50 employees, each representative trade union can appoint union representatives (*délégués syndicaux*) whose duties include representing the union in meetings with management and organising union activities within the company.

A group committee (*comité de groupe*) must be set up at group level (dominant company and subsidiaries) at the request of employee representatives.

The resources to be made available to permit employee representative bodies to fulfil their mission are specified by law and in the collective bargaining agreements (as in other cases, the collective bargaining agreements prevail if their provisions are more generous). These resources include time off during working hours, work council subsidies, periodic information, increased protection of employee representatives against redundancy, etc.

Collective Bargaining Agreements and Agreements Concerning the Organisation of the Elections for Employee Representatives

Collective bargaining agreements are negotiated with the trade unions and cover conditions of employment, working conditions and terms of remuneration.

Specific collective bargaining agreements can be used by a company to organise work patterns on a basis that better reflect the needs of the business (eg working hours calculated on an annual basis). In companies that have union representatives, wage rounds must be conducted each year but there is no obligation for the company and the unions to reach an agreement.

'Pre-electoral agreements' may also be entered into with the unions, covering the organisation of employee representative elections.

EMPLOYMENT CONTRACTS

Open-Ended and Fixed-Term Contracts

In principle, employment contracts are open-ended, but in certain specific cases defined by law an employee can be hired under a fixed-term contract to fill a temporary vacancy within the company.

Employees may be recruited on a part-time basis (in principle, up to 32 hours per week). Specific rules apply to 'part-time contracts'.

At the time of recruitment, new employees must be given a document setting out their main terms and conditions of employment. In certain cases, including fixed-term and part-time contracts, a formal employment contract containing certain compulsory clauses must be signed.

The employment contract can provide for a trial period, to give the company time to ensure that the new employee is capable of performing the work for which he or she has been recruited. The duration and terms of the trial period are generally established in the collective bargaining agreement.

Employment contracts should include all clauses relevant to the employee's position (eg mobility clause, competition clause, exclusivity clause, confidentiality clause, clauses dealing with the question of ownership of employee inventions, etc).

Certain formalities must be carried out by the employer. For example, the social security authorities (URSSAF) must be notified in advance of all recruitments and a personnel register must be kept. Failure to comply with these formalities may qualify as a criminal offence.

In some cases, employers may qualify for recruitment incentives, such as exemption from social security contributions for the first person recruited.

Amendment of the Terms and Conditions of the Initial Employment Contract

An employee cannot refuse to accept any changes in his or her working conditions that the employer considers essential to run the business efficiently. However, any significant changes in terms and conditions affecting, for example, the employee's remuneration package or grade, must be approved by the employee. If the employee refuses to accept the new terms or conditions, his or her contract will be terminated, provided that the change in question is necessary to enable the employer to run the business efficiently. In this case, the employee will be treated as having been made redundant and will be entitled to the related benefits.

In the case of the sale or merger of the company, the employees' contracts will in principle also be transferred to the new employer (Article L 122-12 subparagraph 2 of the Labour Code). However, the new employer will have the right to amend or terminate the contracts, subject to compliance with the provisions of the law or the collective bargaining agreements.

Termination of a Contract of Employment

The main formalities to be observed when an employee resigns (letter of resignation, period of notice, etc) are laid down in the collective bargaining agreements.

Companies wishing to terminate an employee's contract are required to comply with very strict and complex regulations established by law and also with the provisions of the applicable collective bargaining agreement, which generally afford even greater protection to employees.

The legal procedures depend on whether the employee is being dismissed for personal reasons, for professional misconduct or due to the elimination of his or her job; other considerations include the number of employees on the company's payroll and, where applicable, the number of employees affected by the redundancy plan.

In the case of a redundancy plan, employee representatives must be consulted and the labour authorities will also request to examine the plan. Great care should therefore be taken in implementing the related procedures.

In all cases, the employees concerned must be notified in writing of their forthcoming redundancy, providing full details of the reason underlying the decision. There must be 'valid, serious grounds' for making an employee redundant. There is a considerable body of case law clarifying the meaning of 'valid' and 'serious', but judges called on to rule in cases of unfair dismissal tend to adopt their own interpretation, depending on the reasons put forward by the company. A company found guilty of unfair dismissal or failure to comply with the related procedures may be ordered to pay damages or possibly a fine.

Certain categories of employees, such as pregnant women, victims of industrial accidents and employee representatives, enjoy special protection against redundancy.

Different rules apply for termination of a fixed-term contract. The contract may not be terminated in advance except in certain specific cases specified by law (agreement between the parties, *force majeure*, serious professional misconduct, etc).

USE OF TEMPORARY STAFF AND STAFF SHARING

Companies are allowed to use temporary staff or to set up an 'employer group' to share staff.

WAGES, SALARIES AND SOCIAL SECURITY TAXES

Any benefit in kind or cash benefit granted by an employer to an employee in exchange for or in connection with work performed by the employee represents an emolument. There are various types of emoluments, including fixed and/or variable salaries, hourly wages and piece-rate wages.

In principle, employers are free to determine the salary paid to their employees, provided that they comply with certain rules. In particular, the salary must not be below the legal minimum wage (SMIC) or the minimum wage provided for in the collective bargaining agreement. Furthermore, men and women must be paid the same rate for the same job. In addition, the company must not employ discriminatory remuneration policies (based on ethnic origin, sex, political opinions, trade union involvement, etc) and salaries must not be linked to price indices.

Specific rules apply to certain categories of employees, such as school-leavers, apprentices, home-workers and sales representatives (VRP).

Salaries are normally paid monthly and employees must be given a pay-slip.

Employees represent first-tier creditors, meaning that their salaries must be paid before any payments to most other creditors of the company. In addition, in the case of bankruptcy, employees benefit from insurance cover guaranteeing the payment of their salaries.

Social Taxes Payable by the Employer

Certain social security taxes are payable by both the employer and the employee (such as health insurance and pension contributions), while others are payable solely by the employer (covering industrial accident benefits, family allowances, etc). Those paid by the employer represent approximately 45 per cent of the gross remuneration. Employee contributions are withheld at source and both the employer and employee contributions are paid to the URSSAF.

Employers and employees are also required to pay contributions to unemployment benefit schemes and supplementary pension schemes.

Various other payroll-based taxes are also due from the employer, including employment tax (*taxe sur les salaires*) and business tax (*taxe professionnelle*).

Techniques Available to Increase Remunerations while Limiting the Related Social Security Taxes and Other Payroll-Based Taxes

There are a wide range of opportunities to set up cost-efficient incentive plans, depending on the needs and aims of each company. In general, these plans are set up on a company by company basis and are covered by corporate agreements (*accord d'entreprise*).

The main incentive plan is the employee profit-sharing plan (*participation*) which is compulsory for all companies with at least 50 employees.

Voluntary plans include profit-related bonus plans, corporate savings plans, retirement savings plans, stock options, employee share ownership schemes and employee investment funds.

Other employee benefits are exempt from social security and other taxes. Examples include employer contributions to supplementary pension plans, which are partially tax-exempt.

WORKING CONDITIONS

Working Hours

The standard working week is 39 hours. Overtime may be worked in some cases and within certain limits. It is paid at a higher rate and employees are also entitled to additional time off.

Working hours are set by the employer and apply to the entire work-force, except for part-time workers and certain specific employees who may be called on to work different hours. The working day may not exceed 10 hours, except in certain specific cases. No more than 48 hours may be worked per week or 46 hours per week over a period of 12 consecutive weeks.

Companies also have the option of spreading annual working hours unevenly over the year to help them cope with peaks in activity levels. In addition, various forms of shift-working are allowed.

The Labour Code establishes the principle that Sunday represents a day of rest, but various exceptions are allowed.

A bill is being debated in the French Parliament and should be voted in May 1998. This legislation calls for the reduction of the legal working week to 35 working hours on 1 January 2000 for companies with at least 20 employees (and on 1 January 2002 for the others). This reduction could take the form of additional time off for employees. The bill provides financial assistance for companies which negotiate to implement a 35-hour week before 2000.

In the expectation of a second law text submitted to the French Parliament before 2000, the legal work duration remains governed by the ordinance of 16 January 1982 on the 39-hour week.

Holidays

1 May (Labour Day) is the only day which, by law, must constitute a paid day off. However, the collective bargaining agreements generally stipulate that employees may not be required to work on bank holidays.

Employees are entitled to at least 30 working days' paid holiday per year.

The law and the collective bargaining agreements also provide for other paid and unpaid leave, for example at the time of a marriage or other family events, unpaid child care leave, special leave to permit the start-up of a business, etc.

Health and Safety Regulations

The Labour Code contains general provisions applicable to all employees and specific provisions applicable to certain employees or certain jobs. Liability proceedings may be initiated against the chief executive of the company and, in some cases, the company itself, for any breach of these rules.

Employees are required to undergo regular medical check-ups performed by medical officers *(médecin du travail)* who also have various other responsibilities related to employee health and safety.

SOCIAL INSURANCE

Social Insurance Cover Primarily Provided by the Social Security System

The social security system encompasses various social insurance schemes, each with their own administrative and financial structures.

Social security organisations are generally private organisations controlled by government departments *(tutelle)*.

The social security system is financed primarily by salary-based contributions.

General Regime

The main social security regime *(régime général des travailleurs salariés non agricoles)* provides employees other than agricultural workers with various forms of social insurance (health, maternity, disability, industrial accident, widowhood and whole life insurance). It also covers the payment of various forms of family allowances to employees and self-employed persons.

People who are not automatically covered by the general regime may make voluntary contributions to this regime in order to be entitled to health insurance and maternity benefits.

In the case of sickness or accident, social security organisations pay the related medical bills, up to a certain ceiling, and also pay daily allowances to offset the loss of salary. Higher benefits are paid in the case of industrial accidents.

Maternity benefits also cover medical bills and daily allowances to off-set the loss of salary while the employee is on maternity leave.

Disability benefits consist of a pension determined on the degree of invalidity.

Family allowances represent one aspect of a broader policy to support families. They include the basic family allowance, allowances related to the birth of a child (eg young child allowance) and specific means-tested allowances (eg housing allowance).

Other Social Security Regimes

Specific social security regimes have been set up for certain industries (eg railway workers).

Farmers and farm workers are also covered by specific regimes managed by the *mutualité sociale agricole* and other organisations. The benefits payable to farm workers are similar to those under the general regime.

Members of the professions, traders and craftsmen are covered by independent health, maternity and pension insurance regimes (*régimes autonomes*).

Pension Benefits

Salaried employees are entitled to a basic pension funded by the general social security regime. The amount of the pension depends on the age of the person, the number of years in employment and salaries received.

All salaried employees are also entitled to a supplementary pension paid by an institution governed by AGIRC (executive personnel – *cadres*) or ARRCO (executives and other personnel – *cadres* and *non-cadres*).

Employees may also be entitled to other supplementary pension bene-fits under plans set up through a collective agreement or at the employer's discretion. Contributions to these defined-contribution sup-plementary pension plans are voluntary.

INTERNATIONAL MOBILITY

The Status of Foreign Workers Depends on their Country of Origin

Nationals of European Union member states benefit from the principle of free movement of workers between these countries and are not required to obtain a work permit. Under EU rules, an employee who works in France is subject to the French social security regime unless he or she is on secondment.

The situation of nationals of other countries is more complex. A non-EU national wishing to work in France is required to obtain a residence permit and a work permit. The situation regarding social insurance cover differs depending on whether or not France has signed a social security treaty with the country concerned.

In addition, companies that are not established in France and which send employees to France on a temporary basis to perform a service are required to file certain declarations. The conditions of employment of the employees concerned must also comply with the basic requirements of French labour law, in terms of remuneration, working hours and working conditions.

Situation of Employees of French Companies Working Abroad

In general, the employer and the employee decide jointly whether the employee will be covered by French labour law or by the laws of the country of expatriation. Failing that, the applicable law is that of the country corresponding to the employee's normal place of work (Treaty of Rome dated 19 June 1980). In all cases, the rules of law and order of the country of expatriation will apply.

French law stipulates that an employee transferred to a foreign subsidiary and subsequently made redundant by the company must be repatriated by the parent company and given a new position.

Expatriate employees are generally subject to the social security regime applicable in the country of expatriation. However, international social security treaties, EU regulations and various provisions of domestic law allow employees to continue to benefit from French social insurance cover if they are sent to work abroad for a period not exceeding the maximum duration established in the relevant national or international rules.

29

Disputes and Arbitration

Sylvie Le Damany and Catherine Olive,
Coopers & Lybrand CLC Juridique et Fiscal

The overriding considerations in French legal proceedings are the principle of counter-argument (ie all parties shall be in a position to express their claims and defences prior to the handing down of a judgment) and the obligation for the judges to explain the grounds on which judgment is based.

THE JUDICIARY PROCEEDINGS

The decisions of all courts may be reviewed by the *Cour de Cassation* (highest court of the judiciary), which ensures that the law has been appropriately construed and enforced by lower courts, but does not review facts and evidence. Actions before the *Cour de Cassation* require the services of an *avocat aux Conseils* (legal representative before the *Cour de Cassation* and the *Conseil d'Etat*).

In most cases, the principle of judicial review by the *Cour d'Appel* (Court of Appeal) applies.

The procedure is deemed to be conducted by the parties involved (with the exception of criminal matters in particular), ie the parties are responsible for conducting the proceedings under judges' control and judges are strictly bound by the claims and defences of both parties.

Civil Cases

The *tribunaux d'instance* have sole authority over minor disputes, defined as those involving amounts under 30,000 fr and also have exclusive competence over certain matters such as private lease litigation. The procedure before a *tribunal d'instance* is informal and the case is heard by a sole judge.

The *tribunaux de grande instance* are the court of first instance for ordinary jurisdiction and are responsible for hearing all civil cases (as well as commercial cases when there is no commercial court established in the district concerned). They are also the sole competent authority for litigation concerning indirect taxation.

In order to take legal action before a *tribunal de grande instance*, the services of an *avocat* (attorney-at-law) member of the Bar of the district where the *tribunal de grande instance* is located are in principle required.

The procedure is a written one, ie the serving of a summons to appear in court, as well as the arguments and claims of the parties, should be written down and notified in accordance with the legal procedural requirements, in order to be taken into account by the magistrates.

A case coming before a *tribunal de grande instance* under normal circumstances, is heard before a panel of three judges.

Summary proceedings (*référés*) allow for speedy resolutions of cases upon specific conditions provided by procedural rules. This type of procedure, which does not require representation by a lawyer, enables protective or urgent temporary measures to be decided by the presiding judge of the *tribunal de grande instance* or the *tribunal d'instance*.

Appeal against the decisions of the civil lower courts before the *Cours d'Appel* may be lodged for actions with a monetary value of over 13,000 fr and requires the services of an *avoué* (legal court representative). The *avoué* is in most cases involved only in the procedural formalities.

Commercial Cases

The *tribunaux de commerce* (commercial courts) rule on disputes of a commercial nature, as well as commercial insolvency procedures.

The judges are merchants and managers elected by their peers and the procedure is less formal than that before the *tribunal de grande instance*.

The services of a lawyer may be dispensed with; the parties may elect to defend themselves or be represented by a duly empowered person of their choice.

The procedure is deemed to be verbal, ie with the exception of the serving of a summons, claims and defences of the parties need not be presented in writing. In major cases, however, claims and defences of the parties are almost always presented in written form.

As in cases before civil courts, summary proceedings enable protective or urgent temporary measures to be ordered rapidly by the presiding judge of the commercial court.

Appeal rules are identical to those governing appeal against judgments from civil lower courts.

Labour Law Cases

The *conseils de prud'hommes* (labour courts) hear disputes between employers and employees with regard to validity, enforcement and termination of employment contract. Judges are elected by employers and employees.

The procedure is deemed to be verbal but written submissions can always be presented. The services of a lawyer are not legally required.

The procedure before the *conseils de prud'hommes* comprises two phases, conciliation and judgment, at which the attendance of the parties is customary.

Appeals may not be lodged for disputes involving amounts under 21,000 fr and do not require the services of an *avoué*.

Criminal Cases

Criminal sanctions provided under business law and labour law correspond to fines (*contraventions*) and offences of a more serious nature (*délit*). Minor offences are dealt with by the *tribunaux de police* (the criminal branch of the *tribunaux d'instance*), while more serious offences are heard before the *tribunaux correctionnels* (criminal branch of the *tribunaux de grande instance*).

The office of the Public Prosecutor (*Ministre Public*), which represents the state, is party to every criminal trial to request the enforcement of criminal law.

The person (individual or legal entity) who has suffered a prejudice from the infringement could claim for damages before the criminal courts.

As regards more serious offences in complex cases, the hearing before the *tribunaux correctionnels* is preceded by a preliminary investigation conducted by an examining magistrate exclusively dedicated to such matters.

The preliminary investigation is deemed to be secret. The defendant and plaintiff do not have direct access to the information file. Only their respective lawyers are authorised to have access to the related information and can request copies thereof for personal use. They are entitled to deliver copies to their client only if specifically authorised to do so by the examining magistrate.

The court hearing is far more important in criminal cases than in civil or commercial disputes and the defendant is required to be present.

The defendant may elect to either defend himself or be assisted by a lawyer. The plaintiff can also choose to be assisted by a lawyer.

ADMINISTRATIVE COURTS PROCEEDINGS

Administrative courts are under the control of the *Conseil d'Etat* (highest administrative court), which may however rule as court of first instance or court of appeal in some cases.

Administrative courts hear disputes arising from public law between governmental agencies and those under their authority, particularly with regard to tax matters (direct taxation).

The main features of the procedure before the administrative courts are:

- the procedure is not oral: there are no oral testimonies or arguments, and the procedure mainly consists in the communication of requests to the court, which can be answered by memoranda;
- the procedure is directly conducted by the judge, as in criminal cases: the requests and memoranda are communicated by the parties to the judge, who is enabled to divulge them to the other party. The judge is also empowered to demand that the parties answer an argument which has not been raised already by them;
- the public bodies benefit from the *privilège de l'exécutoire:* their individual or regulatory acts are directly enforceable, and actions based on their illegality (including *ultra vires* recourses) do not suspend their enforceability.

ARBITRATION

Under French law, an arbitration clause included in a contract for settlement of a dispute arising from that contract is valid only if the contract is signed between merchants or commercial companies or if the contract involves the interests of international trade.

In the absence of such an arbitration clause or when such clause is prohibited as indicated above, the parties are entitled to submit a matter to arbitration by executing a separate arbitration agreement when the dispute has already arisen.

However, the arbitration procedure may in no case be used for disputes involving the state, the personal capacity of individuals, and under certain conditions, issues concerning state-owned companies.

Procedural rules are flexible:

- the parties decide whether the arbitration tribunal rules at law or on equitable principles;
- when the arbitration tribunal rules at law, the parties are entitled to file an appeal against the arbitration decision before the competent *Cour d'Appel*. However, the parties may waive the right to appeal in the arbitration agreement. In such a case the only possible action against the award is if the procedure can be proved invalid (for serious grounds such as invalidity of the arbitration agreement) before the *Cour d'Appel;*
- on the contrary, if the arbitration tribunal rules on equity the principle is that there is no right of appeal, except if the parties have expressly maintained this option;
- the arbitration tribunal is composed of one arbitrator, or an uneven number of arbitrators; it is customary, however, to appoint three. The prescribed procedural time frame is generally six months, unless otherwise stated in the arbitration agreement. The time frame may be extended subsequently if the parties so agree;
- in the event of procedural difficulties (appointment or dismissal of arbitrators, extension of time frame), the parties may bring the matter before the presiding judge of the *tribunal de grande instance* or the presiding judge of the *tribunal de commerce*;
- arbitration awards are decided by majority vote.

The arbitration award shall, moreover, be submitted to state judges (*exequatur* proceedings), to be enforceable on French territory.

The principal attraction of arbitration is that it offers the possibility to waive the right of appeal in order to obtain a definitive decision promptly and to enable the arbitration tribunal to rule on equitable principles.

Otherwise, the only actual advantage of arbitration is to avoid a public hearing of the case. The recourse to arbitration is far more expensive than bringing the case to State judges insofar as the parties have to remunerate the arbitrators.

ENFORCEMENT IN FRANCE OF DECISIONS HANDED DOWN ABROAD

An official authorisation, or *exequatur*, is also required for the enforcement of a foreign judgment in France, after which the decision handed down becomes enforceable as a *res judicata* (ie a matter settled by judgment).

The French judge may not alter a decision handed down by a foreign judge, but may make the granting of the *exequatur* dependent on the fulfilment of five conditions (save as specifically provided in international conventions): jurisdiction of the foreign tribunal, compliance of the procedure followed before said tribunal to prescribed rules, application of the relevant law in light of French international rules, compliance with international public order and absence of fraudulent evasion of statutory provisions of the law.

30

Establishing a
Distribution Network

*Gilles Semadeni, Coopers & Lybrand CLC
Juridique et Fiscal*

A number of legal issues need to be considered when creating and operating a distribution network. These include legal rules applicable to the selling and the provision of services, compliance with fair competition requirements (see Chapter 31 below concerning restrictive and anti-competitive practices), and consumer information and protection.* Other factors to be considered are the contractual, employment and tax regimes of distributors.

INTERNAL DISTRIBUTION NETWORK

A company may opt to distribute its products or services itself through a salaried sales force. Such sales personnel are subject to standard labour law conditions, or may have the special employment status of VRP (*Voyageurs Représentants Placiers*), ie travelling sales representatives.

VRPs have an exclusive right to sell within particular geographical areas assigned to them. They visit existing and prospective customers and take customer orders, which they then pass on to the company that they represent. Under labour law, VRPs have a right to compensa-

---

* Direct sales to consumers, for example distance-selling, mail order, door-to-door selling and pyramid selling, are governed by specific Consumer Code provisions.

tion for loss of customers if their employer terminates their employment contract unilaterally, given that their work consists of creating and developing a customer base on behalf of their employer.

Setting up an internal distribution network enables a company to maintain full control over the marketing of its products or services. The sales representatives are the company's direct employees and the company thus controls their activity and is free to set prices and conditions of sale.

This method of distribution may, however, prove restrictive and financially costly to the company, as in addition to complying with labour law requirements concerning the sales force, the company has to pay its employees' salaries and social security contributions.

EXTERNAL DISTRIBUTION WORK

In comparison, an external distribution network is made up of independent commercial operators with which the company has no formal hierarchical link. Such operators, either individuals or entities, are free to organise and manage their commercial operations, using their own staff, and themselves bear the personnel costs and taxes related to their business.

Independent operators may be either:

- intermediaries, who market a company's products on behalf of that company and are paid a commission based on the volume of business conducted, while not being liable for any product-related risks; or
- distributors, who market the products on their own behalf and at their own risk, taking their remuneration out of their profit margin on sales of the company's products.

INTERMEDIARIES

Intermediaries are primarily sales agents and commission agents, which represent to varying degrees the companies (principals) whose products or services they sell. It is common to talk of 'complete representation' in the case of sales representatives and 'incomplete representation' in the case of commission agents.

Brokers also act as intermediaries, for example, between a buyer and a seller. Their role is limited, however, to identifying potential customers or suppliers, whom they place in contact with their principal, without ever entering into agreements on behalf of the principal. For this reason, brokers are ill-suited for the purposes of creating a distribution network for products or services, except for businesses where their status is regulated (eg the insurance sector).

Commercial Agency Agreement (*Contrat d'agence commerciale*)

As a general rule, the commercial agent negotiates and/or signs contracts (purchasing, sale, rental, and so forth) in the name and on behalf of his principal.

The commercial agent's status is fully transparent *vis-à-vis* customers, who are aware that the agent has been appointed as such and of the identity of the company represented.

Agreements are deemed to be established directly between the principal and the sales agent's customer. Thus, unlike the case of a distributor, a commercial agent appointed to sell goods does not actually purchase the goods with a view to reselling them; title to the goods is instead transferred directly from the principal to the customer.

Commercial agents must comply with the general conditions of sale and sale prices determined by the company that they represent. They must also follow the principal's instructions, keep accurate accounting records of business conducted on behalf of the principal, to whom the related receipts are transferred.

The principal has the option to assign territories to particular agents on an exclusive basis, thus building up a network of exclusive agents.

Unless otherwise stipulated in the commercial agency agreement, the commercial agent may act on behalf of other companies, provided that those companies are not competitors of an existing principal.

As a result of the independence that they enjoy, commercial agents may generally appoint sub-agents without the prior authorisation of their principal, unless otherwise stipulated in the agency agreement.

It is in fact to a principal's advantage to let the commercial agent act relatively freely and not, for example, to prohibit him from acting on behalf of other principals at the same time, or demand excessively detailed reporting, or dictate the timing of visits to customers, working hours and so forth. If such strict limitations were practised, the commercial agent could be deemed to be an employee of the principal with the resulting obligation to replace the agency agreement by an employment contract.

The agency agreement may require that the commercial agent guarantees payment of all amounts due by customers to the principal (*convention ducroire*, *del credere* agreement). In such cases, the guarantee tends to be limited to the amount of commission payable to the commercial agent.

Commercial agents' remuneration may be fixed or variable. The usual option is a percentage of revenues generated by the commercial agent.

Commercial agents enjoy specific legal protection, particularly concerning their rights in the event of termination of their contracts. Under law no 91.593 of 25 June 1991, in application of EU Directive no 86.653 of 18 December 1986, the principal is required to give advance notice, of between at least one and three months (depending on the term of the agency agreement) of his intention to terminate the agency contract and to pay compensation to the agent, unless the cause of the breach of contract is attributable to the agent. Compensation is payable to the agent both in the event of the cancellation of an open-ended agency agreement and in the event of the non-renewal of a short-term contract.

The courts are free to set the amount of compensation due, which should cover prejudice attributable to the termination of the contract. The norm is for compensation to represent two years' commission income.

Commission Agency Agreement (*Contrat de commission*)

Like the commercial agent, the commission agent (or undisclosed agent) performs legal acts (purchases, sales and so forth) on behalf of the company that is the principal. The commission agent acts in his own name, however, and not in that of the principal, which explains the notion of 'incomplete representation'.

In dealings with the principal, the commission agent acts as an intermediary, ie the principal is deemed to bear the risks arising from contracts entered into by the commission agent and is entitled to the related profits. The commission agent's rights and obligations are therefore similar to those of a commercial agent with regard to the undertaking that he represents (see 'Commercial Agency Agreement' above).

The commission agent's chief obligation is to represent the principal in operations designated by the latter (canvassing for new customers, disbursements and collections, and so forth), in the principal's best interest. To this end, the commission agent must comply with the principal's instructions and conduct business in accordance with the general conditions of sale and/or purchase, and prices stipulated by the principal. Like a commercial agent, the commission agent may not represent any other company which is the principal's competitor.

The commission agent does not own the goods bought or sold on behalf of the principal. Title to the goods is transferred directly from the principal to the customer in the case of a sale, and from the supplier to the principal in the case of a purchase.

The commission agent acts in his own name *vis-à-vis* customers and need not reveal the principal's identity. Similarly, he need not reveal the names of his customers to the principal.

Accordingly, the commission agent is a party to contracts entered into with customers and is personally and, in principle, solely, responsible *vis-à-vis* customers for the related obligations. For example, the commission agent may be held liable if goods held by him and subsequently delivered were to have hidden defects.

Like the commercial agent, the commission agent receives a commission, which may be a lump sum, but which more often is a percentage of the revenues earned by the principal through the agent. In light of the commission agent's more extensive responsibility, the commission is normally greater than that paid to a commercial agent, but the parties are free to determine the amount payable.

The commission agency agreement may be entered into on a short-term or open-ended basis. In the latter case, each of the parties may terminate the agreement unilaterally at any time. If the contract is terminated by the principal, the commission agent is not necessarily entitled to compensation for loss of customers, unlike the commercial agent, nor is non-renewal of a short-term contract grounds for compensation.

DISTRIBUTORS

If a company does not wish to bear the economic risk and cost of distributing its products or services itself, it may use a network of commercial operators, either distributors or franchisees, who act on their own behalf and whose remuneration is taken out of the margin on sales realised by them. Under product distribution contracts, the distributor acquires goods from the supplier which he then resells in his own name and on his own behalf. The supplier company can therefore anticipate transfer of product-related risks, reduce inventory and transport costs, and scale down its accounting. However, it no longer has full control over the marketing of its products through the network, not least of all in respect of deciding resale prices.

The two main types of distribution contracts are exclusive and selective agreements. Franchising is quite different, the related contract conferring more than the right to distribute the franchisor's products. When preparing distribution or franchising contracts, particular care must be taken to avoid anti-competitive arrangements (see Chapter 31).

EXCLUSIVE DISTRIBUTION AGREEMENT (*CONTRAT DE DISTRIBUTION EXCLUSIVE* OR *CONTRAT DE CONCESSION EXCLUSIVE*)

Exclusive distribution agreements give the distributor the exclusive right to market the supplier's products or services in a specific geographical area and/or to specific customers. In return for the exclusive right received, the distributor generally undertakes to market only that supplier's products or services.

Exclusive distribution agreements enable suppliers to build up a distribution network for their products or services and obtain the assurance of regular market outlets for their products or services.

Owing to their exclusivity clauses, contracts of this type often raise problems with regard to competition law and may therefore be used only if they deliver customer service improvements, economic progress etc.

Unlike EU law, whereby conditions governing the validity of exclusive distribution agreements are defined by exemption rules by category (regulation no 1983-83 of 22 June 1983 and, in the case of motor vehicle distribution, regulation no 1475-95 of 21 June 1995), French law does not provide a framework for this type of agreement.

In the majority of cases, the courts recognise the utility of such agreements for the distribution of luxury or prestige products that require substantial investment and appropriate settings, or of highly technical products the sale of which requires specialist advice and after-sales service, and so forth. Those are not the only products marketed on an exclusive basis, of course, but in all cases this form of distribution must be justifiable from an economic standpoint. In practice, exclusive distribution agreements are common in the case of automobile and long-lasting consumer goods, given the related after-sales service requirement.

Like selective distribution and franchising agreements, there are specific rules under French law dealing with exclusive distribution contracts.

These contracts are governed by standard rules of law and case law. It is nevertheless important to note that French law requires full disclosure be made to the distributor, prior to the signature of a formal agreement, concerning the products, know-how, contents of the draft agreement and the supplier's network. This pre-agreement information requirement does not concern solely exclusive distribution contracts, but is likewise applicable to all agreements whereby a trade mark, or corporate or trade name is 'made available' to a party, who takes on an obligation of exclusivity with regard to a significant portion of his business.

The distributor may be required to sell the products on the terms and conditions established by the supplier, but the supplier must allow the distributor the freedom to set minimum resale prices.

If the distributor resells products purchased from the supplier under the conditions of sale set by the latter (eg with regard to warranty), any subsequent deviation from those conditions by the distributor releases the supplier from any liability. The distributor must then fulfil his own obligations towards his customers.

In principle, a distribution contract without a fixed term may be terminated at the supplier's discretion, without payment of compensation. In the case of a distribution contract with a fixed term, the supplier is not obliged to renew the contract at its term. However, French courts often order suppliers to pay compensation when termination of the contract is proved to be unjustified or abusive (eg abrupt termination or termination motivated by the supplier's desire to appropriate the network built up by the distributor).

SELECTIVE DISTRIBUTION AGREEMENT (*CONTRAT DE DISTRIBUTION SELECTIVE*)

Selective distribution agreements may be entered into by suppliers wishing to set up a network of distributors selected on the basis of their capacity to distribute the supplier's products, or to provide maintenance of the supplier's products by virtue of their professional skills or suitable facilities. Suppliers thus have the assurance that their products are distributed in compliance with their quality, technical and corporate image standards, within a cohesive network.

Selective distribution is, in principle, recognised as lawful both in France and at the European Union level, provided that distributor selection is based on criteria concerned purely with effective product marketing. The selection, based on pre-established, objective criteria of a qualitative nature, should not aim to eliminate competitors of the network, but rather to optimise the distribution process by excluding distributors who do not have the required skills. As this type of agreement is not covered by category at the European Union level under an EU exemption rule, the European Court of Justice decides whether criteria are fair or anti-competitive on an individual basis (eg limitation of the number of sales outlets and obligation to buy from an exclusive supplier).

In practice, selective distribution is justified primarily for the distribution of luxury, high-quality, or technically complex products which require that the distributor have special skills and facilities. Examples of such products are perfume, clothing, computers and automobiles.

As in the case of exclusive distribution agreements, French law does not contain specific provisions governing selective distribution contracts. Distributors have the same status as resellers and termination of the agreement is subject to the same principle as exclusive distribution contracts (see above).

FRANCHISING AGREEMENT (*CONTRAT DE FRANCHISE*)

Franchising enables a franchisor who owns a trade mark, trade name, technical and/or commercial know-how, and so forth to grant the right to use such assets to a franchisee, who, in exchange for payment of royalties, is assured of the continued disclosure of the franchisor's know-how.

Franchising enables the franchisor to develop its business and promote its corporate image, backed by internally developed know-how, without having to invest in equipment and human resources. The franchisee makes the necessary investments for business operations, benefiting from the commercial and/or technical experience, assistance and market reputation of the franchisor.

Three forms of franchising exist:

- industrial franchising, whereby the franchisee manufactures the franchisor's products under the franchisor's trade mark, in accordance with the franchisor's instructions;
- services franchising, whereby the franchisee performs services under the trade mark or trade name of the franchisor, in accordance with the latter's instructions;

- distribution franchising, whereby the franchisee sells some of the franchisor's product in an outlet under the franchisor's trade name.

Franchising agreements are provided for at EU level (exemption regulation no 4087-88 of 30 November 1988). Under French law, they are governed by standard legal provisions and case law. Here, too, the accuracy of the information provided to the franchisee prior to entering into a formal contract is of prime importance, as explained above in relation to exclusive distribution contracts. The franchisee operates his business on his own behalf; with respect to a distribution franchise, the franchisee purchases the franchisor's products to resell them.

31

Competition Law

Gilles Semadeni, Marianne Mousseron and Arlette Gastaldy, Coopers & Lybrand CLC Juridique et Fiscal

French competition law is based on the provisions of the Treaty of Rome and the Government Order dated 1 December 1986. The law covers three main areas:

- concentrations;
- anti-competitive practices;
- restraint of trade.

CONTROL OVER CONCENTRATIONS

Controls over concentrations were introduced some 20 years ago, in the Law of 1 January 1977, and are now included in section V of Government Order no 86-1243 dated 1 December 1986.*

Definition of Concentrations

A concentration is any operation which transfers the property or control of all or part of the assets, rights or obligations of a company, or which aims at conferring on a company or group of companies the ability to exercise, directly or indirectly, a decisive influence on one or

---

* The coal and steel industries and the media sector are subject to different regulations. Likewise, this section does not include any discussion of concentrations at European Union level, which are covered exclusively by European controls.

more companies. In practice, the control of concentrations primarily relates to mergers and acquisitions.

French law will only apply, however, if the companies subject to or economically linked to the concentration:

- have together more than 25 per cent of the sales, purchases, or any other transactions on a national market or a substantial part of that market for substitutable goods, products or services; or
- have a total annual turnover (tax excluded) of more than 7 billion fr provided that at least two of the companies in the concentration have an annual turnover of at least 2 billion fr.

In any case, the definition of the relevant market and the extent to which the product or service in question could be substituted for another – raise an issue.

Even if the two thresholds are exceeded, the concentration will not be subject to controls unless it is viewed as being likely to hinder the free play of market forces. To determine whether this is the case, the *Conseil de la Concurrence* (authority responsible for sanctioning anti-competitive practices) will examine the specific features of the markets concerned and the way in which they operate, in order to assess the probability of the concentration resulting in higher prices or a decline in quality without any lowering of prices. Account is also taken of the respective market shares of the expanded company or group and the other domestic market players, as well as of a number of variables such as the technical possibility of imports the competing with domestic products, possible difficulties in obtaining adequate supplies of raw materials, production factors and the magnitude of advertising spending required to penetrate the market or to retain market share.

If a concentration is considered likely to hinder the free play of market forces and is therefore subject to investigation, the *Conseil de la Concurrence* will assess the economic effects in order to determine whether the contribution to 'economic progress' outweighs the negative impact in terms of competition.

Four conditions must be met for the *Conseil de la Concurrence* to consider that this is in fact the case and that the concentration will therefore have a positive net impact on the economy:

- the progress claimed by the parties must be reasonable;
- the progress must benefit the sector as a whole and not simply the companies involved in the project, to the detriment of their competitors in the domestic market or their trading partners;

- the concentration must be an essential element in enabling the claimed progress to be achieved; and
- the claimed progress must be sufficient to outweigh the negative effects in terms of competition.

These issues should be addressed in detail in the notification sent to the Minister of the Economy.

The *Conseil de la Concurrence's* assessment of the benefits and disadvantages of the concentration will also take account of the ability of the companies concerned to compete effectively with international players.

Procedure

Unlike under European Union rules, French law does not contain any requirement for companies to notify the Minister of Economy of a planned concentration. Nevertheless, they have the option of submitting their concentration plans for approval, before or after the event, with the result that controls may be triggered at the initiative either of the parties concerned or of the Minister of Economy.

Notice may be given either in advance, provided that negotiations have reached a stage where the parties concerned are in a position to supply adequate information concerning their plans, or within three months of the legal completion date of the concentration. The parties may also make certain commitments concerning, for example, the protection of jobs or the preservation of free competition.

Companies or groups involved in a concentration that wish to notify the Minister of Economy should submit details of their plans, by registered letter with return receipt requested, to the DGCCRF,* specifying whether they are acting in their own name or on behalf of other companies.

If no reply is received within two months, the concentration or planned concentration can be considered as having been approved, together with the related implied commitments. If the Minister of the Economy submits the project to the *Conseil de la Concurrence* for review, approval can be assumed to be forthcoming if no further communications are received within six months.

In the event that the parties forming a concentration elect not to give notice of their plans, the Minister of Economy can order an investiga-

---

* *Direction Générale de la Concurrence, de la Consommation et de la Répression des Fraudes,* a Government department (Ministry of Economy and Finance) responsible for competition and consumer issues and the prevention of fraud.

tion or submit the project for review by the *Conseil de la Concurrence* if he considers that the link-up is likely to be in breach of the rules governing concentrations. The investigation may be launched before the expiry of the three-month notification period following the concentration completion date.

Companies that are planning or have carried out a concentration are well advised to notify the Minister of Economy, because in this way they will know for certain, after two months (or six months if the project is submitted to the *Conseil de la Concurrence*) whether the operation has been approved. Otherwise, the Minister of Economy can order an investigation or submit the matter to the *Conseil de la Concurrence* at any time in the future, leaving the parties in a state of uncertainty.

In fact, French legal controls over concentrations are such that it is in the company's interest to take the initiative of notifying the authorities of their plans as soon as possible especially in the case of a public tender offer.

Power and Penalties

The Ministry of Economy together with the ministry responsible for the sector concerned can approve the concentration or, after the *Conseil de la Concurrence* has given its opinion, order the companies involved:

- not to proceed further with the proposed concentration or to reverse the situation to how it was before;
- to modify the concentration or to take all necessary and appropriate measures to ensure effective competition; and
- to go ahead with the concentration, subject to conditions which contribute to economic and social progress to compensate for any restrictions on competition resulting from the concentration.

If these orders are not complied with and only in this case, penalties can be imposed. Each company can be fined up to 5 per cent of its annual turnover in France during the previous financial year. No penalties higher than those recommended by the *Conseil de la Concurrence* may be imposed.

ANTI-COMPETITIVE PRACTICES

The principles of free competition and free determination of prices are enshrined in French law. Anti-competitive practices, defined as practices whose purpose or whose result is to distort competition in a relevant market defined on a case by case basis,* are dealt with by the *Conseil de la Concurrence.*†

Competition rules provided for in the order dated 1 December 1986 are similar to the rules in force at European level.

Companies found guilty of anti-competitive practices risk in principle a fine of up to 5 per cent of their annual net turnover generated in France.‡ The Conseil de la Concurrence can decide on its own initiative to investigate suspected cases of anti-competitive practices, but it generally intervenes at the request of the Minister of Economy or of individual companies. In addition, the courts can declare an anti-competitive contract void and order the company concerned to pay damages to the parties that have suffered a loss resulting from such practices.

Anti-Competitive Agreements

Any agreement whose purpose or whose effect is to restrain or distort competition in a given market is said to be anti-competitive. Both explicit or implicit agreements may be sanctioned on this ground, provided that the proof of such practices can be established in some way. Furthermore, both horizontal agreements (ie agreements concluded between players operating at the same level in the economic process) or vertical agreements (ie agreements concluded between players operating at different levels) may fall within the scope of such a definition. For example, the *Conseil de la Concurrence* has been called on to express an opinion on the legality of clauses contained in general conditions of sale, sales co-operation agreements, franchise agreements, exclusive or selective distribution agreements, etc.

The agreements may concern matters such as price-fixing, the dividing up of a market, bid rigging in the case of private or public invitations to tender, exchange of information about competitors' prices and mar-

---

* The market is defined as the meeting point of supply and demand for a specific product or service (*Conseil de la Concurrence* activity report for 1996, p 56).
† The *Conseil de la Concurrence* is composed of seventeen members appointed for renewable six-year terms:
  - Eight current or former members of the *Conseil d'Etat* (highest administrative court), the *Cour de Cassation* (highest court of the judiciary), the *Cour des Comptes* (national audit office) or other government or legal agencies.
  - Four persons selected for their competence in economic matters or competition and consumer issues.
  - Five persons currently or formerly employed in the manufacturing, retailing, craft, service or professional sectors.
‡ Fines levied by the *Conseil de la Concurrence* in 1996 totalled over 106 million fr. They concerned 99 companies or groups and 14 professional organisations.

gins, or boycotts. Certain practices followed by professional organisations, such as the issue of price directives, can also be qualified as anti-competitive.

Each year, the Conseil de la Concurrence conducts investigations in a wide variety of industries and also into public sector practices.

Abuses of Dominant Market Positions

Prohibited abuses of dominant market position are of two types: abuse of a dominant position and abuse of a state of economic dependence.

Abuse of a dominant position

The fact that a company dominates its market is not, in itself, illegal. However, a company may not, even unintentionally, abuse such a position in a way that distorts competition. Examples of abuses include refusal to sell, tied sales, discriminatory conditions of sale or the termination of an established business relationship solely because the customer or supplier refuses to accept unjustified business terms.

Abuse of a state of economic dependence

A state of economic dependence exists where a customer has no alternative source of supply or a supplier has no alternative outlet for its products or services. The abuse of such a state of dependence is illegal only if it distorts competition. The cases in which those rules have been applied remain relatively limited as the *Conseil de la Concurrence* has adopted a restrictive interpretation of the conditions in which they may apply.

Exemptions

French law allows for companies to be exempted from the provisions of the law relating to anti-competitive practices provided that they can demonstrate that they are contributing to economic progress. Although many companies claim immunity on these grounds, they are however, frequently unsuccessful either because the courts consider that these practices do not contribute to economic progress or because the claimed economic progress can be achieved by other means, not involving such anti-competitive practices.

Exemption can also be claimed on the grounds that the anti-competitive practices result from the application of a legislative text or related regulations, but in this case it is necessary to demonstrate that the practices are a direct and necessary consequence of the law or regulation concerned.

Abusively Low Prices to Consumers

Abusively low prices are prohibited, as they are of a nature to threaten certain manufacturing and/or distribution channels. This only applies to prices of products offered for sale to consumers which are unreasonably low compared with the related production, transformation and marketing costs, where it can be established that this pricing policy intentionally or unintentionally eliminates a competitor or its products or limits access to a new entrant on the market. The question as to whether these provisions apply to the pricing of services remains open. However, these provisions do not apply to the resale of products which have not been transformed,* with the exception of sound recordings reproduced on physical media.

RESTRICTIVE PRACTICES

Unlike the legislation governing anti-competitive practices, which applies only where the practice is likely to prevent free competition, restrictive practice legislation applies even in cases where the practice has no impact on the market. The rules are designed to improve market transparency and to prevent certain practices which are abusive and unfair.

Transparency Rules

French law provides that all manufacturers, suppliers of services, wholesalers and importers are required to provide details of their sales offer – including price list and rebate schedule – to any potential buyer of a product or service, at the latter's request. Companies have a fair amount of leeway when it comes to determining their conditions of sale, provided that these are not anti-competitive. In all cases, however, the conditions of sale must include details of the payment terms and the penalties for late payment that will be levied pursuant to the law.

The most common clauses cover (but are not limited to) price, payment terms (certain of which are regulated), reservation of title, delivery lead times, transfer of risk, liability, warranty, applicable law and competent jurisdiction.

Sales co-operation agreements, whereby a specific service is supplied by the buyer to the vendor in exchange for remuneration, must be

---

* The legal provisions applicable to products resold without transformation concern selling at a loss (see 'Transparency Rules').

drawn up and signed prior to the service being rendered, with each party retaining a signed original. Examples of sales co-operation agreements include agreements between a supplier and a retailer providing for promotional displays of the supplier's products, contribution by a supplier to the cost of producing a retailer's promotional leaflets featuring the supplier's products, rental of advertising space, and broadcasting of point-of-sale advertising messages.

The transparent pricing principle also applies to invoices, which must contain certain compulsory information. In particular, the list price of the product must be indicated, with any discounts shown separately. This is essential for products resold without transformation, because the price shown on the purchase invoice is used to determine whether a company is reselling at a loss, a practice that constitutes a criminal offence carrying a heavy fine (see below).

It is also an offence to impose, directly or indirectly, a minimum price or a minimum profit margin for the resale of goods or products or the supply of services.

French law also prohibits discriminatory practices, defined as a practice whereby a producer, trader, manufacturer or craftsman applies to or obtains from a trading partner prices, payment terms, conditions of sale or terms of sale or purchase that are discriminatory and not justified by real consideration, the effect of which is to create a competitive advantage or disadvantage for the trading partner. Discriminatory practices may qualify as anti-competitive if they distort competition (see above).

Abusive and Unfair Commercial Practices

In order to 'promote a climate that favours the development of ethical trading and restore a more balanced relationship between manufacturers and retailers'* a certain number of abusive and unfair practices are prohibited that may result in a liability suit being brought against the company concerned.

Examples of abusive and unfair practices include:

- obtaining or attempting to obtain under threat of delisting special prices, payment terms, methods of sale or commercial co-operation conditions manifestly derogatory to those provided in the supplier's general sales condition;

---

* Introduction to the bill on the *'équilibre et la loyauté des relations commerciales'*, 26 February 1996.

- the complete or partial termination of an established business relationship, without written notice, taking into account previous business dealings or recognised industry practice as established in inter-sector agreements.

Sanctions

Failure to comply with any of the above provisions of French competition law may lead to sanction under either civil or criminal law.

The following matters are sanctioned under criminal law:

- imposed minimum resale prices: a fine of up to 100,000 fr;
- pricing transparency: a fine of up to 100,000 fr in the case of individuals and 500,000 fr for companies;
- invoicing rules: a fine of up to 500,000 fr or 50 per cent of the amount billed or that should have been billed, if this is higher, in the case of individuals and five times this amount for companies;
- reselling at a loss: a fine of up to 500,000 fr or 50 per cent of the amount spent advertising loss leaders, if this is higher, in the case of individuals and five times this amount for companies;
- regulated payment terms: a fine of 500,000 fr.

Civil law governs provisions which aim at establishing balance and fair commercial relationships. Breach of these provisions is sanctioned by the payment of damages to cover the estimated value of the loss suffered by the plaintiff. The mechanism is that applicable to other liability claims, except that the action may be brought not only by the injured party but also by the Public Prosecutor, the Minister of Economy or the President of the *Conseil de la Concurrence*. In this regard, actions brought by the Minister of Economy are increasingly common.

32

Intellectual Property

Régis Carral and Marc Schuler,
Coopers & Lybrand CLC Juridique et Fiscal

The legal protection of intellectual property rights can be analysed under French law depending on whether such protection:

- is subject to registration formalities: trademarks, patent and designs;
- results from the act of creation or the behaviour of the owner: copyright and secrecy.

The main legislative provision concerning intellectual property protection is the Intellectual Property Code (IPC). It has replaced, since 1992, the many texts covering trade marks, patents, designs and copyright which had existed concurrently up to then and which had proved somewhat difficult to reconcile with each other in some circumstances.

Apart from the legal protection mechanisms mentioned, privileged information may also be protected contractually by means of specific provisions notably clauses relating to confidentiality, exclusivity or non-competition.

It should be underlined that although we have limited our analysis to the French protection regimes, specific European and international protection may also be afforded and should be, in practice, taken into account.

PROTECTION SUBJECT TO FORMALITIES

Trade marks

Pursuant to article L711-1 of the IPC, a trade mark is a sign which can be represented graphically and which serves to distinguish products and services from those of other persons and companies.

Trade mark selection

Eligible trade marks may be verbal, expressed in writing or orally, provided that in the latter case, they are capable of graphical or figurative representation.

The selected trade mark must also fulfil the following conditions:

- it must be distinctive, ie the sign concerned must not have any essential link with the product it is used for;
- it must not be excluded under article 6 ter of the revised Paris Convention of 20 March 1883 relating notably to state coats of arms, flags, emblems andofficial inspection and quality signs prohibited by law ('Geneva Cross' and 'Red Cross', the five Olympic circles and the Olympic motto, French and foreign decorations, including the *'Legion d'honneur'*, tobacco brands used for products other than those directly associated with tobacco consumption);
- it is not contrary to public policy or morals;
- it is not deceptive as regards the nature, quality or geographical origin of the product or service;
- it is available for registration; the following are excluded by implication:
  - marks which infringe a mark already registered or of renown;
  - marks which infringe a corporate name, if there is a risk of confusion in the minds of the public;
  - marks which infringe a trade name or commercial name known throughout the country, if there is a risk of confusion in the minds of the public;
  - marks which infringe a protected label of origin or country;
  - marks which infringe copyright;
  - marks which infringe rights related to a protected design;
  - marks which infringe a third party's identity, eg his or her surname, pseudonym or image;
  - marks which infringe the name, image and reputation of a regional authority.

Registration procedure

Under the provisions of article712-1 of the IPC, the ownership of a trade mark results from its registration.

Registration formalities are carried out at the *Institut National de la Propriété Industrielle* (INPI) (trade mark and patents office) or at the clerk of the commercial court or of the higher civil court where the applicant is established or domiciled. Registration forms are available from the INPI.

Applications should include the following information:

- the identity of the applicant;
- a specimen of the trademark;
- a list of the related products or services and their corresponding classes;
- proof of payment of royalties.

Provided that no objection is lodged against the application by a third party within the prescribed deadline, and that the application is not rejected by the INPI, the trade mark will be deemed to have been registered as from the date of filing.

Registration implications

Registration gives the owner the exclusive right to use the trade mark for a ten-year period from the date of filing, which is renewable periodically for an identical term.

For the protection to be *maintained*, however, further action is required. The trade mark holder is required to use the mark constructively for an uninterrupted period of five years, unless he is unable to do so for valid reasons, failing which the trade mark may be deregistered at the request of a third party.

The holder may use the trade mark personally, or may license or assign the related rights. In order to be binding upon third parties, the licence or assignment of contract must be recorded at the *Registre National des Marques* (French trade marks registry).

Exclusive ownership of a trade mark entitles the holder to prevent any third party from using the mark, except in specific cases. Any unauthorised use constitutes infringement, which is punishable under civil or criminal law. The maximum penalties for any act of infringement are two years' imprisonment and/or a 1,000,000 fr fine.

Patents

Patents are used to protect the inventions of private individuals or companies which are intended for industrial purposes.

Patentable inventions

In accordance with article 611-10 of the IPC an invention is patentable provided that:

- the invention is new: an invention is considered as new if it is outside established technical bounds, the latter being all techniques made available to the public before the date of filing of the patent application, in writing or verbally, or through use or any other means, together with the content of applications for patents in France, Europe and internationally, filed prior to the receipt of the application;
- the invention entails inventive activity, ie it derives from methods which are not within established technical bounds in the particular profession;
- the invention has an industrial application, ie it can be manufactured or used in any industry, including agriculture.

In light of these criteria, inventions which fall into the following categories cannot be patented:

- scientific discoveries and theories, and mathematical methods;
- aesthetic creations;
- plans, principles and methods applied in the performance of intellectual or economic activities, games and computer programs;
- presentation of information.

Furthermore, inventions whose publication or implementation is contrary to public policy and morals (eg inventions concerning the human body, including its component parts and products, and knowledge acquired of the total or partial structure of a human gene), and inventions subject to special regimes, such as vegetable products, are considered unpatentable.

Ownership of title

Industrial property rights are owned by the inventor or his successor in title. If several persons created the invention independently of each other, ownership of title lies with the inventor who can prove that he was the first to file a related patent application. Furthermore, if the inventor is an employee, the ownership of title will depend on the conditions in which the invention was created, ie pursuant to an employment contract providing for an inventive activity corresponding to the employee's actual functions, or to the execution of research the employee has been specifically entrusted with, or whether the invention was created independently of the above functions.

Filing procedure

An application for a patent is to be filed with the INPI, containing:

- the request for the patent;
- the identity of the applicant;
- a description and one or several statements defining the object to be patented.

The description of the invention must be sufficiently clear and comprehensive as to permit the invention's execution by any skilled professional.

Following publication in the *Bulletin de la Propriété Industrielle* (official industrial property bulletin), the patent application undergoes examination by the INPI, during which time third parties may object to the registration. Upon completion of the examination and provided that the application is not rejected, the patent is issued and made public.

Patenting implications

A patentee has the exclusive right to use the patented object for a period of 20 years from the date of filing the application. For the patent to be maintained, royalties must be paid annually on the date of filing. After the 20-year period, the invention will be considered as part of the public domain.

Such monopoly of exploitation is subject to effective use of the patent by the patentee. After a three-year period from the date of filing, any company or private individual may obtain a licence to use the patent, if, without legitimate cause, the patentee has not started to use, or made serious preparations for using, the patent within the European Union, or has not marketed the patented object in sufficient quantity as to meet the needs of the French market. Third parties may also apply for a licence if the patent has not been used, or the related product been marketed, for more than three years.

In addition, compulsory licences may be granted 'automatically' if the patented object satisfies a determined general need, particularly in the interests of public health, the economy or national security.

The patentee may use the patent directly, or license or assign it. In order to be binding upon third parties, the related contracts must be recorded at the *Registre National des Brevets* (French patents office). Furthermore, the provisions of the contracts should not give rise to unfair trade practices as specified by French and European Union competition law.

Patent infringement is punishable under civil and criminal law, with a maximum of two years' imprisonment and/or a maximum fine of 1,000,000 fr.

Designs

In addition to patentable industrial inventions, the law also provides protection for ornamental designs, ie those created for purely aesthetic reasons.

Eligible designs

Eligible designs include new designs, new plastic forms or industrial objects distinguishable from their equivalents, either owing to the distinct, recognisable shape which is the essence of their novelty, or by virtue of one or several external features which endow the object with a unique and novel appearance.

Novelty requires that the components of designs, as arranged, laid out, combined or otherwise, have individual particularities. This resembles the definition of originality found within the framework of copyright.

Registration procedure

An application must be filed with the INPI, or with the clerk of the local commercial court nearest to the applicant's residence, stating the identity of the applicant and providing a graphic or photographic illustration of the design(s) in question, together with a brief description, if appropriate. A royalty is due upon registration, its amount being calculated based on the number of designs registered.

It should be noted that a more simple filing procedure exists for designs used in certain sectors which frequently modify the shape and appearance of the related products.

Registration implications

Ownership of the design lies with the creator or his heirs, the act of registration conferring upon the applicant only a putative fatherhood with respect to the creation. Registration of the creation does not establish any right, but is purely declarative. Therefore, even if he does not file for registration, the author of a creation may claim ownership on the basis of copyright.

The law provides for two means of proving a definite date of creation. Priority with regard to a design may be established by consulting private registers subject to INPI certification under article 511-7 of the IPC. The other method involves the use of 'Soleau' double envelopes, obtained from the INPI, in which the author of a creation places a description of the same in each of the compartments, one of which is kept by the INPI for a five-year period, renewable once.

The protection afforded by the registration is valid for a 25-year period from the date of filing, which may be renewed once. If the more simple procedure has been followed, the protection is valid for only three years and the applicant must re-register in accordance with the standard procedure no more than six months before the expiry of the three-year period in order for the protection to be maintained.

The owner may use the creation directly, or license or assign it. In order to be binding upon third parties, the related contracts must be recorded at the *Registre National des Dessins et Modèles* (French designs office).

Any breach of rights related to a registered design constitutes infringement and is punishable under civil and criminal law. Prior to filing, the author of a creation does not enjoy the rights associated with the registration, but may seek copyright protection.

PROTECTION NOT SUBJECT TO FORMALITIES

Copyright

Pursuant to the provisions of articleL111-1 of the IPC, the author of an intellectual work has an intangible right of ownership over that work, by virtue of having created it. The right is exclusive and binding upon third parties.

Copyrighted works

The IPC does not define the characteristics of works eligible for copyright protection, but merely states that all 'intellectual' works are protected, irrespective of their type, form of expression, merit, or destination.

In practice, the courts consistently apply the criterion of originality when assessing whether a work may be protected, rather than taking into account the fact that it may be innovative or, on the contrary, similar to other existing works. An intellectual work is characterised by its author's personal stamp, which makes it unique and distinctive.

A work is deemed to have been created when the author's idea is executed, even incompletely and not at the moment of public disclose. Although eligibility for copyright does not result from disclosure of the work or fulfilment of filing formalities, the author should nevertheless have given some concrete material form to the creation which is the product of his imagination. The idea itself, however, may not be protected, and thus may be used by all.

Authorship

The author is the person under whose name the work is made public, unless proof is provided to the contrary. When there is more than one author, the authors are deemed to be co-owners of the work, the use of which is subject to approval by each co-owner.

However, when the participation of authors or co-authors involves different categories and each personal contribution is distinguishable from the others, each contribution may be used without the consent of the other authors, provided that such use is not prejudicial to the use of the work as a whole.

Furthermore, as an exception to the principle whereby copyright may not be granted to any party other than the effective creator of the work in question, the Code provides that ownership of a work may be attributed to a physical or legal entity when the said work has been created at the initiative of the entity, which supervises the production, publication and disclosure of the work and when the personal contributions of the various contributing authors are inextricably combined in the whole for the purpose of which the work was conceived. A similar principle is applied in the case of software designed by employees in connection with their functions, or in accordance with their employer's instructions, in that the related proprietary rights are attributed to the employer, unless otherwise stipulated.

Copyright entitlements

The intangible property rights which an author holds over his creative work cover intellectual and moral rights as well as property rights.

The moral right of an author consists of his right for his name, his quality and his work to be respected. The right, associated with the persona of the author, is permanent, may be passed on to his heirs, and is not subject to any statute of limitation. This inalienability and indefeasibility implies that the right may be neither assigned nor licensed.

Proprietary rights, which give the author the exclusive right to use his work, may be claimed by the author throughout his lifetime and by his assignees during the calendar year in which the author dies and for 70 years thereafter. After the 70-year period, copyright lapses and the work may then be used without the author or his heirs being entitled to claim any remuneration whatsoever. They nevertheless retain the right to oppose the use of the work in the event of an infringement of the author's moral right.

If the author ceases to use his work personally, but wishes to let a third party use it, he may license or assign all or some of his rights. Some licences or sale agreements concerning proprietary rights are subject to strict formalities and usually involve payment of proportional remuneration to the author.

Any breach of the author's rights constitutes copyright infringement and is punishable under civil and criminal law.

Confidentiality

In addition to legal protection requiring formalities and/or the disclosure to third parties of protected objects, there are specific regimes which provide physical and legal entities with the possibility to preserve the confidentiality of techniques developed by them.

Trade secrets

Manufacturing process   In light of legal doctrine and case law, the concept of manufacturing secrecy is applicable to any means of manufacturing which represents a practical or commercial interest and which, as used in industry, is kept secret from competitors. The focus on manufacturing means that the methods and know-how as to the distribution and marketing of related products and services are excluded.

Manufacturing secrecy requires absolutely that the related knowledge is not readily available to the profession and transcends traditional technical bounds in the industry concerned. The object of secrecy should further represent an improvement on average knowledge, resulting in it having a practical and commercial interest.

Know-how   This concept is broader than that of manufacturing secrecy in that it applies to all the activities of a company, from the production of products and services to the management of the entity. In light of legal doctrine and case law, the salient features of know-how are its transferability, ie its ability to be separated from the persons performing it, and its inaccessibility to persons operating in the same business segment.

Confidentiality implications

Protection through the obligation of confidentiality is founded on the punishment of unauthorised disclosure or use of the protected knowledge.

Pursuant to the provisions of article L152-7 of the Labour Code, the revelation of, or the attempt to reveal, a manufacturing secret by any manager or employee of a company is punishable by a maximum of two years' imprisonment and/or a maximum fine of 200,000 fr. Case law punishes disclosure of a secret not only when the author of the disclosure is effectively employed by the company which owns the secret, but also in cases where the secret learned during employment with a company is revealed by an employee after expiry of his employment contract with that company.

Unauthorised disclosure or use of a manufacturing secret or know-how may also constitute an act of unfair competition and render the author civilly liable, in accordance with article 1382 of the Civil Code.

33

Management Rights and Responsibilities

Marie Supiot and Stéphane Jaffrain,
Coopers & Lybrand CLC Juridique et Fiscal

Under French law, a manager *(dirigeant)* is defined as being any person who has legal or de facto responsibility for running a company and representing it in its dealings with third parties.

For the purpose of this section, managers include:

- the manager *(gérant)* of a *Société Civile*, a *Société en Commandite Simple*, a *Société à Responsabilité Limitée* or a *Société en Commandite par Actions*;
- the chairman and managing director *(Président-Directeur Général)* and the managing director(s) *(Directeur Général)* of a limited liability company with a board of directors *(Société Anonyme à conseil d'administration)* and the president of the management board, or managing director(s) of a limited liability company with a management board and a supervisory board *(Société Anonyme à directoire et conseil de surveillance)*;
- the chairman of a *Société par Actions Simplifiée* (see Chapter 26 for company definitions).

GENERAL AND SPECIFIC MANAGEMENT RIGHTS AND DUTIES

Any manager of a company has the right and the duty to manage the company's affairs and to represent the company in its dealings with third parties. Besides these general powers, managers have specific rights and duties, including the duty to call and, in principle, to chair shareholders' meetings and to disclose certain information to the auditors (in the case of companies that are required to have their accounts audited).

Managers' right to represent the company in its dealings with third parties may be subject to certain restrictions. In *Sociétés Anonymes*, their right to give guarantees is limited by law. In addition, certain contracts between managers and the company are subject to prior approval while others are illegal. More generally, they must manage the company in accordance with its interest and comply with all applicable laws and regulations. A manager who fails to comply with these principles may incur both civil and criminal liability.

RIGHT TO REPRESENT THE COMPANY

The right of managers to represent the company depends on its legal form. The situation also differs depending on whether the issue is viewed from the perspective of managers' dealings with the company or their dealings with third parties.

Sociétés Civiles

In the case of a *Société Civile*, the manager has the right to enter into contracts that are binding on the company within the limits of the company's objects. Any clause in the articles of association limiting the manager's rights will be unenforceable *vis-à-vis* third parties. In *Sociétés Civiles* with more than one manager, each has a separate right to enter into contracts that are binding on the company. The fact that one manager formally objects to a contract to be entered into by another manager will not be enforceable *vis-à-vis* third parties unless it can be proved that they were aware of this manager's objection.

Any contracts entered into by the manager that fall outside the scope of the objectives of the company are not binding on the company.

Sociétés en Nom Collectif and Sociétés en Commandite Simples

The manager of a general or limited partnership has the right, *vis-à-vis* the partners and provided that the articles of association do not include any clause limiting his powers, to carry out any and all acts of management that are in the company's interest. If the company has more than one manager, these rights are vested in each manager separately except that a manager may formally oppose any transaction before it is entered into by another manager. The manager is liable towards the partners for any failure to comply with any clause in the articles of association limiting his powers.

As regards the company's dealings with third parties, the manager has the right to enter into contracts within the limits of the objectives of the company. Any clause limiting his powers are unenforceable *vis-à-vis* third parties; consequently, the partners are jointly and severally liable for contracts entered into by the manager even if the latter has overstepped the rights defined in the memorandum articles of association.

Sociétés à Responsabilité Limitées, Sociétés par Actions Simplifiées, Sociétés en Commandite par Actions and *Sociétés Anonymes*

The powers of management *vis-à-vis* the shareholders of a *Société Anonyme*, a *Société par Actions Simplifiée* or a *Société en Commandite par Actions* are limited to the company's objectives. In a *Société à Responsabilité Limitée* the manager's powers are identical to the manager's powers in a *Société en Nom Collectif*.

As regards the company's dealings with third parties, all actions by the management are binding on the company, even those which fall outside the scope of the objectives of the company. In order to avoid any liability, the company may try to prove that the third parties concerned knew or could not fail to be aware that the commitment given by the managers was not consistent with the company's objectives. This is difficult to prove particularly since the publication of the articles of association does not constitute adequate proof. Any clauses in the articles of association limiting their rights or requiring a double signature are unenforceable *vis-à-vis* third parties.

GUARANTEES GIVEN BY MANAGEMENT ON BEHALF OF A *SOCIETE ANONYME*

Specific rules concerning guarantees given by the management in the company's name exist for *Sociétés Anonymes*. The management's right to give such guarantees depends on the type of *Société Anonyme* and represent an exception to the principle whereby management have the broadest powers to enter into any contracts that are binding on the company. In a *Société Anonyme* with a board of directors, board members, managing directors and other legal representatives may not grant any guarantees without the prior authorisation of the board. The board may place a ceiling on the aggregate amount of guarantees that may be granted by the management and may also set separate limits for each type of guarantee. If a guarantee exceeds either of these amounts, the board's prior authorisation is required.

The same principle applies in the case of a *Société Anonyme* with a management board and a supervisory board, the only difference being that the authorisation is given by the supervisory board.

The above limits do not apply to guarantees granted to the tax or customs authorities.

Members of the management may be held personally liable for any failure to comply with these restrictions and may be required to reimburse the company for any amounts paid out by the latter following a claim made under the unauthorised guarantee.

Shareholders of *Sociétés Anonymes* therefore benefit from a certain amount of protection as regards guarantees given by the management. In addition, creditors who seek a guarantee from the company are required to verify that the management is acting within its powers.

AGREEMENTS BETWEEN A COMPANY AND ITS MANAGEMENT REQUIRING PRIOR APPROVAL

Agreements concluded between a company and its managers are regulated as concerns agreements involving directors, managing director(s), members of the management board or of the supervisory board of a *Société Anonyme*, the manager or member of the supervisory board of a *Société en Commandite par Actions*, the *Gérant* of a *Société à Responsabilité Limitée* or the president and the other managers of a *Société par Actions Simplifiée*.

In the case of a *Société Anonyme*, the prior authorisation of the board of directors or supervisory board is required for any agreement between the company and a member of its management that is not entered into in the normal course of business at arm's length terms. The same principle applies to agreements in which a member of management has an indirect interest or where he deals with the company through a third party. Agreements between companies which have directors or managers in common are also subject to prior authorisation. Any such agreement that is not authorised in advance may be declared null and void, but only if it has adverse consequences for the company. Applications to have an unauthorised agreement declared null and void are statute-barred after a period of three years from the date of signature or the date on which the failure to obtain the necessary authorisation is revealed.

The auditors must be notified of the prior authorisation within one month of the date of signature of the agreement and are required to present a report to shareholders on all such agreements at the annual general meeting. A resolution must also be presented at the annual general meeting, approving the agreements.

The directors concerned do not take part in the vote at either the board meeting or shareholders' meeting. If the agreement is not approved by the shareholders, it will nevertheless remain in effect unless the other party is guilty of fraud. However, the director concerned and, possibly, the other members of the board of directors or supervisory board, will be liable for any adverse consequences suffered by the company.

The same requirement applies in the case of a *Société à Responsabilité Limitée*, except that the agreement is submitted directly to the shareholders' meeting for authorisation and the obligation extends to agreements entered into between the company and its shareholders.

In the case of a *Société en Commandite par Actions*, the authorisation is given by the supervisory board and the auditors are notified by the chairman.

No prior authorisation procedure exists for *Sociétés par Actions Simplifiées*. The approval has to be given by the shareholders. Agreements that have not been approved are binding on the company, but the manager concerned is liable for any adverse consequences suffered by the company.

PROHIBITED AGREEMENTS BETWEEN A COMPANY AND ITS MANAGEMENT

Certain agreements between a *Société Anonyme*, a *Société par Actions Simplifiée*, a *Société à Responsabilité Limitée*, a *Société en Commandite par Actions* and their management are prohibited.

In the case of *Sociétés Anonymes* and *Sociétés par Actions Simplifiées*, directors other than legal entities cannot obtain loans or current account or other advances from the company or any guarantees by the company of their commitments to third parties. The same prohibition applies to the permanent representatives of companies holding seats on the board, the spouse or other direct relatives of a director or any person acting on a director's behalf.

These rules also apply to the manager and shareholders other than legal entities of *Sociétés à Responsabilité Limitées* and to the managers of *Sociétés en Commandite par Actions*.

MANAGEMENT'S CIVIL AND CRIMINAL LIABILITY

Managers in a French company may incur civil or criminal liability. The directors' civil liability is governed by the general principles of French law of tort (fault or negligence causing a loss). Some of the criminal offences for which a manager may be prosecuted are specific to company law while others are to be found in the Penal Code or in specific statutes. A peculiarity of French law is that managers may be held criminally liable for an offence committed by the company's employees, such criminal liability arising as a result of their position.

Civil Liability

In the performance of their corporate functions, all managers may be held civilly liable either *vis-à-vis* third parties or *vis-à-vis* the company or its shareholders.

The civil liability imposed on managers is not regulated by a particular law text. It can be ancillary to a criminal action or result from separate misconduct or negligence on the part of a manager.

Managers' civil liability is generally statute-barred after three years except for *Gérants* of *Sociétés en Nom Collectif* where the statute of limitations is 10 years or, depending on the circumstances, even 30 years.

Shareholders may bring an action against managers either personally, if the latter's action has caused them to suffer a loss, or on behalf of the company if the loss was suffered by the company. Third parties generally do not sue managers but the company itself as represented by the managers.

Criminal Liability

It is a principle under French law that any criminal offence must be expressly qualified as such by a legal provision. Therefore, a manager may not be held criminally liable unless he or the company has breached a rule of law which imposes criminal sanctions, in which case the penalties are those specifically provided for by the rule which was breached. Since 1 March 1994, legal entities may also be prosecuted and held criminally liable for specific offences provided for by law. Therefore, there may be cases where both the company and its managers may be cumulatively sentenced for the same criminal offence, the company as principal offender and the managers as co-offenders or accomplices, for example.

The company may only be held criminally liable if the offence was committed on its behalf by its governing bodies or its legal representatives in the course of their activities for the company, as opposed to offences committed by managers for their own personal benefit or in their capacity as managers without due authority.

A legal entity may only be held criminally liable for intentional offences (as opposed to offences carrying strict liability) if the criminal liability of one or more of its managers can be established.

Legal entities may be sentenced to fines of up to five times – ten times for repeated offences – the amount provided for private individuals; in addition any assets in dispute may be confiscated, and the company may be prohibited from performing certain operations (public offerings, government tenders, etc).

A member of the management who is held criminally liable may be fined or sentenced to a prison term. This may arise in the case of fraud (eg presentation of a fraudulent balance sheet), breach of trust (misappropriation of company's funds) or forgery (modification of minutes of board meetings or shareholders' meetings). However, the most common offences are the misuse of corporate assets (abus de biens sociaux) and the abuse of powers (abus de pouvoirs) – punishable by a fine of up to 2,500,000 fr and five years' imprisonment – and fraudulent bankruptcy (banqueroute).

In addition to the penalties provided for in company law and the bankruptcy laws, a manager found guilty of tax evasion may be sentenced to a term of imprisonment of up to five years and fined 250,000 fr plus an additional fine representing 80 per cent of the tax due.

Management may also be held criminally liable for failure to respect the rights of employees. For example, the offence of impeding the functions of employee representative bodies carries a term of imprisonment of between two months and one year and a fine of between 2,000 fr and 20,000 fr.

Insurance – Delegation of Powers

Civil liability insurance is available but the management cannot insure against criminal liability claims.

To reduce the risk of incurring criminal liability, one solution is to delegate management powers to certain employees. For the delegation of powers to be enforceable vis-à-vis third parties, the following conditions must be met:

- the person to whom the responsibility is transferred must have the professional qualifications and experience, the authority and disciplinary powers and the technical, human and financial resources necessary to carry out the delegated tasks;
- only specific rights and duties may be delegated as opposed to general powers so that the beneficiary may not be granted exactly the same powers as the manager;
- the scope of the delegation must be precisely defined, together with details of the management powers that the employee concerned is authorised to exercise;
- the delegation must be limited in time;
- the delegation must be accepted by the employee concerned. It should be put down in writing, dated, signed and registered with the tax authorities, in order to create a body of proof and firmly establish the date.

A delegation which meets these criteria allows a company to structure various levels of responsibility, thus for instance making each head of department liable for compliance with specific regulations within his field of expertise, and relieving the chairman of the board from any criminal liability for matters over which he has no day-to-day control.

Appendices

Appendix A

Investment Opportunities: how to find them

Véronique Jochum, Corporate Finance, PricewaterhouseCoopers

The search for acquisition candidates can take a number of forms, ranging from a structured search of companies within a predetermined industry sector or size category through to identification of businesses advertised as being for sale in business journals or minitel services.

Table A.1   A Selection of Information Sources on investment opportunities

Sources	Contents
Repreneur	Magazine containing 250 exclusive investment opportunities, plus articles on the acquisition or selling process in France (6 issues/year, only in French)
Reprendre & Transmettre	Publication on French M&A activity with articles on completed deals, financing advice, and investment opportunities (monthly, only in French)
Argus du Fonds de Commerce et d'Industrie	Periodical containing details of businesses and manufacturing sites for sale (6 issues/year, only in French)
PIC International	Publication containing details of investment opportunities classified by regions and articles on doing business in France (monthly, only in French, also available on the Internet)

Table A.1 (*continued*)

Cette Semaine: Les Défaillances	Publication produced by SCRL providing a list of companies in receivership, sorted by region (monthly, only in French)
3615 PMEPMI	Minitel service offering investment opportunities for small and medium-sized companies (only in French)
3615 Défis	Minitel service of the monthly magazine of the same name containing details of businesses for sale and other business opportunities (partnerships, franchises)
3617 Transdev	Minitel service of the monthly magazine of the same name containing details of businesses for sale and other business opportunities (partnerships, franchises, etc)
3615 Crea Club	Minitel service of the *Fédération Française des Clubs de Créateurs et de Repreneurs d'Enterprises* (National Federation of 'setting-up/acquiring a business' Clubs)
3615 Minca	Minitel service of the Ministry of Commerce and Industry with details of investment opportunities

The most productive search is likely to employ a number of methods, including ones identifying companies that are potentially for sale but where no active marketing is taking place, where there is less danger of an auction and where there is less danger of having to overpay.

The most basic search will comprise:

- an analysis of the industry structure and competitive dynamics;
- a review of potential targets matching investment criteria, including details on activities, financials, ownership and competitive positioning.

The above implies having access to databases and publications supplying business and company information for France. Listed on the following page is a selection of the most useful information sources on French companies and markets.

Table A.2 A Selection of Business Information Sources

Sources	Contents
Company Information	
Telefirm	Online directory produced by the Chamber of Commerce and Industry of Paris covering over a million companies. Providing basic information such as address, telephone, legal status, date of incorporation, management, line of business, nominal capital, number of employees (in French and in English)
Firmimport/ Firmexport	Hardcopy and online directory of French importers and exporters, produced by the Chamber of Commerce and Industry of Paris representing 95% of French international trade. Provides details on activity, turnover, export and import figures (in French and in English)
Kompass France	Hardcopy and online directory (also available on CD-Rom) covering over 100,000 companies with extremely detailed information on products and activities (in French and in English)
Infosociétés	Minitel service providing basic information, financials as well as shareholder/shareholding information (only in French)
French Company Handbook	Hardcopy publication by the Herald International Tribune providing one page profiles (company background, important developments, financial highlights, trading details, etc) on 130 of the leading French companies, including all companies in the SBF120 (in English)
Paris Stock Guide	Hardcopy publication by Cofisem on all French companies listed on the Paris Stock Exchange giving details on company activity, financial and trading highlights, etc (in French and in English)
Financial information	
Diane	CD-Rom by Bureau Van Dijk and SCRL containing company accounts and financial ratios for over 250,000 companies with five years of data (in French and in English)
SCRL	Online database providing company accounts and credit reports (only in French)
Dun & Bradstreet	Online database providing company reports including credit ratings (in French and English)

Table A.2 (*continued*)

Inpi Bilans	Minitel service containing annual accounts, financial highlights and key ratios for all SA (société anonyme) and SARL (Société Anonyme à Responsabilité Limitéé) which have filed their accounts with the Register of Commerce and Trade (only in French)

Company Background

Delphes	Online database produced by the ACFCI (Assembly of the Chambers of Commerce and Industry) and the CCIP (Paris Chamber of Commerce and Industry). Provides summaries of articles from approximately 1,000 journals. Focuses mainly on French companies and markets (in French with indexing in English for searching). Provides a photocopying service
Revupresse	Minitel service containing full-text articles of several major French newspapers and journals: *Les Echos, La Tribune, Le Monde, L'Usine Nouvelle, L'Expansion, L'Enterprise,* etc (only in French)
Textline	Online database from Reuters containing news and comments from a wide range of international sources (summaries and full-text articles). Coverage of French publications includes *Les Echos, La Tribune, Le Monde, L'Usine Nouvelle, Emballages, Chimie Actualités, Emballages, Industrie Textile, Points de Vente,* etc (in English and French)
AFP	*Agence France-Press* newswire service providing French and international news (in French and in English)

Market Information

Dafsa	Publishers of market studies and sector overviews on approximately 200 industries (only in French)
Bipe	Publisher of economic reports and market studies with emphasis put on forecasts (in French and in English)
Eurostaf	Publisher of market studies and strategic analysis (only in French)
Xerfi	Publisher of market studies and briefings, over 500 titles available (only in French)
Axétudes (SCRL)	Publisher of market reports and overviews, approximately 30 new titles a year (only in French)

Helpful information on investment conditions in France can also be obtained from several official organisations:

Table A.3   A Selection of Useful Contacts

Organisations	Function
Invest in France Agency	Network of agencies around the world created by the Datar, the French Development agency responsible for assisting foreign investment. Provides investors with information on investing in France and assists them in setting up investment projects
CNPF	*Conseil National du Patronat Français* (the French Employers' National Council) representing 85 trade associations and 170 employers' regional and local unions
ACFCI	*Assemblée des Chambres Françaises de Commerce et D'Industrie* (Assembly of the French Chambers of Commerce and Industry). Chambers of Commerce and Industry are present in all French regions and provide information on markets as well as advice to companies and investors

Appendix B

Contributor Contact Details

*For further details, see the contributors
profiles section at the beginning of the book.*

Association Française des Banques (AFB)
(French Association of Banks)
18 rue Lafayette
75440 Paris cedex 09
France
Tel: +33 (0) 1 48 00 52 52
Fax: +33 (0) 1 48 00 50 10
e-mail: afbcom@afb.fr
Web site: http: //www.afb.fr

Association Française des Investisseurs en Capital (AFIC)
(French Venture Capital Association)
76 avenue Marceau
75008 Paris
France
Tel: +33 (0) 1 47 20 99 09
Fax: +33 (0) 1 47 20 97 48

Chambre de Commerce Française de Grande-Bretagne
(French Chamber of Commerce in Great Britain)
Knightsbridge House, 5th floor
197 Knightsbridge
London SW7 1RB
U.K.
Tel: +44 (0) 171 304 4040
Fax: +44 (0) 304 7034
e-mail: mail@ccfg.co.uk
Web site: http: //www.lille.cci.fr

Coopers & Lybrand CLC Juridique et Fiscal
32 rue Guersant
75017 Paris
Tel: +33 (0) 1 45 72 83 40
Fax: +33 (0) 1 45 72 87 01

Conseil National du Patronat Français (CNPF)
(The National Council of French Employers)
31 avenue Pierre 1er de Serbie
75784 Paris cedex 16
France
Tel: +33 (0) 1 40 69 44 44
Fax: +33 (0) 1 47 23 47 32

Délégation Générale à l'Emploi et à la Formation Professionelle
(DGEFP)
(General Delegation for Employment and Professional Training)
7 Square Max Hymans
75747 Paris cedex 16
France
Tel: +33 (0) 1 44 38 32 83
Fax: +33 (0) 1 44 38 34 14

Ecole Européenne des Affaires de Paris (EAP)
(European School of Management)
6, avenue de la Porte Champerret
75838 Paris cedex 17
France
Tel: +33 (0) 1 44 03 34 58
Fax: +33 (0) 1 44 09 34 71
E-mail: jvasseur@eap.net

E.M.LYON
23 avenue Guy de Collongue
BP 174
69132 Ecully cedex
France
Tel: +33 (0) 4 78 33 78 00
Fax: +33 (0) 4 78 33 61 69
e-mail: tovey@em-lyon.com
Web site http: //www.em-lyon.com

Freight Europe (UK) Ltd
French Rail House
10 Leake Street
London SE1 7NN
U.K.
Tel: +44 (0) 171 203 7020
Fax: +44 (0) 171 401 8778

Healey & Baker
29 St George Street
London W2 3BG
U.K.
Tel: +44 (0) 171 629 9292
Fax: +44 (0) 171 514 2360

11/13 avenue de Friedland
75008 Paris
France
Tel: +33 (0) 1 53 76 92 92
Fax: +33 (0) 1 53 76 05 25

Huglo, Lepage & Associés Conseil
40 rue de Monceau
75008 Paris
France
Tel: +33 (0) 1 56 59.29 59
Fax: +33 (0) 1 56 59 29 39
e-mail: hugloav@imaginet.fr

INSEAD
Boulevard de Constance
77305 Fontainebleau cedex
France
Tel: +33 (0) 1 60 72 43 93
Fax: +33 (0) 1 60 74 55 56
e-mail: olivier.cadot@insead.fr

Invest in France Agency
21–24 Grosvenor Place
London
SW1X 7HU
Tel: +44 (0) 171 8231895
Fax: +44 (0) 171 2358453

PricewaterhouseCoopers
32 rue Guersant
75017 Paris
France
Tel: +33 (0) 1 45 72 80 00
Fax: +33 (0) 1 45 72 22 19

Syndicat des Entreprises de Travail Temporaire (SETT) – *formerly UNETT*
(Union of Temporary Employment Agencies)
56 rue La Fayette
75009 Paris
France
Tel: +33 (0) 1 55 07 85 87
Fax: +33 (0) 1 55 07 85 92

Professeur Jean-Francois Amadieu
Department of Management Studies
Université Paris 1 Panthéon Sorbonne
17 rue de la Sorbonne
75231 Paris Cedex 05
France
Tel/fax: +33 (0) 1 45 50 25 93
e-mail: jamadieu@aol.com

Robin Walden
DTI Export Promoter, Consumer Goods, France
c/o European Directorate
Scottish Trade International
120 Bothwell Street
Glasgow G2 7QP
U.K.
Tel: +44 (0) 141 228 2307
Fax: +44 (0) 141 228 2850
e-mail: robin.walden@scotent.co.uk

Appendix C

Further Sources of Information

General Information

Assemblée des Chambres Françaises de Commerce et d'Industrie (ACFCI)
(Assembly of French Chambers of Commerce and Industry)
45 avenue d'Iéna
75116 Paris
Tel: +33 (0) 1 40 69 37 00
Fax: +33 (0) 1 47 20 61 28
http: //www.lille.cci.fr/ccis/index.html

Bureau d'Informations et de Prévisions Economiques (BIPE)
(Information Bureau for Economic Forecasting)
l'Atrium
6 place Abel Gance
92652 Boulogne Billancourt cedex
Tel: +33 (0) 1 46 94 45 22
Fax: +33 (0) 1 46 94 45 99

Centre d'Études et de Recherches Internationales (CERI)
(Centre of International Studies and Research)
27 rue Saint Guillaume
75341 Paris cedex 07
Tel: +33 (0) 1 44 10 84 84
Fax: +33 (0) 1 44 10 84 50

Centre Français du Commerce Extérieur (CFCE)
(French Centre of Foreign Trade)
10 avenue d'Iéna
75783 Paris cedex 16
Tel: +33 (0) 1 40 73 30 00
Fax: +33 (0) 1 40 73 39 79
http: //www.cfce.fr

Comité National des Conseillers du Commerce Extérieur de la France
(CNCCE)
(National Committee of Foreign Trade Councillors)
22 avenue Franklin Roosevelt
75008 Paris
Tel: +33 (0) 1 43 83 92 96
Fax: +33 (0) 1 42 25 29 87

La documentation française
(French Government Documentation)
29–31 quai Voltaire
75344 Paris cedex 15
Tel: +33 (0) 1 40 15 70 00
36 15 DOCTEL
http: //www.ladocfrancaise.gouv.fr

Ministère des affaires étrangères
(Ministry for Foreign Affairs)
Direction des français à l'étranger
21 bis rue de la Pérousse
75116 Paris
Information for Expatriates
Tel: +33 (0) 1 43 17 69 20
Fax: +33 (0) 1 43 17 63 61
Legal Documents Services
Tel: +33 (0) 1 43 17 65 07

Office des Migrations Internationales (OMI)
(Immigration Office)
44 rue Bargue
75732 Paris cedex 15
Tel: +33 (0) 1 53 69 53 70
Fax: +33 (0) 1 53 69 53 69

Financial and Credit Agencies

Banque de France
(Bank of France)
168 rue de Rivoli
75001 Paris
Tel: +33 (0) 1 42 92 51 91
Fax: +33 (0) 1 42 86 05 54
http: //www.banque-france.fr

Banque Française du Commerce Extérieur (BFCE)
(French Bank of Foreign Trade)
21 boulevard Haussmann
75009 Paris
Tel: +33 (0) 1 48 00 48 00
Fax: +33 (0) 1 48 00 41 51 / +33 (0) 1 48 00 34 20

Banque Mondiale
(World Bank)
Bureau Européen
66 avenue d'Iéna
75116 Paris
Tel: +33 (0) 1 40 69 30 22
Fax: +33 (0) 1 40 69 31 51

Banque Transatlantique
17 boulevard Haussmann
75009 Paris
Tel: +33 (0) 1 40 22 81 77
Fax: +33 (0) 1 40 22 84 37

Crédit National
45 rue Saint Dominique
75008 Paris
Tel: +33 (0) 1 53 89 78 78
Fax: +33 (0) 1 53 89 78 79

Compagnie Française d'Assurance pour le Commerce Extérieur
(COFACE)
(French Assurance Company for Foreign Trade)
12 cours Michelet
La Défense 10
92800 Puteaux
Tel: +33 (0) 1 49 02 10 03 / +33 (0) 1 49 02 17 70
Fax: +33 (0) 1 47 73 77 36 / +33 (0) 1 47 73 81 97
http: //www.coface.fr

Société Française de Garantie de Financement des PME (SOFARIS)
(French Society of Financial Guarantees for Small- and Medium-sized Enterprises)
4 rue de Cambon
75001 Paris
Tel: +33 (0) 1 42 97 57 37 / +33 (0) 1 42 96 43 01
Fax: +33 (0) 1 49 27 08 74 / +33 (0) 1 42 60 51 97
http: //www.finances.gouv.fr/entreprises/sofaris.htm
http: //www.finances.gouv.fr/entreprises/adresses.htm£p9

Ministère de l'industrie et du commerce extérieur
SAEI (Services des Affaires Economiques et Internationales)
(Industry and Foreign Trade Ministry)
68 rue de Bellechasse
75353 Paris cedex 07 SP
Tel: +33 (0) 1 43 19 28 70
Fax: +33 (0) 1 43 19 53 33

Paris Europlace
(Guidance organisation for financial markets and banking)
39 rue Cambon
75001 Paris
Tel: +33 (0) 1 49 27 11 14
Fax: +33 (0) 1 49 27 11 06

Import/export advice

Club des exportateurs
(Exporters Club)
5 rue Paul Cézanne
75008 Paris
Tel: +33 (0) 1 42 65 34 67
Fax: +33 (0) 1 40 74 08 23

France exporte plus
6 rue Jean Jaurès
92807 Puteaux
Tel: +33 (0) 1 49 06 26 88
Fax: +33 (0) 1 49 06 26 99
http: //www.francexport.com

World Trade Centre
Palais des Congrès
2 place de la porte Maillot BP 18
75853 Paris cedex 17
Tel: +33 (0) 1 40 68 14 24 / 25 / 26
Fax: +33 (0) 1 40 68 14 21
http: //www.wtca.org

Industrial and Investment Advice

Agence pour la Coopération Technique, Industrielle et Économique
(ACTIM)
(Agency for Technical, Industrial and Economic Cooperation)
14 avenue d'Eylau
75116 Paris
Tel: +33 (0) 1 44 34 50 00
Fax +33 (0) 1 44 34 50 01
http: //www.cfce.fr

Association pour la Promotion et le Développement Industriel (APRODI)
(Association for the Promotion of Industrial Development)
17 rue Hamelin
75783 Paris cedex 16
Tel: +33 (0) 1 44 05 35 17
Fax: +33 (0) 1 47 55 08 77

Caisse Française de Développement (CFD)
(French Development Bank)
Cité du Retiro
37 rue Boissy d'Anglas
75379 Paris cedex 08
Tel: +33 (0) 1 40 06 30 38 / 31 31
Fax: +33 (0) 1 40 06 38 64
http: //www.cfd.fr

Organisation pour la Coopération et l'Investissement entre la France et
l'Asie (OCIFA)
(Organisation for Investment Cooperation Between France and Asia)
17 rue Hamelin
75783 Paris cedex 16
Tel: +33 (0) 1 44 05 35 28
Fax: +33 (0) 1 47 55 65 94

Organisation des Nations Unis pour le Développement Industriel
(ONUDI)
(United Nations Organisation for Industrial Development)
118 rue de Vaugirard
75006 Paris
Tel: +33 (0) 1 44 39 34 34
Fax: +33 (0) 1 45 48 72 55

Regional Councils and their Development Agencies

Conseil Régional d'Alsace
35 avenue de la Paix
67070 Strasbourg
Tel: +33 (0) 3 88 15 68 67
Fax: +33 (0) 3 88 15 68 15
http: //www.cr-alsace.fr

Conseil Régional d'Aquitaine
14 rue François de Sourdis
33077 Bordeaux cedex
Tel: +33 (0) 5 56 90 53 90
Fax: +33 (0) 5 56 24 72 80 / 99 32 / 73 66
http: //www.cr-aquitaine.fr

Conseil Régional d'Auvergne
13–15 avenue Fontmaure
BP 60
63402 Chamalières cedex
Tel: +33 (0) 4 73 31 85 85
Fax: +33 (0) 4 73 36 73 45
http: //www.cr-auvergne.fr

Conseil Régional de la Basse Normandie
Abbaye aux Dames
place Reine Mathilde
BP 523
14035 Caen
Tel: +33 (0) 2 31 06 98 98
Fax: +33 (0) 2 31 43 75 17

Conseil Régional de Bourgogne
17 boulevard de la Trémouille
BP 1602
21035 Dijon cedex
Tel: +33 (0) 3 80 44 33 00
Fax: +33 (0) 3 80 44 33 30

Conseil Régional de la Bretagne
283 avenue du Général Patton
BP 3166
35031 Rennes cedex
Tel: +33 (0) 2 99 27 10 10
Fax: +33 (0) 2 99 27 11 11
http: //www.cr-cyberbretagne.fr

Conseil Régional du Centre
9 rue Saint Pierre Lantin
45041 Orléans cedex 01
Tel: +33 (0) 2 38 70 30 30
Fax: +33 (0) 2 38 70 31 18

Conseil Régional de la Champagne-Ardenne
5 rue de Jéricho
51034 Chalons en Champagne
Tel: +33 (0) 3 26 70 31 31
Fax: +33 (0) 3 26 70 31 61

Conseil Régional de la Corse
22 cours Grandval
BP 215
20187 Ajaccio
Tel: +33 (0) 4 95 51 64 64
Fax: +33 (0) 4 95 51 67 75

Conseil Régional de la Franche Comté
4 square Castan
25031 Besançon cedex
Tel: +33 (0) 3 81 61 61 61
Fax: +33 (0) 3 81 83 12 92

Conseil Régional de la Haute Normandie
25 boulevard Gambetta
BP 1129
76174 Rouen cedex
Tel: +33 (0) 2 35 52 56 00
Fax: +33 (0) 02 35 52 56 56

Conseil Régional d'Ile de France
35 boulevard des Invalides
75007 Paris
Tel: +33 (0) 1 53 85 53 85
Fax: +33 (0) 1 53 85 53 89

Conseil Régional du Languedoc Roussillon
201 avenue Pompignane
34064 Montpellier cedex
Tel: +33 (0) 4 67 22 80 00
Fax: +33 (0) 4 67 22 81 92
http: //www.cr-languedocroussillon.fr

Conseil Régional du Limousin
27 boulevard de la Corderie
87031 Limoges cedex
Tel: +33 (0) 5 55 45 19 00
Fax: +33 (0) 5 55 45 18 25

Conseil Régional de la Lorraine
A place Gabriel Hocquard
BP 81004
57036 Metz cedex 01
Tel: +33 (0) 3 87 33 60 00
Fax: +33 (0) 3 87 32 89 33
http: //www.cr-lorraine.fr

Conseil Régional des Midi Pyrénées
22 boulevard du Maréchal Juin
31077 Toulouse cedex
Tel: +33 (0) 5 61 33 50 50
Fax: +33 (0) 5 61 33 52 66
http: //www.cr-mip.fr

Conseil Régional du Nord Pas de Calais
7 square Morrison
BP 2035
59014 Lille
Tel: +33 (0) 3 28 82 82 82
Fax: +33 (0) 3 28 82 82 83
http: //www.cr-ndpc.fr

Conseil Régional des Pays de la Loire
1 rue de la Loire
44266 Nantes cedex
Tel: +33 (0) 2 40 41 41 41
Fax: +33 (0) 2 40 47 76 85
http: //www.cr-pays-de-la-loire.fr

Conseil Régional de la Picardie
11 mail Albert 1er
BP 2616
80026 Amiens cedex 01
Tel: +33 (0) 3 22 93 37 37
Fax: +33 (0) 3 22 97 39 00
http: //www.cr-picardie.fr

Conseil Régional du Poitou Charentes
15 rue de l'Ancienne Comédie
BP 575
86021 Poitiers cedex '
Tel: +33 (0) 5 49 55 77 00
Fax: +33 (0) 5 49 55 77 88

Conseil Régional de la Provence Côte d'Azur
27 place Jules Guesde
13481 Marseille cedex 20
Tel: +33 (0) 4 91 57 50 57
Fax: +33 (0) 4 91 57 51 51
http: //www.cr-paca.fr

Conseil Régional du Rhône-Alpes
78 route de Paris
BP 19
69751 Charbonnières les Bains
Tel: +33 (0) 4 72 59 40 00
Fax: +33 (0) 4 72 59 42 18

France Initiative Réseau
(French Research Initiative)
14 rue Delambre
75014 Paris
Tel: +33 (0) 1 43 20 58 03 / 33
Fax: +33 (0) 1 43 20 58 34

Miscellaneous

Association pour la Compensation des Echanges Commerciaux (ACECO)
(Association for the Compensation of Commercial Exchanges)
10 rue Fresnel
75116 Paris
Tel: +33 (0) 1 48 23 50 37 / +33 (0) 1 47 23 50 37
Fax: +33 (0) 01 47 23 79 72

Fédération Française des Sociétés pour le Commerce International
(FFSCI)
(French Federation of International Business Societies)
31 avenue de Pierre ler de Serbie
75784 Paris cedex 16
Tel: +33 (0) 1 40 69 44 43
Fax: +33 (0) 1 47 23 47 32

Institut National de la Propriété Intellectuelle (INPI)
(National Institute for Intellectual Property)
26 bis rue de Léningrad
75800 Paris cedex 08
Tel: +33 (0) 1 42 94 52 52
Fax: +33 (0) 1 42 93 59 30

NOrmes et Regles techniques pour l'EXportation (NORMEX)
(Standard and Technical Regulations for Exporting)
Tour Europe
92049 Paris la Défense cedex 07
Tel: +33 (0) 1 40 73 38 88 / +33 (0) 1 42 91 55 55
Fax: +33 (0) 1 42 91 56 56

Additional Websites

www.admifrance.gouv.fr/	French government website index, links to all the ministries
www.paris-anglo.com/index.html	Paris info pages for foreign business residents
www.nomade.fr/	French information search site (in French)
www.paris.org/	A mass of information on Paris hotels, restaurants, museums, courses, etc
www.assemblee-nat.fr/	National Assembly home page – good links page (in French).

Index

Index of Advertisers